How They Got Away with It

HOW THEY GOT AWAY WITH IT

White Collar Criminals and the Financial Meltdown

EDITED BY

SUSAN WILL, STEPHEN HANDELMAN,

AND DAVID C. BROTHERTON

Columbia University Press   *New York*

Columbia University Press
Publishers Since 1893
New York   Chichester, West Sussex
cup.columbia.edu

Cover photos: © adam eastland/Alamy, © Sieda Preis/Getty Images
Cover design: Marc Cohen

Library of Congress Cataloging-in-Publication Data

How they got away with it : white collar criminals and the financial meltdown / edited by
Susan Will, Stephen Handelman, and David C. Brotherton.
    p. cm.
  Includes index.
    ISBN 978-0-231-15690-5 (cloth : alk. paper)—ISBN 978-0-231-15691-2 (pbk. : alk.
paper)—ISBN 978-0-231-52766-8 (ebook)
    1. White collar crimes.   2. Commercial crimes.   3. Commercial criminals.
4. Financial crises.   I. Will, Susan.   II. Handelman, Stephen.   III. Brotherton, David.

  HV6768.H69 2013
  364.16'80973—dc23

                                                                        2012017414

Columbia University Press books are printed on permanent and durable acid-free paper.
This book is printed on paper with recycled content.

Printed in the United States of America
c 10 9 8 7 6 5 4 3 2 1
p 10 9 8 7 6 5 4 3 2 1

References to Internet Web sites (URLs) were accurate at the time of writing. Neither the
author nor Columbia University Press is responsible for URLs that may have expired or
changed since the manuscript was prepared.

To the victims
of corporate malfeasance

CONTENTS

Contents

Contents

ACKNOWLEDGMENTS

We thank the McCormick Foundation for their financial support and the staff of John Jay College of Criminal Justice's Center on Media, Crime, and Justice, who organized the April 2008 conference for journalists, academics, and other specialists, "How Do They Get Away with It? Tracking Financial Crime in the New Era," which gave attention to the developing economic events.

We also thank our graduate research assistant, Alex Holden, who provided invaluable assistance. His organizational skills, attention to detail, and sheer endurance greatly facilitated the completion of this book. We greatly appreciate his devotion to this endeavor.

Finally, we thank the editors and staff at Columbia University Press who worked with us. In particular, we are grateful for Edward Wade's patience and editorial attention to detail and the masterful copyediting by Ron Harris and Julie Palmer Hoffman.

INTRODUCTION

In a 2011 *New York Times* article, the authors ask why no bankers have gone to prison for activities related to the financial meltdown (Morgenson and Story, "In Financial Crisis, No Prosecutions of Top Figures," April 14, 2011). Such a question, raised by one of the leading newspapers in the United States, goes to the heart of this volume: How did the movers and shakers of a world financial and economic system make the decisions they did, creating untold social harm to millions, and yet fail to be held accountable by our various governments?

This book grew out of an initiative we took at John Jay College of Criminal Justice in 2008 to organize a conference for journalists, academics, and practitioners that would shed a criminological light on one of the biggest economic crises in U.S. history. Given that we were located in the eye of the storm (a twenty- minute subway ride from Wall Street) and as faculty members of the largest college of criminal justice in the nation (with a commitment to "educating for justice"), we felt compelled to put into context the social, political, and economic processes behind the meltdown and show culturally how this epoch had come about. At the time, we thought that academics were paying scant attention to the extraordinary events of 2007–2008. Although hundreds of column inches, hours of broadcast time, and millions of cyber pixels were produced by investigative and other journalists, there was too little commentary or serious analysis from those of us who were supposedly trained to investigate scientifically the nature, type, and meanings behind the egregious transgressions that constituted this most recent rupture in the fabric of global capitalism.

Needless to say, the conference was a tremendous success. As financial regulators, journalists, criminal investigators, criminologists, sociologists, rehabilitated Ponzi schemers, and accountants aired their perspectives, participated in heated debates, and dialogued with rapt audiences of several hundred students, faculty, and lay members of the public, it was clear that we needed to produce a compilation of the contributions heard that day. But we also felt called to push the exploration further, with rigorous analysis of the criminality that lay behind much of the crisis—an aspect that while frequently touched upon by journalists and commentators has not received the attention it merits.

Some of the authors who contributed essays to this volume were present at the event. Others sent us their analyses on hearing of our intention to launch such a project. The result, we believe, is an extraordinary document that will well serve students, academics, and laypersons alike in their quest to understand the complexity of the issues behind the system's partial collapse and the policies that we might consider if history is not to move so assuredly from tragedy to farce.

In the opening section of the book, we have assembled contributions addressing the roots of the crisis as their foundational theme. Here David O. Friedrichs, Saskia Sassen, Susan Will, and Jock Young, through their respective disciplines, pursue a series of distinctive inquiries that have emerged from the seismic shifts in the world's political economy located at its financial heart. Friedrichs begins by asking: Who or what is responsible for the financial economic debacle? The author makes clear that the crisis falls classically within the purview of white collar criminology and goes on to suggest several reasons why hardly a single perpetrator spent a night in one of the United States' infamously overflowing prisons.

Sassen makes her particular mark on this intriguing discussion by analyzing how the restructuring of capitalism has almost inevitably led to the present set of contradictions, what she calls its "radical reshuffling" (p. 26) characterized by two sets of logics that intersect with such devastating consequences. The first logic is that associated with "privatization," one of the many tentacles of neoliberalism as both an ideology and a practice. The second logic is that of the expansion and proliferation of "extreme zones of profit extraction" (p. 26) now famously contained in her notion of global cities. These two logics produce conditions, beliefs, policies, cultures, and spaces that give rise to the now-ubiquitous dynamic of financialization—a reference to the ascendancy of finance capital over industrial capital and the consequent liquid culture of superexploitation that now overdetermines outsourced, overproducing, and undercompensated labor.

Will, a criminologist, suggests that Ponzi scheme practices are not the exception but the rule in contemporary capitalism. From the operations of Sanford and Madoff to the institutionalized promises of public pensions, Ponzi-like properties abound in the way we do business as well as in the provisions of the social contract. Will makes the important point that with the U.S. government so impossibly intertwined with the goals, motives, and culture of the financial economy, the people have lost the guardian of their supposed interests. Thus, we have moved irrevocably from a government of, by, and for the people to one that is beholden to the profit-based diktats of financial corporations, stockholder interests, and the well-connected individuals who occupy America's boardrooms, many of whom now seem to routinely shuttle between their desks in the White House and their offices on Wall Street.

Rounding out this opening section, Young complements Will's insights and argues that the present crisis must be seen as a facet of the generalized condition of anomie that has afflicted the United States for many a decade. Young invokes Merton's renowned 1930s sociological analysis of the impossibility for many citizens of reaching the mythic American Dream, despite the key role of this concept in the nation's ideology, and he underlines Merton's well-respected conclusion that this contradiction has consistently produced a moral crisis of immense proportions. It is this moral crisis, according to Young, which is reflected in the culture of the present financial-economic crisis, as we watch the wanton criminality of the well-heeled who, for the most part, are feted and extolled by a craven culture of excess, greed, and human speculation. As Young explains, "great wealth, as Merton pointed out, is itself seen as a sign of some inner virtue, regardless of how it has been accumulated" (p. 77). This virtuous accumulation was present in the unabashed lifestyle of Madoff et al., consistently packaged and circulated by such entities as the News Corporation, whose dynastic heads during the summer of 2011 were exposed for their venality. These business cultural practices, according to Young, cannot be otherwise in "advanced" societies whose class structures have become more unequal than at any time since World War II.

In Part II, we deal with the enablers of fraud and begin with Gilbert Geis's chapter on the unaccountability of external auditors. Where were the external auditors during and before the Great Economic Meltdown? Geis asks. It is a question that is constantly posed in a world that is supposedly kept rational by an array of checks and balances, only to see mounting evidence of impunity for those manipulating the levers of institutional power and privilege for purely personal gain. Thus Geis concludes, not unexpectedly, that from the huge corporate watchdogs, some of which are no longer with us, to the small-time accountant, there has been a fairly consistent pattern of choosing not to bite the hand that feeds one.

Consequently, when we wonder how the largest bankruptcy in U.S. history was allowed to happen (i.e., Lehman's) or how Bernie Madoff's operations received a clean bill of health for more than 40 years, we have to penetrate the criminal tendencies of the auditing profession and its vulnerability to seduction through the tried and tested means of financial gain, shared culture, ideological consensus, political expediency, and the general trappings of power. Harold Barnett, in his contribution, similarly takes on another vexing question regarding the exponential growth of the fraudulent subprime loan industry: How was this toxic business allowed to proliferate and contribute to mortgage-related losses that ballooned from $945 billion in 2008 to $4 trillion a year later? What is meant by predatory lending and how did this practice of blatant financial criminality become so rife in the previously cautious world of bankers, mortgage brokers, and loan analysts? The answer is clear, according to Barnett: It is the logical end result of a long cycle of deregulation. Nothing was done unknowingly. The loans industry conceived, packaged, and processed fraudulent loan upon fraudulent loan while the ratings agencies looked on in approval, thumbing their noses at any notion of due diligence let alone civic responsibility.

David Shapiro's contribution sheds light on the "secret financial world" of "alpha" managers and astonishing returns (p. 130) and how the absence of effective forensic accounting and oversight masks the fraudulent practices of many such players in this subterranean sphere of the economy. Shapiro argues that there is an increased blurring of the lines between illegitimate Ponzi schemers and legitimate hedge fund managers; while the former intentionally make misleading statements to their clients and to the authorities, the latter merely do so accidentally—as if it were an accepted foible of professionals increasingly operating in an unaccountable world of smoke and mirrors.

In Part III, we turn to the theme of perverted justice, and here we begin with the analysis of Laureen Snider, who comments on whether regulation is possible given the rapidly evolving technology of Wall Street–related industries and their increasingly fragmented if rhizomatic character. Undoubtedly, Snider demonstrates that there are objective hurdles that make regulation difficult, but the failure to regulate has led to 12 percent of market trades outside of any regulation, occupying what are ominously called "dark pools" (p. 163). Of course, in this antiregulation, antigovernment, neoconservative climate such difficulties simply become self-fulfilling prophecies. But when the political will is present, no amount of technological sophistication will get in the way of fact-finding and oversight.

As Snider presciently states, compared with the normative presence of CCTV monitors and other types of observatory devices used to combat theft and destruction of private property, "no surveillance cameras have been installed in executive boardrooms; nor have police, forensic accountants, or regulatory officials been empowered to routinely use 'panoptic' surveillance or digitally mine the online activities of CEOs" (p. 155).

Adding significantly to this section are contributions from William Black and Justin O'Brien. Black's contribution is important not least because it comes from someone who has been there before: Black was involved as a high-level regulator during the 1980s savings and loan crisis and is able to place the current epidemic of fraud and financial malfeasance in both a personal and historical perspective. He argues that the major law enforcement and financial control agencies prior to the meltdown neither had the resources nor the political will to mount any serious campaign to prosecute the wrongdoers and fight against a level of mortgage fraud that was already an epidemic by 2006. Taking aim at the neoliberal zealotry he says, "Private markets do not 'discipline' firms reporting record profits; instead they compete to fund them" (p. 175).

O'Brien focuses on the dynamics of regulatory reform and, in particular, on the effectiveness of "creative enforcement," that is, the legal strategies used by prosecutors to ensure corporate compliance. Again, O'Brien is very skeptical of society's will to bring in rules that have any desired impact in the corporate domain not only because of the inherent difficulties of such regulation but also because of the collapse of professional obligations among lawyers, auditors, and a host of regulatory workers who should at all times be protecting the public interest. The long-heard plaintive cry of "too much regulation stunts investment," the mantra of almost every business lobbyist (including the U.S. Chamber of Commerce), has apparently become the stuff of common sense.

The results can be seen all around us: in the massive rise in home foreclosures, in the irrational opposition of the Republican Party to an increase in the national debt limit, and in the continued payment of obscene bonuses to financial executives whose lack of scruples is only matched by their belief in the sanctified position of "The Street."

The final section takes us outside of the United States and brings reports from Britain, the Netherlands, Portugal, Greece, and China. This small but important foray onto the global terrain of the crisis demonstrates the need for many more comparative and multiperspectival analyses of the financial and economic skullduggery that has come to define our current epoch.

Steve Tombs and David Whyte discuss what might be called the political economy of regulation based on the recent experience of Britain. Approaching the subject through a Marxist lens, they argue that it is impossible to grasp the overt and latent impacts and intentions of financial regulation without an understanding that such controls are always designed to promote more efficient capital accumulation (or improve capitalism as a system). Thus in the United Kingdom's context, what has been mischaracterized as an era of deregulation under the governments of Margaret Thatcher and New Labour (Tony Blair et al.) were really epochs of reregulation designed to shore up capitalist contradictions rather than simply a retreat by the state before the logic of laissez-faire ideology. Does this mean that all such efforts at regulation are worthless? Not at all, reply the authors; but it does mean that we need to discern the politics of controls and the class nature of the regimes from which they emerge, dispensing with the naive assumption (at best) that the logics of financial markets will not always be about the relative power of capital as both a social and economic relation.

Moving on to the Netherlands, Hans Nelen and Luuk Ritzen discuss the impact of the crisis on one of Europe's "healthiest" economies. They argue that even here, despite its relatively low unemployment rate (around 5 percent) and generally high standards of living, the "meltdown" had significant effects, particularly in the real estate industry, which is of great importance to the Dutch, who live in Europe's most densely populated country. The authors analyze the "crime-facilitative" aspects of the real estate sector, using a rational-choice perspective to assess the opportunities and restraints for crime in the country's property market over the recent decade.

They conclude that while the crisis helped to diminish the speculative values of the market (and therefore acted as a kind of corrective), it also provided for more possibilities to commit fraud. In particular, they point to the corrupting influence of key legal institutional actors, such as notaries public who have an extraordinarily powerful function quite unlike those in the same profession in the United States.

Although it is not mentioned in Chapter 12, we should also note that the extreme insecurity occasioned by the crisis and the cultural climate which led up to it have helped to produce a rapid rise of anti-immigrant sentiment reflected in an openly racist and xenophobic political party (the Freedom Party) currently participating in the country's coalition government.

In Chapter 13, Portugal's Rita Faria, José Cruz, Andre Lamas Leite, and Pedro Sousa discuss the rise of economic and financial crimes in their country, one of the members of the infamous PIGS of Europe, as Portugal, Ireland, Greece, and Spain, the sickest economies in the euro zone, have been labeled by the media. The authors point out that with Portugal facing rampant unemployment (for the first time going above 12 percent in its 30 years of democracy), falling living standards due to drastic austerity budgets, and weak political leadership, the tendency has been to loosen economic controls in the hope that the private sector will take advantage of its new market freedoms. Nonetheless, both the crisis and the response to the crisis have produced new possibilities for white collar crime.

But Portugal is a relatively recent democracy (coming about after the antifascist, anticolonial revolution of 1974, which saw the overthrow of the more than 40-years-long dictatorial eras of Marcelo Caetano and Antonio Salazar), and its legal codes have yet to catch up to new economic realities. In particular, the country's judicial codes and lack of political will have failed to address the extraordinary power now concentrated in national and international elites, as referred to in the work of numerous authors in this book. Thus Portugal is an important test case to be studied in this political-economic climate, and as the authors aver, the country is just at the beginning of this critical task.

Greece, as Sophia Vidali tells us, offers an example of how a corrupt Greek political system served as a petri dish for criminality on the part of major financial players—both domestic and international—and made Greece especially vulnerable to financial meltdown. The long-standing collusion between the public and private sectors, along with the manipulation of statistics on Greece's economic health in order to smooth its accession to the euro zone, created a bubble in the Greek economy that became all too easy to puncture. The consequences continue to be grave, as Greece's economic illnesses now threaten to infect the rest of the euro zone.

The final chapter in this section, by Hongming Cheng, reflects on the exponential rise of financial fraud in the fastest growing economy in the world. Cheng adopts a conflict perspective based on the classical white collar studies of Donald Black and Edwin Sutherland and analyzes the differential treatment of those convicted of fraud in Chinese society. The author asserts that the pervasiveness of such practices that are both directly and indirectly linked to the overall economic crisis of the West has had a "major impact on the lifeblood of . . . society" (p. 296). Cheng discovers through both interviews and archival resources that family origins explain why such severe treatment, including the death sentence, is meted out to the poor for fraud convictions; whereas for the offspring of the elites, whom he calls the "blue bloods" or second-generation progeny of party or government leaders, there are few lasting consequences, if any. Those coming from such privileged backgrounds who are involved in these cases (if indeed they ever come to light) are shielded by a plethora of "connection networks" and "protective umbrellas" (p. 307) as afforded by the bizarre combination of a one-party "Communist" state practicing the policies of neoliberalism.

In the epilogue, we attempt to bring together the multiple strands of inquiry to assess whether, in the face of continued evidence that financial misbehavior remains largely unpunished, those who pushed the envelope in 2008 (and their heirs) can "still get away with it." Readers of the essays in this volume will have their own answers. But the editors will be satisfied if this rich collection of essays and viewpoints inspires other scholars and researchers to delve deeper into the disturbing questions posed by the gravest financial meltdown since the Great Depression.

[PART I]

ROOTS OF THE CRISIS

While the vulnerabilities that created the potential for crisis were years in the making, it was the collapse of the housing bubble—fueled by low interest rates, easy and available credit, scant regulation, and toxic mortgages—that was the spark that ignited a string of events, which led to a full-blown crisis in the fall of 2008. . . . When the bubble burst, hundreds of billions of dollars in losses in mortgages and mortgage-related securities shook markets as well as financial institutions that had significant exposures to those mortgages and had borrowed heavily against them. This happened not just in the United States but around the world.

—(Financial Crisis Inquiry Commission, *Final Report of the National Commission on the Causes of the Financial and Economic Crisis in the United States,* Official Government Edition 2011, xvi).

WALL STREET

Crime Never Sleeps

DAVID O. FRIEDRICHS

The global economic and financial crisis that began in 2007, and reached an especially intense apex in the fall of 2008, has been widely described as the worst such crisis since the Great Depression of the 1930s. If the financial meltdown has multiple dimensions and involves a variety of causes, fraudulent misrepresentations in many different forms and on many different levels were clearly at the center of this catastrophe.

Analysis of, and commentary on, the global economic crisis has poured forth from a wide range of sources; and in the academic realm, in particular, from historians, economists, political scientists, law professors, and many others. Overall, to date, criminology and criminal justice have not had a high profile in the avalanche of analysis and commentary. It is a core premise of this chapter that criminologists should be well qualified to make useful and unique contributions to understanding the financial crisis and should be able to frame the ongoing dialogue on the optimal response to the crisis in a form that constructively complements the dominant voices in this dialogue. It is obviously difficult to overstate what is at stake in arriving at the most comprehensive understanding of the causes of the crisis and the importance of the perspectives, policies, and practices that might impose fundamental constraints on a similar crisis in the future.

The objectives of this chapter are as follows. First, to address the financial crisis as crime in conceptual terms: If crime—and, more specifically, white collar crime—played a central role in this crisis, in what sense of the term *crime* was this the case, and what form of white collar crime was involved? Second, to address the financial crisis as crime in contextual terms: How should the consequences of crime on Wall Street be understood in relation to the consequences of crime on Main Street? And third, to address the financial crisis as crime in critical terms: What kinds of transformative perspective and policy initiatives are needed if we are to minimize the chances of a catastrophic financial crisis in the future?

In the wake of the financial crisis, many excellent books, along with countless articles and columns, on how and why this crisis occurred have been produced (e.g., Cassidy 2010; Johnson and Kwak 2010; Lowenstein 2010; Prins 2009; Roubini and Mihm 2010; Stiglitz 2010). Those who have written these books have included highly respected economists and financial journalists. Although some of the key dimensions of these analyses must be included here, the overriding objective is to complement rather than to duplicate these efforts. Accordingly, the goal is to apply a specifically criminological framework—one rooted in the traditions of white collar crime and critical criminological scholarship—to the financial crisis. But both of these traditions within criminology have always drawn upon an especially broad range of sources. Similarly, the interdisciplinary character of this anthology recognizes that the financial crisis and the wrongdoing associated with it can be understood in a sophisticated way only by drawing upon many different academic and professional perspectives.

Muckraking journalists and investigative reporters have made and continue to make important contributions to our understanding of crime in high places, in part because of both the resources and the special access available to them to investigate this world. The segment of the media that covers the financial industry did not always collectively and skeptically question the claims made by spokespersons for this industry. But white collar and critical criminologists need not be apologetic about drawing upon the work of those journalists who have been at the forefront of exposing fraud in the financial industry, as well as the contributions of those from a range of academic disciplines. The complexity of sophisticated crimes perpetrated by powerful institutions and individuals requires an interdisciplinary approach.

Criminology, throughout its history and into the present, has focused disproportionately on conventional forms of crime and delinquency and on their control. The belief that conventional crime and delinquency result in significant social harm, and accordingly should be addressed, is a core raison d'être for the field of criminology. But criminologists who focus upon white collar crime have long believed that by many standard measures the harms caused by such crime outweigh those caused by conventional forms of crime and delinquency. Accordingly, criminologists who specialize in white collar crime have been disturbed and puzzled by the lack of proportionality in the field: That is, a great deal of criminological attention and research focuses upon less consequential forms of crime, and far less attention and research are focused upon the most consequential forms of crime. Elsewhere, I have referred to this situation in terms of an "inverse hypothesis," where the proportion of criminological attention to a form of crime varies inversely with the objectively identifiable level of harm caused by such crime (Friedrichs 2007, 5). Of course this "hypothesis" may be regarded as somewhat hyperbolic by some, but I believe there is a strong measure of truth to it.

The Causes of the Financial Crisis—and Attributing Responsibility

Who or what is to blame for this economic and financial crisis? The list is very long and includes Wall Street, Washington, and Main Street (Kowitt 2008; Morris 2008; Ritholtz 2009). In the simplest and most colloquial terms, Wall Street is blamed for unsound, highly risky practices; Washington is blamed for regulatory failure and bad policies; and Main Street is blamed for living beyond its means. The specific list of blameworthy parties and institutions in relation to the financial crisis can be expanded almost indefinitely (Gibbs 2009). It includes, but is not necessarily limited to, recent presidents; cabinet secretaries; high-level legislators; regulatory agency chairs and staff; government-sponsored entities (e.g., Fannie Mae and Freddie Mac) and their directors and staff; financial industry lobbyists; investment bankers; credit rating agencies; insurance division chiefs; major home builders; and mortgage lenders. Corporate boards played a role, as they are ridden with conflicts of interest, have awarded unwarranted and exorbitant compensation packages, and have failed to effectively oversee excessively risky practices (Ritholtz 2009). "Risk officers" who had the specific responsibility of overseeing and evaluating the risks in banking investments obviously did a very poor job (Story and Dash 2009). Lawyers—as legislators, as regulators, as judges, and as counselors—played a key role in drafting legislation, disregarding dangerous initiatives, blocking shareholder lawsuits, and sanctioning highly questionable deals as legally sound (Carter 2009).

Other entities and parties can also be blamed, ranging from high-level economists, hedge fund managers, and media-show promoters to traders and leaders of countries such as China and Iceland who adopted or promoted practices that contributed to the economic crisis and financial meltdown. In the view of some prominent behavioral economists, the classic economic model of a "rational man" is wrong. The financial crisis must be understood as reflecting, among other things, the "animal spirits" of human beings and their strong tendency to act in irrational ways, independent of economic motivations (Akerlof and Shiller 2009). The much-invoked fundamental human concept of "greed," as well as "delusional optimism," was clearly involved (Ehrenreich 2008). The recent era embraced with abandon a "fundamentalist" belief in the unlimited potential of free markets and their capacity to be self-regulatory. Broad dimensions of human nature, psychology, and ideology contributed to speculative bubbles, the acceptance of excessive risk, and inevitable catastrophic financial failures and meltdowns.

Given the extraordinary breadth of assigning blame for the financial crisis, how can "crime" and "criminality" be disentangled from all of this? Which, if any, of the parties invoked in the preceding paragraphs are criminals who belong behind bars? Should all the financial institutions and entities involved be criminally prosecuted? Of course, the reality is that few (if any) of those identified earlier intended to cause a financial catastrophe; and few (if any) will be criminally prosecuted for their actions. What is really involved is a complex, broad spectrum or continuum of actions with varying degrees of intent, liability, and wrongfulness.

But the central thesis here is that the structure of the present financial system, its culture, and its collective practices and policies are fundamentally criminal and criminogenic. The harms emanating from this financial system are exponentially greater than those emanating from the disadvantaged environments that generate a disproportionate percentage of conventional crime. Accordingly, on various levels, there is much at stake in more fully and directly recognizing and identifying many core policies and practices of the financial system for what they are: *crimes* on a very large scale.

Analysis of the financial crisis should adopt as a starting point this recognition, and work through both the moral and the practical implications of this premise. Let us begin by considering the populist or rhetorical (as opposed to analytical) use of the terms *crime* and *criminal* in relation to the financial crisis, before moving on to a conceptual analysis of these terms in relation to white collar crime.

The Financial Crisis as Crime, as White Collar Crime, and as Finance Crime

The term *crime* has been widely applied to the activities of individuals and institutions regarded as having played a central role in causing the financial crisis. Those who have invoked this term include political officials, public commentators, cartoonists, and ordinary citizens. Michael Moore's 2009 documentary *Capitalism: A Love Story* opens with shots of conventional bank robberies but then turns to the "robberies" committed by investment banks, with Moore's proclamation outside the Goldman Sachs building that "crimes have been committed in this building," and his attempt to enter and carry out a citizen's arrest of the perpetrators. He marks off investment banking office buildings with yellow police tape announcing "Crime Scene: Do Not Cross." Danny Schechter's 2010 documentary *Plunder: The Crime of Our Time* invokes the term *crime* not only in its subtitle but throughout. A protester calls for a "Jailout, Not Bailout"; Wall Street is described as a "crime scene" and as being engaged in a Ponzi scheme that has produced the biggest financial crime in history, stealing far more than has the Mafia. In the course of a one-hour documentary, the terms *crime, fraud, white collar crime,* and *financial crime* are all invoked in relation to the financial meltdown. The very title of Charles Ferguson's 2010 documentary *Inside Job* is also associated with crime, with the clear claim that the financial meltdown of 2008 is best understood as a fraud on a massive scale (or "bank heist") committed by those operating inside the financial (and political) system.

The Nobel laureate economist and *New York Times* columnist Paul Krugman (2010b) characterizes the activities on Wall Street as "looting" and "a racket." Former Senator Ted Kaufman has specifically demanded that we root out the "fraud and potential criminal conduct" that "were at the heart of the financial crisis" (Rich 2010). One could cite many other such examples. It seems worthwhile to sort through some of the key terms.

Despite its ubiquity in popular culture, *crime* is, in fact, applied in a broad range of different ways (Kauzlarich and Friedrichs 2005). A violation of the criminal law is arguably the most widely accepted meaning of the term. In relation to the financial crisis, two key points arise. First (as noted by *Plunder* and uniformly by students of white collar crime), corporate and financial elite interests have always exercised formidable influence over which activities do and do not get defined as crime by substantive criminal law and have historically been largely successful in shielding many of their blatantly exploitative practices from being prohibited by law or criminalized. Only in 2010, for example, do we very belatedly have federal legislation prohibiting the imposition of overdraft protection and associated fees, in fine print, on debit card customers without their specific consent. Banks had earned some $27 billion annually from overdraft fees, overwhelmingly from their least affluent and least sophisticated customers (Johnson and Kwak 2010, 196). And second, even when financial elites are charged with violations of the substantive criminal law in relation to their activities, it is generally far more challenging to adjudicate such cases and arrive at a formal finding that a crime has in fact occurred than in the case of conventional crime offenders. Two hedge fund managers for Bear Stearns, the first high-level Wall Street executives criminally indicted in the wake of the financial meltdown, were acquitted in the fall of 2009 because their well-funded defense team was able to persuade a jury that their actions took the form of poor investment decisions and not intentional criminal fraud (Kouwe and Slater 2009). Such outcomes have the potential to discourage prosecutors from initiating criminal prosecutions against financial elites.

Although mainstream criminology has for the most part adopted the legalistic conception of crime for purposes of studying crime and criminological phenomena, criminology has a long tradition of suggesting alternative conceptions of crime. The founding father of white collar crime scholarship, Edwin Sutherland (1945), famously incorporated violations of civil and administrative laws in his definition of white collar crime, and engaged in a celebrated debate with Paul Tappan (1947) on the legitimacy of extending the definition of *crime* beyond violations of the criminal law. Herman Schwendinger and Julia Schwendinger (1972) set forth a humanistic conception of crime in relation to demonstrably harmful activities, arguing that one should not cede to the capitalist state a monopoly over the definition of crime. More recently still, some British criminologists have argued that we should abandon our focus on the notion of crime itself and should shift our focus to the more appropriate category of "social harm" (Hillyard et al. 2004).

In relation to the financial meltdown, it is worth noting, then, that the invocation of the term *crime* ranges from references to apparent violations of existing criminal law and violations of some other body of law to activities that are demonstrably harmful and should be classified as crimes even if they are not specified as such by existing law. One could take this further by acknowledging that the term has a populist dimension when it is simply used in popular discourse in reference to practices and policies the speaker regards as abhorrent.

If the perception exists that crime was involved in the financial meltdown, clearly it was not conventional or street crime (although a significant slice of it occurred on a "street"—Wall Street!). So it is widely understood, by members of the public as well as by professional commentators, that white collar crime is involved. But if this is true, what does this mean, and what form or forms of white collar crime were involved? As was suggested earlier, the proper definition of the term *white collar crime* has a long and contentious history (e.g., Friedrichs 2010b; Geis 2007; Helmkamp, Ball, and Townsend 1996). But since the 1970s, in particular, two core types of white collar crime have been widely recognized: corporate crime and occupational crime. Corporate crime is defined most concisely as illegal and harmful financially driven acts committed by officers and employees of corporations primarily to benefit corporate interests. Occupational crime is most concisely defined as illegal or harmful financially driven acts committed within the context of a legitimate, respectable occupation primarily to benefit those who commit the acts. Both types played at least some role in bringing about the financial crisis. When I produced the first edition of my text *Trusted Criminals: White Collar Crime in Contemporary Society*, written in the early 1990s and published in 1996, it seemed necessary to recognize that beyond these core types, significant cognate, hybrid, and marginal forms of white collar crime that did not fit neatly into these categories also had to be identified and delineated. At least some of these cognate, hybrid, and marginal forms of white collar crime were central to the financial meltdown.

The term *finance crime* in the original edition of my text referred to "large-scale illegality that occurs in the world of finance and financial institutions" (Friedrichs 1996, 156). More specifically, I noted that such crime stands apart from corporate and occupational crime insofar as "vastly larger financial stakes are involved . . . [it is intertwined with] financial networks . . . [and it] threatens the integrity of the economic system itself" (Friedrichs 1996, 156). The stakes, as we have learned, are in the hundreds of billions of dollars—or in the trillions by some measures—far more money than is typically involved in corporate crime and occupational crime, certainly relative to the number of organizations and individuals involved. Although the worst corporate crimes can have a substantial impact on the economy, they do not have the diffuse, devastating impact of finance crimes. The proportion of harmful, unproductive activity—in the sense of no measurable benefit for society—relative to beneficial, productive activity, is significantly greater for finance crime than for corporate and occupational crime. This type of crime has an especially broad network of parties, both horizontal and vertical. If some of the most significant finance crimes are committed on behalf of financial institutions, such as major investment banks, then the top executives of these institutions benefit disproportionately, arguably exponentially, more than the top executives in corporate crime. One can argue that the finance crimes at the center of the financial crisis are the single most complex form of white collar crime. Their complexity contributes to the paradoxical fact that, relative to the harm done, finance crime has been the most difficult form of white collar crime to define by law, to regulate and contain, and to prosecute or adjudicate successfully.

If it is clear that white collar crime was one of the core forces at the center of the financial crisis, it is surely important to understand what white collar crime in the financial world has in common with, and how it differs from, white collar crime in other contexts. In simply referring to this activity as "white collar crime" or "fraud," it becomes conflated with a broad range of illegal or unethical activities, for the most part of far narrower scope. The unique dimensions and extraordinary consequences of finance crime come into sharper relief when it is separated clearly from the broad range of activities characterized as white collar crime or fraud.

Other students of white collar crime have recognized that white collar crime in the financial industry is distinctive. William Black (2005), for example, has adopted the term *control fraud*, where the corporation becomes a weapon used to commit fraud. Stephen Rosoff, Henry Pontell, and Robert Tillman (2010) have invoked the terms *securities fraud* (e.g., insider trading and stock manipulation) and *fiduciary fraud* (i.e., crime in the banking, insurance, and pension fund industries).

The task for students of white collar crime is to refine and explore systematically and empirically the relative utility of competing formulations in this realm. A coherent and sophisticated understanding of the forms of white collar crime that occurred within the financial crisis requires a typological approach that delineates as fully as possible the attributes of these forms of crime that are both common to and distinctive from other forms of white collar crime. We should never lose sight of the fact that a typological approach can gloss over complexities and ambiguities in the most significant manifestations of white collar crime (Haines 2007). The premise here is that typologies provide a necessary point of departure for any meaningful discussion of white collar crime, despite the inevitably arbitrary and limited dimensions of any typological scheme.

"Bank Robbery": From Without and from Within

Famously, during the savings and loan crisis of the 1980s, California banking regulator Bill Crawford commented that the "best way to rob a bank is to own one" (Calavita and Pontell 1990, 321). The looting of the savings and loans by their owners generated losses vastly greater than those from conventional bank robberies. In the case of the recent financial meltdown, with the investment banks (not thrifts) playing such a central role, it may be more accurate to suggest that the best way to commit bank robbery is to *control* such a bank. This form of bank robbery is "robbery" of many different parties—including clients and customers, investors, and ordinary taxpayers—*by* the banks, not robbery *of* the banks. The top executives of the major investment banks, from Lehman Brothers to Goldman Sachs, were not best described as owning these banks, although they often held a significant number of their shares. But they certainly ran and controlled them. Here again the claim is made that the losses caused by these investment banking executives vastly exceeded—by at least some measures on a level exponentially greater than the losses involved in the savings and loan catastrophe—the losses involved in conventional bank robberies.

Bank robbery is a quintessential form of crime in the public imagination. Those who rob banks range from polished professional bank robbers to opportunistic or desperate amateurs (McCluskey 2009). But they are more often than not hapless individuals, possibly unemployed, afflicted with a substance abuse or gambling problem, committing a crime where the take often ranges from a few hundred to a few thousand dollars and more often than not results in arrest and subsequent long prison sentences, to be served in maximum-security prisons. Conventional bank robbers who commit multiple bank robberies are almost certain to be caught sooner or later. Most such bank robberies involve lone, unarmed individuals making an oral demand or passing a note. Violence is rare (less than 5 percent of bank robberies involve violence), and deaths are very rare (Weisel 2007). The total annual take from all bank robberies in the United States over the past few years has been in the range of $25 million to $60 million (Weisel 2007). Although this is not an insignificant sum, it is a very small fraction of the losses incurred by the reckless (and often fraudulent) conduct of major financial institutions, including investment banks.

The intent here is not to dismiss the various forms of harm involved in conventional bank robberies, which are surely traumatic for many of the victims, but rather to place such robbery within the broader context of other forms of "bank robbery," and to call for more appropriate proportionality in the popular, legal, and justice system responses to these different forms of crime.

Finance Crime on a Grand Scale and the Case of Goldman Sachs

In the two most recent editions of my text *Trusted Criminals*, I have included a box entitled "Investment Banks: Wealth Producers or Large-Scale Fraudsters?" Investment banks are prestigious and powerful financial institutions, with high-level executives who are richly compensated. They present themselves as central players in the creation of wealth in capitalist societies who put the interests of their clients first. In *The Greed Merchants*, former investment banker Philip Augar (2005) challenged this characterization and sought to demonstrate that the investment banks are riddled with conflicts of interest and, all too often, put their own interests and profits ahead of everything else. Specifically, the wages for the investment banking industry for the period from 1980 to 2000 amounted to a staggering $500 billion, with shareholders and customers subsidizing a vast proportion of this payout (Augar 2005, 62). Since 2000, payouts increased even more dramatically (Johnson and Kwak 2010; Morris 2008; Prins 2009).

By simultaneously advising both buyers and sellers in merger transactions, investment banking institutions are obviously involved in a conflict of interest. Indeed, they aggressively promote mergers—even when such mergers impose great costs or losses on investors, employees, and consumers—because they generate huge fees for investment banks. They allocate hot initial public offering (IPO) shares to top executives of corporations, expecting that in return these executives will steer lucrative corporate business to the investment banking houses.

Major investment banks were deeply implicated in the corporate scandals involving Enron, WorldCom, and other corporations that vastly misrepresented their finances (Augar 2005; Sale 2004). They were accused of either inadequately overseeing huge loans to such corporations or being directly complicit in fraudulent applications of these loans. Among other things, they had helped structure controversial and sometimes illegal off-balance-sheet partnerships. High-level employees of these banks were accused of having misled investors in relation to the prospects of telecommunications companies, and the banks themselves were charged with having failed to supervise some trading accounts that lost large sums of money.

Investment banks were very much in the midst of the current financial crisis (Johnson and Kwak 2010; Prins 2009; Ritholtz 2009). I restrict myself here to focusing on just one of these investment banks. Goldman Sachs has been widely recognized as an iconic American investment bank, perhaps *the* iconic investment bank. It has been phenomenally successful over a long period of time and has generated enormous wealth for its partners and employees. Its senior officers have also been a pervasive presence, especially in the recent era, in the highest ranks of the United States government. Two recent Treasury secretaries came from the firm. In the spring of 2010, Goldman Sachs received a great deal of unwanted attention following the civil fraud filing against it by the Securities and Exchange Commission (SEC), reports of an ongoing criminal fraud investigation by the Department of Justice, and a high-profile Senate hearing (Story 2010; Story and Morgenson 2010; Taibbi 2010). Among other forms of wrongdoing, Goldman Sachs was accused of selling to investors "synthetic collateralized debt obligations [CDOs]" that were designed to fail and then betting against these opaque investments (Gandel 2010a). In July 2010, Goldman Sachs agreed to pay $550 million to settle the SEC complaint (Chan and

Story 2010). In that same month, an arbitration panel ordered Goldman Sachs to pay more than $20 million to investors defrauded by the Bayou Group, a hedge fund from which Goldman earned millions of dollars of fees for clearing trades (Craig 2010). The arbitration panel accepted the claim that Goldman had serious concerns about Bayou but failed to alert investors. During this period the meltdown of the Greek economy and the resulting impact on the European Union was also a big story. Goldman Sachs was shown to have collected hundreds of millions of dollars in fees over a period of years for helping Greece conceal its mounting debt and then to have made more money betting on the failure of the Greek economy (Schwartz and Dash 2010). In the United States, Goldman Sachs created CDOs that ultimately were repackaged as structured investment vehicles (SIVs)—all highly complex financial instruments—and sold to many American municipalities and counties, leading to huge losses when the housing market collapsed (Gandel 2010b). As a consequence, vital services had to be cut and fees imposed on residents of these municipalities and counties. Journalist Matt Taibbi (2009) demonstrated that Goldman Sachs played a central role, over much of the course of the past century, in major manipulations of the financial markets, profiting very richly while complicit in the "high gas prices, rising consumer-credit rates, half-eaten pension funds, mass layoffs, future taxes to pay off bailouts," and other immense costs to the American citizenry.

According to this analysis, Goldman Sachs was involved in a vast "investment pyramid" or "pump-and-dump" scheme, persuading ordinary investors to purchase investments that the bank knew to be defective and that would decline greatly in future value. Traditional guidelines for underwriting companies were abandoned, and stocks in new companies with extremely doubtful prospects were increasingly sold to investors. Goldman engaged in "laddering," the practice of manipulating share prices in new offerings; and "spinning," the practice of offering executives in new public companies shares at exceptionally low prices, in return for promised future business. Practices such as these contributed to the creation of a huge internet bubble, which wiped out some $5 trillion of wealth on the NASDAQ alone. Penalties imposed on firms such as Goldman Sachs for wrongful practices were so small relative to the profits that they could not be said to act as any deterrent.

According to Taibbi (2009), Goldman Sachs also played a central role in the manipulation of the oil market, which led to a dramatic rise in the cost of gas at the pump, not traceable to a shortage of supply or an increase in demand. Starting in 1991, Goldman Sachs invested heavily in the food commodities market, in effect profiting greatly by "gaming" this market, with the ultimate consequence of an estimated one billion more people worldwide left hungry or even starving (Kaufman 2010). The worldwide price of food rose some 80 percent between 2005 and 2008, with millions of American households bearing a heavy burden from this rise. Goldman Sachs has continued to pay billions of dollars of compensation in the midst of the devastating financial meltdown to which it contributed, and it has continued to benefit hugely from "bailout" initiatives due to its contacts at the highest levels of the government. Moreover, it has positioned itself to profit immensely from a proposed, emerging carbon credits market. Throughout most of its history, Goldman Sachs has epitomized ultrarespectability and has enjoyed a high level of trust. If the preceding critique is accurate, however, it should more properly be regarded as a form of organized crime. And if some of its key activities over the years were fraudulent, then they need to be legislatively defined as such and therefore classified as criminal.

Criminogenic Conditions Contributing to the Global Financial Crisis

If we are to diminish the chances of a repeat of the 2008 financial meltdown, and more broadly the global financial crisis linked to this meltdown, we must identify the conditions that were central to this crisis and the policies needed to address them effectively. Within the context of a specifically criminological framework, it is necessary to identify *criminogenic* conditions. Broadly defined, the concept of "criminogenic conditions" refers to conditions that promote criminal activities and actions. Thus, the notion of crime is extended beyond the strictly legalistic notion of violation of the criminal law to encompass demonstrably harmful activities and actions that often are not specifically encompassed in the criminal codes, as a reflection of the influence of powerful and privileged segments of society.

Many of the proposed or selectively implemented financial reforms implicitly, if not explicitly, acknowledge criminogenic dimensions of a wide range of policies, practices, and conditions in the financial industry, and do so without specifically invoking this concept. The criminogenic conditions complicit in the financial meltdown include financial organizations that are either "too big to fail" or too interconnected to challenge without harming financial structures. They also include exorbitant executive compensation and bonuses; excessive leveraging in relation to investments; "innovative," complex, and excessively risky financial products or instruments; and pervasive conflicts of interest involving entities that supposedly provide some form of oversight of the activities of financial institutions, including boards of directors, auditing firms, and credit-rating agencies.

The fact that the government has felt obliged to bail out financial institutions and corporations deemed too big to fail and has, furthermore, imposed no significant negative consequences in relation to the other criminogenic conditions just mentioned has created a situation of "moral hazard." That is to say, incentives exist for financial institutions and executives to continue taking huge risks and paying huge bonuses, with potentially catastrophic consequences for the economy, because the upside vastly outweighs the downside, with the costs of failure shifted to third parties. Other criminogenic conditions contributing to the financial meltdown include a weak or ineffective regulatory system; an inherently corrupt political system where wealthy financial institutions and corporations have far too much influence; and, more broadly, "free market" fundamentalism. Proponents of such fundamentalism advocate a largely, if not wholly, unregulated market as the most efficient and productive model for the economy. The argument here is that we must collectively focus on how these conditions very specifically promote criminal practices. The second task is to address which practices might be specifically criminalized and what the benefits and the drawbacks would be of such criminalization.

Transformative Public Policies and the Full Acknowledgment of Financial Industry Practices as Crimes

It is widely agreed that the financial crisis requires an effective response and the adoption of appropriate policies. But what sort of policies? One division exists between those who favor incremental and targeted reform policies and those who call for transformative and systemic policies. Just prior to the 2008 presidential election, Robert Kuttner (2008) argued persuasively that President Barack Obama's administration needed to adopt transformative policies in the midst of extraordinary and exceptionally challenging historical circumstances. In this regard, transformative public policies are indeed called for in response to the financial crisis, and the specific *criminalization* of practices at the center of the financial meltdown should be one dimension of this transformative policy shift.

The history of the development of criminal law incorporates disproportionate attention to some minor or inconsequential forms of harm, while either disregarding or legitimizing and supporting large-scale forms of demonstrable harm. William J. Chambliss (1976), in a frequently cited analysis, traced the origins of vagrancy laws to the Black Death in the fourteenth century, when the elite landowning classes feared that the devastating loss of life among the laboring classes would make it difficult to keep their enterprises going. Vagrancy laws were thus intended to ensure that cheap labor would continue to be available, as those unwilling to work would be subject to penal sanctions. Although prosecutions for vagrancy in the contemporary era are rare, homeless people continue to be prosecuted for such "offenses" as panhandling and loitering. Many other recent examples could be cited, such as the criminalization of marijuana use.

The history of penal policies is, in a parallel vein, one of harsh punishments imposed on individuals for minor offenses, while the rich and the powerful committed large-scale crimes (e.g., in relation to the slave trade and colonialism) with impunity. Many desperately poor people convicted of relatively minor property crimes such as shoplifting, picking pockets, and stealing incidental items of food or clothing were transported to penal colonies from the United Kingdom to Australia to serve long sentences, with some of the offenders as young as 9 years of age (Hilton and Hood 1999). Although over a long period of time the specific policies associated with transportation were abandoned, it remains the case that early in the twenty-first century in the United States well over two million people are incarcerated, with a not insignificant proportion of these imprisoned for relatively minor offenses involving property or drugs.

In the late nineteenth century, a growing number of politicians and social commentators recognized that the large monopolistic trusts exemplified by John D. Rockefeller's Standard Oil were harmful to American consumers, farmers, small businessmen, and, more broadly, the U.S. economy. This recognition led to the adoption of the Sherman Antitrust Act, which prohibited (and criminalized) anticompetitive practices. It is not necessary to revisit the long (and uneven) history of the implementation of this act to acknowledge its significance in creating a more level playing field for American businesses. Nevertheless, oligopolies, conglomerates, and multinationals have, in at least some important respects, counterbalanced the formal purpose of the Sherman Antitrust Act to produce a "fairer" marketplace by giving large and powerful entities immense competitive advantages. That said, we would be far worse off without this act.

If in an earlier era it was recognized that monopolies were too harmful to be allowed to exist, and accordingly had to be outlawed, then it follows that in the contemporary era we must recognize that the criminogenic conditions that have had such demonstrably harmful consequences in bringing about a massive financial meltdown should be outlawed to the extent possible. In relatively recent times, we have criminalized environmental pollution, the creation of unsafe working places, and the distribution of harmful products, although still in a fairly limited way (Friedrichs 2010b). A truly effective response to the current financial crisis would have to be quite direct and uncompromising in acknowledging the inherently criminal character of the financial industry as presently organized, and the criminogenic conditions promoted by many of its core policies and practices.

All financial reform initiatives generate concerns about unintended or negative consequences. This is especially true for any criminalization initiatives. When public policy initiatives are promoted in response to the whole range of conventional forms of crime, there tends to be little concern with potential unintended or negative consequences of such policies. Tough new legislation in response to street crime, to drug dealing, to sexual predation (especially directed at children) is politically popular and generates little effective opposition. But such policies have led recently to the vast expansion of the prison population and those under the supervision of the criminal justice system. Some criminologists have explored the negative consequences of these policies. As just one example, in *Imprisoning Communities: How Mass Incarceration Makes Disadvantaged Neighborhoods Worse* (2007), Todd Clear documents the claim made in the subtitle to his book. But a broad popular or political concern with such consequences is relatively absent.

Concern about negative and unintended consequences of initiatives directed at the harmful practices and policies of major corporations and financial institutions is immense. It is fueled particularly by the vast economic resources and political influence of these organizations. There can be no question that proposed transformative policies directed at the financial industry, if implemented, will carry huge costs, starting with greatly diminished profits for major financial institutions. All sophisticated proponents of transformative policies recognize such direct costs as well as many potential residual costs and unanticipated consequences. But the fundamental premise of such proponents is quite simple: The costs of failing to adopt and implement such policies, to society as a whole and to a broad swath of taxpayers, workers, homeowners, investors, and savers, are certain to be far greater than any negative and unintended consequences.

Paul Krugman, in one of his *New York Times* columns (2010a), has put the matter concisely: "We've devoted far too large a share of our wealth, far too much of the nation's talent, to the business of devising and peddling complex financial schemes—schemes that have a tendency to blow up the economy. Ending this state of affairs will hurt the financial industry. So?"

The financial reform measures passed in 2010 by the U.S. Congress are incremental, technical, and limited. Certainly some elements of the reform measures are needed and may have some beneficial effects. But the history of such reforms is that over time they will be gamed, watered down, and selectively enforced. New regulatory agencies and initiatives are always subject to the enduring problem of "agency capture." That is, they are "captured" and virtually controlled by the industry they are supposed to regulate. Only transformative policies are likely to have an enduring effect (Friedrichs 2010a). Such policies implemented by the Roosevelt administration in the 1930s—including the passage of the Glass-Steagall Act of 1933 and the establishment of the SEC—did make a difference over a period of many decades. Ultimately the Reagan conservative "counterrevolution"—including the passage of the Garn-St. Germain Act of 1982 and the enfeebling of the SEC—led to a systemic erosion of the controls rooted in the New Deal policies (Hagan 2010). Subsequent administrations, including those of Bill Clinton and George W. Bush, adopted further deregulatory initiatives.

Concluding Observations

In a world of growing interdependence and diminishing resources, the current architecture of high finance is not sustainable. Going forward, the harmful effects of this architecture will be progressively amplified, with broad and catastrophic consequences. The specific, direct harms that can be linked to the financial system activities are well understood: millions of lost homes, jobs, and savings, along with broad and devastating effects on the physical and mental well-being of millions of people. It is impossible to explore larger issues here that can be linked to all this, such as the dramatic increase in the unequal distribution of wealth and income, the case that high income is not earned, for the most part, in terms of merit and effort, and the multiple harmful effects on society and its citizens of intensifying socioeconomic inequality. More narrowly, it has been a core argument of this chapter that unless the inherently criminal and criminogenic nature of the present architecture of the system of high finance in our society is fully recognized and addressed, we are destined to endure ongoing cycles of financial crises, with often devastating losses imposed on a wide range of people—but with those at the top of the financial system coming out ahead.

This analysis does not suffer from the illusion that formally characterizing policies and practices at the heart of the financial industry as crime is a realizable objective in the near term. Rather, the case being set forth here is that broadly diffused *recognition* of this activity as criminal is a crucial starting point for transformative public policies that will ultimately prove essential to minimizing the chances of future catastrophic financial meltdowns. A transformative collective consciousness about the nature of crime in relation to harm is part of this. We must transform our understanding of crime and adopt an understanding that accords appropriate societal attention to the whole range of criminal activities proportional to their identifiable harm. It remains the case that activities with relatively mild harmful consequences for society are accorded much attention and treated harshly, whereas activities with demonstrably major harmful consequences for society are accorded little attention and only very selectively addressed.

Admittedly, a call for a radical reordering of our consciousness of crime and our response to it is an ambitious project. Many might insist it is wholly unrealizable. But whether or not it can be realized, it should be at the center of our dialogue about the financial system and the harm emanating from it.

A Postscript: How They Got Away with It

At this writing not a single high-level private- or public-sector executive or official has been convicted of criminal charges in relation to a financial meltdown that has been described as having obliterated trillions of dollars of value. How is this possible, in an era when our prisons are filled with a record number of offenders, many of whom have been convicted of relatively inconsequential crimes? A concise (and contextual) answer to the core question posed in the title of this book—"How they got away with it"—can readily be produced by any serious student of white collar crime. First, because the illegitimate and harmful activities in the financial sector were intertwined with legitimate and beneficial activities, it is on some level challenging to disentangle one from the other. There is nothing legitimate, beneficial, or productive about an inner-city mugging, but this is not necessarily the case with the securitization of mortgage loans by Wall Street investment banking houses.

Second, the media (and the popular culture itself) has a long history of highlighting conventional crime—especially sensational, violent crime—over white collar crime, which tends to direct the public to demand political responses. Third, the Wall Street "crooks"—despite being widely castigated as such—continue to enjoy a relative degree of immunity from formal identification and processing as criminals, significantly protected by their ultrarespectable status. Bernard Madoff avoided serious scrutiny of his suspect investment fund, over a period of many years, due in part to his highly respected status (as a former chair of NASDAQ, among other things). Fourth, the ties between the high-level financial sector and the high-level political sector—greased by large campaign donations and multimillion-dollar lobbying—provide a further measure of relative immunity from criminal investigations and prosecutions.

Fifth, the complex and diffuse nature of Wall Street wrongdoing (relative to most conventional crime) confronts potential investigators and criminal prosecutors with formidable challenges. And sixth, following up on this point, much greater resources must be devoted to investigating and prosecuting Wall Street cases relative to conventional criminal cases. It is clear that, otherwise, any hope of success in such investigations will be compromised by the vast resources available to stifle investigations and defeat prosecutorial initiatives.

A Brief Update on Wall Street Crime: February, 2012

In his State of the Union address in January 2012, President Barack Obama announced the establishment of a new prosecutorial entity to address financial sector crimes that contributed to the financial meltdown. Phil Angelides (2012), chairperson of the Financial Crisis Inquiry Commission, asserted that if Wall Street is to face justice, a real commitment of substantial resources to this entity will be necessary. And if we hope to deter future malfeasance, criminal prosecutions must be vigorously pursued. As of early 2012, no Wall Street executives or their firms have been successfully prosecuted for practices they engaged in leading up to the meltdown that had occurred. Some high-profile insider trading cases were pursued—most prominently the conviction and imprisonment of hedge fund billionaire Raj Rajaratnam—but individuals from various quarters have criticized the privileging of these prosecutions over the prosecutions of fraudulent investment banking practices. Federal Judge Jed Rakoff refused to sign off on an SEC civil settlement with Citigroup that allowed the bank to fork over hundreds of millions of dollars without admitting any wrongdoing. Such settlements have been quite common. And key figures in the subprime mortgage collapse, such as Angelo Mozillo of Countrywide, have been allowed to make civil settlements that were largely paid by other parties and did not in any way put a significant dent into the huge fortunes acquired during the subprime mortgage mania.

Substantial lobbying efforts from Wall Street to rescind provisions of the Dodd-Frank Act, which places restrictions on excessively risky (but often highly profitable) investment bank activities, are under way. The bankruptcy of MF Global (headed by former New Jersey governor and Goldman Sachs CEO Jon Corzine), with over $1 billion of customers' funds missing, is an ominous warning that little has changed since the financial meltdown. In March 2012, a Goldman Sachs executive director, Greg Smith (2012), inspired a firestorm of commentary with his *New York Times* op-ed "Why I Am Leaving Goldman Sachs." He alleged that the "morally bankrupt" culture of Goldman Sachs continued to promote aggressively "ripping off" the investment bank's own clients in the interest of making the most possible money from them. In April 2012 the manager of a major institutional investment firm, Sequoia Fund, criticized Goldman Sachs' renomination of James Johnson, former CEO of Fannie Mae, to its board, since Johnson was at the center of several major corporate governance debacles (Sorkin 2012). And the outbreak of Occupy Wall Street protests—with the failure to prosecute Wall Street crime as one theme of these protests—was just one sign of widespread and justifiable public anger toward both Wall Street and Washington. It is crystal clear that an effective response to the criminogenic nature of Wall Street is far from being realized. Altogether, in Spring 2012, crime on Wall Street was still wide awake and had hardly been put to sleep.

References

Akerlof, George, and Robert J. Shiller. 2009. *Animal Spirits: How Human Psychology Drives the Economy, and Why It Matters for Global Capitalism.* Princeton, N.J.: Princeton University Press.

Angelides, Phil. 2012. "Will Wall Street Ever Face Justice?" *New York Times* (March 2): A25.

Augar, Philip. 2005. *The Greed Merchants.* London: Penguin.

Black, William. 2005. *The Best Way to Rob a Bank Is to Own One.* Austin: University of Texas Press.

Calavita, Kitty, and Henry N. Pontell. 1990. "'Heads I Win, Tails You Lose': Deregulation, Crime, and Crisis in the Savings and Loan Industry." *Crime & Delinquency* 3:309–41.

Carter, Terry. 2009. "How Lawyers Enabled the Meltdown." *ABA Journal*, January, 34–39.

Cassidy, John. 2010. *How Markets Fail: The Logic of Economic Calamities.* New York: Farrar, Straus, and Giroux.

Chambliss, William J. 1976. "The State and Criminal Law." In *Whose Law, What Order?*, edited by William J. Chambliss and Milton Mankoff, 66–106. New York: Wiley.

Chan, Sewell, and Louise Story. 2010. "S.E.C. Settling Its Complaints with Goldman." *New York Times*, July 16.

Clear, Todd R. 2007. *Imprisoning Communities: How Mass Incarceration Makes Disadvantaged Neighborhoods Worse.* New York: Oxford University Press.

Craig, Susanne. 2010. "Bayou Case Casts Cloud on Goldman." *New York Times*, October 22.

Ehrenreich, Barbara. 2008. "The Power of Negative Thinking." *New York Times*, September 24.

Friedrichs, David O. 1996. *Trusted Criminals: White Collar Crime in Contemporary Society.* Belmont, Calif.: Wadsworth.

———. 2007. "Transnational Crime and Global Criminology: Definitional, Typological, and Contextual Conundrums." *Social Justice* 34:4–18.

———. 2010a. "Mortgage Origination Fraud and the Global Economic Crisis: Incremental Versus Transformative Policy Initiatives." *Criminology & Public Policy* 9:627–32.

———. 2010b. *Trusted Criminals: White Collar Crime in Contemporary Society.* 4th ed. Belmont, Calif.: Wadsworth/Cengage Learning.

Gandel, Stephen. 2010a. "The Case Against Goldman Sachs." *Time*, May 3, 30–37.

———. 2010b. "How Goldman Trashed a Town." *Time*, July 5, 32–33.

Geis, Gilbert. 2007. *White-Collar and Corporate Crime.* Upper Saddle River, N.J.: Pearson.

Gibbs, Nancy. 2009. "25 People to Blame." *Time,* February 23, 20–25.

Hagan, John. 2010. *Who Are the Criminals? The Politics of Crime Policy from the Age of Roosevelt to the Age of Reagan.* Princeton, N.J.: Princeton University Press.

Haines, Fiona. 2007. "Crime? What Crime? Tales of the Collapse of HIH." In *International Handbook of White-Collar and Corporate Crime,* edited by Henry N. Pontell and Gilbert Geis, 523–39. New York: Springer.

Helmkamp, James, Richard Ball, and Kitty Townsend, eds. 1996. *Definitional Dilemma: Can and Should There Be a Universal Definition of White-Collar Crime?* Morgantown, W.Va.: National White Collar Crime Center.

Hillyard, Paddy, Christina Pantazis, Steve Tombs, and Dave Gordon, eds. 2004. *Beyond Criminology: Taking Harm Seriously.* London: Pluto Press.

Hilton, Phillip, and Susan Hood. 1999. *Caught in the Act: Unusual Offenses of Port Arthur Convicts.* Port Arthur, Tasmania: Port Arthur Historic Site Management Authority.

Johnson, Simon, and James Kwak. 2010. *13 Bankers: The Wall Street Takeover and the Next Financial Meltdown.* New York: Pantheon Books.

Kaufman, Frederick. 2010. "The Food Bubble." *Harper's Magazine,* July, 27–34.

Kauzlarich, David, and David O. Friedrichs. 2005. "Crime, Definitions of." In *Encyclopedia of Criminology,* edited by Richard A. Wright and J. Mitchell Miller, 1:273–75. New York: Routledge.

Kouwe, Zachery, and Dan Slater. 2009. "2 Bear Stearns Fund Leaders Are Acquitted." *New York Times,* November 11.

Kowitt, Beth. 2008. "The Blame Game." *Fortune,* October 27, 14.

Krugman, Paul. 2010a. "Don't Cry for Wall Street." *New York Times,* April 25.

———. 2010b. "Looters in Loafers." *New York Times,* April 19.

Kuttner, Robert. 2008. *Obama's Challenge: America's Economic Crisis and the Power of a Transformative Presidency.* White River Junction, Vt.: Chelsea Green.

Lowenstein, Roger. 2010. *The End of Wall Street.* New York: Penguin.

McCluskey, John D. 2009. "Robbery." In *21st Century Criminology: A Reference Handbook,* edited by J. Mitchell Miller, 507–14. Los Angeles: Sage.

Morris, Charles R. 2008. *The Trillion Dollar Meltdown: Easy Money, High Rollers, and the Great Credit Crash.* New York: Public Affairs.

Prins, Nomi. 2009. *It Takes a Pillage: Behind the Bailouts, Bonuses, and Backroom Deals from Washington to Wall Street.* Hoboken, N.J.: Wiley.

Rich, Frank. 2010. "Fight on, Goldman Sachs!" *New York Times,* April 25.

Ritholtz, Barry, with Aaron Task. 2009. *Bailout Nation: How Greed and Easy Money Corrupted Wall Street and Shook the World Economy.* Hoboken, N.J.: Wiley.

Rosoff, Stephen M., Henry N. Pontell, and Robert H. Tillman. 2010. *Profit Without Honor: White-Collar Crime and the Looting of America.* 5th ed. Upper Saddle River, N.J.: Pearson.

Roubini, Nouriel, and Stephen Mihm. 2010. *Crisis Economics: A Crash Course in the Future of Finance.* New York: Penguin.

Sale, Hillary A. 2004. "Banks: The Forgotten Partners in Fraud." *University of Cincinnati Law Review* 73:139–77.

Schwartz, Nelson D., and Eric Dash. 2010. "Banks Bet Greek Defaults on Debt They Helped Hide." *New York Times*, February 25.

Schwendinger, Herman, and Julia Schwendinger. 1972. "The Continuing Debate on the Legalistic Approach to the Definition of Crime." *Issues in Criminology* 7 (1): 71–81.

Smith, Greg. 2012. "Why I Am Leaving Goldman Sachs." *New York Times* (March 14): A27.

Sorkin, Andrew Ross. 2012. " 'Tainted,' But Sheltered on Boards." *New York Times* (April 24): B1.

Stiglitz, Joseph E. 2010. *Freefall: America, Free Markets, and the Sinking of the World Economy*. New York: Norton.

Story, Louise. 2010. "Prosecutors Start Inquiry at Goldman." *New York Times*, April 30.

Story, Louise, and Eric Dash. 2009. "Bank of America Outs Head of Risk Oversight." *New York Times*, June 5, B1.

Story, Louise, and Gretchen Morgenson. 2010. "S.E.C. Accuses Goldman of Fraud in Housing Deal." *New York Times*, April 17.

Sutherland, Edwin H. 1945. "Is 'White-Collar Crime' Crime?" *American Sociological Review* 10:132–39.

Taibbi, Matt. 2009. "The Great American Bubble Machine." *Rolling Stone*, July, 9–23, 52–61, 98–101.

———. 2010. "The Feds vs. Goldman." *Rolling Stone*, May 13, 40–41.

Tappan, Paul. 1947. "Who Is the Criminal?" *American Sociological Review* 12:96–102.

Weisel, Deborah Lamm. 2007. *Bank Robbery*. Washington, D.C.: U.S. Department of Justice, Office of Community Oriented Policing Services.

[2]

THE LOGICS OF FINANCE

Abuse of Power and Systemic Crisis

SASKIA SASSEN

The end of the Cold War launched one of the most brutal economic phases of the modern era. Following a period of Keynesian-led relative redistribution in developed market economies, a mix of government action and corporate economic interests led to a radical reshuffling of capitalism. Two logics organized this reshuffling. One is systemic and gets wired into most countries' economic and (de)regulatory policies—most important, privatization and the lifting of tariffs. We can see this in the unsettling and debordering of existing arrangements within the deep structures of capitalist economies. This unsettling took place through the implementation of specific fiscal and monetary policies in most countries around the world, albeit with variable degrees of intensity. The effect was to open global ground for new or sharply expanded modes of profit extraction even in unlikely domains, such as subprime mortgages on modest residences, or through unlikely instruments, such as credit default swaps, a key component of the shadow banking system (Sassen 2008a; 2010).

The second logic is the transformation of growing areas of the world into extreme zones for these new or sharply expanded modes of profit extraction. The most familiar contexts are global cities and the spaces for outsourced work. These have become thick *local* settings that contain the diverse conditions that *global* firms need—diverse labor markets, specific deregulations and guarantees of contract, and particular infrastructures and built environments. Other local settings for global capitalism exist, notably the vast areas of land in Africa and central Asia purchased to grow food, mine for rare metals, and extract water (Sassen 2010).

Critical to both these logics is the invention of extremely complex financial and organizational instruments to engage in what are, ultimately, new forms of obtaining profit.[1] Many of the components of the post-1989 global economy were already present or being elaborated in the early 1980s. Just as the silent revolutions of 1989 are the iconic representation of a political process that had been building for a long time, the corporate globalizing of the late 1980s had also begun many years earlier. But the fall of the Soviet empire in 1989 made a major difference, most notably by giving these innovations the run of the world through the legitimating mantra of "the market knows best." As a result, a new kind of global economy formed, one centered on global firms using *national* governments to make *private global* space for them (Sassen 2008b, chapters 4 and 5). This contrasts with the international economy of the post–World War I era, one centered on international trade and capital flows governed in large part by states, no matter their unequal power to do so. Both periods are marked by the concentration of power. The difference in the current period is private actors' extreme power and national governments' extensive participation in making this private global space.

This chapter permits the examination of only a few aspects of the dominant economic tendencies of the last decades and of ways to go beyond their deeply destructive character.[2] The first section focuses on the capacity of finance to impose its logics across economic sectors. This financialization is a matter not just of the volume of finance but, more important, of its logic getting wired into a growing number of economic sectors. Here I am particularly interested in examining the capacity of financial institutions to invent instruments that allow them to build high financial value from modest assets, often at a high cost to the owners of those modest assets. Next, I focus on the particulars of the current crisis and what it reveals about a system and its limitations—more a crisis of panic than a response to subprime mortgage losses and more a question of abuse from the top than of irresponsible consumers. I conclude with suggestions for what can be done now to lay the groundwork for a better, more distributive future.

Advanced Capitalism and Its Mechanisms for Primitive Accumulation

The history of the era following the 1989 revolutions in countries that were once part of the Soviet sphere of influence is usually depicted as the spread of liberal political reforms and the end of antidemocratic approaches to government (the "End of History"). But the more profound and wider effect of those revolutions has been on our post-1989 economic history. At the end of the Cold War, the free market was pronounced victorious, and neoliberalism was declared the best growth policy for countries. All of this points to a systemic feature of advanced capitalism, one that may have been held in check by the Cold War but that rose to its full capacity for expansion and destruction once freed from territorial restraints. The celebration of free-market economics enabled finance to enter a new phase in the 1990s, one that legitimized the financialization of growing sectors of the economy. Among its several major negative effects was that "shareholder value," rather than quality of product or magnitude of sales, became the leading criterion for firms' success.

One of the ironic consequences of the growing complexity of finance was the implementation of advanced financial forms of primitive accumulation. It took work, but advanced financial innovators and firms succeeded in articulating enormously complex financial and organizational instruments with elementary forms of extraction.[3]

Corporate outsourcing of jobs to low-wage countries is one example of this articulation. A large literature documents various links in the long chains that connect outsourced jobs to shareholders' gains, firms' profits, and consumers' access to lower-cost products and services. Less attention is paid to the fact that to implement this outsourcing, global firms have had to develop complex organizational structures, using enormously expensive and talented experts. The purpose of this complexity and talent is to extract labor at lower cost than is possible in the firms' home countries. Furthermore, this organizational innovation encompasses the use of types of unskilled labor that would be already fairly low domestically, given the active dismantling of labor unions. To achieve this simple gain took complex reorganization of production processes and distribution, new legislation or regulation in home and destination countries, and so on.

The insidious element is that millions of saved cents per hour of labor actually translate into a particular categorical positive: gains for shareholders. The decreased cost can also contribute to increases in firms' profit margins and consumers' savings, but the invention of instruments to transform savings of labor costs into a more highly valued corporate share was crucial to the strategy.

Similarly, the financial sector created complicated financial instruments to extract profit from even very modest households. Securitization was a key bit of financial engineering. It enabled financial firms in the 1980s to bundle millions of credit cardholders' debt and home mortgages and develop investment instruments. This is the prehistory of what we now refer to as the subprime mortgage crisis. In early 2000, a type of subprime mortgage was developed that became catastrophic for modest-income households. Subprime mortgages can be valuable instruments for modest-income households, enabling them to buy a house or obtain a second mortgage or a mortgage on an already-paid-for home. What had been a state project became a financial project after 2000.

Presented with the possibility (which turned out to be mostly a deception) of owning a house, modest-income people will put whatever savings or future earnings they have into a down payment. The small savings or future earnings of modest-income households or the ownership of a modest house was used to enter into a contract. And it was the contract that mattered, not the house itself or the mortgage payments: the contract was necessary to develop a financial instrument that could profit investors. By 2004 the strategy was so successful with investors that mortgage sellers did not even ask for a full credit report or down payment, just a signature on the contract. In a financial world overwhelmed by speculative capital, all that mattered was the contract representing the material asset (the house). Indeed subprime mortgage sellers were, we now know, indifferent to whether those households could make monthly payments. Speed and numbers mattered, so the premium was on selling subprime mortgages to as many households as possible, including those who qualified for a regular mortgage that would have afforded them more protections but would have taken much longer to process. For the "innovation" to work, sellers needed to bundle at least 500 contracts (mortgages) as quickly as possible into an instrument that combined high-grade debt and to sell it on the high-finance circuit. The negative effects on households, on neighborhoods, and on cities received no consideration.

From the investors' perspective, the key was the growing demand for asset-backed securities in a market where the outstanding value of derivatives was $600 trillion, more than ten times the value of global gross domestic product (GDP). To address this demand, investors could use even subprime mortgage debt as an asset. But the low quality of this debt necessitated cutting each mortgage into multiple tiny slices and mixing them with high-grade debt: no matter the tiny slices, it could still be sold as an asset-backed security. The result was an enormously complex and opaque instrument. Tracing all the components of these bundled assets is difficult, and in many instances impossible, as was the case with now defunct Lehman Brothers, whose value still has not been established by a team of top-level experts for the company's bankruptcy proceedings.

The lethal threat to these households was that payment of monthly mortgages mattered less, if at all, to the sellers of those mortgages than securing a certain number of loans, within a short time span, to be bundled into "investment products." The use of complex sequences of "products" delinked the creditworthiness of the home buyer from investors' profit. Second, the accelerated buying and selling of these instruments in the high-finance circuit enabled profit making while passing on the risk. Investors made hundreds of billions of dollars in profits on these mixed instruments merely by including a bit of asset—those houses—in mostly speculative instruments that could then be sold as *asset*-backed securities. Millions of those modest households have gone bankrupt and continue to do so and to lose their homes and savings, and many investors made enormous profits.

The insidious element of these transactions, as with the outsourcing of labor, is that a very large number of mortgages sold to modest-income people (who mostly did not ask for them) can actually translate into a categorical positive: profits for the high-finance investor. It took serious financial engineering to make this possible, just as it did to increase corporate shareholder value through outsourcing jobs. The millions of bankruptcies among subprime mortgage holders in 2006 and 2007 did not affect investors directly: Only those firms that held on to these mortgages suffered. Most investors did not hold on and thus made profits. But within the logic of finance, it is also possible to make a good profit by betting against the success of an innovation, predicting failure.[4] That type of profit making also happened. Further, anxious investors began to think about cashing in their credit-default swaps, which led to an actual investor's crisis because the funds were insufficient to meet these vastly larger obligations than the subprime mortgage.

In short, the so-called subprime crisis was not due to irresponsible households taking on mortgages they could not afford, as is still commonly asserted in the United States and in the rest of the world. It was a foreclosure crisis for homeowners. But for the financial sector it was at that point merely a crisis of *confidence,* as the numbers of foreclosures exploded in August 2007 and it became evident that it was impossible to trace the toxic component in their investments.

Multiple conditions, including the decline in housing prices, led to extremely negative outcomes for households, including foreclosure. From 2005 to 2010, over 9.3 million mortgage foreclosure notices were sent to households in the United States; this can amount to about 35 million people. In 2008, for instance, on average, 10,000 U.S. households lost their home to foreclosure every day. Not all foreclosures lead to eviction, or at least not promptly; and some households may have been sent more than one foreclosure. The available evidence shows that by 2010, over 7 million of these households were no longer in the foreclosed home. There are still an estimated 4 million households that could be in trouble until 2014. This is a brutal form of primitive accumulation achieved through an enormously complex sequence of instruments using vast talent pools in finance, law, accounting, and mathematics.

For millions of modest-income people, the impact was catastrophic. New York City offers an example, in microcosm. Table 2.1 shows how white residents of New York, who have a far higher average income than all the other groups in the city, were far less likely to have subprime mortgages than all other groups, just 9.1 percent of all mortgages taken in 2006, compared with 13.6 percent for Asian Americans, 28.6 percent for Hispanic Americans, and 40.7 percent for African Americans. The table also shows that all groups, regardless of incidence, experienced high growth rates in subprime borrowing from 2002 to 2006. If we consider the most acute period, from 2002 to 2005, subprime borrowing more than doubled for whites, tripled for Asians and Hispanics, and quadrupled for blacks.

The subprime mortgage instrument developed in these years is just one example illustrating how financial institutions can make major additions to financial value on very modest assets and future losses of assets, and most important, with a disregard for social outcomes and even for the national economy. This disregard is legal, notwithstanding its pernicious effects.

Finally, we should remember that the complexity of the meaning of "gains" in finance contrasts with traditional banking gains. In traditional

Table 2.1
Rate of Conventional Subprime Lending by Race in New York City, 2002–2006
(in percent)

	2002	2003	2004	2005	2006
White	4.6	6.2	7.2	11.2	9.1
Black	13.4	20.5	35.2	47.1	40.7
Hispanic	11.9	18.1	27.6	39.3	28.6
Asian	4.2	6.2	9.4	18.3	13.6

SOURCE: Furman Center for Real Estate and Urban Policy, 2007.

banking, the gain is on the sale of money the bank has, whereas in finance the gain comes from the sale of money the institution does not have. As a result, finance needs to "make" capital, which means creating speculative instruments and the financialization of nonfinancial sectors, subjects I return to later and develop more fully elsewhere (Sassen 2008b, chapter 5; 2010).

Crisis as Systemic Logic

Financial profit either can be promptly materialized as a nonfinancial asset, such as a dam or a telecommunications infrastructure, or can keep being used on increasingly speculative high-risk financial instruments. The latter, facilitated by the use of electronic networks, software, high-frequency trading, and many new derivative-based instruments, has been dominant for the last 20 years and has generated the extremely high levels of financialization now evident in several major developed countries (Sassen 2008b, chapter 7). To give a sense of the orders of magnitude that the financial system has created over the last two decades, the total (notional) value of outstanding derivatives, which are a form of complex debt and the most common financial instrument, was more than $600 trillion in the early 2000s. This created a demand for asset-backed securities among investors.

Financial assets have grown far more rapidly than the overall economy of developed countries, as measured by GDP.[5] This is not necessarily bad, especially if the growing financial capital is transformed into large-scale public-benefit projects—for example, a rapid transit system or the development of solar energy. But in the period that began in the 1980s, this was

rare, except for some extreme cases with few, if any, general public benefits, such as the building up of Dubai in a very short period of time. Mostly,
finance developed more speculative and complex instruments. Historically, this seems to be part of the logic of finance: As it grows and gains
power, it does not use its power well. Furthermore, Arrighi (1994) has
argued that when speculative finance becomes dominant in a historic
period, it signals the decay of that period.

In the United States, the source of many organizational and financial
innovations, the value of financial assets by 2006—before the 2007 crisis
deepened—exceeded GDP by 450 percent (McKinsey & Company 2008).
In the European Union (EU), the corresponding figure was 356 percent,
with the United Kingdom well above the EU average at 440 percent. More
generally, the number of countries where financial assets exceeded the
value of their GDP more than doubled from thirty-three in 1990 to seventy-
two in 2006.

These numbers illustrate that the period beginning in the late 1980s
and continuing to the present time constitutes an extreme moment. But is
it anomalous? I argue that it is not. Furthermore, it is not created by exog-
enous factors, as the notion of crisis suggests. Recurrent crises are characteristic of this particular type of financial system. Since the first crises of
this phase occurred in the 1980s, the U.S. government has given the financial industry the instruments to continue its leveraging stampede, as
in the savings and loan crisis and the New York stock market crash of
1987. We have had five major bailouts since the 1980s, the decade when the
new financial phase began. Each time, taxpayers' money was used to
pump liquidity into the financial system; and the financial industry used it
to leverage, aiming at more speculation and gain. It did not use it to pay off
its debt because the industry is about debt.

The financialization of a growing number of economic sectors since the
1980s has become both a sign of the power of this financial logic and the
sign that it is exhausting its growth potential in the current phase insofar
as finance needs to use and invade other economic sectors in order to
grow. Once it has subjected much of the economy to its logic, it reaches
some type of limit, and the downward curve is likely to set in. One acute
illustration of this is the development of instruments by some financial
firms that bet on growth in a sector and simultaneously bet against that
sector. This clearly is not made public, but every now and then we gain an
insight into how it might work. In one recent case, Goldman Sachs sold

derivatives to the Greek government and then developed instruments for another client that would deliver profits if that government went bankrupt. This led to the filing of a lawsuit against Goldman Sachs by the U.S. government in 2010. The firm settled out of court to avoid making public too much information about its procedures.

The current crisis contains features that suggest that financialized capitalism has reached the limits of its own logic for this phase. It has been extremely successful at extracting value from all economic sectors through their financialization; however, when everything has become financialized, finance can no longer extract value. Therefore, it needs nonfinancialized sectors to build on. In this context, one of the last frontiers for financial extraction is modest-income households, of which there are a billion or more worldwide, and bailouts through taxpayers' money—which is real, old-fashioned, not financialized money.[6]

Credit default swaps are a critical factor in the current financial crisis and yet another innovation. These instruments reached a value of $62 trillion by 2007, more than the $54 trillion of global GDP, and led to massive high finance losses in September 2008. The critical factor for the financial sector is not the millions of subprime mortgage foreclosures, because the overall value of foreclosures was relatively small for global financiers. It was not knowing what might next turn out to be a toxic asset, given the impossibility of tracing the toxic component in complex investment instruments. As already indicated, the housing crisis for millions of people was only a crisis of confidence among investors. The homeowners' crisis (valued at a few hundred billion dollars) was the little tail that wagged the enormous dog of trust in the financial system. In other words, this type of financial system has more of the social in it than is suggested by the technical complexity of its instruments and electronic platforms (Sassen 2008b, chapter 7).

The language of crisis remains ambiguous, as is evident in the following events and trends. A first point is that what we call crisis has enormous variability. Since the 1980s, there have been several financial crises. Some are well known, such as the 1987 New York stock market crash and the 1997 Asian meltdown. Others have received less attention, such as the financial crises that occurred in more than seventy countries during the 1980s and 1990s as they deregulated their financial systems. These are usually referred to as adjustment crises; the language of "adjustment" suggests they are good crises as they move a country toward economic development. Typically, the term *financial crisis* is used to describe an event that has a deleterious effect on the leading sectors of finance rather than on a country's institutions and people. National "adjustment" crises involved a far larger region of the globe than did the "financial" crises of 1987 and 1997. Yet the miseries they inflicted on middle-income people in the countries where they occurred, and the resulting destruction of often well-functioning national economic sectors, have largely been invisible to the global eye. These individual-country adjustment crises intersected with global concerns and interests only when there were strong financial links with global firms and investors, as was the case with the 1994 Mexico crisis and the 2001 Argentine crisis.

A second point arises from data that present the period after the 1997 so-called Asian financial crisis as a fairly stable one—until the current financial crisis. One element of this representation is that after a country goes through an adjustment crisis, what follows can be measured as "stability" and even prosperity according to conventional indicators. Except for a few major global crises, such as the dot-com crisis and the Argentine sovereign default, the post-1997 period was one of considerable financial stability.

But behind this "stability" is the savage sorting of winners and losers described in the prior section. It is easier to track winners than to track the often slow sinking into poverty of households, small firms, and government agencies (such as health and education) that are not part of the new glamour sectors (finance and trade). The postadjustment losers became relatively invisible globally over the last twenty years. Every now and then they became visible, as when members of the traditional middle class in Argentina engaged in food riots in Buenos Aires (and elsewhere) in the mid-1990s (after adjustment!), breaking into food shops just to get food—something that was previously unheard of in Argentina and took many by surprise. Such rare events also make visible the very incomplete character of postadjustment stability and the new "prosperity" praised by global regulators and media.

Thus, we need to disaggregate the often-touted fact that in 2006 and 2007, most countries had a GDP growth rate of 4 percent a year or more, a rate much higher than that of previous decades. Behind that measure lays the making of extreme forms of wealth and poverty. In contrast, a 4 percent GDP growth rate in the Keynesian years described the massive growth of a middle class.

Also left out of this macro-level picture of relative stability in the post–Asian financial crisis decade is the critical fact that "crisis" is a structural feature of deregulated, interconnected, and electronic financial markets. Two points are worth mentioning in this regard. One is the sharp growth in the extent to which nonfinancial economic sectors were financialized, leading to the overall growth of financial assets as a share of sector value. That is to say, if crisis is a structural feature of current financial markets, then the more that nonfinancial economic sectors experience financialization, the more susceptible they become to a financial crisis, regardless of their product. As a result, the potential for instability even in strong economic sectors is high, particularly in countries with sophisticated financial systems and high levels of financialization, such as the United States and the United Kingdom. Germany, which has weathered the financial crisis much better than the United States and the United Kingdom, has a manufacturing economy and a fairly low level of financialization—175 percent to GDP compared with 450 percent in the United States.

Let me illustrate with an example from the current crisis and another from the 1997 Asian crisis. When the current crisis hit the United States, many healthy firms, with good capitalization, strong demand for their goods and services, and good profit levels, were brought down by the financial crisis. Large U.S. corporations, from Coca-Cola and Pepsi to IBM and Microsoft, were doing fine in terms of capital reserves, profits, market presence, and so on, but the financial crisis still hit them, directly via devalued stock and other financial holdings and indirectly through the impact of the crisis on consumer demand and credit access. Highly financialized sectors such as the housing market and commercial property market suffered directly and immediately. Previously, basically healthy nonfinancial firms were affected in many countries that underwent adjustment crises: These adjustments were aimed at securing the conditions for globally linked financial markets, but they ruined firms in the nonfinancial sector.

We saw this also in the 1997 Asian financial crisis. Thousands of healthy manufacturing firms were destroyed in South Korea—firms whose products were in strong demand in national and foreign markets and that had the workforces and the machines to fill worldwide orders but had to close because credit dried up. This prevented them from paying the up-front costs of production and caused the unemployment of more than a million factory workers (Sassen 2001, chapter 4).

Two Separate Crises

The financial crisis of 2008, which followed the crisis of confidence in late 2007, had markedly different impacts across the world. Figure 2.1 compares the major global financial crises since the 1980s. It shows the extent to which financial leveraging has made the current crisis more acute than the other three major crises since the 1980s and up to 2008; not captured in this graph, however, is what eventually became the European sovereign debt crisis. Figure 2.1 shows that financial leveraging added another 20 percent to the underlying banking crisis, thereby bringing the current financial crisis up to an equivalent of 40 percent of global GDP, compared with earlier crises, which rarely went beyond 20 percent.

International Monetary Fund (IMF) data (Figure 2.2) show the extent to which Asia is in a very different position from the United States and Europe. Its current crisis is economic rather than financial. But interlinked global markets have brought a crisis made largely in the United States and to a lesser extent in the European Union to Asia.

As indicated earlier, the critical component that brought the financial system to a momentary standstill was the classic bursting of a speculative bubble: the $62 trillion dollar credit default swap crisis that exploded in September 2008, a full year after the subprime mortgage crisis of August 2007. The decrease in house prices, the high rate of mortgage foreclosures, the declines in global trade, and the growth of unemployment all alerted investors by 2008 that something was not right. This in turn led those who had bought credit default swaps as a sort of insurance to want to cash in. Figure 2.3 shows the extremely sharp growth in the value of these swaps from 2001 to 2007. But default swaps were not insurance; they were derivatives, which means that the sellers of the swaps did not have the capital needed to back these instruments up, which would have been required had they really constituted insurance. The sellers had not expected the downturn or the desire of buyers to cash in. This catapulted much of the financial sector into crisis. However, not everybody lost; investors such as George Soros made large profits by going against the trend.

Credit default swaps are part of what is referred to as the shadow banking system. According to some analysts, the shadow banking system accounted for 70 percent of banking at the time that the crisis exploded. The shadow banking system is not informal, illegal, or clandestine. It is in the open, but it thrives on the opaqueness of investment instruments. This

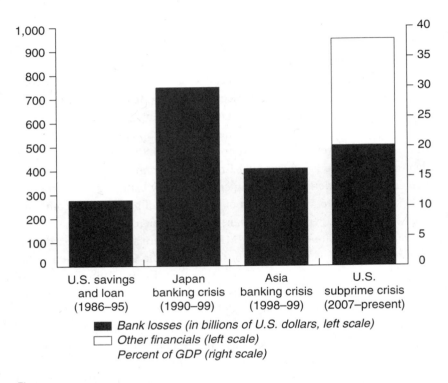

Figure 2.1
Comparison of financial crises. Note: U.S. subprime costs represent staff estimates of losses on banks and other financial institutions. All costs are in real 2007
dollars. Asia includes Indonesia, Korea, the Philippines, and Thailand. Sources:
World Bank and IMF staff estimates.

opaqueness facilitates the recoding of instruments (a derivative recoded as
insurance), which permits practices that are now, after the fact, viewed as
bordering on the illegal. For instance, it is now clear that credit default
swaps were sold as a type of insurance. From the perspective of the financial system this makes a significant difference: Had they constituted insurance, the law would require that they be backed by capital reserves and
be subject to considerable regulation. Turning them into derivatives was
de facto deregulation and eliminated the capital-reserves requirement.
Credit default swaps would not have grown so fast and reached such extreme values if they had needed to meet capital-reserves requirements,
which would have reduced much of the impact of the September 2008

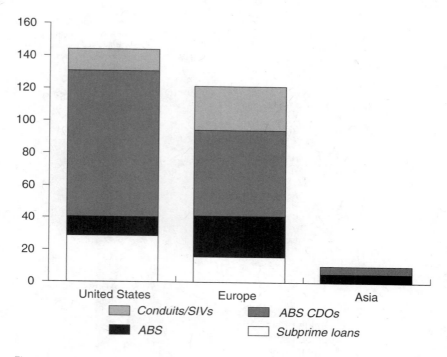

Figure 2.2
Expected bank losses as of March 2008 (in billions of U.S. dollars). Note: ABS = asset-backed security, CDO = collateralized debt obligation, SIV = structured investment vehicle. Source: Goldman Sachs, UBS, and IMF staff estimates.

crisis. Because they were derivatives, they could have an almost vertical growth curve beginning as recently as 2001. For that same reason, most swap sellers lacked the capital needed to back their obligations, ie. the swaps they sold in.

In short, there were several distinct crises. The millions of home fore-closures were a signal that something was wrong, but in itself, this crisis could not have brought down the financial system. It led to a crisis of confidence in the investor community, which in turn led those who had bought swaps as insurance against what they saw as the end of the cycle, to want to cash in those swaps. And the sellers of swaps, not ready for such a massive sudden disbursement in turn went into crisis. The decision to bail out banks with taxpayers' money with no guarantees from banks that they would re-circulate bailout funds in the economy, in turn led to further

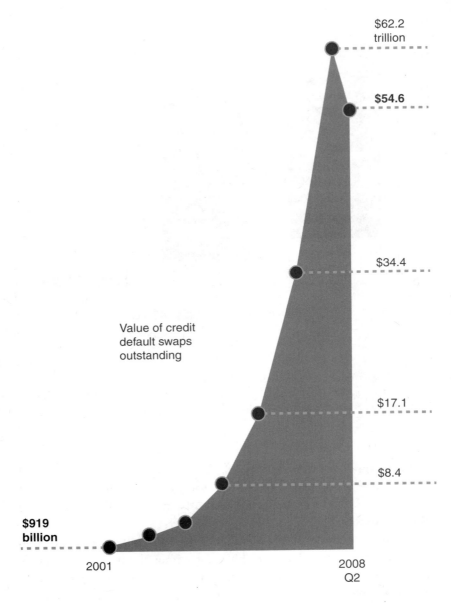

$62.2 trillion

$54.6

$34.4

Value of credit
default swaps
outstanding

$17.1

$8.4

**$919
billion**

2001

2008
Q2

Figure 2.3
Rising risk: the credit default swap market nearly doubled each year from 2001
through 2007. Source: Value of credit default swaps outstanding according to International Swaps and Derivatives Association data (Varchaver and Benner 2008).

declines in growth and rising poverty of citizens and governments. It pushed already over-indebted governments and households over the edge. The long present sovereign debt was formally recognized.

We all need debt, whether we are a firm, a household, or a country. But do we need this level of debt? More important, do we need such complex instruments to finance basic needs for firms and households?

No. Many of these needs can be met with traditional banking loans. We need finance because it "creates" capital, and large-scale projects need vast amounts of capital. At this point, only finance can reach these orders of magnitude, but it needs to be brought down into actual material processes to deliver its goods. And in this last cycle it never did. Furthermore, one major problem of the current phase is that finance entered domains—such as consumer loans and home mortgages—where traditional banking would have been a safer option for consumers. We need to expand and strengthen regulated banking and make finance less invasive and aggressive.

Changing Our Understanding of Growth and Prosperity

One important difference between the current crisis and other post-1980 crises is the order of magnitude that speculative instruments have made possible. A second important difference involves the larger economic landscape: the stronger recognition that we need to act now, because international treaties are not enough. A third difference is the wider recognition that the extremes of wealth and poverty have become problematic. We now know there is no "trickle-down" of profits secured by the richer segments of society. In fact, more concretely, epidemics resulting from poverty and inadequate health care will also affect the rich.

The extreme character of the current crisis and the fact that we have recognized other major crises—most important, climate change—creates an opening for the establishment of novel criteria for economic benefit. Yes, we need financial institutions: Finance has the capacity to make capital. However, financial capital has been used during the last decade for extremely speculative investments that largely served to enrich the already wealthy. Instead, we must use that new capital for large-scale investments in public goods, to develop manufacturing sectors, to green our economies.

This combination of goals creates an opportunity to reorient financial capital to meet a broad range of needs. As an example, financial capital helped a half-million people lift themselves out of poverty in China and India, but it did so via investments in manufacturing, infrastructure, and other material economies. Using financial capital to expand material economic sectors and to green our economies is distributive—the opposite of using financial capital to make more financial capital, which leads to massive concentrations of wealth and power.

In principle, a serious effort to use financial capital to develop the material economy carries with it an opportunity to green those investments. In that sense, the current financial crisis, which has partly paralyzed the further financialization of our economies, can be a positive factor in the development of green economies.

This mixture of conditions should also provide the opportunity to upgrade vast parts of our economies worldwide, but the search for profits at all costs has a boomerang effect. For example, the development of more profitable ways to raise cattle and pigs led to serious health threats. In the United Kingdom, the largely discarded practice of using nonsellable parts of diseased animals (such as spines) to make animal feed in the 1970s and 1980s was linked to the outbreak of so-called mad cow disease (Creutzfeldt-Jakob disease) in the 1990s among humans who consumed meat products. The H5N1 (or bird flu) virus that spread across the globe from China, including the Hong Kong Special Administrative District, in the late 1990s has been linked to substandard private housing conditions where many poor people raised chickens for human consumption. And more recently swine flu (H1N1) has been associated with the unsanitary conditions in which pigs are raised to maximize profits. If we add to this the enormous levels of workplace injuries across the world—from the U.S. meatpacking industry to the dismantling of huge ironclad ships by unprotected workers in India—we begin to see the vast costs to society and to economies that result from narrow criteria for understanding and defining profitability.

The greater our capacity to produce wealth has become over the last 20 years (and finance has played a critical role here), the more radical the condition of poverty has become. It used to be that being poor meant a plot of land that did not produce much. Today the two billion people living in extreme poverty own nothing but their bodies—not even a stable shack that might be called home. The fact is that we have the capacity to feed everybody on the globe, but feeding is not the priority of economic actors, so we have more hunger than ever before. We have all heard about the abusive conditions under which diamonds are extracted, and how those profits get re-routed for armed warfare rather than for development. Not as many may have heard about rare earths, key metals needed for electronic components (notably cell phones) and for green batteries, which are often mined by unprotected workers who use their naked hands to extract the minerals, live in conditions of poverty, and die too young from poisoning to have been able to pass on the news of their abuse to the wider world. Finally, there is the well-established fact that discovering oil in a poor country becomes the formula for the creation of even more poverty and a small elite of the super rich.

We need to change the logics through which we define genuine prosperity. The triple crisis we confront should become an opportunity to reorient our enormous capacities to make capital and to produce what is urgently needed in both the global south and the global north.

Notes

1. I develop this proposition in Sassen (2008a).

2. For a fuller development, see Sassen (2010).

3. This is only one component of the financial system. There are many components of finance that consist of interactions between rich and powerful investors where these mechanisms of primitive accumulation are not an issue. And there are some other major components that also are subject to the mechanism of primitive accumulation, notably pension funds and mutual funds, which often have to pay multiple little fees and commissions that contribute to significant and unwarranted losses for the pensioners and the consumers who buy shares in mutual funds.

4. They speculated against these instruments. That is to say, they betted against the sustainability of instruments based on getting low-income people to sign off on mortgage contracts regardless of their capacity to pay. This suggests that many of the damaging aspects of these instruments for the households were known in the financial community.

5. More detail can be found in my article "A Bad Idea: A Financial Solution to the Financial Crisis" at http://www.huffingtonpost.com/saskia-sassen/a-bad-idea -using-a-financ_b_145283.html.

6. Elsewhere (Sassen 2008a) I examine data that show the potential for global finance to use this particular type of subprime mortgage worldwide, given its invention of instruments that delink the capacity to pay the mortgage from investors' profit.

References

Arrighi, Giovanni. 1994. *The Long Twentieth Century: Money, Power, and the Origins of Our Times*. London: Verso.

Furman Center for Real Estate and Urban Policy. 2007. *State of New York City's Housing and Neighborhoods*. http://furmancenter.org/research/sonychan/2007-report/ (accessed November 28, 2008).

International Monetary Fund. 2008. *Global Financial Stability Report: Containing Systemic Risks and Restoring Financial Soundness*. Washington, D.C.: International Monetary Fund. http://www.imf.org/external/pubs/ft/gfsr/2008/01/pdf/text.pdf (accessed August 28, 2008).

McKinsey & Company. 2008. *Mapping Global Capital Markets Fourth Annual Report*. McKinsey Global Institute. http://www.mckinsey.com/mgi/reports/pdfs/Mapping_Global/ MGI_Mapping_Global_full_Report.pdf (accessed November 28, 2008).

Sassen, Saskia. 2001. *The Global City: New York, London, Tokyo*. Princeton N.J.: Princeton University Press.

———. 2008a. "Mortgage Capital and Its Particularities: A New Frontier for Global Finance." *Journal of International Affairs* 62 (1): 187–212.

———. 2008b. *Territory, Authority, Rights: From Medieval to Global Assemblages*. Princeton, N.J.: Princeton University Press.

———. 2010. "A Savage Sorting of Winners and Losers: Contemporary Versions of Primitive Accumulation." *Globalizations* 7 (1–2): 23–50.

Varchaver, Nicholas, and Katie Benner. 2008. "The $55 Trillion Question: Special Report Issue 1: America's Money Crisis." http://money.cnn.com/2008/09/30/magazines/fortune/varchaver_derivatives_short.fortune/index.htm.

[3]

AMERICA'S PONZI CULTURE

SUSAN WILL

Writing about the American economy for *Harper's* during the 1980s, L. J. Davis submitted article after article about Ponzi schemes despite his editor's complaints. "It's the same story over and over again," the editor said. "I can't keep printing the same story. Can't you find something that's not a Ponzi scheme?" (Davis 2002).

In fact, Davis saw what most people failed to see or did not want to see: Ponzi schemes were everywhere. Clever operators like Bernard Madoff, R. Allen Stanford, and—much earlier—Charles Ponzi represented the most iconic examples. But they were small fries compared with the smoke-and-mirrors practices of large corporations and government entities that encouraged and facilitated a "Ponzi culture" that has created massive harm to the U.S. economy.

By normalizing leverage, speculation, and bubbles, Ponzi culture discourages fiscal conservativism and counters the proverbial wisdom of saving for a rainy day. It creates a casino economy that is fueled by the belief that through speculation individuals can reap huge profits and live beyond what their salaries alone would allow.[1] Despite recessions triggered by a succession of crises, from the savings and loan scandal of the late 1980s to the deflation of the dot.com bubble and the financial meltdown of 2006–2010, the Ponzi culture still finds willing believers in the illusion that huge returns on meager investments are available without any risk.

Ponzi schemes, named after Charles Ponzi, the architect of a fraudulent international postal reply coupon scheme in 1920, are unsustainable investment scams that rely on an ever-increasing influx of participants and money (American Institute of Certified Public Accountants 2007). Ponzi operators appeal to a variety of needs and emotions to lure victims: greed, ego, the fear of losing opportunities for financial security, and the urge to increase wealth and status. They promise abnormally consistent and/or high rates of return on short-term fictitious investments. In fact, victims' funds are not used for their stated purpose and early investors are paid not from profits but from money obtained from subsequent participants.[2]

Since Ponzi scams, though illegal, are structurally similar to accepted practices in the financial market (Dorn 2010, 27; see recent book by Henriques 2011), such as the fractionalized reserve system, it is difficult for people to recognize them for what they are. With the benefit of hindsight, most can recognize the schemes perpetrated by Bernard Madoff, R. Allen Stanford, Marc Dreier, and Kenneth I. Starr as Ponzis. But such scams are more difficult to recognize when they are cloaked in traditional economic activities.

Take, for example, the purchase of a home. Americans have been conditioned in recent decades to believe that home ownership is the key to the American Dream and that home values will always increase. So they were unlikely to recognize that the promises of cheap no-money-down mortgages offered at the height of the housing bubble in the 1990s and 2000s were effectively little more than Ponzi schemes.

That's why several economists have extended the definition of a Ponzi beyond the activities of individual swindlers to include business operations and government programs. For them the telltale signs of a classic Ponzi scam are dependency on future contributors (Samuelson 1967), rapid growth (Black 2005), and extreme leverage (Roubini 2009). Nobel Prize–winning economist Paul Samuelson (1967), for example, contends that social security is *actuarially* unsound because "[e]veryone who reaches retirement age is given benefit privileges that far exceed anything he has paid in." As with traditional Ponzis, as long as there are more young people paying into the system than retirees taking money out, the system will survive. But once new members and cash dwindle, the system will be in crisis.

William K. Black (2009), a contributor to this volume (see Chapter 9), asserted on PBS's "Bill Moyers Journal" that the entire U.S. financial system is a Ponzi scheme. Economics professor Nouriel Roubini (2009) echoed

Black with his claim that Americans live in "a 'Made-off' and Ponzi bubble economy of overleveraged components that are all on the edge of collapse." According to him, the United States' willingness to issue trillions of dollars of new debt to pay for the recession and private losses of corporations risks turning the U.S. economy into an unsustainable Ponzi.

If we accept that Ponzi schemes depend upon a constant influx of investors and money and operate in a manner that ensures at least some of the funds are used to cover returns promised to earlier investors while the enterprise is ultimately unsustainable, we must indeed broaden what is considered to be a Ponzi to include the housing bubble, many pension plans, Social Security, and fractionalized reserve banking, among others. These ventures generally escape the Ponzi label because they are tightly interwoven within the fabric of finance capitalism's casino economy. Many of these endeavors are legal. Some skirt the boundaries of law and what is reasonable and ethical. Others clearly violate the law.

It is not surprising that news of the economic crisis during the first decade of the twenty-first century made headlines at about the same time as stories about elaborate Ponzi schemes operated by individuals such as Madoff, Dreier, and Stanford appeared in the press. Both were products of an underlying Ponzi culture. Like the proverbial house of cards, the collapse of the unsustainable Ponzi elements of the housing and finance markets leads to the failure of other unsustainable practices, because they cannot attract new investors and feign growth.

In this essay I argue that a Ponzi culture emerged in the United States during the second half of the twentieth century—a pivotal period in U.S. social and economic history—and laid the foundation for the financial crisis during the first decade of the twenty-first century. Its development was aided by governmental and financial service industry actions that directly and indirectly encouraged credit, the accumulation of debt, speculation, and gambling.

Ponzi Culture

In the biological sciences, culture is a medium conducive for growth. Culture in the social sciences is generally understood as arising from social practices that are transmitted through primary groups within a community. These social practices allow "individuals in a community (to) develop an understanding of how the world works and make decisions based on that understanding" (Wilson as cited by Cohen 2010). Gramsci (1971) argues that cultural values do not simply arise from a group; instead, they reflect the hegemonic arrangements within the social order that strongly favor the interests of the dominant group.[3] Financial culture in particular is influenced and shaped by giant corporations whose major concern is to accumulate wealth (Parenti 1999). In this essay, Ponzi culture is defined as the hegemonic arrangement that facilitates and encourages speculation, unsustainable debt, and bubbles.

Although Ponzi cultures have appeared throughout history, the latest iteration took root and spread as survivors of the Great Depression—members of a generation that downplayed speculation and risk, rejected the accumulation of unsustainable debt, and therefore would not purchase something they could not afford—were succeeded by those with vague or no memories of the events leading up to 1930s and their consequences.

As changes in the cultural environment provided the attitudes and rationale that normalized borrowing and speculation, the ability to recognize bubbles and Ponzis diminished. Post–World War II prosperity led to a loosening of lending standards and the development of universal credit cards. This in turn led to and fed an addiction to hyperconsumption. The transition from a manufacturing economy to a casino economy predated state governments' sponsorship of gambling venues for leisure activity and profit by only a few years.

In sum, Ponzi culture's three legs—debt, speculation or gambling, and the belief in rapid "investment" growth—facilitated the creation of financial bubbles. To the extent that this environment not only encourages and normalizes gambling, speculation, unsustainable deficit spending, and financial risk taking but also facilitates and encourages fraud, it is criminogenic (Needleman and Needleman 1979).

The shift in attitude toward gambling was assisted when state governments, looking for new sources of revenue, entered into lucrative revenue-generating endeavors that were once the domain of organized crime: numbers games and casinos. With states encouraging citizens to participate in these newly legalized forms of gaming to benefit schools or other government services, the number of gambling outlets dramatically increased. During the 1990s, the number of riverboat and dockside casinos rose from zero to nearly 100. Ten years after the 1989 Supreme Court decision that Native Americans could operate casinos on their reservations, the number of Native American casinos reached 260. Nearly "125 million Americans gambled in 1998—a figure that represents most of the adult population" (Shiller as quoted in *American Journal of Economics and Sociology* 2000, 539).

Gambling and risk taking on Wall Street has an aura of respectability. Most people do not equate "investing" in stocks as engaging in speculation, much less gambling. This was particularly true after 401(k)s were introduced to supplement or replace traditional pension plans in the 1980s. Citizens were encouraged to invest their 401(k)s in the stock market and saw their pension plans invested there. President George W. Bush even proposed placing a portion of Social Security in the stock market.

After the SEC deregulated brokerage commissions on May 1, 1975, the general public was welcomed into one of the main venues of the casino economy. Ordinary people were encouraged to protect their wealth from inflation by investing in products that would appreciate along with, or ahead of, the cost of living (Ferguson 2008b). It seemed to make sense to borrow in order to maximize stock and real estate holdings as long as investments generated higher rates of return than the cost of interest payments. Moreover, the message was sent that within financial markets, risk taking is generally perceived as a positive—an integral ingredient of innovation and the pursuit of profit (Dorn 2010, 25).

In the casino economy, as in traditional casinos, where technically anyone can win, the advantage clearly belongs to the house. The notion that anyone can win is part of the seduction and a hegemonic component of the casino economy that convinces those who are not wealthy to participate in financial activities that are bound to disadvantage them, and it increases the gap between the rich and poor (Hiltzik 2009). For investment schemes and frauds to work, participants must buy not only into the scheme but into the legitimacy of the social, cultural, and economic system that supports it. In this environment, victims willingly hand over their money to someone who promises them high returns, and they are, at least initially, happy to do so. If something goes wrong, they blame themselves.

"Just One Word: Plastics. There is a Great Future in Plastics. Just Think About It."

When Mr. McGuire uttered those words in the 1967 film *The Graduate*, the economy was still growing. But the shift to finance capitalism was already under way. Little did he (or anyone watching the film) know that plastic bank cards held more promise for young Benjamin Braddock than did the manufacture of plastic products. And even fewer could predict that the technological innovations hyped by America's industrialists would ultimately make it cheaper for American employers to use low-wage labor abroad than to pay U.S. workers middle-class wages (Reich 2010). As manufacturing left the United States, workers increasingly earned incomes by providing services or by playing in finance capitalism's casino. Individuals, companies, and government agencies became increasingly reliant on debt and leverage.

Bank of America's introduction of the first national all-purpose revolving credit bank cards in 1966 profoundly changed how people viewed consumption, money, and debt.[4] Once the profitability of this new product was recognized, banks bombarded individuals with offers of magical plastic cards that made it easy for them to spend money they did not have. The timing was fortuitous: During the 1970s and 1980s, the incomes and standards of living of working-class and middle-class families were threatened by the offshore migration of manufacturing and by the federal government attempts to control inflation by undermining unions and suppressing wages. The downward pressure on wages would normally constrain consumption, but the widespread availability of credit cards encouraged American families to continue spending as if their incomes were keeping pace with economic growth (Reich 2010). At the time, this seemed to be a win-win situation. Consumers could maintain the trappings of an elevated standard of living, even though their salaries stagnated or lost ground. Bankers had a new source of revenue, and the economy grew as a result of the consumer spending. Although Marx warned against fictitious capital, credit permitted workers to continue to purchase the products they produced in ways he would not have predicted.

Credit cards transformed the United States into a consumer society that lived beyond its means. U.S. revolving debt reached a high of $957.5 billion in 2008, and the total American consumer debt was $2.4 trillion by 2010 (Federal Reserve 2011), or $7,800 of debt for every man, woman, and child (money-zine.com n.d.). Sixty percent of consumers barely kept their heads above water or relied on deficit spending in 2009 (Bureau of Labor Statistics 2010).[5] The ratio of household debt to disposable income increased from less than 40 percent in 1952 to a peak of 133 percent in 2007. While indebtedness became the norm and created the illusion of economic growth, its long-term consequences were harmful for families. Increased household debt necessitated longer working hours and dual incomes (Reich 2010).[6]

The type of credit extended, and debt accrued, changed significantly during the new millennium. In previous years, nonmortgage consumer credit—auto loans, credit card loans, and other consumer loans—made large contributions to the country's economic growth rate. However, in the early years of the twenty-first century, home equity loans and cash-out mortgage refinancing provided a larger and cheaper share of funding for consumers and, as will be discussed later, were part of the housing Ponzi scheme (Eichner, Kohn, and Palumbo 2010, 10–11).

Hyman Minsky

Of the many ideas offered by the late economist Hyman Minsky, two concepts within his financial instability hypothesis are pertinent to the discussion of the financial meltdown and the Ponzi culture: First, prolonged periods of financial stability breed instability; and second, the accumulation of debt, bubbles, and Ponzi schemes are intrinsically related to the financial instability of the capitalist system.

Periods of financial stability or "good times," Minsky argued, lead investors to believe that stability and profit making are inherent characteristics of the financial system. Impatient with normal rates of return and desiring growth, they experiment, innovate, use greater leverage, and adopt risky financial tactics that lead them toward financial structures that emphasize speculative and Ponzi finance (Nesvetailova 2008, 2–3; Dorn 2010; Galbraith 2009; Norris 2011).

The fact that several innovative instruments and transactions closely associated with the financial crisis of 2008 did not exist just a few years earlier—including asset-backed securities, CDOs, SIVs, and subprime securitizations—lend support to Minsky's contention.[7] These investments were extremely lucrative for a while, were allowed to grow rapidly (unsustainably) through leverage, and became part of a bubble or assisted in the creation of bubbles.

In outlining how the accumulation of debt could lead to financial instability and financial crisis, Minsky identified three categories of borrowers—hedge, speculative, and Ponzi—according to the difficulty each faces in repaying their debt (Wolfson 2002). Hedge borrowers can meet interest and principal from cash flow. When hedge financing dominates the economy, it is in a state of equilibrium (McCulley 2009). Speculative borrowers have difficulties meeting some payments and need to refinance some short-term liabilities. Ponzi borrowers consume more than they take in and cannot service either interest or principal payments on their debts. They need their investments to continually increase in value (they need a bubble) to be able to refinance their debt (McCulley 2009; Roubini 2009; Wolfson 2002). As speculative and Ponzi borrowers dominate the economy, it becomes increasingly unstable.

The process of moving from a hedge position to a speculative Ponzi one is as follows:

Financial positions previously sustainable from historical cash flows— hedge positions—are replaced by those which, it is known in advance, will require refinancing at some future point. These are speculative bets. Then there is an imperceptible transition, as speculative positions morph into positions that can only be financed by new borrowing on an ever-increasing scale. This is the Ponzi scheme, the end stage, which must collapse once it is recognized to exist. (Galbraith 2009, 91–92)

Speculative and Ponzi borrowers buy into elements of the Ponzi culture. The rise of the U.S. debt-to-GDP ratio of households, financial firms, and corporations is 350 percent higher than what existed in 1929, and the increase of U.S. households' debt-to-income ratio to 135 percent in 2009 was evidence, according to Roubini (2009), that the United States is a Ponzi borrower.

Paul McCulley (2009), executive director of an investment management company, applied Minsky's three categories of borrowers to the housing bubble. Hedge borrowers are the individuals who take out traditional 30-year mortgages. The speculative borrowers, believing in consistently rising house prices, take out interest-only loans that require a balloon payment at maturity, which will require them to refinance. Speculative borrowers can afford to pay more for a house than a hedge borrower with the same income. Thus, speculative borrowers drive up housing prices and inflate a bubble. With housing prices going up, lenders wanting to make money create exotic loans, such as negative amortization, for Ponzi borrowers who cannot even afford to pay the interest payments in full.

The Housing Bubble Ponzi Scheme

Confronted with a decreasing rate of home sales and ownership because the pool of qualified borrowers had reached its limit, President Bill Clinton's administration, along with the housing industry, developed "The National Homeownership Strategy: Partners in the American Dream" in 1994–1995 with the goal of increasing home ownership to a record high level within the subsequent 6 years. To achieve this, the federal government encouraged creative public and private financing for individuals who otherwise would not qualify for conventional loans—those with insufficient resources and questionable credit and employment histories.[8] They sold the program by drawing on studies touting "democratization of credit"—the notion that a property-owning democracy was socially and politically stable because "high rates of home ownership generate financial wealth for borrowers, reduce crime and stimulate economic growth" (Morgenson 2007). Furthermore, "a worker mortgaged up to the hilt," as David Harvey (1976, 272) noted, "is a pillar of social stability, and schemes to promote home ownership within the working class has long recognized this basic fact."

President George W. Bush continued the push to increase home ownership, declaring that "We want everybody in America to own their own home" (Ferguson 2008b). However, anyone who could qualify for and wanted a traditional mortgage already had one by 2003 (Hinojosa in Breslauer 2008). To expand the housing market, Bush signed the American Dream Downpayment Act that year and challenged lenders to create 5.5 million new minority homeowners by the end of the decade. The Department of Housing and Urban Development (HUD) pressured Fannie Mae and Freddie Mac to support the subprime market. As a result, between 2000 and 2006, the share of undocumented subprime contracts rose from 17 percent to 44 percent (Ferguson 2008b).

Both federal programs were welcomed not only by those connected to the housing industry, ranging from ordinary realtors to banks and finance companies, but also by individuals previously excluded from the housing market. Flexible creative financing—among them, adjustable rate mortgages (ARMs), subprime mortgages, and loans with zero down—encouraged by federal programs, succeeded in increasing the percentage of households owning homes from 64 percent in 1995 to almost 70 percent at the peak of the bubble (Nocera 2010; Ferguson

2008b),[9] and minority ownership increased by 3.1 million between 2002 and 2007 (Ferguson 2008a, 266).

Countless individuals were lured by the media-hyped promises of generous real estate profits. Cable network shows such as "Flip This House" (on A&E) and "Flip That House" (on TLC), and stories of friends, neighbors, and coworkers making huge profits from buying and selling homes, encouraged many Americans to buy into the Ponzi culture's illusion of ever-increasing home prices. Taking out loans they could ill afford, many became Ponzi borrowers. The housing market expanded as loose mortgage standards facilitated a speculation frenzy that fed the housing bubble in the years leading up to 2007. Subprime mortgages and loans with nontraditional terms (for example, "alt-A" loans) issued without consideration to borrowers' ability to repay increasingly replaced standard 30-year mortgages (Eichner et al. 2010).[10] The housing boom's 40–50 percent contribution to the GDP's growth served the federal government's interest by camouflaging weak job and income growth (Henwood 2006).

In addition to homebuyers taking advantage of loose lending standards, American households refinanced their homes between 2002 and 2007 in great numbers based on perceived increases in their home equity. Refinancing permitted them to extract $2.3 trillion from their homes to finance their lifestyle (Reich 2010).[11] These equity withdrawals "accounted for 30 percent of the growth in consumption over [a] six-year period" (Henwood 2008). Enjoying the illusion of a healthy economy, the federal government had little interest in curtailing these equity withdrawals that helped families spend more than they earned. Furthermore, borrowing was so prevalent between 2002 through 2007 that the growth of household debt exceeded growth of income (Eichner et al. 2010, 11). To sustain the new debt load, income needed to increase to cover principal and interest on home mortgages.

Timid, prudent, and skeptical consumers who distrusted innovative mortgages appeared to lose ground to their more adventurous friends who speculated or became Ponzi borrowers. That "no one had ever seen a national real estate bubble" led individuals to believe it would not occur (Streitfeld 2010). Many of those who hesitated eventually succumbed to the Ponzi culture, based on the reasoning that it did not make sense for banks to lend money if they believed the loans would not be repaid.

When the bubble burst, most borrowers were left in a perfect trap, having bought so completely into the Ponzi culture that they did realize the dire financial straits they were in.[12] An Arizona man, who bought three houses and parcels of land, using earlier deals to finance subsequent ones, is a case in point. He was "taught in real estate that you use your leverage to grow"; therefore, it was inconceivable to him that his property values could fall, as they did, from $265,000 to $65,000 (Streitfeld 2010). He and other Ponzi borrowers had ignored two crucial factors: First, the housing bubble, like all Ponzi schemes, relied on increasing numbers of people entering the market and on rising real estate values. Even with the assistance of federal programs that enticed marginal borrowers, the market was bound to become saturated and the housing bubble would collapse.

Second, the growth of household debt greatly exceeded income growth. Zero-percent-down mortgages, negative amortization, and low initial teaser rates, or the prospect of using the increasing value of their homes as "money trees," had effectively lured borrowers into a massive Ponzi scheme (Roubini 2009). Once the market collapsed, these purchasers no longer could afford the payments.

Financial consultant Janet Tavakoli (2008) examined how Wall Street's unregulated shadow banking industry aggressively sought and encouraged mortgages to be packaged into profitable CDOs. She contends that mortgage lenders and investment banks replicated a classic Ponzi scheme:

> The largest Ponzi scheme in the history of the capital markets is the relationship between failed mortgage lenders and investment banks that securitized the risky overpriced loans and sold these packages to other investors—a Ponzi scheme by every definition applied to Madoff. . . . Investment banks raised money from new investors to pay back old investors (mortgage lenders' dividends to shareholders and creditors of mortgage lenders which often included themselves). When mortgage lenders imploded, investment banks sped up opaque securitizations to offload worthless tranches of CDOs mixed in with others to careless socalled sophisticated investors along with naive investors. Raising money from new investors to pay back old investors, even if you are the old investor covering up losses, is a Ponzi scheme.

In other words, Tavaloki continued, these "mortgage lenders paid high dividends to shareholders (old investors) and interest on credit lines to Wall Street (old investors) with money raised from new securities investors." Wall Street used the new money to hide losses and pay enormous bonuses (Tavakoli 2009). Unfortunately, "speculative" units and adventurous Ponzi traders, who do whatever it takes to attract more and more investments to survive, tend to edge out conservatively operated units that do not produce high yields (Dorn 2010).

Pension Ponzis

Madoff's declaration in a *New York Times Magazine* interview that "the whole government is a Ponzi scheme" (Fishman 2011) might be interpreted either as a case of "it takes one to know one" or as invoking the "condemning the condemner" technique of neutralization. The former seems more likely. State and federal governments are notorious for "borrowing from Peter to pay Paul" when faced with unfunded obligations. Not wanting to raise taxes, if they see a surplus in another account, they will use those funds.

Pension plans are particularly susceptible to becoming Ponzis, because contributions accrued over the work life to be paid out sometime in the future are tempting sources of money to use now. Recently, several public figures with inside knowledge have identified states and government agencies that engaged in Ponzis or Ponzi-like activities (that is, legal Ponzis) by failing to set aside adequate funds for their workers' defined-benefit pension plans and for their public service retirees' promised medical coverage. Instead, as in a traditional Ponzi, they pay retirees' pensions with funds collected from current employees who believe they are contributing to their own retirement accounts. With baby boomers retiring in ever greater numbers and no longer contributing to retirement funds, several states facing growing debt will likely place the burden on future taxpayers and workers (Rauh 2011).

Former New York City Public Schools Chancellor Joel Klein (2011) called teachers' defined-benefit pension plan a Ponzi scheme because, instead of creating a pension reserve, politicians needing money now choose to underfund or defund the pension plan. Thus, current teachers' money is used to fund current retirees.

Illinois Appellate Court Justice Thomas E. Hoffman, chair of the judicial retirement system and a trustee of the Illinois State Board of Investment, which oversees three retirement systems—the Illinois State Employees' Retirement System, the Illinois Judges' Retirement System, and the Illinois General Assembly Retirement System—alleges that all three "are nothing more than state-operated Ponzi schemes" (Burr 2011). Illinois has failed to make any of its required annual contributions to the systems for fiscal year 2010–2011. It too is staying afloat by using current employees' contributions to pay current retirees but is expected to go broke in 10 years.

In August 2010, the SEC accused New Jersey of engaging in securities fraud for its failure to disclose to bond buyers that it underfunded its Teachers' Pension and Annuity Fund and the Public Employees' Retirement System. The state allegedly overstated its pension assets by $2.4 billion when it used figures inflated from the 1999 technology bubble instead of 2001 values in creating its benefit enhancement fund (Scannell and Neuman 2010). To make matters worse, New Jersey was to contribute about $3 billion a year to the funds, but it "never contributed more than 30 percent of its required contribution between 2000 and 2006," and it completely skipped its payment to the system in 2009 (Scannell and Neuman 2010, A2). To meet their future obligations, the pension funds should have had assets of $112 billion; they had only $66 billion (Pérez-Peña 2010).

Although New Jersey is the only state targeted by an SEC action, twenty-one other states are believed to severely underfund their public sector retirement benefits (Pew Center on the States 2010). Seven states (notably Illinois) and six big cities will have insufficient funds to pay for promised benefits past the year 2020 (Rauh 2011). Instead of blaming poor decision making by government executives and legislators, public services employees tend to be scapegoated for obtaining "extravagant" benefits.

Many states have also created Ponzi-like structures to fund medical care for public service retirees. Unlike pensions, which are at least partially prefunded through contributions to large investment pools, retiree health care operates on a "pay-as-you-go" basis out of annual government budgets. Increasingly, states use these funds to meet pressing current obligations and shift responsibility for retirees' medical payments to some nebulous time in the future. New York state and local governments, for example, have not set aside the promised $205 billion in postretirement health benefits for their public service employees (McMahon 2010). Just like Ponzi operators, the state is transferring "wealth from future taxpayers to current government employees and retirees" instead of using funds for their intended purposes (McMahon 2010, i).

The Government Accounting Standards Board's (GASB) new accounting standards require state and local governments to calculate and disclose the long-term costs of keeping all of their retiree health care promises. However, the GASB allows a form of accounting for these promises that hides debt and violates the principles of financial accounting (Rauh 2011). Eventually, states and local governments will have to confront this hidden debt.

Private Sector Pensions

The situation is no better in the private sector. A 1980 amendment to the Employee Retirement Income Security Act allows any company in a multi-employer plan to assume that other members will continue to pay into the fund. Those who do not and leave the plan, as has occurred in growing numbers in recent years, are required to pay a withdrawal penalty. The penalties rarely cover the cost of withdrawal; therefore, the cost for the remaining companies increases. Accounting changes proposed by the Financial Accounting Standard Board may force businesses to confront the Ponzi-style nature of multiemployer pension plans as new rules will likely require companies to recognize their withdrawal penalty as a liability on either their income statement or balance sheet. In doing so, many companies will show that their withdrawal liabilities exceed their assets.

The Pension Benefit Guarantee Corporation (PBGC) was created in 1974 as a government insurance plan to protect "the pensions of approximately 44 million workers and retirees in more than 29,000 private defined benefit pension plans" (Solomon 2010). It promises to pay a fixed monthly sum to retirees for life when U.S. businesses underfund or fail to pay their share to their workers' retirement plan. PBGC is funded from premium fees paid by pension plans, by assets from plans it takes over, by recoveries from plan sponsors' bankruptcy estates and by investments.

When the recession worsened, an increasing number of U.S. companies, such as Circuit City, the IndyMac Bank, and Lehman Brothers, needed their pensions to be rescued, placing PBGC at risk. Its deficit increased from $11.2 billion in fiscal year 2008 to $21.9 billion in fiscal year 2009 (Solomon 2010). Its obligation to cover future pension losses from financially troubled companies more than tripled from $47 billion at the end of fiscal year 2008 to about $168 billion at the end of 2009 (Solomon 2010). Single-employer plans promised more than $121 billion in benefits but had only $99.4 billion in assets to pay out,[13] and multi-employer plans promised $3 billion in promised benefits, with only $1.6 billion in assets to cover benefits (Hall 2011). The Government Accountability Office believes PBGC is at high risk of failure because it cannot refuse to provide insurance and only Congress can change its premium structure (Hall 2011).

Fractional Reserve Banking

Audiences watching performances of *Peter Pan* are asked to declare that they believe in fairies to save Tinkerbell. In a similar fashion, U.S. citizens were asked, after the country discontinued the gold standard in 1971, to believe that paper currency and checks have value. Today, the U.S. currency, as part of the fractional reserve money system, is backed by the full faith and trust in the federal government.

The fractional reserve money system was developed by John Law, a Scottish economist and gambler, to replace gold as currency. The system allows banks to keep only a small proportion of deposits on hand to satisfy depositors' demands, lend the rest profitably, and issue banknotes supported by a fraction of their value in gold. As originally designed, a bank holding "$10 in gold could safely print and loan out about $100 in paper money"[14] (Langrick n.d.).

Canadian economic commentator Roger Langrick argues that the fractional reserve system is fundamentally flawed because it keeps the total national and private debt greater than the money available to repay it. The more a nation expands, the more debt goes into the system because the expansion is financed with money borrowed to cover the principle and interest. Thus, any nation that uses the system fulfills Minsky's definition of a Ponzi borrower. The only way in which the borrower can return what he or she owes is if the bank prints more money and then lends it with interest (Langrick n.d.). The focus is not on sustainability but on making money in the hope of staying ahead of debt.

Since financial banking relies on the fractional reserve system, Ponzi schemes are embedded within legitimate financial banking (Hansen and Movahedi 2010, 371). Generally, they borrow on a day-to-day basis to have enough money to cover their longer-term obligations (Dorn 2010, 25). A shortage or withdrawal of short-term finance often creates a problem or crisis for them as demonstrated during the savings and loan crisis of the 1980s and 1990s, by the current crisis in the United States, and by banks in Iceland, Ireland, Greece, and Portugal.

Conclusion

In providing a hospitable environment for speculation, unsustainable debt, and bubbles, Ponzi culture supplied the conditions that led to financial meltdown, threatened the economy, concentrated wealth, and increased the gap between the haves and have-nots. The culture's legal Ponzi schemes threatened the economy by encouraging questionable behavior, desensitizing individuals to the dangers of illegal Ponzi schemes, and obscuring the existence of structural and institutional Ponzis in the housing market and financial system.

Average Americans, wanting to maintain or improve their economic position, were seduced by the hegemonic rhetoric that told of new financial opportunities and the prospect of producing wealth like the "big boys." In buying into the housing bubble and other financial schemes, they contributed to the Ponzi culture and unwittingly supported the alliance between government and the financial sector. Unfortunately, average Americans generally lost more than they gained and became the biggest losers as the financial meltdown consolidated wealth in the hands of fewer and fewer individuals and increased the numbers of those poor and struggling.

Ponzi culture is a product of the symbiotic relationship between government and financial institutions. Ponzi-inflated earnings produce the illusion of a healthy economy and increase tax revenue without raising taxes. Since state and federal governments depend upon the financial service industry for economic growth and have much to gain from increased real estate prices, construction of new houses, and general consumer spending, they are reluctant to create and enforce regulations that would hinder profits. Furthermore, federal and state governments operated their own versions of a Ponzi scheme. The financial sector benefits from its close relationship with government as it depends upon the state to create legislation and programs that favor them (for example, government guarantees on loans and the "National Homeowner Strategy").

No matter how closely government interests are aligned with business interests, Calavita, Pontell, and Tillman (1997) claim that the state will crack down on businesses only when their activities threaten the economy, as it did during the 1980s savings and loan scandal. Then, regulators and prosecutors took action against criminal operators whose actions threatened the larger financial system. A process of reregulation took place that temporarily undermined the widespread acceptance of the casino economy's Ponzi culture. As could be expected, within a few years, financial institutions fought back and obtained even greater deregulation, including the enactment of the Gramm-Leach-Bililey Act of 1999, which repealed the Glass–Steagall Act that separated commercial from investment banking.

Even though the U.S. economy has suffered greatly during the current meltdown—an unknown number of individuals have lost their jobs and homes and hundreds of banks and subprime lenders have failed—major financial institutions, especially the corporate financial players who violated and skirted the laws, have not suffered the consequences of their actions.[15] By focusing on prosecutions of individual Ponzi operators such as Madoff and Dreier, the state diverts attention from the harmful, and in some cases criminal, activity embodied by structural and institutional Ponzis.

When the unsustainable schemes operated by Madoff, Stanford, and Dreier collapsed, their targets learned they were Ponzi victims and knew whom to blame. Victims of the housing bubble and other institutionalized Ponzi schemes rarely understand or are told that they participated in a Ponzi. It is difficult for them to comprehend that they were victims of Ponzis operated by the country's most respected financial institutions. If, after all, these institutions perpetrated Ponzis, why would they receive government bailouts that remove the consequences for risky behavior and violate one of the cardinal principles of capitalism, namely, that firms that repeatedly make bad decisions will cease to exist?

Ponzi culture still predominates. Though it is true that culture is slow to change, without making fundamental longer-term changes, the United States is doomed to repeat the patterns of financial crisis with increasing frequency, and the consequences of the next crash will have harsher consequences. As long as the U.S. financial system continues to enjoy an unchallenged symbiotic relationship with government, neither party has the incentive to change the culture. The weakness in the symbiotic pairing is that although government finds it beneficial to assist the financial industry, it still has to preserve its survival both economically and through the approval of its citizens. The trick here is for citizens to recognize that they are living in a Ponzi culture that is disadvantaging them, and that they have the right to protection by the government. For much too long, Ponzi culture has allowed the U.S. government to shirk its responsibility to protect its citizens from the consequences of Ponzis.

Notes

1. French economist and Nobel Prize–winner Maurice Allais dubbed an economy that emphasizes windfall profits made from bets on speculative endeavors a "casino economy" (Bates 1989).

2. Pyramid schemes, also known as franchise fraud or chain referral schemes, are closely related to Ponzis. They differ in that profit is realized from the sale of new distributorships, not the sale of the purported product.

3. Gramsci (1971, 161) asserts that hegemony cannot be separated from economics and is exercised by the dominant group in the "decisive nucleus of economic activity."

4. Although individual merchants issued credit cards to be used only in their establishments for years, and Diners Club in 1950 and American Express in 1958 issued credit cards designed for travel and entertainment associated with business travelers, it was not until Bank of America introduced its BankAmericard in California in 1958 and nationwide in 1965–1966 that average citizens had access to a ready line of credit that could be used anywhere.

5. Households in the lowest 40 percent of the U.S. income distribution spent more than they earned. The average income for household in the lowest quintile was $9,956 and their average expenditure was $21,611. Households in the middle quintile earned only slightly more than they spent—their medium pretax earnings was $46,012, while their medium annual expenditure was $41,150. The average consumption for households in the next highest quintile was $56,879 and their average earnings were $73,417. The highest quintile's average income was $157,631; its households spent on average $94,244 (Bureau of Labor Statistics 2010).

6. In 1966, only 24 percent of mothers with small children worked outside of the home; by the late 1990s, more than 60 percent of these mothers did. By the mid-2000s, male earners worked approximately 100 hours more each year than they had two decades earlier, and the typical female worker put in about 200 more hours. Despite that, the average male earns less in 2010, adjusted for inflation, than he did 30 years ago (Reich 2010).

7. This is not to imply that innovation is bad or that these instruments are inherently problematic or fraudulent. It was how they were used that created problems. Chairman of the Federal Reserve Ben Bernanke, when questioned by a member of the Financial Crisis Inquiry Commission about the role of financial innovation in the economy, provided an unexpected response: "Innovation is not always a good thing." He went on to say that innovations can have unpredictable

consequences and are used primarily "to take unfair advantage rather than to create a more efficient market" and thus they create systemic risks (Chan 2010, B3).

8. Over the years, the federal government encouraged home ownership in multiple ways ranging from making mortgage interest payments tax deductible to creating agencies explicitly designed to make it easier for people to buy homes. Many federal programs and agencies began as New Deal initiatives: the Federal Home Loan Bank Board (which oversees and encourages savings and loans for homebuyers); federal deposit insurance; the Home Owners' Loan Corporation (which extended mortgage terms to 15 years); Fannie Mae; and in 1935 the Federal Housing Administration provided federally backed insurance for lenders and allowed for 80 percent mortgages to be paid over 20 to 25 years. Together, these programs increased home ownership from 43 to 62 percent between 1940 and 1960 (Ferguson, 2008b).

9. As a result of these unsustainable policies, the percentage of Americans owning homes dropped to 66.8 percent in May 31, 2011, and is expected to decline to levels last seen in the 1980s (Streitfeld 2011).

10. More than 75 percent of "subprime mortgages [that] originated from 2003 to 2007 were teaser 'short-term hybrid' loans," which reset in a couple of years (Eichner, Kohn, and Palumbo 2010, 15).

11. Henwood (2008) estimates that homeowners withdrew as much as $5 trillion in home equity between 2001 and 2007.

12. Not only borrowers but all home owners were hurt by decreasing house values and foreclosures. Wealth was redistributed and the gap between the haves and have-nots increased

13. A single-employer plan is not portable to another employer. However, multi-employer pension plans allow employees to accumulate credit toward retirement from work with several different employers.

14. The conversion of notes to gold ended in the 1930s. It was replaced by checks and credit and a national accounting system of credits and debits (Langrick n.d.).

15. Only Lee B. Farkas, the former chairman of Taylor, Bean & Whitaker, has been tried and found guilty of securities, bank, and wire fraud for his role in a $2.9 billion scheme that led to the 2009 collapse of Colonial Bank (Protess 2011). Two former Bear Stearns hedge fund managers, Ralph R. Cioffi and Matthew M. Tannin, were found not guilty of securities fraud in November 2009 (Kouwe and Slater 2009); there were indications that a few additional individuals may be prosecuted. President Barack Obama announced in his 2012 State of the Union address that he was expanding a federal task force to crack down on financial firms that engaged in "abusive lending and packaging of risky mortgages that led to the housing crisis" (Wyatt and Dewan 2012). Bearing in mind that many firms and individuals have already been investigated (for example, Mozilo, Countrywide, Goldman Sachs, and Washington Mutual have reached settlements with the government), one questions what will be accomplished. That the new federal-state working group on misconduct in the residential mortgage-backed securities market filed charges against three Credit Suisse traders for inflating the value of mortgage bonds in late 2007, a mere three weeks after its formation was

announced seem impressive. However, on closer examination there seems to be a bit of misdirection. The case is more about embezzlement from a bank by its employees than causes of the housing market collapse and harm to homeowners (Henning 2012).

References

American Institute of Certified Public Accountants. 2007. "Business Valuation and Forensic & Litigation Services Practice Aid 07-1, Forensic Accounting—Fraud Investigations." *American Institute of Certified Public Accountants.* http://www.aicpa.org/InterestAreas/ForensicAndValuation/Resources/PractAids Guidance/DownloadableDocuments/PA%2007–1_Forensic_Accounting_Fraud_Investigations.pdf (accessed August 8, 2010).

American Journal of Economics and Sociology. 2000. "Book Review: Shiller, Robert J. *Irrational Exuberance.* Princeton University Press. Princeton, NJ." *American Journal of Economics and Sociology,* July, 539.

Bates, James. 1989. "Columbia S&L Puts Its Loss at $226.3 Million." *Los Angeles Times,* October 26, D1–D2.

Black, William. 2005. *The Best Way to Rob a Bank Is to Own One.* Austin: University of Texas Press.

Breslauer, Brenda (producer). 2008. "Credit and Credibility." *Now with David Brancaccio,* November 21.

Bureau of Labor Statisitics. 2010. *Consumer Expenditure Survey, 2009, Quintiles of Income Before Taxes.* Washington, DC: United States Department of Labor. http://www.bls.gov/cex/2007/share/quintile.pdf (accessed March 17, 2011).

Burr, Barry B. 2010. "Are Illinois Plans Just Ponzi Schemes?" *Pensions & Investments,* November 29. http://www.pionline.com/article/20101129/PRINTSUB /311299996 (accessed February 11, 2011).

Calavita, Kitty, Henry N. Pontell, and Robert H. Tillman. 1997. *Big Money Crime: Fraud and Politics in the Savings and Loan Crisis.* Berkeley: University of California Press.

Chan, Sewell. 2010. "Bernanke Says He Failed to See Financial Flaws." *New York Times,* September 2, B3.

Cohen, Patrica. 2010. "'Culture of Poverty' Makes a Comeback." *New York Times,* October 17.

Coleman, James W. 1987. "Towards an Integrated Theory of White-Collar Crime." *American Journal of Sociology* 93 (2): 406–39.

Davis, Lawrence J. 2002. "The Same Old Story." *Daily Deal,* February 21.

Dorn, Nicholas. 2010. "The Governance of Securities: Ponzi Finance, Regulatory Convergence, Credit Crunch." *British Journal of Criminology* 50:23–45.

Eichner, Matthew J., Donald L. Kohn, and Michael G. Palumbo. 2010. "Financial Statistics for the United States and the Crisis: What Did They Get Right, What Did They Miss, and How Should They Change?" *Federal Reserve Board: Finance and Economic Discussion Series: 2010–20 Screen Reader Version,* April 15. http://

www.federalreserve.gov/pubs/feds/2010/201020/index.html (accessed August 5, 2010).

Federal Reserve. 2011. "G19 Consumer Credit." *Federal Reserve Statistical Release.* March 7. http://www.federalreserve.gov/releases/g19/Current/ (accessed March 17, 2011).

Fishman, Steve. 2011. "The Madoff Tapes." *New York Times Magazine,* February 27.

Ferguson, Niall. 2008a. *The Ascent of Money: A Financial History of the World.* New York: Penguin Press.

———. 2008b. "Wall Street Lays Another Egg." *Vanity Fair,* December, 190. http://www.vanityfair.com/politics/features/2008/12/banks200812-2 (accessed January 29, 2011, via Academic OneFile).

Galbraith, James K. 2009. "Who Are These Economists Anyway?" *Thought & Action,* (Fall): 85–97.

Gramsci, Antonio. 1971. *Selections from the Prison Notebooks,* edited and translated by Quitin Hoare and Geofrey Nowell Smith. New York: International Publishers.

Hall, Kevin G. 2011. "Business Fights Obama's Fix for Sick Corporate Pensions." *Miami Herald,* March 7. http://www.miamiherald.com/2011/03/07/v-print/2102619/business-fights-obamas-fix-for.html (accessed March 17, 2011).

Hansen, Lisa L., and Siamak Movahedi. 2010. "Wall Street Scandals: The Myth of Individual Greed." *Sociological Forum* 25 (2): 367–74.

Harvey, David. 1976. "Labor, Capital, and Class Struggle Around the Built Environment in Advanced Capitalist Societies." *Politics & Society* 6:265–95.

Henning, Peter J. 2012. "Bank Is Victim in Financial Crisis Case, Not Homeowners." *New York Times,* February 6. http://dealbook.nytimes.com/2012/02/06/bank-is-victim-in-financial-crisis-case-not-homeowers/?scp=1&sq=financial%20crime%20prosecution&st=cse (accessed February 9, 2012).

Henriques, Diana B. 2011. *The Wizard of Lies: Bernie Madoff and the Death of Trust.* New York: Times Books.

Henwood, Doug. 2006. "Leaking Bubble." *The Nation,* March 27.

———. 2008. "Crisis of a Gilded Age." *The Nation,* October 13.

Hiltzik, Michael. 2009. "The Belief That the Wealthy Are Worthy Is Waning." *Los Angeles Times,* March 19. http://articles.latimes.com/2009/mar/19/business/fi-hiltzik19 (accessed August 11, 2010).

Klein, Joel. 2011. "Opinion: Why Teacher Pensions Don't Work." *Wall Street Journal,* January 10. http://online.wsj.com/article/SB10001424052748704415104576066192958395176.html (accessed January 10, 2011).

Kouwe, Zachary, and Dan Slater. 2009. "2 Bear Stearns Fund Leaders Are Acquitted." *New York Times,* November 11. http://www.nytimes.com/2009/11/11/business/11bear.html (accessed April 20, 2011).

Langrick, Roger. n.d. "A Monetary System for the New Millennium." http://www.worldtrans.org/whole/monetarysystem.html (accessed July 18, 2010).

McCulley, Paul. 2009. "The Shadow Banking System and Hyman Minsky's Economic Journey." *PIMCO: Global Central Bank Focus,* May. http://media.pimco-global.com/pdfs/pdf/GCB%20Focus%20May%202009.pdf?WT.cg_n=PIMCO-US&WT.ti=GCB%20Focus%20May%202009.pdf (accessed March 29, 2011).

McMahon, E. J. 2010. *Iceberg Ahead: The Hidden Cost of Public-Sector Retiree Health Benefits in New York*. Special Report. New York: Empire Center for New York Public Policy.

money-zine.com. n.d. *Consumer Debt Statisitics*. http://www.money-zine.com /Financial-Planning/Debt-Consolidation/Consumer-Debt-Statistics/ (accessed March 17, 2011).

Morgenson, Gretchen. 2007. "Fair Game; Home Loans: A Nightmare Grows Darker." *New York Times*, April 8.

Needleman, Martin L., and Carolyn Needleman. 1979. "Organizational Crime: Two Models of Criminogenesis." *Sociological Quarterly* 20:517–28.

Nesvetailova, Anastasia. 2008. "Ponzi Finance and Global Liquidity Meltdown: Lessons from Minsky." Working Paper CUTP/002. London: City University of London, Center for International Politics, February. http://www.city.ac.uk/— data/assets/pdf_file/0005/83993/CUWPTP002.pdf (accessed July 18, 2010).

Nocera, Joe. 2010. "Widespread Fear Freezes Housing Market." *New York Times*, August 27.

Norris, Floyd. 2011. "2 Meltdowns with Much in Common." *New York Times*, March 18, B1, B4.

Parenti, Michael. 1999. "Reflections on the Politics of Culture." *Monthly Review*, February, 11–18.

Pérez-Peña, Richard. 2010. "Behind Fraud Charges, New Jersey's Deep Crisis." *New York Times*, August 19.

Pew Center on the States. 2010. *The Trillion Dollar Gap: Underfunded State Retirement Systems and the Road to Reform*. Washington, D.C.: Pew Charitable Trusts.

Protess, Ben. 2011. "Leader of Big Mortgage Lender Guilty of $2.9 Billion Fraud." *New York Times*, April 19. http://www.nytimes.com/2011/04/20/business /20fraud.html?_r=1&nl=todaysheadlines&emc=tha25 (accessed April 19, 2011).

Rauh, Josh. 2011. "Statement of Professor Joshua Rauh for the Hearing on 'The Role of Public Employee Pensions in Contributing to State Insolvency and the Possibility of a State Bankruptcy Chapter.' Before the Subcommittee on Courts, Commercial, and Administrative Law." February 14. http://judiciary.house. gov/hearings/pdf/Rauh02142011.pdf.

Reich, Robert B. 2010. "How to End the Great Recession." *New York Times*, September 2, A21.

Roubini, Nouriel. 2009. "The United States of Ponzi: Behold the Madoff in the Mirror." *Forbes*, March 19.

Samuelson, Paul. 1967. "Social Security, a Ponzi Scheme That Works." *Newsweek*, February 12, 88.

Scannell, Kara, and Jeannette Neuman. 2010. "SEC Sues New Jersey as States' Finances Stir Fears." *Wall Street Journal*, August 19, A2.

Solomon, John. 2010. "No Guarantees at the Pension Benefit Guarantee Corporation." *Public Integrity*, May 3. http://www.publicintegrity.org/articles/entry/2061/ (accessed March 26, 2011).

Streitfeld, David. 2010. "Debts Rise, and Go Unpaid, as Bust Erodes Home Equity." *New York Times*, August 12, A1, A3.

————. 2011. "House Prices Are Set to Hit Another Low." *New York Times*, May 31, A1, A3.

Tavakoli, Janet. 2008. "Madoff Deserves Lots of Company." *Tavakoli Structured Finance*, December 13. http://www.tavakolistructuredfinance.com/TSF11.html (accessed February 22, 2011).

————. 2009. "Washington's Bipartisan Betrayal: The 2015 Financial Global Financial Crisis." *Huffington Post*, December 31. http://www.huffingtonpost.com /janet-tavakoli/washingtons-bipartisan-be_b_408308.html (accessed February 22, 2011).

Wolfson, Martin H. 2002. "Minsky's Theory of Financial Crises in a Global Context." *Journal of Economic Issues* 36 (2): 393–400.

Wyatt, Edward and Shaila Dewan. 2012. "New Housing Task Force Will Zero In on Wall St." *New York Times*, January 25. http://www.nytimes.com/2012/01/26 /business/new-housing-task-force-takes-aim-at-wall-st.html?pagewanted=2& sq=financial%20crime%20prosecution&st=cse&scp=6 (accessed February 9, 2012.

[4]

BERNIE MADOFF, FINANCE CAPITAL, AND THE ANOMIC SOCIETY

JOCK YOUNG

Bernie Madoff was, before he went to jail, considered a solid and reputable citizen. A man well thought of in the world of finance, he worked out of offices in the prestigious Lipstick Building at the corner of Third Avenue and East 53rd Street in midtown Manhattan, the world center of finance capitalism. He was for a time chair of NASDAQ and, as would later prove ironic, of the National Society of Security Dealers, which regulated members of his profession. A noted philanthropist, he lived in great luxury with a penthouse apartment on the Upper East Side and houses in Palm Beach and the French Riviera. Madoff was considered so good at what he did that people jostled and cajoled to gain his company and to invest with him.

He was in no way a marginal man; he was well adjusted and integrated into society. Yet he committed what some have called one of the greatest thefts in history through a Ponzi scheme that stretched across the globe. In this essay, I argue that Bernie Madoff was not only well integrated into the financial and social circles of his class but that his behavior was neither strange nor particularly deviant. It must be understood within the context of the values and practices of present-day finance capital. Rather than being an outlier, Madoff's career is something of a metaphor of our times.

Bernie Madoff, Finance Capital, and the Anomic Society

The Bernie Madoff "Puzzle"

What can one make of Bernie Madoff? How many average American thieves would it take to steal $60 billion? He is a bit of a puzzle for the criminologist: He is the right gender to be sure but the wrong class, ethnicity, and age; we usually spend our time looking down, not up, the social structure when analyzing criminal behavior. I am not one who believes that there is a general theory of crime that can explain everything. Such endeavors usually end up in vacuous abstractions, for instance, Gotttfredson and Hirschi's (1990) grandly named *General Theory of Crime*. But there are formal similarities, for example, the Ponzi scheme as a con trick is only an upmarket version of the guy on the street corner with three cards or three tumblers and one concealed marble. You have a mark, the likely investor; a shill, who plays on the cupidity of the mark and his or her desire for easy money; a chief compliance officer; and the con man himself, Mr. Madoff. And there are cultural parallels: subcultures that thrive on risk, which go to the very edge of legitimacy and often drift over it, and those who, whether high or low in the class structure, see extravagance as a style of life and eschew utilitarian notions of wealth (see Katz 1988).

Robert K. Merton, possibly the greatest American sociologist of the twentieth century, writing in 1938, at the end of the Great Depression, published an article entitled "Social Structure and Anomie," which was to become the most cited paper in the history of sociology. His argument centered on the American Dream and its relationship with the high rate of crime in America—a rate much higher than in many far poorer countries. Merton (1938) saw the Dream as the key legitimation of American society— the notion that the United States, unlike the Old World, was not class-bound, that success could be within the grasp of any citizen provided he or she worked hard and had talent. Such a dream persists to this day. After all, it was a major theme in the electoral campaigns of both the candidates in the 2008 presidential election.

Merton saw, however, three problems: first, that there was an overemphasis on success, particularly, financial success, without a proper regard for means or indeed any ends more substantial than that of making money; second, that success had no limits, no arrival point, that the ends moved incessantly forward; and third, that there were, in fact, limited possibilities for social mobility, particularly for those low in the class structure. All three of these defects in the American Dream he saw as leading, in certain circumstances, to crime.

The effects of the first extended throughout the class structure; the second impacted those at the very top of society; the last affected those at the bottom. Thus, from Marx, Merton took the idea of society in contradiction; from Durkheim, the notion of the "sickness of infinity," the pursuit of incessant ends; and from Simmel, the emphasis on monetary rather than substantial ends. All in all, he saw in American society a particular degree of instability or anomie, and he found that there were two sorts of anomie— that of the advantaged and that of the disadvantaged (see Young 1974). Both types were seen to frequently lead to crime. Indeed the United States' propensity to have a high rate of crime compared with other advanced industrial societies was considered a result of this instability.

Interestingly, Merton's examples of crime tend to dwell as much on white collar crime, fraud, insider dealing, and the like as on conventional crime, although subsequent interpretations of his work have very largely focused on the latter and at the bottom of the social structure.

Merton was particularly critical of the imbalance in the American value system. Thus, at the end of his short essay he writes: "The social order we have described necessarily produces this strain towards dissolution" (1938, 681). This is a far cry from modern "strain theory," which interprets his work as something like a minor pain in a ligament. He also notes, "A stable social structure demands a balanced distribution of affect among its various segments." The overwhelming shift in emphasis from means to ends leads to "a breakdown in the regulatory structure. With the resulting attenuation of the institutional imperatives, there occurs an approximation of the situation erroneously held by the utilitarians to be typical of society in general, wherein calculations of advantage and fear of punishment are the sole regulating agencies. In such situations, as Hobbes observed, force and fraud come to constitute the sole virtues in view of their relative efficiency in attaining goals. These were for Hobbes, of course, not culturally derived (Merton 1938, 682). And on top of this tendency to deceit and falsehood, there is an unsustainable degree of unpredictability in the system.

"Insofar as one of the most general functions of social organization is to provide a basis for calculability and a regularity of behavior, it is increasingly limited in effectiveness as these elements of the structure become dissociated. At the extreme, predictability virtually disappears and what may be properly termed cultural chaos or anomie appears" (Merton 1938, 682).

Thus Merton's assessment, grounded in the Great Depression, pointed to the fundamental imbalances and contradictions of capitalism, with American capitalism being something of an extreme case. He was critical of the normative context of the market and its social surround. He noted two consequences amongst others that are particularly relevant to the present: first, the tendency to fraud and, second, the unpredictability of the system.

The Predictions of James Q. Wilson and Eric Hobsbawm

Let us now fast-forward to the present. I wish to argue that not only was the exposure of Bernie Madoff's gross misdemeanors the result of the financial crisis but that in many ways it epitomized the causes of the crisis. Commentators as diverse as James Q. Wilson (1997), the author of *The Moral Sense* and former Ronald Reagan Professor of Public Policy at Pepperdine University, and Eric Hobsbawm (1994), the renowned Marxist historian, have pointed out how neoliberal values threaten the fabric of society. Hobsbawm accurately predicted a coming crisis as values of trust, hard work, and willingness to postpone immediate gratification became replaced by values that actively disdained the very elements that made the system possible. He pointed to how Adam Smith, the grand theorist of capitalism, stressed that although the pursuit of individual advantage was the fuel that propelled capitalism forward, it relied on what he called "habits of labor" to flourish. Among these were savings and investment, norms of obedience and loyalty, including the loyalty of executives to their firm, pride in achievement, and customs of mutual trust. Thus he writes:

> As we take for granted the air we breathe, and which makes possible all our activities, so capitalism took for granted the atmosphere in which it operates, and which it had inherited from the past. It only discovered how essential it had been when the air becomes thin. In other words capitalism succeeded because it was not just capitalist. Profit maximization and accumulation were necessary conditions for its success but not sufficient ones. (Hobsbawm 1994, 343)

Such an institutional unraveling can be seen in the attitudes of owners and workers to their work. Once upon a time, both entrepreneurs and workers were proud of the fruits of their labor, whether it was motorcars, forks and spoons, or Wedgewood china (see Sennett 1998). Today, labor is outsourced, financial "products" replace manufacturing, and the successful firm reduces its labor force and increases its profits, while little is made in the United States outside of the arms industry.

Hobsbawm, in his evocation of Adam Smith, puts bones upon Merton's means-and-ends schema. All of this argues for a market that is not detached but is socially embedded, where both means and ends have substantial social resonance and value. It demands a regulation that is external and internal—both in terms of regulatory bodies and informal workaday norms and ideals. It demands respect for the product of labor, for the firm, and for colleagues in the workforce. But what has occurred is precisely the opposite of this: widespread deregulation propelled by the politics of neoliberalism and intellectually justified by the strange belief of economists in the rational market.

The Myth of the Rational Market

> I can calculate the motions of heavenly bodies, but not the madness of people.
> —Isaac Newton, in 1721, after he had lost the equivalent today of $4 million in the 1720 South Sea bubble.

Rational market theory basically argues that the market has a wisdom that stockbrokers, governments, and corporations do not and that the free, unencumbered market will bring rationality to human economic affairs (see Fox 2009). Following Hayek, it stresses that the market is too complex to be understood by planners, who are unable to assess demand and effectively generate delivery. The agents on the ground—the realtor, the person shipping goods, the commodity broker, and the consumer—has "a special knowledge of circumstances of the fleeting moment" that central planners could not hope to emulate. Furthermore, this knowledge is communicated by the prices that the market generates. Capitalism's supposed superiority over the planned economies of socialism and communism is its ability, when unhindered, in a situation of individual and economic freedom, to create a near-perfect system or at least, in former U.K. Prime Minister Margaret Thatcher's stern words, a world for which "there is no alternative."

For the economist, such a system of perfection is also an object of mathematical beauty (see Krugman 2009). For it is possible—or so it is argued—to express this entity, even in its seeming randomness, by statistical equation and predictability as certain as the movement of bodies in the physical universe. Such an expression of physics envy has its parallels in the positivist movement in the other social "sciences" (see Young 2011). It is particularly prevalent in economics because of the easy availability of regular numerical data. The common tendency is to create a model abstracted from reality and to believe that human behavior can be predicted from its constellation of determinants.

Orthodox economics is the most developed and curious example of what C. Wright Mills called "abstracted empiricism," abstracting social reality from the surrounding social structure, culture, and history. The image of the perfect market, when unencumbered by social intervention, greatly encourages this process of creating abstract models. Such an abstraction is especially pernicious in economics and particularly encourages the denial of the importance of normative and legal regulation (means, ends, social norms of trust and contract), which as we have seen is the bedrock of stable economic relationships.

The abstracted model led to the beautiful equation where even the seemingly unpredictable nature of the stock market was seen to succumb to statistical analysis, and the pricing of the risks involved in increasingly complex and unstable financial packages was seen to be amenable to the rigor and precision of mathematics. In an interesting twist of fate, while Merton senior (R. K. Merton), as we have seen, viewed the uncontrolled market as unpredictable, his son (R. C. Merton) became renowned for his elegant mathematical presentation of its predictability. The younger Merton trained as an applied mathematician and with only a smattering of economics got into MIT, where he was roped into working for Paul Samuelson, the renowned economist. Despite, or maybe because of, his lack of training in the discipline, he eventually became the joint winner of the Nobel Prize in Economics in 1997 with the famous Black-Scholes-Merton formula and a key player in the increasingly dominant world of mathematical finance.

The notion of the perfect market running with mathematical precision became generally accepted in academic economics and had great influence on the world of financial practice. James Galbraith, in another father-son story, pointed out that such a consensus in economics was contested by his father, John Galbraith, in the older man's magnum opus, *The New Industrial Estate*, in 1967. The book, although "a huge public success . . . was the target of a sustained and largely successful attack by mainstream economists, and . . . disappeared from view during the neo-liberal revival." It was dismissed, he argued, because "it represented a vast threat to their modes of thought, for it sought to replace (in part) an economics of markets with an economics of organizations—of corporations, governments, unions and other parties—of structures of governance, countervailing power and the efficacy of group effort and shared objectives" (Galbraith 2009, 93). The younger Galbraith is hugely cynical about the consensus, noting both its palpable failure, given the size and intensity of the 2007 recession, and its predilection for mathematics:

> To be sure mathematics is beautiful or can be [but] the clumsy mathematics of the modern mainstream journal article is not like this. It is more like a tedious high school problem set. The purpose, one suspects, is to intimidate and not to clarify. And with reason: an idea that would come across as simple-minded in English can be made "impressive-looking" with a sufficient string of Greek symbols. Particularly if the idea that "capitalism is a perfect or near-perfect system" would not stand the laugh test once stated plainly. (Galbraith 2009, 86)

James Galbraith has argued that it is impossible to understand the recent recession by looking at the behavior of the market alone. For it was not only a lack of regulation but the behavior of the major players in the process and their involvement in gross fraud and deception that led to the crisis. He interestingly calls for the need to set up a satisfactory social surround to the marketplace and for the study of its workings, including a "new criminology" that would bridge the gap between traditional economics and criminology:

> In the present crisis, the vapor trails of fraud and corruption are everywhere: from the terms of the original mortgages to the appraisals of the houses on which they are based; to the ratings of the securities issued against those mortgages; to the gross negligence of the regulators; to the notion that the risks could be laid off by credit-default swaps, a substitute

for insurance that lacked the critical ingredients of a traditional insurance policy, namely, loss reserves. None of this was foreseen by mainstream economists, who generally find crime a topic beneath their dignity. In unraveling all of this now, it is worth remembering that the resolution of the savings and loan scandal saw over a thousand industry insiders convicted and imprisoned. Plainly the intersection of economics and criminology remains a vital field for research going forward. (Galbraith 2009, 94)

The World of the Wealthy Top Percent

There is a world where money comes miraculously out of ATM machines and platinum cards; where work has disappeared and labor is what people who serve you do; where the major activity is leisure and shopping; where manufacturing has been replaced by the artifice of financial products. There are no workers making profits, only investors shrewd enough to collect them. It is easy not only to see Madoff as a symbol of all of this but to regard his financial setup in the Lipstick Building in Manhattan as something of a satire. Below his legitimate brokerage business was a whole floor, the seventeenth, devoted to deception, to smoke and mirrors with nothing in it but an old beat-up computer and accounts retrospectively made up as investments by a loyal, overpaid staff, ill educated and unlikely to find a job elsewhere. Nothing happened, except money passing hands, a good return at an extraordinary regular rate; if everyone half-knew it was fishy, they managed to suppress their suspicions under the near-mystical inducement of unearned income. And Madoff himself was the conjurer—benign, mysterious, charitable—who made money for his adoring clients magically out of nothing.

There have been two biographies published so far of Bernie Madoff, written by Erin Arvedlund (2009) and Jerry Oppenheimer (2009). Both describe him as well integrated socially and occupationally in the world of the very rich (for how else could he have garnered clients?). But they seem to suggest that his business practices were distant from those of normal finance and that his pursuit of extravagance and ornamental expenditure was somewhat unusual. Yet it is not at all strange for managers of hedge funds, by skillful if stealthy bookkeeping, to shift funds from one account to another in order to maintain a reasonable return for their clients. These are mini-Ponzis, if you like, which come and go. After all, this was probably why Madoff's scheme started in the first place. And it should be noted that there is little doubt that if the financial crisis had not occurred, with its widespread withdrawal of funds by large investors, the scheme would still be in operation.

The Ponzi scheme itself is surely not a million miles away from the normal *modus vivendi* of banks, which are permitted to lend money many times the level of their reserves, or, indeed, of the housing bubble, where people were induced to borrow money on the "inevitable" rise in house prices that were dependent on a constant run of new buyers entering the market. Moreover, the financial sector makes a great point of its acumen in running as close to the border between legality and illegality (and sometimes beyond) as is possible. Activities ranging from those of the most humble accountant to those of the managers of the great hedge funds exemplify this. The only other major institutions that dwell in such margins are the military and, persistently, the police.

Lastly, of course, Madoff was the "greatest thief in history" only if you ignore the activities of our great corporations, which regularly employ an army of lawyers in order to ward off tax payments, whose financial centers have been outsourced to distant tax havens, and whose own day-to-day activities are frequently on the wrong side of the law. As Matt Taibbi (2011, 41) said of Goldman Sachs: "They weren't murderers or anything; they had merely stolen more money than most people can rationally conceive of, from their own customers, in a few blinks of an eye. But then they went one step further. They came to Washington, took an oath before Congress, and lied about it."

Furthermore, as extravagant and unusual their lifestyles were, it is difficult to see how Madoff, his wife Ruth, and his extended family were particularly different from their peers who also passed time in, say, the golf clubs of Palm Beach, at luxury resorts on the Riviera, or at charity get-togethers on New York's Upper East Side. Madoff's extravagances were renowned: the rack upon rack of Savile Row suits that he showed proudly to guests; his several boats all named Bull (including one $7 million yacht berthed in the Antibes and one $2.2 million antique motor yacht docked on the gold coast of Florida); the two Rolex watches he wore on his left wrist (his rule was to never spend more than $80,000 on a watch), one set to New York time and the other registering the time in his London office (perhaps he found it difficult to add five to eastern standard time); not to mention his $2,000 slacks. Ruth matched her husband's luxurious tastes: a $4,000 little blue jacket; a $150,000-a-day spending spree during the run-up to the holidays, a habit she'd held since the early 1990s and which her staff referred to as "Ruth's twelve days of Christmas"; and a favored $7,500 Birkin bag on her arm. As for the rest of the family, their lives were facilitated by private planes, beautiful houses, the best hotels, and bottomless corporate American Express cards.

But none of this was exceptional in the milieu within which the family circulated. They existed in a world of wealth and extravagance where what is implausible and extraordinary to the vast majority of people was commonplace. Their environment, in short, was like them: spoiled and expensive.

Let us take, for example, the Palm Beach Country Club in Florida, which was ravaged by the Ponzi scheme. This is an island of wealth, with an initiation fee of more than $300,000 and a long waiting list; one assessment of its worth was that one third of club members had invested a collective $1 billion with Madoff by 2008. It has to be remembered that it was the cupidity of Madoff's clients that was the real motor behind the scheme and that it was they who benefited year in and year out until the final collapse. Anyone with an ounce of sense, particularly the big players, must have been only too aware that it was impossible to keep a level rate of return in a fluctuating stock market and that the rate of payment was extremely unlikely. Yet once Madoff was arrested, his greedy Palm Beach investors considered themselves, with breathtaking hypocrisy, victims. It was this transformation of their greed into the mantle of victimization, once Madoff was arrested, that was the greatest act of hypocrisy.

As Matthew Yeager, an astute analyst of the Madoff affair wrote: "In a document which was not filed in the criminal case against Bernard Madoff, the Government lists all the various investors, funds, pension trusts, and foundations who were victimized by Madoff. It literally reads like the investment portfolio of the American ruling class" (2010, 21). This is a class that would have delighted Veblen, arrogant in its wealth, blatant in its extravagance, narrow in its horizons, using philanthropy as a display of its humanity—albeit with tax deductions and frequently in lieu of public taxes and social obligations. Indeed in the United States, in particular, great wealth, as Merton pointed out, is itself seen as a sign of some inner virtue, regardless of how it has been accumulated. Moreover, for Madoff and his associates, charity seemed like some attempt at redemption—allowing on one side public approbation while on the other effectively soothing the conscience.

There were relatively poor victims who deserve our concern, but they played more of a role in the rhetoric of victimization than they did in the proportion of losses. Even some of the "less" wealthy clients lost millions of dollars, which scarcely vindicates their claims of being the average American family. They had, in many cases, done well over the years from the Ponzi scheme. Their notion of destitution was having been left with the assets of a normal middle class family. I certainly would not have grumbled at their spare change.

The Paradox of the American Dream

Merton in his early radical phase portrayed the American Dream as an ideology that served to hold society together, a counterpoise to the actual values that tended to break it apart (see Young 2010). It was, in his words, "a sop," which prevented rebellion, a dream that legitimated the social order, which promised social mobility despite the actualities of a rigid class structure. Nowadays the contrast between the dream and the reality has become considerably sharper. The United States is the most unequal of all the liberal democracies and is becoming more unequal. It has the lowest rate of social mobility and yet the highest expectations (Blanden, Gregg, and Machin 1995). As the comedian George Carlin has put it, the only people who believe in the American Dream are asleep. But it is a dream where the dreamers, once awakened, are anguished by their realization that something seriously is wrong and look around desperately for people to blame and for groups to despise. The financial crisis severely hastened this.

At the same time as Merton was writing about the impact of anomie and inequality on upper and working class crime, Svend Ranulf was exploring the impact of the economic crisis on the lower middle class. His pioneering study *Moral Indignation and Middle Class Psychology* (1938/1964) focused, in part, on the rise of National Socialism in Germany and the resentment conjured up by a threatened lower middle class. This involved both intense scapegoating and punitiveness. It would be absurd to suggest that anything like such an extreme situation could occur today, but parallel problems have arisen since the recession that play the same tune, albeit in a minor key. There is a widespread "fear of falling" among upper working class and middle class families, particularly in the United States. Let me briefly list some of the contributory factors:

1. There has been a substantial fall in house prices after a decade of increases that provided a sense of economic well-being and a comfort zone that encouraged high consumer spending despite the static nature of incomes during this period; the result was a buildup of massive credit card debt. The carpet has been pulled out from under this sense of security; consciousness of debt has replaced a sense of upward mobility.

2. Some 11.1 million U.S. households have negative equity, about 23 percent of which is held in home mortgages. That is to say, these owners would still owe money if they were able to sell their houses. Nearly one half of mortgages held in Arizona fall in this category. Similarly high percentages of negative equity are reported in Florida, California, and Michigan. On top of this, a further 2.4 million homes across the nation are financed with only 5 percent equity, putting them on the edge of tipping.

3. Retirement savings have been severely hit by the fall of stock prices, as has the money saved to get the kids through college. The possibility of class failure, of families falling into the ranks of the poor and the despised "underclass," becomes an increasing possibility.

4. There is widespread unemployment, while part-time and short-contract work is increasingly common.

5. There is a decline in real wages.

The vortex of prejudice set in such a current of economic distress engenders a multitude of moral panics and scapegoats. The lives of the poor and of the culturally diverse are regular targets. One glance at the tabloid newspapers or the extraordinary television dramas on law and order each side of the Atlantic readily substantiates this. The anger of the middle classes surfaces in the large and increasingly powerful, extreme right-wing parties of Europe and the tea-baggers of the United States and stirs up the vitriol of politicians. Charles Blow (2011), in an article in the *New York Times*, pointed to the most reprehensible statements about African Americans, Hispanics, and gays publicly made by Republican politicians in the preceding few months. One suggested that the threat of illegal immigrants was comparable to that of Hitler in World War II and that border guards should be allowed to "shoot to kill"; one compared pregnant illegal immigrants to "multiplying rats"; another argued that funds to HIV-AIDS victims should be cut off because "they lived a perverted life style"; whilst another—and I forbear to communicate the details—compared the Black unemployed to dogs.

Conclusion: From Moral Crisis to Financial Crisis; from Financial Crisis to Moral Panic

I began this essay by pointing to the moral crisis of late twentieth-century capitalism, which gave rise to an undermining of the social norms and regulations that held the market in check and maintained its sustenance. I have touched neither on the material reasons for this nor on the class struggle that this has engendered (see Harvey 2005; Wood 2005), choosing instead to concentrate on the moral dimensions. I have endeavored to show how such a moral crisis has in turn generated moral panic and resentment in sections of the population. It has, furthermore, created feelings of injustice, often misplaced in their targets and evidenced in moral panics that dwell on the poor, the diverse, and the immigrant (Young, 2011).

Lastly, I have attempted to place Bernie Madoff in this dismal story. I have argued that far from him being a deviant outlier to the system, he dramatically presents the spirit and practice of finance capitalism. The two principal biographies so far of Bernie Madoff, written by Arvedlund (2009) and Oppenheimer (2009), wonder what made him tick, as if there were some mysterious elements of malice and deceit residing within his personality. In fact, he was perfectly normal. What made him tick was finance capital in the twenty-first century and the narcissistic values of a callous and undeserving elite.

References

Arvedlund, Erin. 2009. *Madoff: The Man Who Stole $65 Billion*. London: Penguin.

Blanden, Joe, Paul Gregg, and Stephen Machin. 1995. *Intergenerational Mobility in Europe and North America*. London: London School of Economics, Centre for Economic Performance.

Blow, Charles M. 2011. "Silliness and Sleight of Hand." *New York Times*, April 30, A21.

Fox, Justin. 2009. *The Myth of the Rational Market*. New York: Harper Collins.

Galbraith, James K. 2008. *The Predator State*. New York: Free Press.

————. 2009. "Who Are These Economists Anyway?" *Thought and Action* 25 (Fall): 85–97.

Galbraith, John K. 1967/2007. *The New Industrial State*. Princeton, N.J.: Princeton University Press.

Gottfredson, Michael, and Travis Hirschi. 1990. *A General Theory of Crime*. Stanford, Calif.: Stanford University Press.

Harvey, David. 2005. *The New Imperialism*. Oxford: Oxford University Press.

Hobsbawm, Eric. 1994. *The Age of Extremes*. London: Michael Joseph.

Katz, Jack. 1988. *The Seductions of Crime*. New York: Basic Books.

Krugman, Paul. 2009. "How Did Economists Get It Wrong?" *New York Times Magazine*, September 6.

Merton, Robert K. 1938. "Social Structure and Anomie." *American Sociological Review* 3:672–82.

Oppenheimer, Jerry. 2009. *Madoff with the Money*. Hoboken, N.J.: Wiley.

Ranulf, Svend. 1938/1964. *Moral Indignation and Middle Class Psychology*. New York: Schocken.

Sennett, Richard. 1998. *The Corrosion of Character*. New York: W. W. Norton.

Taibbi, Matt. 2011. "The People vs. Goldman Sachs." *Rolling Stone*, May 26, 41–46.

Wilson, James Q. 1997. *The Moral Sense*. New York: Simon & Schuster.

Wood, Ellen Meiksins. 2005. *Empire of Capital*. New York: Verso.

Yeager, Matthew. 2010. "The Perils of Capital Accumulation: Bernie Madoff and the American Ruling Class." Paper presented at the Annual Meetings of American Society of Criminology, November, San Francisco.

Young, Jock. 1974. "New Directions in Subcultural Theory." In *Approaches to Sociology*, edited by John Rex. London: Routledge.

————. 2010. "R. K. Merton." In *Fifty Key Thinkers in Criminology*, edited by Keith Hayward, Shadd Maruna, and Jayne Mooney, 88–99. London: Routledge.

————. 2011. *The Criminological Imagination*. Cambridge: Polity.

————. 2012. "Moral Panics and the Transgressive Other." *Crime, Media, Culture* 7(3): 245–558.

[PART II]

ENABLERS OF FRAUD

In 80% of cases, according to the FBI, fraud involves industry insiders. For example, property flipping can involve buyers, real estate agents, appraisers, and complicit closing agents. In a "silent second," the buyer, with the collusion of a loan officer and without the knowledge of the first mortgage lender, disguises the existence of a second mortgage to hide the fact that no down payment has been made.

—(Financial Crisis Inquiry Commission, Final Report of the National Commission on the Causes of the Financial and Economic Crisis in the United States, Official Government Edition, 2011, 160)

UNACCOUNTABLE EXTERNAL AUDITORS AND THEIR ROLE IN THE ECONOMIC MELTDOWN

GILBERT GEIS

The SEC has been pelted, deservedly, with criticism for its abject failure to monitor the financial crimes and shenanigans engaged in by investment banks and other irresponsible entities whose reckless behavior collectively triggered what become known as "the Great Economic Meltdown." The SEC, ideologically identified with the Republican Party, became an appetizing target when the Democrats came to power. The SEC's negligent and overmatched chairman, Christopher Cox, had reflected the George W. Bush administration's indifferent attitude toward the self-indulgent excesses of real estate brokers and financial institutions involved in the subprime lending racket and toward Wall Street investment firms that were avidly marketing toxic mortgage derivatives. The peddlers of these polluted and often largely incomprehensible papers, not coincidentally, were reaping extremely high profits.

There were, as well, other corporate and partnership culprits who participated in the affairs leading to the meltdown that have largely remained out of the limelight. One group of these organizations—the external auditing firms that are supposed to provide detailed and accurate information about the financial situation of their clients—constitutes the subject matter of the present chapter.

Public faith "depends upon the public perception of the outside auditor as an independent professional," the U.S. Supreme Court observed in *United States v. Arthur Young & Co.* The court in that case ruled that "endowing the work papers of an independent auditor with work-product immunity would destroy the appearance of auditor's independence by creating the impression that the auditor is an advocate for the client" (*United States v. Arthur Young & Co.* 1984, 819). Unfortunately, making the work papers transparent did little to undermine suspicion regarding auditor independence.

Of all the outside auditors of the large firms and banks whose irresponsible and possibly criminal behavior contributed to the meltdown, only Ernst & Young came under close scrutiny for its failure to detect and/or protest the audacious and deceptive accounting maneuvers of its client.[1] This was noted in a nine-volume, 2,220-page report by Anton R. Valukas, a court-appointed examiner, who pinpointed the irresponsible endorsement by Ernst & Young of Lehman Brothers practices (Valukas 2010). Lehman had moved $50 billion in losses off its books in what was known internally as a Repo 105. Repo is shorthand for repurchase, the arrangement under which "sold" toxic holdings would be reclaimed after the audit was completed. (The number 105 in its name reflects the fact that the assets became worth 105 percent of what Lehman had sold them for.) Valukas's report noted that although Repo 105 was not inherently improper, Lehman Brothers' use of the tactic violated accounting principles that require all legitimate transactions to have a business purpose. In Lehman's case, the bankruptcy examiner said that Repo 105 was employed solely to manipulate financial information. It was noted, too, that a Lehman senior vice president, Matthew Lee, had met with two members of the audit team and blown the whistle on the questionable accounting maneuver. Lee, who had been with Lehman for 14 years, was fired soon after, and the firm had to go to England to obtain a legal opinion supporting its accounting maneuvers since it could locate no American law firm willing to do so (*In re: Lehman Brothers Holdings Inc.* 2010).

The focus on Ernst & Young's alleged wrongdoing in connection with the largest bankruptcy in American history was a consequence of what in effect was a coroner's examination of Lehman's demise (Valukas 2010). But the other malefactors closely linked to the financial crisis—and there were many—were able to protect themselves from equally penetrating scrutiny. In the case of Bank of America, for instance, six repo transactions hid from view billions of dollars of debt in order to meet financial targets, but the SEC apparently declined to go forward with any legal action because the amount involved was significantly less than in the Lehman case (Rapoport 2010).

Ernst & Young may or may not find itself in a criminal court. At the time of writing, except for the auditor in the Bernie Madoff Ponzi scheme, only PricewaterhouseCoopers (PwC), the European external accountant for Lehman Brothers International (Europe), took a significant financial (but not criminal) hit in the aftermath of the economic meltdown. PwC agreed to pay about $22 billion to some 6,500 unsecured creditors of the European branch of Lehman Brothers (Thomson 2010). Many observers considered the PwC penalty as merely the price that sometimes has to be paid for doing business—or rather, monkey business.

The role of accountants in the economic recession—actually a depression, although it appears to be politically incorrect to describe it that way (Posner 2009)—has barely been considered. An exception was an article in the business section of the *New York Times* that dealt with the loose rules promulgated and still defended by professional organizations such as the Financial Accounting Standards Board. The article carried the telling headline "Accountants Misled Us into Crisis." The story jumps to a headline inside that may prove prescient if effective remedial measures are not put in place. It read: "It Could Happen Again" (Norris 2009, B4).

In the following pages, I provide evidence to support the argument that a radical overhaul in the U.S. system of external auditing of corporate financial affairs is necessary.

The Rakoff Remedy

One of the developments in the meltdown cleanup involved the merger of Bank of America, nudged rather strenuously by the U.S. Department of the Treasury, with a near-bankrupt Merrill Lynch. Bank of America, itself the recipient of a loan from the government, failed to tell its shareholders, who had to approve the blending of the two companies, that Merrill Lynch would dole out huge—some would call them obscene—bonuses that would reduce its value to its purchaser. In the fourth quarter of 2008, Merrill Lynch suffered losses of $15 billion, yet it allocated $3.6 billion of its funds for executive bonuses. Charged in civil court by the SEC for having hidden these facts from its stockholders, Bank of America agreed to settle the case by paying a $33 million penalty.

For the deal to be clinched, a federal district judge had to approve. Judge Jed Rakoff, reputed to be something of a curmudgeon, rebelled. He wanted to know, among other things, why the company was expropriating money from shareholders to pay the fine rather than getting the funds from the lawyers who had failed to mention the bonuses in the proxy statement. Or as Rakoff noted, why not penalize Bank of America executives who either knowingly or negligently let this happen? Rakoff refused to approve the settlement (*SEC v. Bank of America* 2009).

Five months later, however, Rakoff "reluctantly" agreed to a $150 million settlement, thereby expropriating even more of the shareholders' money than in the original plan. Conceding that the new agreement was "far from ideal," he apparently relented because it seemed likely that the New York attorney general would press a criminal case against Bank of America and individuals involved in the merger arrangements. The charges never were forthcoming. A pair of investigative reporters maintained that Secretary of the Treasury Timothy Geithner and New York State Attorney General Andrew Cuomo had cut a deal not to charge the corporations or their executives criminally because it would roil an already unsettled marketplace (Morgenson and Story 2011b). The same two reporters subsequently noted that the Department of Justice had adopted guidelines favoring a "deferred prosecution" approach to white-collar criminals, whereby they would be put on warning to behave thereafter or to face a delayed prosecution (Morgenson and Story 2011a).

Particularly noteworthy was an item in the Bank of America settlement that received no coverage in the media. The parties had agreed to submit proposed bonuses to a nonbinding vote by shareholders within the following 3 years and, during the same time period, to appoint an independent "disclosure counsel" who would report solely to the audit committee of Bank of America's Board of Directors on the adequacy of the bank's public disclosures. Rakoff added a further element to the oversight proposal that was especially interesting:

> In order to further strengthen these prophylactic measures, the Court suggested at the hearing on February 8, 2010 that the independent auditor and the disclosure counsel not just be chosen in consultation with the S.E.C. but rather be fully acceptable to the S.E.C. with the Court having the final say if the two sides could not agree on the selection. The parties, by letter dated February 16, 2010, have subsequently agreed to

these suggestions, which will therefore need to be incorporated in a revised Proposed Consent judgment to be presented to the Court. (*SEC v. Bank of America* 2010, 3)

Rakoff's recognition of the key role that can be—but often has not been—played by external auditors in scrupulously monitoring the financial affairs of their clients attests to a very significant subplot in both the recent economic meltdown and earlier business scandals.

The Madoff Maelstrom

It was a difficult task for the media, especially television, to get a firm grasp on the ingredients that constituted the Great Economic Meltdown. Arcane financial transactions, such as synthetic CDOs, do not make for rousing images. Also, no attention was paid to the matter that had moved Judge Rakoff to try to fashion a remedy. Despite flagrant mismanagement and irresponsible risk taking by insurance giants such as the American International Group (AIG) and by investment banks such as Goldman Sachs, Bear Stearns, and Lehman Brothers, the question never arose as to why outside auditors had not spotted the accounting chicanery that marked the perhaps illegal and certainly ill-advised corporate activities. Nor were there questions about why they had not alerted government officials and the public to what was occurring.

Bernard Madoff attracted the most intense media and prosecutorial scrutiny, in part because the Ponzi scheme he operated was so brazen and simple-minded, and many of its victims were so well known. Madoff himself was a person whose glamorous lifestyle could be depicted in terms vivid enough to satisfy viewers and readers (see, e.g., Arvedlund 2009; Kirtzman 2009; Kotz 2009; LeBor 2009; Markopolos 2010; Oppenheimer 2009; Ross 2009; Sander 2009; Strober and Strober 2009). The Madoff case was the only instance in the meltdown that addressed a basic question: Where were the external auditors while all this was going on?

Madoff allegedly cheated about 8,000 investors in his scheme of somewhere between $15 billion and $65 billion. The exact figure varies with the source. He operated over a span of 40 years, paying off those who sought to cash out with funds secured from new clients, and he sent regular statements to investors detailing their holdings and their illusory high level of profits.

It apparently never occurred to Madoff's clients to exercise due diligence that would involve checking out the person or organization responsible for auditing his company's books. Had they done so, they would have learned that the Madoff enterprise was audited by Friehling & Horowitz, a firm that occupied a 13-foot-by-18-foot storefront office in the village of New City, about 30 miles north of Manhattan. David G. Friehling, 49, the only professional accountant in the office, had been auditing Madoff's books since 1991. Jeremy Horowitz, Friehling's father-in-law and cofounder of the firm, had retired to Florida. He died of cancer on the day that Madoff received a 150-year prison sentence.

Friehling proved an easy target for the authorities. Prosecutors noted that he had signed off on a report to the SEC indicating that Madoff's firm had $1.09 billion in assets and $425 million in liabilities. The figures were phony. He pled guilty in November 2009 to single counts each of securities and investment advisor fraud, four counts of making false filings with the SEC, and three counts of obstructing and impeding the administration of the federal tax laws—the last on the ground that he prepared phony tax returns for Madoff and unidentified others. Friehling was fined $3.18 million, the sum representing his fees from Madoff and his investment in the company. He said that at no time had he been aware that Madoff was operating a Ponzi scheme. Friehling sought to support this claim by pointing out that he had lost about $500,000 in personal investments in Bernard L. Madoff Investment Securities. He said that he took the documents that were presented to him from the Madoff operation at face value and rubber-stamped them. For this amiable activity, Friehling was paid between $12,000 and $14,500 monthly from 2004 to 2007. He agreed to cooperate with the prosecution in other Madoff-related cases, and as a result his sentencing was postponed (Bharara 2010). He faces the maximum possible statutory term of 114 years (Bray 2009, C3).

Stanford Investment Bank

Madoff's Ponzi peer was Texas billionaire R. Allen Stanford, the 59-year-old head of Stanford International Bank (SIB). Along with his chief financial officer, James M. Davis, Stanford carried out what the SEC described as a massive, ongoing fraud. Like Madoff, he appears to have played fast and loose with auditing activity. The Stanford group is headquartered in St. John's, the capital of the island-nation of Antigua and Barbuda, a locale that fits the description novelist Somerset Maugham once applied to the French Riviera: "a sunny place for shady people." Antigua has long been considered an attractive site for U.S. citizens who, illegally, pursue off-shore internet gambling (Pontell, Brown, and Geis 2007). It was also the temporary refuge of Robert Vesco, who sought without success to buy the island of Barbuda from Antigua and thereby to avoid extradition to the United States, where he had been charged with egregious financial frauds (Herzog 1987).

SIB had sold approximately $8 billion of what it called "certificates of deposit" to Central American and North American investors. Stanford was tripped up, ironically, when he claimed to have had nothing to do with Madoff. SEC investigators knew better, since they had learned that Stanford had deposited some of the funds invested with him in Madoff's company. So careless was Stanford that SIB claimed that its "diversified portfolio" had returned precisely identical results in consecutive years, a claim that an expert hired by the SEC labeled impossible.

Alex Dalmady, an investigative blogger, first exposed SIB in an article published in a Venezuelan financial magazine, *VerEconomy Monthly*. Dalmady titled the piece "Duck Tales," playing on the old saw that if something looks like a duck and quacks like a duck—or, analogously if things look decidedly crooked—then the former is a duck and the latter is a scam. Dalmady pointed out that the SIB auditor was an island firm whose principal was a 72-year-old man who had been examining the company's books for at least a decade, despite the fact that PwC and KPMG both had offices in Antigua. Dalmady indicated that a Spanish proverb was appropriate to the Stanford situation: "Hecha la ley, hecha la trampa"—if there's a law, there's a loophole (Dalmady 2009, 14).

The SEC complaint briefly summarized the auditing farce that characterized Stanford's operation:

The impossible results are made even more suspicious by the fact that, contrary to assurances provided to investors, at most only two people— Stanford and Davis—knew the details concerning the bulk of SIB's investment portfolio. For example, its long-standing auditor is reportedly retained based on a "relationship of trust" between the head of the auditing firm and Stanford. (*SEC v. Stanford International Bank, Ltd.* 2009, 2)

An Autopsy on Arthur Andersen

The cozy relationship between the Enron Corporation and Arthur Andersen, LLP, its auditor and consultant, may have made for jolly social events and interchangeable job movement between the two companies, but it also contributed significantly to the demise of both organizations (Squires et al. 2003; Swartz and Watkins 2003; Toffler and Reingold 2003). It is arguable whether the prosecutors inflicted what reasonably could be regarded as a death penalty upon the companies or whether their departure from among the living was a matter of suicide.

Arthur Andersen, a limited partnership, was founded in 1913. By 2000, it was one of the "Big Five" (as the auditing kingpins were known from 1989 to 1998, when Price Waterhouse merged with Coopers and Lybrand and the group subsequently became known as the Big Five) in the country's auditing industry, with 340 offices in thirty-four countries, 85,000 employees, and $9.3 billion in annual revenues worldwide. Andersen had worked for and with Enron since 1985 and at the end was receiving $52 million a year in auditing and consulting fees from Enron, its major client.

In time, government authorities essentially got fed up with Arthur Andersen's repetitive wrongdoing. In 1997, the company had been the defendant in more than thirty lawsuits regarding advice it had provided investors who lost hundreds of millions of dollars following the collapse of Colonial Realty in West Hartford, Connecticut. Andersen paid out more than $90 million to settle the case. A year before its troubles regarding Enron, the auditing company paid $110 million to settle a class action suit brought by shareholders of Sunbeam. Andersen's accountants also had failed to detect a Ponzi scheme run by the Baptist Foundation of America. That cost the firm $217 million to settle claims. Then there was a $229 million payment in a 2001 suit involving an earnings statement by Waste Management that Andersen had "knowingly or recklessly" inflated by $1.4 billion by recourse to unacceptable accounting methods (Laufer 2006, 45). The SEC director of enforcement, Richard Walker, noted that the Waste Management lawbreaking was rooted in the fact that "Arthur

Andersen and its management failed to stand up to company managers" (Laufer 2006, 45). As part of that settlement, Andersen was enjoined against engaging in such behavior. The U.S. deputy attorney general noted that in finally deciding to prosecute Andersen criminally, his office had taken into account many considerations, "including the seriousness of the alleged offense" and "the firm's history of wrongdoing" (Laufer 2006, 45).

The prosecution of Andersen for its work with Enron chose to focus on the shredding of relevant papers in Andersen offices in Houston, Portland (Oregon), Chicago, and London after its attorneys and managers had learned that the government was suspicious of Enron. More than a ton of documents were destroyed as well as some 30,000 e-mails and computer files (Chase 2003).

After Andersen lost the case, its clients fled to other firms and the company went under. The episode demonstrates how vulnerable a company that depends on a reputation for integrity is to a shaming criminal charge (Chaney and Philipich 2002). The U.S. Supreme Court ruled that Andersen had been unjustly convicted because the government had not adequately proven that the shredding was no more than a routine business activity (*Arthur Andersen LLP v. United States* 2005; Spalding and Morrison 2006). But it was too late: The Big Five was now the Big Four.

Stephen Rosoff and his colleagues aptly sum up the Enron-Andersen events this way: "The company now acknowledges that it made what it terms 'errors of judgment.' One could respond that wearing a striped tie with a plaid shirt is an 'error in judgment.' What Arthur Andersen did is *a crime*" (Rosoff, Pontell, and Tillman 2007, 310).

A former employee offered a telling account of his experiences on his first job as an auditor for an Arthur Andersen team. Vincent Daniels, who later would make a killing betting short on the downfall of investment firms, was struck by the opacity of Solomon Brothers' books. Neither he nor his Andersen colleagues could understand what Solomon was doing and why it was doing it. He concluded that there was no way for an accountant assigned to such a task to determine accurately whether the company was making money or losing money, that their books were giant black boxes with hidden gears that were in constant motion. His manager, who had no better comprehension of the true picture, finally told Daniel to stop asking questions and just do the best he could, that that was what he had been hired for (Lewis 2010).

This brief vignette, multiplied many times, lies behind the recent observation of Richard Posner, a conservative federal judge and highly regarded economist: "accountants, since they are paid by the firm they audit, are reluctant to flag their clients' default risks. Granted, often those risks are not disclosed in the documents the accountants review in an audit, but sometimes they are" (Posner 2009, 94).

Posner's observation that information is often camouflaged so that accountants are unable to make an accurate assessment of the true state of a company's financial condition comport with the above-cited lament by Vince Daniels in his effort to audit Solomon Brothers and is a theme often echoed. When Arthur Young & Co. was alleged to have mishandled its audit of the Vernon Savings and Loan Association, Young's CEO flatly declared that "skilled management can virtually always fool the auditor" ("Study to Show Accountants Failed to Detect S&L Fraud" 1989, 21). Similarly, when in 1982 the American Association of Certified Public Accountants mandated stricter auditing rules, it also stressed that "we are acknowledging our responsibility in this regard, but we are trying to write this in a way that also acknowledges the limits of an audit as well" (Berg 1982, 1). A Peat Marwick partner made the same point: "So long as there are dishonest people in this world," he said, "there are going to be audit failures" (Berg 1987, B9).

These are depressing disclaimers and they inevitably raise the question: Why bother at all with an "independent" external audit of a corporation? On the upside, it seems very likely that some corporations some of the time (especially, perhaps, when those times are prosperous) go out of their way to offer honest appraisals of their financial condition and operations. But the naysayers routinely emphasize that an outsider who depends on the accuracy of the external auditor's examination in regard to the true condition of a company will be gulled if the company chooses to conceal relevant facts. The auditor's report then becomes no more than a fig leaf. It seems obvious that a better way of dealing with such situations is required. Or perhaps consideration ought to be given to abandoning the practice altogether.

As disturbing as the Arthur Andersen revelations were, more fuel was added by a study that concluded that Andersen was no worse that the handful of other accounting firms who were responsible for external audits of almost every large corporation in America. Theodore Eisenberg and Jonathan Macey, using selected restatements from 1997 to 2001 as a gauge of auditing malfeasance, concluded that "firms will capture the teams of

auditors assigned to prepare financial statements and cause these accountants to acquiesce in inappropriately aggressive accounting treatment, or even
to pro-actively participate in the design of materially misleading accounting
statements." More to the point, Andersen's clients' restatement rates were
statistically no different than other firms (Eisenberg and Macey 2004, 264).

Eisenberg and Macey found no evidence that the accounting firms compete with one another in regard to the quality of their work. Part of what
reasonably can be seen as an emergent and growing irresponsibility among
external auditors is attributed to the move toward limited liability partnerships. Without this arrangement, the partners themselves could have been
held personally liable in lawsuits, a situation that made them, according to
the authors, a good deal more careful and encouraged them to more scrupulously monitor the work being conducted by every member of the firm.

The Savings and Loan Swindles

The savings and loan collapses of the 1980s and 1990s involved a number of
what one postmortem labeled "hired guns"—a category, according to this
autopsy, that was led by accountants (Calavita, Pontell, and Tillman 1997).
By 1990, twenty-one certified public accountants had been sued by the federal government for their role in the thrift debacle, fourteen of whom worked
for Big Six companies. One prosecutor called the accounting negligence of
Arthur Young & Co. "the K-Mart blue light special" (Waldman 1990, 49).
Arthur Andersen had endorsed the bookkeeping of the Financial Corporation of America before the institution had to be taken over, costing taxpayers
$2 billion. Deloitte, Haskins & Sells approved the books of CenTrust in
Florida at a time when the owners were jacking up assets by a series of
round-robin trades that wildly inflated the value of the properties involved.
Similarly, Touche Ross confirmed the viability of the Beverly Hills Savings
and Loan not long before it went belly up (Calavita et al. 1997).

Sarbanes-Oxley

Jeffrey Skilling, the former CEO of Enron who was convicted of twenty-
five counts of fraud, persistently sought to exonerate himself from complicity in the company's finagling of its books by repeating that he was not

an accountant and therefore did not possess adequate expertise to comprehend the crooked auditing schemes that were practiced. Skilling's disclaimer was a major ingredient that fed into what is regarded as one of the most powerful elements of the reformist Sarbanes-Oxley Act of 2002 (formally the Public Company Reform and Investor Protection Act), enacted in the wake of (and only because of) the Enron–Arthur Andersen and associated scandals. The act holds chief executives and chief financial officers responsible for the accuracy of audits of companies with annual earnings of $1.2 billion or more. The two executives have to sign off on the reports that go forward to the SEC, and they can be held criminally responsible if the reports that they endorsed are found to be fraudulent.

The Sarbanes-Oxley Act requirements are monitored by an SEC-appointed five-person Public Company Accounting Oversight Board (PCAOB), which is dubbed by some wits as "Peek-a-Boo." The board survived a challenge on constitutional grounds that focused on what was claimed to be a violation of the separation of powers based on the fact that the board was appointed by the SEC rather than by the president—the latter requiring Senate approval. The Supreme Court in 2010 ruled that only minor rearrangements would be necessary to satisfactorily remedy what its challengers saw as its inadequacy (*Free Enterprise Fund v. Public Company Accounting Oversight Board* 2010).

Title II of the act established standards for external auditor independence, seeking to limit conflicts of interest. Section 201 of the title restricts auditing companies from conducting other kinds of business with the same client, such as providing bookkeeping services, conducting actuarial activities, engaging in management, or providing various other forms of consulting (Fletcher and Plette 2003; Prentice and Bredeson 2008; Thibodeau and Freir 2007). An empirical inquiry found a positive correlation between the fees generated by an external auditor and nonauditing consulting services and company audit aberrancy (Frankel, Johnson, and Nelson 2002; but for a contrary conclusion, see DeFord, Raghunandan, and Subramanyam 2002; see also, generally, Ashbaugh 2004).

Title II also addresses the new auditor approval requirement and specifies that a company cannot be audited for more than five consecutive fiscal years by the lead or coordinating auditor having primary responsibility or by the person responsible for reviewing the audit. Also if the CEO, CFO, or controller of a company had worked for an auditing group within the past year, that group could not be hired as the company's out-side auditor. The act addresses circumstances that contributed to the Arthur Andersen–Enron debacle and, had they been in place, could possibly have prevented that occurrence. However, skilled attorneys are notably adept in finding ways around laws and regulations aimed at curbing corporate behavior.

An Unhealthy HealthSouth

The CEO of HealthSouth became the first person charged with violation of the Sarbanes-Oxley requirement that its financial reports be certified as accurate by its executive officers. The indictment charged that since 1999, the company, located in Birmingham, Alabama, and one of the nation's largest health care providers, employing more than 50,000 people worldwide, had misstated its earnings by at least $1.4 billion (Johnson 2003, A1). The apparent impetus for the fraud was the insistence of Richard M. Scrushy, the company's founder, CEO, and chairman of the board, that the company had to appear to meet or exceed the earnings expectations established by Wall Street analysts. When earnings did not reach that level, Scrushy's orders were to fix things so that they would. In accordance with the requirement of the Sarbanes-Oxley Act, Scrushy and Davis had certified under oath that the earnings report contained "no untrue statement of a material fact." The indictment maintained that the HealthSouth financial position was overstated by 4,722 percent (Johnson 2003, A1). Scrushy, however, was acquitted in a jury trial, perhaps because he had developed a very positive image in Birmingham through philanthropic donations (Morse, Terhune, and Carms 2005, 8). Soon after, he received a 6-years-and-10-months prison sentence when convicted of giving Alabama Governor Don Siegelman half a million dollars in exchange for appointment to a seat on the board that regulated hospitals (Lewis 2010).

A major question raised by the HealthSouth case was whether the Sarbanes-Oxley Act, when employed as the basis for a criminal prosecution, could effectively produce the result it sought by punishing a wrongdoer and, much more difficult to determine, whether it could inhibit others from engaging in the same kind of illegal behavior (Taylor 2005). Certainly, the subsequent economic meltdown strongly suggested that allegedly independent auditors, persons with considerable outsider access to the details of the financial condition of corporations, had woefully failed to alert others to situations that foretold impending doom.

The Dodd-Frank Economic Reform Measure

One provision in the 2,000-page economic reform package that worked its way through Congress and a Senate-House reconciliation committee before being signed into law by President Barack Obama in 2010 is particularly pertinent to the thesis of this chapter. One of the problems said to contribute to the onset of the meltdown was the wrongheaded ratings of toxic derivatives by Standard & Poor's, Moody's, and Fitch, the three leading organizations that determine the relative risk of investment offerings.

The Dodd-Frank bill sought to alleviate this unseemly situation with a provision that allowed bond holders to sue raters if they thought they had been misled by malfeasance. In addition, rather than continue to permit issuers to choose which rating organization to deal with, an investor board overseen by the SEC will make the assignment in the future in regard to which group will assign letter evaluations of which bonds. Given a choice, companies sensibly have sought to deal with the most friendly and accommodating group to evaluate their products. For their part, rating agencies, who are extremely well paid for this activity, have been much too careful about not alienating actual and potential customers by taking hard-nosed positions. This conflict of interest was exacerbated by the fact that the instruments that they were rating were often as incomprehensible to the raters as they were to their issuers.

Recommendation and Conclusion

The performance of external auditors, to put it kindly, has left a good deal to be desired. Less kindly, a friend of the writer, a corporate executive who asked for anonymity, said that a single word could best summarize for her the current situation of external auditors: That word was "whores." It is no longer fashionable, much less sensible, to parrot the Adam Smith platitude that capitalism, left unattended by government oversight, invariably will in time cure itself of whatever ails it. Taken literally, this position would advocate the total elimination of outside auditors, who could be viewed as superfluous interference with the health and vitality of what should be an unfettered market.

It could be argued that ridding the business world of the necessity for outside audits is a good idea—but for reasons other than Smith's economic axioms. Audits represent an expensive enterprise that fails to achieve its purpose. External auditors too often create a "Potemkin Village" that hides the real state of a firm's finances, and in so doing they dupe those who might rely on what they report to the authorities and the public. Compare, for instance, the sage, albeit utopian, advice offered to external auditors by Warren Buffett. The man famously regarded as one of the nation's top financial sages has three standards:

1. If the auditor were solely responsible for preparation of the company's financial statements, would they have been done differently?—and if "differently," the auditor should explain both management's argument and his own;
2. If the auditor were an investor, would he have received the information essential to understanding the company's financial performance during the reporting period?;
3. Is the company following the same audit procedure that the auditor would if he himself were CEO? If not, what are the differences and why? (Buffett 2007, 612)

More generally, researchers stress that "auditors must come to appreciate the profound impact of self-serving biases on judgment" (Bazeman, Loewenstein, and Moore 2002, 103).

The core problem is, of course, conflict of interest. Because they are the hirelings of those they audit, and because they cherish the lucrative assignments they receive, external auditors are much too likely to tread carefully, to turn a blind eye, to avoid confrontations, when they sense or know they might be pinpointing wrongdoing. They feed placebos to the public and hope that nobody will be the wiser.

If we accept the premise that outside accounting scrutiny by qualified independent auditors of corporate financial matters is devoutly to be desired, how might we better achieve this objective? Can the current conflict of interest be overcome?

A partial answer to this question can be extrapolated from the two pathways that have been laid out by innovations discussed in the earlier pages of this chapter: First is Judge Rakoff's negotiated settlement with Bank of America, which stipulated that the outside auditor and the disclosure counsel be fully acceptable to the SEC and, in the event of a dispute over the selection, that the matter be settled by the court. Second, the provision in the Dodd-Frank economic reform measure that requires the SEC, rather than the company, to select the organization that will rate its bonds has potential.

A similar approach should be initiated in regard to external auditors. Companies should be assessed fees that are deposited in the coffers of an independent body that assumes full responsibility for the assignment and review of auditing work. Such a body, which might be called the Oversight Board, should have its own staff of skilled accountants and investigators and might well include lawyers who are given the power to file and try civil and criminal law suits against offending corporations. Funds recovered in such suits should be fed into the board's operating budget. If an auditing team can justify the need for more financial support to follow disconcerting information, the board should be in a position to underwrite such extra funds. The Oversight Board also ought to encourage the work of newcomers to the auditing enterprise and foster their growth so that there comes to be a much larger corps of companies competing for business.

Notes

The author wishes to thank Mary Dodge for her comments and suggestions on this essay.

1. In 1989, the firm of Ernst & Whitney merged with Arthur Young to create Ernst & Young.

References

Arthur Andersen LLP v. United States, 544 U.S. 696 (2005).
Arvedlund, Erin. 2009. *Too Good to Be True: The Rise and Fall of Bernie Madoff.* New York: Portfolio.

Ashbaugh, Holly. 2004. "Ethical Issues Related to Provision of Audit and Non-Audit Services: Evidence from Academic Research." *Journal of Business Ethics* 2:143–48.

Bazeman, Max, George Loewenstein, and Don A. Moore. 2002. "Why Good Accountants Do Bad Audits." *Harvard Business Review* 80:96–103.

Berg, Eric. 1982. "New Audit Rule to Require Search for Client Fraud." *New York Times*, February 16, 1, 32.

———. 1987. "Critics Fault Accountants for Not Blowing Whistles." *New York Times*, July 5, B9.

Bharara, Preet. 2010. Personal communication to Judge Alvin Hellerstein, August 20.

Bray, Chad. 2009. "Madoff Auditor Says He Was Duped, Too." *Wall Street Journal*, November 4, C3.

Buffett, Warren. 2007. "Advice to Outside Auditors." In *Honest Work: A Business Ethics Reader*, edited by Joanne B. Ciulla, Clancy Martin, and Robert C. Solomon, 612. New York: Oxford University Press.

Calavita, Kitty, Henry N. Pontell, and Robert H. Tillman. 1997. *Big Money Crime: Fraud and Politics in the Savings and Loan Crisis.* Berkeley: University of California Press.

Chaney, Paul K., and Kirk L. Philipich. 2002. "Shredded Reputation: The Cost of Audit Failures." *Journal of Accounting Research* 40:1221–45.

Chase, Christopher R. 2003. "To Shred or Not to Shred: Document Retention Policies and Federal Obstruction of Justice Statutes." *Fordham Journal of Corporate & Financial Law* 8:721–63.

Dalmady, Alex. 2009. "Duck Tales." *VerEconomy Monthly*, January, 11–15.

DeFord, Mark L., Kannan Raghunandan, and K. R. Subramanyam. 2002. "Do Non-Audit Service Fees Impair Auditor Independence?" *Journal of Accounting Research* 40:1247–1274.

Eisenberg, Theodore, and Jonathan R. Macey. 2004. "Was Arthur Andersen Different? An Empirical Examination of Major Accounting Firms' Audits of Large Clients." *Journal of Empirical Legal Studies* 1:263–300.

Fletcher, William H., and Theodore N. Plette. 2003. *The Sarbanes-Oxley Act: Implementation, Significance, and Impact.* New York: Nova Science.

Frankel, Richard M., Marilyn F. Johnson, and Karen K. Nelson. 2002. "The Relationship Between Auditor's Fees for Non-Audit Activities and Earnings Management." *Accounting Research* 77:2–13.

Free Enterprise Fund v. Public Company Accounting Oversight Board, 129 S. Ct. 2378 (2010).

Herzog, Arthur. 1987. *Vesco: From Wall Street to Castro's Cuba: The Rise, Fall and, Exile of the King of White Collar Crime.* New York: Doubleday.

Johnson, Carrie. 2003. "Health South Founder Is Charged with Fraud." *Washington Post*, November 5, A1.

Kirtzman, Andrew. 2009. *Betrayal: The Life and Lies of Bernie Madoff.* New York: HarperCollins.

Kotz, H. David. 2009. *Investigation of Failure of SEC to Uncover Bernard Madoff's Ponzi Scheme.* Washington, D.C.: U.S. Securities and Exchange Commission, Office of Investigations.

Laufer, William S. 2006. *Corporate Bodies and Guilty Minds: The Failure of Corporate Criminal Liability*. Chicago: University of Chicago Press.

LeBor, Adam. 2009. *The Believers: How America Fell for Bernie Madoff's $65 Million Investment Fraud*. London: Weidenfeld & Nicolson.

In re: Lehman Brothers Holdings Inc. Chapter 11 Case No. 081355 (JMF), U.S. Bankruptcy Court (S.D. N.Y. 2010).

Lewis, Michael. 2010. *The Big Short: Inside the Doomsday Machine*. New York: W. W. Norton.

Markopolos, Harry. 2010. *No One Would Listen: A True Financial Thriller*. Hoboken, N.J.: John Wiley.

Morgenson, Gretchen, and Louise Story. 2011a. "Behind the Gentler Approach to Banks by US." *New York Times*, July 8, A1, B7.

———. 2011b. "A Financial Crisis with Little Guilt: After Widespread Reckless Banking a Dearth of Prosecutions." *New York Times*, April 14, A1, B10–11.

Morse, Dan, Chad Terhune, and Ann Carms, 2005. "HealthSouth's Scrushy Is Acquitted." *Wall Street Journal*, June 29, A1.

Norris, Floyd. 2009. "Accountants Misled Us into Crisis." *New York Times*, September 11, B1, B4.

Oppenheimer, Jerry. 2009. *Madoff with the Money*. Hoboken, N.J.: Wiley.

Pontell, Henry N., Gregory C. Brown, and Gilbert Geis. 2007. "Offshore Internet Gambling and the World Trade Organization: Is It a Crime or a Commodity?" *International Journal of Cyber-Criminology* 1:119–36.

Posner, Richard A. 2009. *A Failure of Capitalism: The Crisis of '08 and the Descent into Depression*. Cambridge, Mass.: Harvard University Press.

Prentice, Robert A., and Dean Bredeson. 2008. *Student's Guide to the Sarbanes-Oxley Act*. Mason, Ohio: Houston/West.

Rapoport, Michael. 2010. "B of A Admits Hiding Debt." *Wall Street Journal*, July 10–11, A1, A2.

Rosoff, Stephen M., Henry N. Pontell, and Robert Tillman. 2007. *Profit Without Honor: White-Collar Crime and the Looting of America*. 4th. ed. Upper Saddle River, N.J.: Prentice Hall.

Ross, Brian. 2009. *The Madoff Chronicles: Inside the Secret World of Bernie and Ruth Madoff*. New York: Hyperion.

Sander, Peter J. 2009. *Madoff: Corruption, Deceit, and the Making of the World's Most Notorious Ponzi Scheme*. Guilford, Conn.: Lyons Press.

SEC v. Bank of America. 09 CIV 6829 (JSR) (S.D. N.Y. 2009).

SEC v. Bank of America. 10 CIV 0219 (JSR) (S.D.N.Y. 2010).

SEC v. Stanford International Bank. 3–09CV0298-L (N.D. TX 2009).

Spalding, Albert D., Jr., and Mary Ashby Morrison. 2006. "Criminal Liability for Document Shredding After Arthur Andersen, LLP." *American Business Law Journal* 43:647–88.

Squires, Susan E., Cynthia Smith, Lorna MacDougall, and William B. Yeack. 2003. *Arthur Andersen: Shifting Values, Unexpected Consequences*. Upper Saddle River, N.J.: Prentice Hall.

Strober, Deborah H., and Gerald S. Strober. 2009. *Catastrophe: The Story of Bernard L. Madoff, the Man Who Swindled the World*. Beverly Hills, Calif.: Phoenix Books.

"Study to Show Accountants Failed to Detect S&L Fraud." 1989. *Los Angeles Times,* January 8, 21.

Swartz, Mimi, and Sherron Watkins. 2003. *Power Failure: The Inside Story of the Collapse of Enron.* New York: Doubleday.

Taylor, Jaclyn. 2005. "Fluke or Failure? Assessing the Sarbanes-Oxley Act After *United States v. Scrushy.*" *University of Missouri Kansas City Law Review* 74:411–34.

Thibodeau, Jay, and Deborah Freir. 2007. *Auditing After Sarbanes-Oxley: Illustrative Cases.* Boston: McGraw-Hill/Irwin.

Thomson, Ainsely. 2010. "Auditors for Lehman Aim to Return $22 Billion." *Wall Street Journal,* June 16, A3.

Toffler, Barbara Ley, and Jennifer Reingold. 2003. *Final Accounting: Ambition, Greed, and the Fall of Arthur Andersen.* New York: Broadway Books.

United States v. Arthur Young & Co. 465 U.S. 805 (1984).

Valukas, Anton R. 2010. *Lehman Brothers Holdings, Inc. Chapter 11 Proceedings: Examiner's Report.* New York: United States District Court, Southern District of New York.

Waldman, Michael. 1990. *Who Robbed America? A Citizen's Guide to the Savings & Loan Scandal.* New York: Random House.

[6]

AND SOME WITH A FOUNTAIN PEN

*Mortgage Fraud, Securitization,
and the Subprime Bubble*

HAROLD C. BARNETT

In 2006, an elderly African American couple lost their home to a foreclosure rescue scheme in Chicago's North Lawndale neighborhood when a
fraudulent subprime loan issued to Charlotte Delaney was used to strip
their equity. Ms. Delaney was the office manager for the real estate agency
that perpetuated the fraud. This loan, funded by subprime lender MILA
(Mortgage Investment Lending Association) and securitized by Goldman
Sachs, was one among many 2006 vintage subprime loans characterized
by fraud and misrepresentation. It also was the subject of a lawsuit to return the property to the homeowners.[1] Following this loan from origination to securitization highlighted the relationship between mortgage
fraud and the financial meltdown (Barnett 2009). Assigning responsibility for this and other similar loans is at the center of many post meltdown
lawsuits.

Inspection of fraudulent loan files provides a unique perspective on lenders' claims of prudent underwriting and securitizers' claims of due diligence. Examination of the Delaney file revealed glaring evidence of fraud
and extremely lax underwriting by MILA. Even though Goldman Sachs
included MILA loans in a mortgage-backed security (MBS) issued in May
2006, when subpoenaed for its record of due diligence on MILA, Goldman Sachs provided none.

Fraudulent subprime loans were a central element of the subprime bubble and its subsequent collapse. They have also been central to official investigations of the meltdown. In a program called Operation Stolen Dreams, the Department of Justice brought together federal and state agencies in a nationwide push to "investigate, prosecute, and bring to justice swiftly those whose fraudulent activities contributed to the real estate market collapse" (Dollar 2010). By 2010, Operation Stolen Dreams had led to the prosecution of mortgage fraud accounting for $2.3 billion in losses (Dollar 2010).

Attorneys general of several states achieved an $8.6 billion settlement with Bank of America to resolve predatory lending claims against Countrywide Financial.[2] Recently, the Massachusetts attorney general signed a $102 million settlement with Morgan Stanley related to lending practices by New Century Financial (*In re: Morgan Stanley* 2010). These settlements have targeted funds for loan modifications.

Investor lawsuits have to contend with denial of access to loan files, the best source of information to document misrepresentation by underwriters. In 2010 the Federal Housing Finance Agency, conservator of Fannie Mae and Freddie Mac, issued sixty-four subpoenas to lenders to obtain documentation on private-label MBSs held by the enterprises. These loan documents would help determine whether misrepresentations, breaches of warranties, or other acts or omissions would require repurchase of the loans (Federal Housing Finance Agency 2010).

Other investors who lack subpoena power have sued lenders and securitizers to force the repurchase of $25.6 billion in loans they allege were tainted by misrepresentation. Lawsuits brought by the Federal Home Loan Banks (FHLB) of Pittsburg, Seattle, and San Francisco echoed allegations of misrepresentation and limited access to loan files found in these enterprise law suits. On the basis of FHLB complaints, Compass Point estimates that MBS underwriters could face a liability of $46.6 to $89.3 billion (Compass Point Research and Trading, LLC 2010). The website D&O Diary identifies some 215 subprime and credit crisis–related securities lawsuits (LaCroix 2010).

This chapter traces the thread of mortgage fraud from origination through securitization to the creation of the collateralized debt obligations that facilitated bets against housing debt. The goal is to highlight the centrality of mortgage fraud to the creation and collapse of the subprime bubble and the subsequent financial meltdown. In the first sections, I examine the relationship between the subprime mortgage market and mortgage fraud and define the latter to include subprime loans that could not reasonably be expected to be repaid. I draw on Hyman Minsky's model of financial instability to show the interconnections between fraudulent loans and a subprime bubble.

The subsequent section then provides a brief overview of MILA and the fraudulent Delaney loan. It illustrates the failure of the origination and underwriting systems to stem the exponential growth in misrepresentation and fraud associated with 2006 vintage subprime loans, the proximate cause of the subprime bubble collapse in 2007. The originate-to-distribute model that fed fraudulent loans to securitizers is the subject of the following section. The story of MILA is supplemented by that of New Century, the second largest subprime originator and a major provider of loans to Goldman Sachs. New Century's growth strategy and financial behavior was broadly similar to that of MILA. Both continued to originate loans despite evidence that they were unsustainable.

The final sections examine the role of Goldman Sachs in securitizing loan pools that contained fraudulent loans and facilitating bets that the borrowers would default. I argue that Goldman Sachs had sufficient information to know that the risk associated with its MBS was in excess of that implied by the risk ratings assigned to these bonds. I also show that the magnitude of fraudulent subprime loans was sufficient to collapse the subprime bubble and initiate the subsequent financial meltdown.

A Subprime Bubble

Many factors contributed significantly to the growth in subprime mortgage originations and to an environment conducive to unsustainable lending and mortgage fraud. They include capital inflows seeking higher yields, easy monetary policy, lax regulatory oversight of financial institutions, and the creation of new products during an era of deregulation. Additional factors include the government's promotion of affordable housing and home ownership, Fannie Mae and Freddie Mac purchases of MBS to satisfy affordable housing goals, credit rating agencies' monopoly power as nationally recognized statistical rating organizations, and incentives for banks to hold AAA-rated securities. Finally, major contributing factors were regulators' denial of the possibility of a national housing bubble and a disconnect and lack of communication between those constructing and rating structured investment vehicles and those observing credit standards, underwriting standards, and borrower characteristics.

Hyman Minsky's (1992) model of financial instability demonstrates the connection between unsustainable subprime lending and a financial bubble.[3] The model focuses on the balance between growth in income and growth in debt obligations. In an economic expansion that is fed by capital inflows and easy monetary policy, borrowers increase debt to purchase real estate or other assets in anticipation of short-term capital gains. Their expectations are fulfilled so long as the rate of increase in the value of the assets held exceeds the rate of interest on borrowed funds. Accelerated growth breeds optimism and expansion of debt. But an economic event, such as a decrease in the rate of return to the speculative asset, can shift the balance between income and debt and turn optimistic borrowers into distressed sellers. The bubble created by leveraged asset purchases may then burst.

Minsky (1992) describes three distinct income-debt relationships: hedge, speculative, and Ponzi finance. An economic unit engaged in hedge finance can fulfill all of its contractual payment obligations through its cash flow. The greater the unit's equity position in asset ownership, the more likely that it is engaged in hedge finance. In the mortgage market, hedge finance units generally have sufficient net worth to make a 20 percent down payment. An economic unit engaged in speculative finance can meet its debt obligation out of current income but cannot repay principal out of current cash flow. Refinance of debt is necessary when principal repayments come due. These units include borrowers who take interest-only loans or who borrow in anticipation of increased future income.

An economic unit engaged in Ponzi finance does not have sufficient cash flow or current income to cover interest due or repayment of principal on outstanding debt. They either have to sell assets or borrow to meet financial obligations. Ponzi finance units afford the lowest margin of safety to their debt holders. These units include borrowers who qualify at teaser or low rates, which then reset, and borrowers with negative amortization or underwater loans.

A subprime bubble began in 2003–2004 with a significant weakening of lending standards and ended with the collapse of subprime lending in 2007. In 2006, the peak year for mortgage originations, $3 trillion in mortgage loans were extended to all borrowers. Twenty-one percent of these were subprime mortgages (Zandi 2009, 43). Subprime lending grew by 324 percent from $190 billion in 2001 to $615 billion in 2006. In contrast, conforming loans, those that conformed to Fannie Mae and Freddie Mac guidelines, decreased from $1,433 billion in 2001 to $1,040 billion in 2006 (Ashcraft and Schuermann 2008, 2).

On average, in 2006, subprime borrowers put 5 percent down to purchase or refinance, while many put no money down. Roughly $250 billion, or half of the loans, were stated-income no-money-down ARM products, also known as "liar loans," for which the lender did not verify borrower's income (Zandi 2009, 33–34). Total debt equaled 42 percent of the borrower's stated income but a larger unknown share of actual income. Three-quarters of the borrowers had 2-year ARMs. Subprime lenders had developed an appetite for risk. Investors chasing higher yields believed that this layered risk was manageable. A full 75 percent of subprime loans were securitized, up from a 45 percent securitization rate in 2001 (Ashcraft and Schuermann 2008, 2).

The expansion in subprime lending was sustained by home price appreciation from 2000 to 2005.[4] Price appreciation increased equity and offered homeowners the opportunity to cash out their recently created wealth. Appreciation allowed homeowners to refinance to lower teaser rates when their income could not cover mounting debt. It also increased monthly housing payments relative to income. The increase in property valuations afforded attractive returns to investors as well as to quick turn-around speculators and flippers who saw an opportunity for a high return with little or no cash investment.

The peak and subsequent decline in home prices had predictable impacts. Homeowners who previously could refinance to mask unsustainable debt were now left with the unappealing options of a quick sale, delinquency, or default. Within 12 months of their origination, 4.7 percent of 2005 vintage mortgages were seriously delinquent or in foreclosure. The rate increased to 7.8 percent for the 2006 vintage and rose to 10 percent for 2007 vintage loans (OFHEO 2008, 9). The rate of early payment default, that is, default within 6 months or less of closing, also increased. All this clearly indicated that lenders had been making riskier, less sustainable loans. Easier lending guidelines and looser underwriting standards fed the buying frenzy that supported housing price inflation. The decrease in home price appreciation was followed by a tightening of credit, which caused further declines in home prices.

As rates of delinquency and early payment default rose, securitizers increasingly returned loans to lenders for repurchase. Lender lines of credit dried up along with lender capital. By spring 2007, the largest subprime lenders had declared bankruptcy or been acquired, and subprime MBS were subject to substantial credit downgrades. Losses associated with the unsustainable debt that pumped up the subprime bubble were then amplified by side bets against housing and contributed to the financial meltdown of 2008.

The collapse of the subprime bubble and associated subprime foreclosures preceded the recession of 2008. Much subprime debt was unsustainable before the economic slowdown. In contrast, foreclosures on prime fixed-rate mortgages were more closely in step with the rise in unemployment. Statistics from the Making Home Affordable Program indicate that 60 percent of permanent loan modifications were the result of loss of income (Dunne and Fee 2010).

Subprime Lending and Mortgage Fraud

Subprime lending was praised for making home ownership possible for people whose poor credit histories otherwise excluded them from the market (Gramlich 2004).[5] Subprime borrowers, however, paid interest rates and fees that were higher than average. They also faced substantial prepayment penalties if they refinanced into a cheaper product when or if their credit improved, which left many borrowers essentially locked into high interest rate mortgages. Rising home prices, however, allowed subsequent refinance—a safety valve—if the borrower needed additional financial relief. For Wall Street, the subprime mortgage was a highly profitable financial product that could be originated and securitized to earn huge fees. Risk associated with delinquency and default was to be passed on to investors.

In contrast to this benign view, community reinvestment groups had long characterized subprime mortgages as a vehicle for predatory lending that disproportionately targeted African American and Hispanic borrowers.[6] Although the Community Reinvestment Act of 1977 outlawed redlining, the banks that made prime loans did not expand their branch networks into minority neighborhoods (Immergluck and Wiles 1999). Instead, these neighborhoods were served by independent mortgage brokers who specialized in subprime lending, by the subprime divisions of national lenders such as Wells Fargo, and by national subprime lenders like Household International, which would become affiliates of major bank-holding companies.

Predatory lending is characterized by the following practices: making unaffordable loans based on the borrower's assets rather than on the borrower's ability to repay the obligation; inducing a borrower to repeatedly refinance a loan in order to charge high points and fees each time the loan is refinanced; and/or engaging in fraud or deception to conceal the true nature of the loan obligation from an unsuspecting or unsophisticated borrower. Significantly, Fannie Mae estimated that up to half of the borrowers with subprime mortgages could have qualified for loans with better terms (Ashcraft and Schuermann 2008, 70–71).

Targeting home equity, predatory lending thrives in an environment of appreciating home values, loose lending guidelines, and lax underwriting. However, since growth in household income did not keep pace with increases in mortgage and consumer debt loads, many subprime households became Ponzi finance units. Financial obligations, as a percentage of disposable income, increased for both prime and subprime borrowers between 2001 and 2006. Although the ratio for prime borrowers grew, it remained in the 12 to 13 percent range. In contrast, the ratio of debt to disposable income for subprime borrowers was nearly 30 percent in 2001 and increased to over 35 percent by 2006 (Zandi 2009, 228). Predictably, the rate of serious delinquency for subprime loans increased four-fold between the first quarters of 2001 and 2003, dipped slightly in the third quarter of 2005, and increased exponentially in 2007. An increase in subprime borrowers entering foreclosure followed a similar path after the first quarter of 2004 (OFHEO 2008, 5).

In 2006, the FBI Financial Crimes Report warned that mortgage fraud was "pervasive and growing" (Federal Bureau of Investigation 2006, 13–15). The growth in subprime lending combined with appreciation in property values to create a "ripe and expanding market for the unscrupulous" (Cox 2006, 608).

The characteristics of subprime lending that make it a tool for predatory practices also enable mortgage fraud. It is easier to misrepresent the true nature of a transaction when there are minimal documentation requirements, loose lending standards, lax underwriting, a willingness to make exceptions, and a focus on collateral rather than on borrower characteristics. A loan is considered fraudulent when the application and associated documentation contains representations of material fact that are false and on reasonable grounds are not believed to be true. Furthermore, these false representations are made with the intent that a lender-investor will fund or purchase the loan. The lender-investor, who is ignorant of the false representations and reasonably believes them to be true, acts upon them and, consequently, suffers economic loss. Lying on a loan application is fraud whether or not the lender-investor suffers a loss. However, a loss often motivates the search for fraud and misrepresentation.

For the purpose of this analysis, I recognize three conceptualizations of mortgage fraud. The first involves predatory lending, which is usually differentiated from mortgage fraud in that the former victimizes the borrower while the latter victimizes the lender. A predatory lender is considered a perpetrator of fraud when a borrower is induced, convinced, or misled into signing a loan where income, credit, or assets are misrepresented and the loan is unsustainable. Second, Ashcraft and Schuermann (2008) argue that the borrower is the perpetrator (predatory borrowing) when a real estate transaction involves a willful misrepresentation of material fact on the borrower's part and without the lender's knowledge. Finally, there is a consensual middle ground where a mortgage broker or lender, with a borrower's active or passive consent, makes material misrepresentations to approve a loan that the borrower cannot reasonably be expected to repay given the borrower's current financial circumstances. This last category of unsustainable loans is a result of competitive subprime lending. These loans are originated to sell for securitization.

Mortgage fraud is generally categorized as fraud for profit or fraud for housing. Fraud for profit consists of illegal actions taken jointly by a borrower and real estate insiders to inflate the value of property and to borrow with no intention of repayment. The FBI reports that 80 percent of losses from such fraud involve collaboration or collusion with industry insiders. Most of the recent Operation Stolen Dreams prosecutions fall into the fraud-for-profit category. Foreclosure rescue and equity skimming were common frauds in the housing market of 2003–2007 (Cox 2006) and were involved in the case that initiated this research.

The FBI defines fraud for housing as an illegal act perpetrated solely by the borrower to acquire and maintain ownership of a house under false pretenses. This typically entails the misrepresentation of income or employment to qualify for a loan or a misrepresentation of occupancy (Federal Bureau of Investigation 2006, 9, 13). While some frauds for housing or housing equity were perpetrated by borrowers acting alone, as implied by the FBI definition, others fell into the predatory or competitive subprime lending categories. When more broadly defined, fraud for housing was a significant source of the unsustainable subprime loans that triggered the collapse of the subprime bubble.

Misrepresentation of income to obtain a stated income loan became commonplace after 2000. One lender who reviewed a sample of 100 stated income loans found that, when compared with IRS figures, almost 60 percent of the stated amounts were exaggerated by more than 50 percent (BasePoint Analytics LLC 2007, 5).

Many fraud-for-housing loans were originated through misrepresentation and with the lender fully aware that the loans were unsustainable. There were benefits to all parties. Some borrowers participated in the hope of speculative gain. Mortgage brokers could earn fees and commissions from lenders. Lenders could sell the loans they generated to securitizers. Many rationalized these loans by saying that an improvement in the borrower's credit rating or a rise in property values could enable refinancing of these otherwise unsustainable debts. But the fact remains that this was fraud. The borrowers' qualifications for the loan and their ability to pay were misrepresented.

Originating and Underwriting Fraudulent Loans

The North Lawndale home I referred to earlier was purchased by Henderson Hall in 1993 with joint titleholder Mary Hawthorne. When Hall left his job for medical reasons, the couple fell behind on their mortgage payments and were threatened with foreclosure. Hall and Hawthorne thought they had found a way out of their dilemma when they received a solicitation from Unity Management Development Corporation, which promised to "stall" the foreclosure proceedings. Unity agreed to buy their property and lease it back to them.[7] Hall and Hawthorne were left with the impression that this was some form of refinance. They signed papers including a contract to sell their home for $235,000, a sale-leaseback contract, and a promissory note for $100,000, although they never received that sum from Unity and were not aware of that additional debt.

On January 13, 2006, the property was sold to Charlotte Delaney, Unity's office manager, for $235,000. The purchase was financed with no-money-down, stated income loans from MILA. Hall and Hawthorne's mortgage was paid off, but roughly $82,000 of equity was kept by various participants in what amounted to an equity skimming scheme. MILA sold Delaney's first mortgage to Goldman Sachs, which included it in a $1.5 billion securitized mortgage trust. Delaney made no payments on the mortgage, and by spring 2006 the property was in foreclosure. The Delaney loan was just one of a growing number of early payment defaults associated with 2006 vintage subprime loans.

For Fitch Ratings, subprime residential mortgage-backed securities (RMBSs) issued in 2006 were remarkable for early payment default. Fitch analyzed a sample of 2006 loans and concluded that "poor underwriting quality and fraud may account for as much as one-quarter of the underperformance of recent vintage subprime RMBS" (Fitch Ratings 2007, 2). No-money-down and stated income mortgage products were vehicles for misrepresentation or fraud by participants throughout the origination process. Underwriting fell victim to competitive pressure to speed up the approval process through reliance on Automated Underwriting Systems (AUS) and the use of validation rather than verification[8] to ease heavy underwriting workloads. An earlier study by BasePoint Analytics LLC (2007) also attributed a substantial portion of early payment defaults to fraudulent misrepresentations on the original application.

MILA, an aggressive subprime lender, developed an AUS to enhance its growth and efficiency in loan origination (Broberg 2004). The MILA AUS was used to approve high-risk loans to Delaney. It deemed that Delaney's 720 FICO score was sufficient to balance the layered risk of a no-down-payment, interest-only, and stated income loan to a self-employed borrower. The risk she posed as a borrower would have been even greater had she not misrepresented herself as an owner-occupant rather than as an investor. Clearly, credit scores lose their power to predict default risk when other information provided by the borrower is false. A cursory examination of the Delaney file by a knowledgeable underwriter would have revealed the fraudulent nature of the loan and the transaction. [9]

The red flag that by itself should have resulted in rejection of the loan was documentation of a prior lien on the property—the $100,000 promissory note unwittingly signed by Hall and Hawthorne with no evidence that the debt was discharged. With this outstanding debt, MILA's $188,000 loan to Delaney became a second lien, and its $47,000 loan became a third lien. There was $325,000 in debt on a $235,000 property.

The Department of Housing and Urban Development mandatory settlement disclosure statement (the HUD-1) forwarded to MILA for funding lists Hall and Hawthorne's actual mortgage plus an additional mortgage lien of $70,472.54 to be paid off at closing. The loan file does not contain any payoff information for this lien or other information to establish its existence. It is evident that this phantom lien was entered to help account for the $82,000 in equity stolen from Hall and Hawthorne.

There were additional inconsistencies in the loan file. Delaney's stated income on her loan application was not sufficient and was increased on a MILA worksheet to satisfy the lender's guidelines. Furthermore, Delaney reported no reserves on her loan application. One test of the reasonableness of stated income is the relationship between a person's stated income and assets.

Despite multiple red flags, MILA approved and funded $235,000 in loans to Delaney. The loan facilitated two interrelated frauds. First, Unity, Delaney, and accomplices defrauded MILA by taking out a $235,000 loan with no intention of repayment. Second, the loan allowed Unity to strip $82,000 in equity from Hall and Hawthorne by using their home as collateral for the MILA loan.

The Originate-to-Distribute Model

I supplement limited sources on MILA with publicly available information on New Century Financial Corporation, the second largest subprime originator. Both originated subprime loans that were securitized by Goldman Sachs in 2006, and both declared bankruptcy in the spring of 2007.

MILA funded $1.5 billion in loans in 2003 and grew threefold to fund $4.5 billion mostly subprime loans in 2006 (Frishberg 2008). New Century entered the mortgage business in 1996 with a volume of $337 million. By 2002 it was funding $14 billion in subprime loans and grew dramatically to fund $60 billion loans in 2006 (*In re: New Century* 2008, 1). Both

MILA and New Century were in the business of originating loans for distribution to securitizers. They agreed to repurchase loans under several conditions, including early payment default. Investors usually were given up to 90 days to return a loan to the lender.

Both lenders developed specialized AUS mortgage origination software to automate underwriting and generate rapid loan commitments (*In re: MILA* 2008, 7). They both faced several insurmountable problems in developing a robust AUS algorithm that could minimize default. First, there was virtually no historical data to predict default rates for new products with zero-down-payment and stated income features. Credit scores were increased marginally to account for the fact that these and other new features increased the risk of default. But the credit score differentials lacked predictive value since they were derived from populations who shared few characteristics with the newer, high-risk borrowers. Second, model predictions of default risk assumed that the AUS was using accurate information about income, assets, credit, and property values. Credit scores cannot accurately predict risk if the AUS is fed inaccurate data (Fitch Ratings 2007, 3). In the absence of a procedure to streamline the time-intensive task of data verification, an increased rate of loan origination and approval would increase the rate of delinquency and default. Borrower and property information were neither validated nor verified. New Century performed quality control on its loans only after they were funded (*In re: New Century* 2008, 66).

MILA's financial health was in peril as early as 2004, a circumstance not unique among subprime lenders (*In re: MILA* 2008, 5). A lender's profits reflect the spread between the cost of short-term money and the mortgage rate. The spread between the two widened after 2001 when short-term interest rates fell. It then began to shrink between 2004 and late 2005, as short-term rates rose while mortgage rates remained relatively flat. Competition for borrowers also increased while the rate of growth in originations had slowed from 83 percent in 2003, to 78 percent in 2004, and finally to 24 percent in 2005. The rate became a negative 66 percent in 2006 (Zimmerman 2007, 10, 17).

As subprime loan originations began to top out, lenders needed new products that would expand the pool of eligible borrowers. An expanded pool generally meant a higher risk pool. Between 2002 and 2006, the percentage of subprime loans with less than 20 percent owner equity went from 45.3 percent to 62.8 percent. The percentage of ARMs increased from 73.5 percent in 2002 to 80.9 percent in 2005 and then decreased in 2006. Increasingly, lenders offered interest-only features and 40-year amortizations to minimize monthly payments, allowing a borrower to qualify with lower income. Low documentation loans rose from 30.5 percent of the total in 2002 to 42.9 percent in 2005 (Zimmerman 2007, 10).

A growing percentage of high-risk subprime loans that were clearly unsustainable appeared on the landscape. New Century's experience with Morgan Stanley, the subject of an unfair lending suit brought by the Massachusetts attorney general (*In re: Morgan Stanley* 2010), was a typical case. The firm was the largest provider of a warehouse line of credit to New Century.[10] When Morgan Stanley examined 2005 vintage New Century loans in 2006, it found that when an interest rate resets, the ratio of debt to income would exceed the maximum acceptable to the bank. New Century was originating loans with knowledge that they could be affordable only if refinanced. Since refinancing could not be assumed and applied in qualifying the borrower, the loans were originated as unsustainable. New Century continued to originate these loans and Morgan Stanley, despite knowing what it did, continued to purchase and securitize them.

The suit also revealed that New Century was qualifying borrowers with clearly exaggerated income. Borrowers' stated income averaged $115,000, some 42 percent higher than income on fully documented loans. Moreover, a third of New Century loans securitized in 2006 and 2007 were for more than 100 percent of property value. About 19 percent of these had loan-to-value ratios of more than 120 percent. Also, few of the loans that New Century approved with exceptions had sufficient compensating factors. During 2006–2007, Morgan Stanley waived exceptions and purchased large numbers of loans that violated New Century guidelines without sufficient compensating factors (*In re: Morgan Stanley* 2010, 10; *In re: New Century* 2008, 4). New Century performed quality control only after loans were funded. Unsustainable fraudulent loans were either retained in New Century's loan portfolio or were securitized. Loans returned to New Century might be sold to other investors for securitization. Loans that were nonperforming or did not conform to New Century underwriting guidelines might be sold for securitization at a discount (*In re: New Century* 2008, 66–67; Morgenson 2010).

The origination and sale of unsustainable loans became insurmountable problems for both MILA and New Century. MILA repurchases, which represented 0.53 percent of loan sale in 2002, had risen to 1.27 percent in

2004. The lender projected that its loan repurchases as a percentage of total loan sales would triple in 2005 through 2007. By March 2005, MILA was delaying payments to conserve cash (*In re: MILA* 2008, 4–5). By mid-2004, New Century also was aware of an alarming and steady increase in early payment default loans, but the company continued to feed investors' demand (*In re: New Century* 2008, 4).

Overwhelmed by demands to repurchase loans and cut off from necessary short-term funding, MILA ceased operation in April 2007 and declared bankruptcy in July 2007. By 2008, creditor claims had ballooned to nearly $2 billion (Frishberg 2008; Grunbaum 2008). New Century filed for bankruptcy protection in April 2007. Bankruptcy trustees claimed that both lenders understated losses associated with loan repurchases and overstated earnings. MILA's bankruptcy trustee alleges that MILA was insolvent as early as 2004 (*In re: MILA* 2008, 6). New Century's bankruptcy examiner alleges that the lender engaged in wide-ranging accounting practices in 2005 and 2006 that produced material misstatements of firm finances, particularly in relationship to loan repurchases (*In re: New Century* 2008, 5, 8). In under-reporting the extent of loan repurchases and overstating net revenues, both lenders misrepresented to investors the sustainability of their loan originations and their capacity to honor the representations and warranties associated with the loans they sold to securitizers.

Securitizing Subprime Risk and Fraud

Accepting the dictum that "volume outpaces bad debt all day long," subprime originators MILA and New Century escalated the speed of origination and approval and attempted to hide the threat that mounting loan repurchases posed to their solvency.[11] Goldman Sachs profited by securitizing their loans and then arranged bets against the housing market as MILA, New Century, and scores of subprime lenders ceased operations.[12] In the first instance, Goldman Sachs, through acts of omission or commission, included fraudulent subprime loans in the MBS it sold to investors. In the second instance, it recognized that these same loans had the highest probability of delinquency and default and referenced them in collateralized debt obligations.

An MBS is a pool of loans with priority of payment structured into tranches. The risk associated with each tranche or slice is based on the loss-absorbing value of tranches that are subordinate (lower in the structure) and on additional collateral and enhancement. The senior tranches, usually accounting for about 80 percent of total value, receive the highest S&P/Moody AAA ratings and are the last to suffer loss. The subordinate mezzanine tranches have lower credit ratings. Mezzanine tranches at the bottom receive the lowest investment grade rating and are first to absorb loss from delinquency and default. Securitizers and credit rating agencies anticipate that there will be some unsustainable and fraudulent subprime loans, and they adjust enhancements accordingly to achieve the desired risk ratings. Underestimating the extent of these loans will cause investors to experience greater than anticipated loss and requires a ratings downgrade.

The structure of risk in an MBS mirrors Minsky's income-debt relationships. The mortgage debt of hedge finance units has the highest reliability and stability, characteristics that justify a AAA rating. Pools with a greater percentage of speculative finance unit loans will require more subordination and collateral. MBS with a greater percentage of Ponzi finance unit loans will require even more subordination and collateral. Since losses associated with bad loans sink to the bottom, underestimating the extent of loans to actual or potential Ponzi units in the pool must inevitably result in greater than predicted losses to holders of mezzanine tranches. As the value of subordinate tranches are reduced through delinquency and default, more senior tranches become subject to a greater risk of loss.

Goldman Sachs sponsored some $45.7 billion in subprime securitizations between 2002 and 2006.[13] Moody's Investor Services projected losses of about $9.4 billion on $27 billion in Goldman Sachs MBS issued in 2005–2007, a 35 percent loss in value. Projected losses for Goldman Sachs MBS issued in 2005 were generally in the 10 to 30 percent range. For those issued in 2006–2007, projected losses were in the 30 to 50 percent range and exhibited a clear upward trend.[14] Goldman Sachs purchased about one-third of its loans from New Century, Fremont Investment & Loan, Long Beach Mortgage (a subsidiary of Washington Mutual), and WMC Mortgage (owned by GE Money). These originators accounted for at least a third of Goldman Sachs MBS' projected losses and roughly 60 percent of the subprime loans downgraded by Moody's in its historic action of July 2007.[15] Goldman Sachs issued its last MBS in early 2007, at the same time it was facilitating bets against the subprime market.

The Delaney loan was one of a pool of loans originated by MILA and was included in a $1.5 billion Goldman Sachs MBS issued in May 2006.[16]

The prospectus for GSAMP Trust 2006-HE3 reported sufficient credit enhancements and subordinations, such that at least $1.2 billion of its sub-prime certificates had the highest credit ratings. Mezzanine tranches valued at around $311 million were rated AAA/Aa1 down to BBB+/Baa3. The highest-tier tranche included some prime loans to boost its credit rating. In 2010, Moody's projected that this MBS lost 38 percent of its value.

A confidential March 2007 presentation to the Goldman Sachs Board of Directors reveals how the firm viewed the market in 2006 and is broadly consistent with what they told investors. Goldman Sachs told the board that it was placing emphasis on a borrower's ability to make current payments, the proliferation of affordability products to achieve lower payments for borrowers, the widening of credit to include first-time borrowers, and an increase in alternative documentation. In the first half of 2006, Goldman Sachs had increased long positions but was becoming more vigilant on early payment defaults. In the second half of 2006, it reported deterioration in underwriting standards and increased fraud, a beginning of widespread mortgage originator defaults, and a decrease in profitability as the bids for subprime loans fell below origination costs.

In response to this, Goldman Sachs said it stepped up its due diligence on originators, scaled back the purchase of riskier loans, reduced collateralized debt obligation activity, and reversed a long market position. As of March 2007, it ceased purchasing new subprime loan pools, reduced warehouse lending, and noted that early payment default claims continued to increase.[17]

In the same presentation, Goldman Sachs tracked New Century stock prices to draw a timeline of the subprime meltdown. The firm should have been aware of New Century's mounting repurchase problems despite the lender's attempts to hide these escalating obligations. Goldman Sachs was a New Century customer for "scratch-and-dent" loans, which were loans that a lender had to repurchase due to violation of representations and warranties or that had documentation deficiencies. Goldman Sachs purchased and securitized some $740 million in scratch-and-dent loans in 2005–2006, including at least $168 million from New Century.[18] The percentage of New Century loans that were deficient and needed to be sold at a discount rose from 0.4 percent of its total loan volume in 2004 to 2.1 percent in 2006 (*In re: New Century* 2008, 67–68).

The prospectus for the GSAMP Trust 2006-HE3 containing the MILA loans provided potential investors with Goldman Sachs's comprehensive disclosure of risk factors. Investors were informed that the loans were riskier than those underwritten with Fannie Mae and Freddie Mac guidelines. Investors were told that borrowers may have impaired or unsubstantiated credit histories and that, as a result, the loans could experience higher rates of delinquency, default, and foreclosure. Further, it was disclosed that borrowers increasingly financed their homes with new mortgage products, such as stated income and no-money-down loans. There is little historical data with respect to these new mortgage products. As borrowers faced potentially higher monthly payments, it was possible that delinquencies and defaults could exceed anticipated levels.

The prospectus for GSAMP Trust 2006-NC2, packaging New Century loans and issued about 6 months later, in the second half of 2006, advised investors of additional risks.[19] The prospectus noted that ARMs were underwritten on the basis of a judgment that the borrower initially would have the ability to make monthly payments. However, the borrower's income might not be sufficient to continue payments as the size of the payment increased. In other words, the borrower is qualified on a teaser rate, as opposed to the fully indexed rate, and might not have sufficient income to make monthly payments when the rate increased. Moreover, the loans might not conform to the originator's underwriting standards. Compensating factors could warrant Goldman Sachs to make exceptions to these guidelines and purchase the loans. (As noted above, Morgan Stanley found that exceptions were often not justified by compensating factors.) In addition, investors were informed that stated income loans did not involve verification by the originator. Employment was verified and income should be consistent with employment.

Anticipating the collapse of the subprime bubble, the prospectus for GSAMP Trust 2007-NC1, another pool of New Century loans, noted recently increased levels of delinquency and default in the subprime mortgage market. Combined with deterioration in general real estate market conditions, this had resulted in originators being required to repurchase an increasingly greater number of mortgage loans due to early payment default and other violations of representations and warranties. Deterioration in the financial performance of many subprime lenders had followed and in some cases had caused them to cease operation. Investors faced a heightened risk since the originators might not be able to repurchase loans that did not satisfy their representations and warranties.

With twenty-twenty hindsight, and in light of the recitation of risk, it is relevant to ask why investors were still buying subprime MBS. It appears that many investors did not read past the first page of the prospectus, which stated that some 80 percent of the tranches were rated AAA. If they read the sections on risk and due diligence, they might have asked whether Goldman Sachs was acting to minimize risk and feed accurate data to credit rating agencies for risk assessments.

The prospectus for the MBS that contained the Delaney loan typically assured investors that Goldman Sachs would conduct a review of the mortgage loan originator prior to purchasing loans. The review would cover select financial information to allow a credit and risk assessment, and it would include an examination of the originator's underwriting guidelines, discussion with senior-level management, and background checks. The underwriting guidelines review would consider mortgage loan origination processes and systems. In addition, the review would consider origination practices by jurisdiction, historical loan–level loss experience, quality control practices, and significant litigation. The prospectus stated that the scope of the mortgage loan due diligence would depend on the credit quality of the mortgage loans, which would lead one to expect a more intensive due diligence, since the 2006 vintage subprime loans were extended to an increasingly riskier pool of borrowers.

Due diligence is supposed to provide assurance that the characteristics of the loans purchased for securitization are what the lenders say they are. Contractors are hired to sample loan pools and reject loans that do not meet guidelines or exceed the limits of acceptable compensating factors. Ratings agencies then use summary loan characteristics as reported by the lenders to help structure the MBS and assess the risk of default. The rating agencies are not provided with the loan-level data that are less subject to manipulation.

In the case that initiated this research, the attorney for Hall and Hawthorne subpoenaed Goldman Sachs for records of all due diligence associated with subprime originator MILA. Goldman provided no documentation to establish that it had performed the due diligence promised in the prospectus.

Goldman Sachs told its Board of Directors that it stepped up due diligence in the second half of 2006. However, anecdotal evidence indicates that Goldman Sachs, like its competitors, was willing to scale back the scrutiny of loan originators so that it could buy more loans to securitize. The firm reportedly agreed to reduce the percentage of loans that were reviewed before a deal closed and agreed to not reject as unacceptable more than 5 percent of the loans in a pool (Gordon 2009c). Anecdotal evidence also suggests that due diligence firms overrode the bulk of challenges to shaky loans (Gordon 2009a).

The high rate of delinquency and default associated with the 2006 vintage of subprime loans leaves no doubt that fraudulent loans were purchased and securitized to sell to investors. Goldman Sachs was aware of deteriorating loan quality and should have been aware of an increase in fraudulent loan originations. They bought and securitized these loans to stay competitive, warned investors of the increased risk involved, and then allowed these facts to be obscured with the imprimatur of a AAA rating.

At the peak of the subprime bubble in late 2006 and early 2007, senior tranches in Goldman Sachs MBS continued to receive AAA ratings despite acknowledgments of increased risk, the end of home price appreciation, rising interest rates, and increasing delinquencies and defaults. Credit rating agencies received loan pool summary data from Goldman Sachs rather than the loan-level data that would have allowed a more accurate risk assessment. These guarantors of credit quality began to lower their standards in 2004 and were competing for the profitable investment banks' business. They published their models and allowed investment banks latitude to "game" the ratings system. They used historic loan performance data that investors were told were outdated and assigned the highest ratings despite deteriorating loan quality and increased risk (Smith 2008). When S&P announced a change in its ratings model in May 2006, it said that application of the new model would not be retroactive, and MBS issuance increased before the application date (Lewis 2010, 94). The credit rating agencies mirrored the behavior of the investment banks who were willing to buy unsustainable and fraudulent loans to securitize and of lenders who were eager to originate those loans to sell to the investment banks.

Betting on Mortgage Fraud

By the end of 2006, Goldman Sachs was acting to reverse its long position in the subprime market. It sold nearly $28 billion of 2006 vintage bonds, including $10 billion issued in October 2006 (Gordon 2009b). At the same time it was facilitating bets on a subprime market decline through issuance of synthetic collateral debt obligations, CDOs. Synthetic CDO amplified the impact of mortgage fraud on the subprime meltdown. CDOs are used to securitize the mezzanine MBS tranches that are difficult to sell due to their lower credit ratings. Synthetic CDOs, in contrast, do not contain MBS loans or tranches. They are comprised of credit default swaps that are side bets on MBS, usually on mezzanine tranches. These synthetic CDOs refer to a specific MBS tranche, and their creation does not require the origination and securitization of new loans. Supply is limited only by investor demand for a high yield.

An estimated 20 to 25 percent of synthetic CDOs were intended to guarantee actual risk faced by mortgage-related bondholders, while the remaining 75 to 80 percent were side bets on the value of the referenced MBS tranches. They were called credit default swaps rather than insurance to avoid the regulation that applied to insurance products (Greenberger 2010, 16).

As noted, fraudulent loans and their promised payments sink to the bottom in the MBS tranche structure. A CDO comprised of the mezzanine slices of MBS is therefore likely to contain a concentration of these loans. However, credit rating agencies often applied the same incorrect assumptions of uncorrelated risk and diversification to a CDO as to an MBS and rated 80 percent of the pool AAA. Through this financial alchemy, a collateralized debt obligation comprised of BBB-rated slices of MBS becomes a AAA-rated investment.

Goldman Sachs and other banks designed synthetic CDOs for bets against the subprime mortgage market. ABACUS 2007-AC1, the centerpiece of the SEC fraud suit against Goldman Sachs, made reference to ninety BBB-rated tranches from existing MBSs issued over the previous 18 months.[20] These synthetic instruments were designed with the assistance of hedge fund Paulson & Company, which paid insurance premiums to provide an income stream to the purchaser. The purchaser would effectively provide insurance against default of the referenced tranches. In this unregulated market, the insurer was not subject to any capital requirements to guarantee that it could meet its obligations in case of default by subprime borrowers. This would add another layer of Ponzi finance.

The referenced tranches would maximize the likelihood of failure. They would be taken from MBS with loans from states such as California and

Florida that had the highest rates of home price appreciation, loans made by aggressive lenders such as Long Beach, and loans with minimal documentation (Lewis 2010, 97–98). They would include loans to the first-time home buyers, speculators, and no-money-down borrowers that Fitch would associate with early payment default loans and Moody's would identify in its July 2007 downgrade. These were selection criteria that would most likely make reference to fraudulent loans with the highest rate of default.

Credit agencies rated 48 percent of $1 billion in ABACUS tranches AAA even though they were made up entirely of BBB-rated tranches, the worst performing loans in each pool. ABACUS designer Fabrice Tourre told a Senate subcommittee that CDO buyers "should include fewer sophisticated hedge funds" (Efrati and Scannell 2010). The preferred buyer was one who was less likely to look at the details behind the ratings. By October 2007, 99 percent of ABACUS tranches were worthless and several other Goldman Sachs issues were either withdrawn or downgraded to junk.

A synthetic CDO amplifies the debt associated with a referenced pool of bad loans. The impact of a downgrade is also amplified. An Option One Mortgage slice worth $38 million appeared in more than thirty debt pools and ultimately caused roughly $280 million in losses, a 7.4 bad loan loss multiplier (Mollenkamp and Ng 2010). The Financial Crisis Inquiry Commission (2010) provides examples of other tranches with amplification in the range of three to six times. When the value of MBS fell due to default by fraudulent Ponzi unit borrowers, a magnified loss was suffered by the holders of synthetic CDO debt.

The magnitude of subprime mortgage fraud was sufficient to initiate deflation of the subprime bubble and a broader financial meltdown. One recent estimate puts 2006 fraudulent originations at roughly $30 billion (Whelan 2010). Compass Point (2010) estimates liability to repurchase loans originated in 2005–2007 that involve misrepresentation at between $46.6 and $89.3 billion. The lower estimate is for losses suffered within 18 months of origination and could net out the impact of recession. A synthetic CDO will amplify the impact of default, variously by a factor of three to seven. These fraudulent loan values combined with some amplification would have accounted for a significant percentage of the $945 billion in losses estimated by the International Monetary Fund (IMF) in early 2008.

The impact of subprime losses reverberated through the financial system. Subprime originators went bankrupt, and Moody's and S&P downgraded hundreds of subprime issues. The lack of transparency in the CDO market created considerable uncertainty as to which banks held the down-graded MBS and CDOs and raised questions as to whether those who had provided the guarantees against default, such as American International Group, had the capital to satisfy their obligations. The credit system seized up, and the federal government acted to supplement bank capital with tax-payer funds and guarantees. The economy went into recession in December 2007, and the decrease in income, employment, and housing prices resulted in mounting delinquencies, defaults, and foreclosures in all segments of the mortgage market. The IMF estimate of mortgage-related loss grew from $945 billion in April 2008 (Lewis 2010, 225) to $1.4 trillion in October 2008 and then to $4 trillion in April 2009 (Gilmore 2009).

Concluding Remarks

The subprime bubble was a final act of free market greed at the end of a cycle of deregulation. Subprime lenders knew that they were originating and packaging fraudulent loans. Securitizers, like Goldman Sachs, stated the nature of the risk but not the degree. Pending lawsuits may provide an opportunity to determine in more detail who knew that fraud was being perpetrated on borrowers and investors. Holding corporations liable will not, by itself, deter fraud if those responsible can leave with millions in questionable gains. The absence of effective regulation and oversight of the financial system set the stage for the subprime bubble. It is an open question whether newly passed financial regulation can and will be used to constrain financial fraud and the next bubble.

Notes

1. The lawsuit was brought by Attorney John Elson, Bluhm Legal Clinic, Northwestern University School of Law.

2. The complaint was filed by California's attorney general. States joining in the settlement include Florida, Illinois, Iowa, Arizona, Connecticut, Michigan, North Carolina, Ohio, and Texas (ElBoghdady 2008; Reuters 2008).

3. Kindleberger and Aliber (2005, 24–30) use Minsky to interpret financial crises in the United States, Great Britain, and other market economies over the past three centuries. Tymoigne (2010) has applied the model to the recent bubble.

4. The home purchase price index rose about 6.9 percent through 2000–2001, 7.6 percent over the next 2 years, and about 9.4 percent to the end of 2005. The

rate of appreciation fell to 3.9 percent at the end of 2006 and 0.5 percent by the end of 2007 (OFHEO 2008).

5. Gramlich was one of the few Fed governors concerned about predatory lending. He recognized that some borrowers were excluded from prime loans for reasons other than bad credit.

6. A summary of this argument is provided by the National Community Reinvestment Coalition civil rights complaint against Fitch and Moody's rating services, submitted to the Department of Housing and Urban Development on November 17, 2008. More recently, see Illinois Attorney General (2010) for the suit against Countrywide Financial.

7. The details of the case are from the complaint in *Hall v. Unity Management Development Corp., et al.*, Circuit Court of Cook County Illinois, Chancery Division, Case 7CH36731 and Expert Report of Harold C. Barnett, PhD, September 2, 2009.

8. Validation involves a simple check or acceptance of the information provided by the borrower or loan officer. In contrast, verification involves the time-intensive task of documenting the accuracy of the information.

9. A more detailed discussion of the loan file and red flags is provided in Barnett (2009).

10. A warehouse line of credit is a short-term loan, in this case from Morgan Stanley to New Century, the mortgage lender. The mortgage lender uses loan documents as collateral for the warehouse line/loan. When the loan is sold to an investor, the line of credit is paid off.

11. Observation attributed to top New Century officials by Gordon (2009c).

12. The Mortgage Lender Implode-O-Meter lists 209 nonprime lenders or lending divisions that suspended operations, closed, or were sold between November 2006 and the announced rescue of Countrywide Financial Corp. by Bank of America in January 2008 (as reported on http://ml-implode.com as of November 9, 2010).

13. Data are from the prospectus for GSAMP Trust 2007-NC1, available online via the Edgar database at http://www.sec.gov/edgar/searchedgar/companysearch .html.

14. Calculations by author based on Moody's Investor Service, "Moody's Current Loss Projections for 2005–2008 Jumbo, Alt-A, Option ARM and Subprime RMBS," posted July 23, 2010; and Moody's posting of ratings actions for Goldman Sachs GSAMP Trusts rated by Moody's for the period 2005–2007 at http://v3 .moody's.com/researchandratings.

15. In July 2007, Moody's and Standard & Poor's announced that they would review and downgrade $17.2 billion in residential MBSs issued in 2006. This was the credit rating agencies' first official recognition that there was a "mountain of bad debt held by investors" working its way through the financial system (Rosner 2007).

16. The details of the Goldman MBS are taken from the prospectus for GSAMP Trust 2006-HE3, available online via the Edgar database at http://www.sec.gov /edgar/searchedgar/companysearch.html.

17. Presentation to GS Board of Directors, Subprime Mortgage Business, March 26, 2007, Exhibit #22, Senate Permanent Subcommittee on Investigation.

18. Author's calculations from the Moody's database referred to in note 14.

19. Prospectus for GSAMP Trust 2006-NC2, available online via the Edgar database at http://www.sec.gov/edgar/searchedgar/companysearch.html.

20. The flip book for ABACUS 2007-AC1 is from Senate Permanent Subcommittee on Investigations, Hearing Four: The Role of Investment Banks, Exhibits, posted April 23, 2010, at http://levin.senate.gov/senate/investigations/index.html.

References

Ashcraft, Adam B., and Til Schuermann. 2008. "Understanding the Securitization of Subprime Mortgage Credit." *Federal Reserve Bank of New York Staff Reports*, March.

Barnett, Harold C. 2009. "And Some with a Fountain Pen: The Securitization of Mortgage Fraud." Paper presented at the Annual Meeting of the American Society for Criminology, November 5, Philadelphia, Penn. http://ssrn.com/abstract =1612330.

BasePoint Analytics LLC. 2007. "Early Payment Default—Links to Fraud and Impact of Mortgage Lenders and Investment Banks." White paper. Carlsbad, Calif.: BasePoint Analytics.

Broberg, Brad. 2004. "Mortgage Firm Founder Has Little Time to Waste." *Puget Sound Business Journal*, October 15.

Compass Point Research and Trading, LLC. 2010. "Mortgage Repurchases Part II: Private Label RMBS Investors Take Aim—Quantifying the Risks." August 17. Available as Private Label RMBS litigation at api.ning.com.

Cox, Prentiss. 2006. "Foreclosure Equity Stripping: Legal Theories and Strategies to Attack a Growing Problem." *Clearinghouse Review Journal of Poverty Law and Policy*, March–April, 605–26.

Dollar, Rachel. 2010. "Florida Cracks Down on Mortgage Fraud." *Mortgage Fraud Blog*, June 29. http://mortgagefraudblog.com/perp-walk/item/13314-operation _stolen_dreams_a_nationwide_crackdown_of_mortgage_fraud.

Dunne, Tim, and Kyle Fee. 2010. "Changes in Foreclosure and Unemployment Across States." Federal Reserve Bank of Cleveland, July. http://www.clevelandfed .org/research/trends/2010/0710/01regact.cfm.

ElBoghdady, Dina. 2008. "Bank of America to Modify Mortgages from Countrywide." *Washington Post*, October 7. http://www.washingtonpost.com/wp-dyn /content/article/2008/10/06/AR2008100601150.html.

Efrati, Amir, and Kara Scannell. 2010. "Trader's Testimony Raises Legal Issues." *Wall Street Journal*, April 28. http://online.wsj.com/article/SB10001424052748 703832204575210610576774470.html.

Federal Bureau of Investigation. 2006. "Financial Crimes Report to the Public Fiscal Year 2006." http://www.fbi.gov/publications/financial/fcs_report2006 /financial_crime_2006.htm.

Federal Housing Finance Agency (FHFA). 2010. "FHFA Issues Subpoenas for PLS Documents." News release, July 12.

Financial Crisis Inquiry Commission. 2010. "Amplification." Hearings on the Role of Derivatives in the Financial Crisis, charts and graphs, June 30. http://fcic-static.law.stanford.edu/cdn_media/fcic-testimony/2010–0630-chart-amplification.pdf.

Fitch Ratings. 2007. "The Impact of Poor Underwriting Practices and Fraud in Subprime RMBS Performance." *US Residential Mortgage Special Report*, November 28.

Frishberg, Manny. 2008. "One-Minute Mortgage." *Seattle Metropolitan Magazine*, June. http://www.seattlemet.com/real-estate/articles/0608-rainmaker/.

Gilmore, Grainne. 2009. "Toxic Debts Could Reach $4 Trillion, IMF to Warn." *Times*, April 9.

Gordon, Greg. 2009a. "How Goldman Secretly Bet on the U.S. Housing Crash." *McClatchy Washington Bureau*, November 1.

———. 2009b. "Why Did Blue-Chip Goldman Take a Walk on Subprime's Wild Side?" *McClatchy Washington Bureau*, November 4.

———. 2009c. "Why Did Goldman Stop Scrutinizing Loans It Bought?" *McClatchy Washington Bureau*, November 1.

Gramlich, Edward M. 2004. Remarks at the Financial Services Roundtable Annual Housing Policy Meeting, Chicago, Illinois, May 21. http://www.federalreserve.gov/Boarddocs/Speeches/2004/20040521/default.htm.

Greenberger, Michael. 2010. "The Role of Derivatives in the Financial Crisis." Testimony before the Financial Crisis Inquiry Commission, June 30. http://fcic-static.law.stanford.edu/cdn_media/fcic-testimony/2010–0630-Greenberger.pdf.

Grunbaum, Rami. 2008. "Lawsuit Raises New Questions About Demise of Subprime Lender MILA." *Seattle Times*, October 5.

Hall v. Unity Management Development Corp., et al. Circuit Court of Cook County Illinois, Chancery Division, Case 7CH36731.

Illinois Attorney General. 2010. "Madigan Sues Countrywide for Discrimination Against African American and Latino Borrowers." Press release, June 29.

Immergluck, Dan, and Marti Wiles. 1999. "Two Steps Back: The Dual Mortgage Market, Predatory Lending, and the Undoing of Community Development." Woodstock Institute, Chicago, November. http://www.woodstockinst.org/publications/research-reports/.

In re: MILA, Inc. United States Bankruptcy Court. Western District of Washington at Seattle, Case No. 07–13050-SJS, 2008.

In re: Morgan Stanley & Co. Inc. Suffolk Superior Court, Civil Action No. 10–2538, June 24, 2010.

In re: New Century TRS Holdings, Inc. Final Report of Michael J. Missal, Bankruptcy Court Examiner, February 29, 2008.

Kindleberger, Charles P., and Robert Aliber. 2005. *Manias, Panics, and Crashes.* Hoboken, N.J.: Wiley.

LaCroix, Kevin M. 2010. "Subprime and Credit Crisis-Related Securities Class Action Lawsuits." D&O Diary, June 3. http://www.oakbridgeins.com/clients/blog/subprimeresolution.doc.

Lewis, Michael. 2010. *The Big Short*. New York: Norton.

Minsky, Hyman P. 1992. "The Financial Instability Hypothesis." Jerome Levy Economics Institute Working Paper 74, May. http://ssrn.com/abstract=161024.

Mollenkamp, Carrick, and Serena Ng. 2010. "How a Little Subprime Lending Had a Big Impact." *Wall Street Journal*, May 3.

Morgenson, Gretchen. 2010. "Seeing vs. Doing." *New York Times*, July 25.

Office of Federal Housing Enterprise Oversight (OFHEO). 2008. "Mortgage Markets and the Enterprise in 2007." Research paper, July. http://www.fhfa.gov/webfiles/1164/MME2007revised.pdf.

Reuters. 2008. "B of A in $8.6 Billion Settlement Over Countrywide Loans." October 6. http://www.reuters.com/article/2008/10/06/sppage012-bng287494-oisbn-idUSBNG28749420081006.

Rosner, Joshua. 2007. "Stopping the Subprime Crisis." *New York Times*, July 25.

Smith, Elliot Blair. 2008. "'Raced to the Bottom' at Moody's, S&P Secured Subprime's Boom, Bust." *Bloomberg*, September 25.

Tymoigne, Eric. 2010. "Detecting Ponzi Finance: An Evolutionary Approach to the Measure of Financial Fragility." Jerome Levy Economics Institute Working Paper 605, June..

U.S. Senate, Permanent Subcommittee on Investigations. 2010. "Wall Street and the Financial Crisis: The Role of Investment Banks." Memorandum prepared by Carl Levin and Tom Coburn, April 26, 111th Cong., 2d sess.

Whelan, Robbie. 2010. "Mortgage Fraud Is Rising, with a Twist." *Wall Street Journal*, August 23.

Zandi, Mark. 2009. *Financial Shock*. Upper Saddle River, N.J.: FT Press.

Zimmerman, Thomas. 2007. "The U.S. Subprime Market: An Industry in Turmoil." UBS presentation to American Enterprise Institute, March.

[7]

GENERATING THE ALPHA RETURN

How Ponzi Schemes Lure the Unwary in an Unregulated Market

DAVID SHAPIRO

Why do Ponzi schemes flourish? Does it take a financial crisis, such as the one that overcame the U.S. economy in 2007–2008, to expose them? As the crisis grew, many Ponzi swindlers' investment schemes were exposed as fictions when requests for redemptions from investors dwarfed available cash and access to capital. But many hedge and private equity fund investments also collapsed in value as underappreciated credit and market risks in these investments were recognized. The nature of today's unregulated or lightly regulated market often makes the distinctions between outright fraud and high-risk vehicles hard to discern. The Ponzi manager makes intentionally false and materially misleading statements, whereas the hedge and private equity funds' managers make accidentally or inadvertently false and materially misleading statements. Obviously, it is difficult for an outsider to tell the difference. In the following essay, I examine the differences and similarities by looking at the characteristics of a largely secret financial world where the mystique of the alpha manager and alpha returns reigns supreme, often to the detriment of investors. The article concludes with a number of recommendations that, if followed, will alert investors to the presence of Ponzi schemes, such as requiring that all funds be subjected to special-purpose confidential audits under the supervision of forensic accountants and fraud investigators.

The Distinctions Between Hedge and Private Equity Funds and Ponzi Schemes

Hedge and Private Equity Funds

Investment advisors, investment funds, broker-dealers, and accredited (i.e., high net worth) or qualified (i.e., institutional) investors are the main players in the hedge and private-equity funds industry. Savings from investors are converted into fund assets that earn a rate of return that will enrich both investors and fund managers. Hedge and private equity fund investments are commonly deemed riskier but potentially more profitable alternatives to ordinary retail investing, such as mutual funds.

Hedge funds and private equity funds are pools of investment capital that are largely unregulated by federal, state, and local authorities. In contrast, mutual funds or registered investment companies are subject to a comparatively rigorous federal regulatory framework. Hedge and private equity funds are lawful devices in market opportunity or exploitation enterprises that serve accredited investors and qualified purchasers. Generally, the funds themselves are not public filers subject to periodic reporting obligations, though the managers of these funds may be public filers (e.g., the Blackstone Group LP, the Fortress Investment Group LLC). In addition, registration obligations governed by federal or state investment advisor regulatory regimes may affect their operations.

Essentially, the hedge and private equity funds manager's role is defined in an investment agreement with investors that delineates the rights and obligations of the parties. The means and methods by which funds' managers realize investment objectives are generally described without rigorous detail to prevent free riders. If the strategies to obtain superior performance were disclosed in detail in documents released to investors, actual and potential, the economic need for the manager would be adversely affected; that is, an investor could take the investment advice and make investments himself or hire someone else on the cheap.

Hedge fund managers may use trading techniques such as short sales or purchases of exotic financial instruments, including credit default swaps, to obtain returns on investments for their clients and earn either management fees (based on the value of assets under management) and incentive fees (based on the profitability of the investments). The hedge fund is primarily a trader of financial instruments through public exchanges (the retail network) or over the counter (the broker-dealer network). It exploits market vulnerabilities: for example, opportunities through arbitraging price discrepancies between legitimate financial instruments in different markets or locations.

The private equity fund primarily invests in legitimate businesses, whether publicly or privately held. A manager's fees are based on the profitability of the fund and its component investments, which may not be realized for several years. Thus, the private equity focus is more long-term than the comparatively short-term focus of hedge funds.

As these investments become complementary, the distinctions between hedge funds and private equity funds have begun to blur. Both hedge funds and private equity funds managed by publicly traded entities are subject to the same scrutiny as any publicly traded entity (e.g., Fortress Investment Group LLC). Importantly, a Ponzi scheme would not likely survive the audit requirements imposed on public filers (e.g., Sarbanes-Oxley Section 404 audits of internal controls), so the likelihood of a fund manager perpetrating a significant Ponzi scheme within a publicly traded enterprise is remote. The survivability of a Ponzi scheme depends on the lack of independent and objective oversight. Entities under the umbrella of publicly reporting enterprises are subjected to rigorous auditing of both their financial statements and their systems of internal control. To evade detection from such an audit would require either corrupt auditors or an immaterial Ponzi scheme; auditors may not test immaterial transactions and entities even within publicly traded enterprises.

Ponzi Schemes

Ponzi schemes are broadly interpreted as faux investment vehicles characterized by fraudulent, embezzling management. The Ponzi manager not only markets fraudulently with intentional misrepresentations about the bona fides of the vehicle (e.g., its historical rates of return, investment strategies) but also operates fraudulently by misappropriating assets contributed by investors. That is, the Ponzi manager commits fraud by inducing investors to contribute assets, usually cash, to the vehicle under false pretenses and continues swindling of investors by mischaracterizing the financial performance of the vehicle (e.g., lying about the revenues and expenses of the vehicle), so as both to get new investors and to cajole current investors to leave their investments in the vehicle.

Essentially, the Ponzi scheme is theft by deception. A Ponzi manager misrepresents the performance of the investments in a fund in order to ensure a sufficient stream of investment capital that can be paid out to investors and disguised as extremely high returns. The scheme is fraudulently marketed as a highly successful trading operation in the style of hedge funds and in fact is generally directed at the kind of well-to-do investor who is engaged with legitimate hedge and private equity funds, although many Ponzis have been marketed to middle class and working class individuals. But while Ponzi managers "talk the talk" of legitimate hedge and private equity fund managers, they do not "walk the walk."

Regulatory authorities can also be deceived by them. Although Ponzi managers are rarely public filers, some may be registered with government agencies. For example, the Madoff enterprise (Bernard L. Madoff Investment Securities LLC) was both a federally registered broker-dealer and a federally registered investment advisor.[1] A telltale distinction lies, however, in how Ponzi managers amass their wealth. Traditionally, the earnings of hedge fund and private equity fund managers depend on the number of assets under management or high profits. But the lack of adequate regulation over the hedge fund and private equity industry enables Ponzi managers to develop customized, unorthodox agreements with investors. For example, Madoff was purportedly remunerated by (among other things) trading commissions. Though hedge funds and private equity funds are unregulated or lightly regulated, the managers of these devices generally do not obtain remuneration from investors in the form of trading commissions.

The key to prolonging a Ponzi scheme is to minimize investors' request for redemption since the Ponzi manager lacks an equity cushion to satisfy such requests. Therefore, the manager needs to persuade investors to maintain (or increase) their investments in the funds over the long-term. This persuasion is accomplished through misrepresentations of investment performance typically by intentionally overstating returns on investment.

Another important distinction between hedge and private equity funds and illegal Ponzi schemes is that the former are conduits to place investors' savings into lawful activities under the supervision of legitimate investment managers, whether they be hedge fund purchases of credit derivative instruments protecting against default (e.g., John Paulson)[2] or investments in the equity of closely held companies later offered to public shareholders (e.g., Caribou Coffee). In contrast, the Ponzi scheme is a device to fraudulently impersonate such an investment fund and steal investors' savings.

Method of Operation: High Performance

Legitimate fund management requires, among other functions, the following:

1. Administration (e.g., maintaining books and records of investors' accounts, including proprietary and related party accounts of the manager);
2. Brokerage (e.g., executing, clearing, and settling trades);
3. Custodianship (e.g., safeguarding assets).

These functions may be outsourced to third parties, such as prime brokers, who execute trades and provide credit. To the extent that these functions are performed by one enterprise, the risk of concealing a Ponzi-type scheme or other fraudulent activity is increased. However, the use of independent parties to assist an investment manager does not provide absolute assurance against fraudulent reports of the fund's performance.

The Ponzi manager and hedge and private equity fund managers all shield information. But legitimate financial managers use their resources, skills, and relationships to reap high returns on investment funds. They exploit market opportunities ahead of other market participants as a result of data generated in-house or received from external parties. Hedge and private equity fund managers demand secrecy to protect proprietary information regarding trade secrets, trading positions, trading algorithms, risks assumed, related party transactions, and so forth, though the risk of inadequate disclosure of third-party service entities (e.g., undisclosed related parties), even in the cases of hedge and private equity funds, unfortunately exists. In contrast, the Ponzi manager requires opacity to avoid detection. Neither registration with a regulator nor audit by an independent public accountant provides absolute assurance that economic reality is consistent with the manager's assertions. Ponzi fraud thrives in a fertile soil of incomplete disclosure and lack of transparency. Secrecy holds investors at bay, making them vulnerable. Although opacity in legitimate high-risk investment vehicles enables them to gain real competitive advantage not only with respect to its peers/rivals and investors/clients but also in public opinion, secrecy tends to inflate the performance of managers and raise their value in the highly competitive investment marketplace. This works to the benefit of the architects of Ponzis.

Leverage

Leverage is money borrowed from investors, banks, and others entities to amplify or multiply absolute return on investments. For example, if a proposed investment offers a 10 percent return within 6 months, then borrowing at 3 percent for the same period provides the fund with seven cents additional profit on each dollar borrowed. Leverage may dwarf capital. Leverage increases the risk of inadequate capital (liquidity risk) to cushion against near-term adverse changes in market and credit risks. This may become manifest as a shortage of liquidity—that is, an inability to pay current liabilities with current assets (e.g., demands for more collateral from lenders). Although private equity funds may limit the amount of debt that they may incur in the investment agreement with their investors, hedge fund managers, in particular, depend on leverage. As more money is borrowed, the ratio of debt to equity increases, potentially creating an inadequately capitalized fund. Ponzi schemes are not only inadequately capitalized, they may be inherently insolvent from inception—that is, the total value of the Ponzi fund assets is exceeded by its liabilities, leaving no equity cushion whatsoever.

Specialized Skills

Specialized skills place the best managers ahead of the competition. They provide the mojo in the vernacular of traders. The skills may include specialized degrees or extensive experience in finance, and they are put to use in the analysis of public and nonpublic data and to identify, among other things, undervalued companies and arbitrage opportunities. Mathematical prowess has become an especially valued skill in today's market, enabling quant hedge funds, for instance, to employ algorithmic arbitrage trading among different markets. The promotion of this skill may represent economic reality in the case of John Paulson or be unsoundly but perhaps plausibly founded on the practice of taking public positions in support of high technology to enhance trading activities, as exemplified by Madoff in relation to the NASDAQ. Moreover, managers and the media tend to promote the role of specialized skill sets as a rational basis for social acceptance of the legitimacy of alpha returns, whereas the roles and risks of leverage and privileged relationships (e.g., uneven playing field, insider trading, and luck) are downplayed or seem less noteworthy than managers' mojo.

Although managers' professional credibility may be enhanced by credentials in finance, educational degrees, or stints at an investment banking firm, how they use these skills and experience is not widely known. There is no published manual explaining how to transform cash into oodles of more cash within a short period: The investment manager making oodles of money seems to be a mysterious agent.

Privileged Relationships

The successful manager cultivates a network of influential parties ranging from public officials to wealthy investors from whom material nonpublic information may be obtained and not disclosed to outsiders. (The nature and extent of John Paulson's partnership with Goldman Sachs is a prime example of this.) Although managers have relationships with influential businesspeople, politicians, and others, the role of privileged relationships tends to be downplayed lest others become suspicious that the market is significantly rigged or gamed.

The mystique of highly successful managers depends on investors not quite knowing enough. If managers or others empowered investors to know enough about how the successful manager makes enormous amounts of money, managers would likely lose not only their competitive advantage but also their livelihood (and in the case of Ponzi managers, their liberty). Those who know how the game is played do not tell its secrets.

Alpha Return

Theoretically, managers earn money based on both profitability of the fund—that is, incentive income for reported excess returns—and size or reported value of investments managed. Therefore, the manager's right to compensation requires supporting accounting data presented and disclosed in the income statements and balance sheets. The key to understanding the legitimacy of managers' compensation is to grasp the implications of unrealized capital appreciation gains: An unrealized gain reflects an investment that has been revalued higher than its previously reported value, yet the investment is still held by the reporting entity (i.e., a holding gain).

Whereas realized capital gains generally result in the manager actually holding more cash (or the legal right to cash), unrealized gains do not increase a manager's actual cash holdings.[3] If a reported increase in the value of assets under management or return on these assets does not confer either increases in actual cash or the right to actual cash, the holding gain may be illusory or Ponzi-like. For example, a long or short position marked to market for a gain on December 31 may become an unprofitable position weeks, a day, or a fraction of a second later.[4] Additionally, valuations of investments in illiquid markets may become subjective and unreliable as investments are marked to model in lieu of a robust market.

In contrast, realized gains include profits from trading financial instruments, such as securities and credit derivatives. Managers with specialized skills or inside knowledge may identify under- or overpriced instruments and effectively buy low and sell high (covered sales) or sell high and buy low (short sales). Investors are unlikely to possess sufficient data to monitor the integrity of this process. As a result, investors learn the results of the manager's investment processes through monthly or quarterly reports but are unable to verify the truthfulness of these reports.

Transparency

Many phenomena seem mystical at first blush (e.g., solar eclipse), yet become understandable after subjected to the rigors of the scientific method. However, when the phenomenon of high performance (alpha returns) is subjected to the rigors of generally accepted auditing standards, the application of which results in a clean opinion by the auditor (the alleged alpha return is fairly represented), the issue of transparency is not always resolved. For example, the audit may be deficient as in the case of Madoff's accounting firm, Friehling & Horowitz, or the auditor may be fictitious as in the case of Bayou Funds' Richmond-Fairfield Associates. The perennial issue of "who guards the guardians?" remains.

Transparency promotes an understanding of the subprocesses involved in high-performance investments. It provides knowledge deeper than sell-high, buy-low, by addressing questions of how the investment manager knows when, where, and what to buy and when, where, and what to sell. It exposes the workings of the black box. Transparency would also expose hedge and private equity funds and their managers to competitors, dulling their competitive edge, however obtained.

A successful Ponzi scheme needs to be protected against transparency and the volatility of actual market conditions, which explains why the operator generally uses investment vehicles for which the values cannot be readily corroborated or independently verified by the investors. Therefore, investors rely exclusively on the performance assessment scheme selected by the Ponzi manager. Interestingly, it was Madoff's purported use of the split-strike conversion strategy, among other things, that tipped off Harry Markopolos to the lack of bona fides of the Madoff enterprise.[5] Madoff promotional materials apparently attempted to persuade potential investors of the legitimacy and superiority of his investment strategy and investment vehicles by including purported details of the historical performance of his vehicles against Standard & Poor's (S&P) publicly traded indices. The benchmarks to which Madoff referred ironically highlighted the unlikelihood that his investments could have achieved these reported returns. After Markopolos tested this conversion strategy against actual market conditions, he concluded that Madoff and his agents significantly overstated the company's profitability. Specifically, the actual volume of S&P derivative contracts was way too light to support the profits Madoff claimed in his promotional materials.[6] In effect, Madoff concealed material information about his purported high performance.

By analogy, a fund promoting a return on domestic certificates of deposit of 10 percent during a period when others were offering 3 percent on the same type of financial instrument would theoretically not attract much investor savings as it would lack credibility. However, a fund promoting an equivalent return by exotic means such as arbitrage across global markets may cause the investor to suspend disbelief. Unsurprisingly, many funds are incorporated or registered offshore to avoid excessive regulation and facilitate minimization of income taxation by U.S. authorities. However, seemingly legitimate economic reasons may also serve as cover or concealment for illicit investment activities. For example, according to the SEC, Robert Allen Stanford used an Antiguan-based bank that he had controlled to fleece investors. He deceived them into believing that their investments were earning extraordinary rates of return from opportunities available offshore while diverting their funds for his personal expenses.[7]

Insider Status: Exploiting Vulnerability

Insiders, such as key management personnel of managing entities, are positioned to benefit from the investment process. They have access to confidential information, including trading positions and strategies. Armed with such information, insiders can buy low and sell high or sell high and buy low. Moreover, these insiders significantly influence market pricing of assets.

Specifically, the insider is a person possessing material nonpublic information on behalf of the manager and customers' trading positions. This type of information may be obtained in numerous legitimate ways but used illegitimately. The stereotypical example is an officer or director of a corporation engaging in insider trading by using nonpublic information. Other examples include a market maker using front-running and a broker-dealer paying co-location fees to a market or exchange to obtain advance access to orders and using flash trading in exploitation of the broker-dealer's customers. Additionally, an individual not in one of these positions may be informed or tipped by an associate or a friend who is in one of these positions.

The expression "it's not what you know but who you know" offers wise guidance. Since the mechanics of making profitable investments are obvious (buy assets at low prices and sell at high prices), while the details of how to exploit highs and lows are not, investors willingly pay a premium to managers who seem to perform as if they had inside information.

Managers do not expressly sell inside information or their privileged relationships to their client investors; they sell their specialized skills. The risk of civil and criminal litigation for securities fraud, breach of fiduciary duty, and so forth from misusing inside information or privileged relationships has encouraged managers to explain and sell their alpha returns by referencing their purportedly exceptional investment management techniques, which makes a better narrative for public consumption.

Even publicly traded market participants with hedge and private equity funds, such as the Goldman Sachs Group (www2.goldmansachs.com), that report exceptional, high-performance results leave investors in the dark as to how these gains occurred, including whether they were based on insider information. Investors cannot practically obtain sufficient and timely detail from analysis of public filings, including financial statements, to make these alpha returns transparent. Hence, a mystique of specialized skill and privileged relationships is borne and sustained. Frankly, the investor may not care much how managers make alpha returns (as deep knowledge of these means and methods is not accessible and transparent to them anyway), so long as these managers actually report and return alpha profitability to them. As with sausage-making, the gourmand need not observe to enjoy the results. It is likely Madoff's investors believed the same—until reality struck.

Managers provide sufficient data to withstand legal challenges from SEC and Commodity Futures Trading Commission (CFTC) regulators, but they do not provide investors with enough information to enable them to understand and replicate the investment strategy. This not only protects trade secrets of apparently legitimate managers, such as John Paulson, but it provides cover to Ponzi managers, such as Bernie Madoff, for whom a requirement to provide all of the details necessary for a complete understanding of their investment strategies would unmask their fraud. As a result, the pedigree or background of the manager (e.g., Goldman Sachs alumni, former NASDAQ board member) becomes more useful to the investor than a narrative of strategy and technique with accompanying tables and charts: After all, he must know what he is doing; look where he has been.

The manager is ideally positioned to exploit the investor's excessive trust, a vulnerability that is not satisfactorily remedied in the lightly regulated regime of hedge and private equity fund investments, founded on the assumption that high net-worth individuals and institutional investors can take care of themselves. The asymmetry of information between the managerial class and investor class puts the latter at severe disadvantage.

Information and Communication

Transparent communication is crucial. Initially, the investor receives documentation such as an offering memorandum from the fund sponsor describing the proposed investment strategy. Underlying the financial statements may be an audit report. However, the absence of an audit report would not be unusual, especially in the lightly regulated regime of hedge and private equity fund investments. The value of audit reports may be questionable. Not only are they expensive to purchase, they lack the focus of competently performed fraud or forensic audit that would directly and deeply target and challenge management assumptions, estimates, and biases.

The three general approaches managers may select to convey data to investors are window dressing, big bath, and neutrality:

1. Window dressing
The manager puts a positive spin on the data (which may support investors' excessive optimism). For example, a reporting entity that has a spike in earnings in one period may also take overstated reserves or charges against these earnings in successive periods to smooth expected earnings.

2. Big bath
The manager places a negative spin on data (which may support investors' excessive pessimism). For example, a reporting entity that has a drop in earnings may decide to write off or write down certain assets, which will lower net income for the year. In essence, this technique cleans up the balance sheet during a bad period in hopes of showing a profit in the next.

3. Neutrality
The data may be converted to information neutral to the natural bias of the data. This process emphasizes the inherent probative value of the data (which may support investors' rationalism). For example, a reporting entity undergoing an SEC audit of its financial reporting minimizes window dressing and big bath techniques to reduce litigation risk.

These approaches are not mutually exclusive. The manager directly or indirectly controls the processing of data into information with the intent of affecting investors' responses. Investor expectations are managed; financial and nonfinancial reports are manipulated, whether in good faith or bad faith. Though recognition, disclosure, and presentation may be regulated by government rules and guided by general principles of the accounting profession, investors are not generally able to challenge the completeness and accuracy of financial and nonfinancial reporting in general-purpose reports produced by management. Moreover, the principles of recognition, disclosure, and presentation are not rigid but flexible (e.g., fair value determinations). The investors are expected to trust in the managers' integrity to report honestly and objectively.

Technology

As the use of computer hardware and software has grown immensely over the past decades, the ability of a manager to construct forged documentation and data has also increased (e.g., in the Parmalat scandal, bank statements were forged; in the Madoff scandal, it was account statements).[8] Therefore, the authenticity of documentation is a critical issue. Moreover, the possibility of collusion between manager and service provider exponentially decreases the likelihood of detecting fraudulent accounting or of identifying misleading corroborative data. Therefore, there are two primary questions regarding the data:

1. Are the data valid and consistent with internal documentation? For example, is the valuation of an investment supported by an internal worksheet that includes all of the essential data? Investments in nonpublic entities by a private equity fund may be valued under a discounted cash flow analysis requiring certain assumptions, such as expected growth of revenues and a discount rate.
2. Are the data sound and consistent with economic reality? For example, are trading activities recorded in the internal daily blotter of traders consistent with brokerage statements prepared by a third party? Sales and other exchanges or swaps of assets by hedge funds should be supported by third-party confirmations.

Unfortunately, the general-purpose financial reports that investors receive do not contain the corroborative data. The investor must trust but cannot verify. The issue of the reliability of data supporting managers' reports on investment returns goes to the heart of the market economy on which these returns are founded: As regulated and unregulated markets depend on accuracy of disclosure, investors cannot obtain fair return on their investments unless they are armed with reliable and relevant data concerning manager performance. Otherwise, the Madoffs can blend in and effectively indirectly exploit the Paulsons of the financial world.

The risk of bias in a manager's manipulation of accounting and corroborative data is intrinsic to both legitimate funds and illicit funds. For example, a manager may prepare statements relating the values of assets and investments that are supported by nonexistent market or model data, as in the case of the Madoff enterprise, or unreliable information, as with AIG's credit default swaps. Whether the manager intentionally misrepresents the values of assets is an issue for criminal or civil litigation. However, the investor is not really served by catastrophic errors in judgment: Either way the investor suffers steep losses.

The investor is no better served by a manager's mistakes than by a manager's fraud. Investigations into managers' communications to investors too often result in the following dilemma: The manager asserts unawareness of wrongfulness, and the investor asserts deficient manager selection and monitoring of investment vehicles. Discovering evidence to resolve these assertions is time consuming and expensive. What is required is an expanded use of technology to enhance preventive measures that promote verifiable, objective, and timely reporting by managers to investors.

Asset Pricing: The Bubble

The level of credit available affects the market pricing of assets. In a fractional reserve banking system, credit is highly expandable, potentially producing many dollars of capital in search of profitability greater than the cost of capital. Moreover, an abundance of credit increases liquidity, enabling the bidding up in asset values.

Asset prices rising significantly above their intrinsic, fundamental, or true value create asset bubbles; that is, they are priced at irrationally high, artificial levels. Asset bubbles create continual gains—both realized and unrealized—as reporting entities sell or revalue investments at prices increasingly greater than historical or acquisition costs. This has the effect of raising investors' demands and expectations: If normal return on investment is 8 percent, then a superior or alpha return on investment must be higher. Yield-hungry investors chase alpha returns.

These conditions create a wonderful opportunity for hedge and private equity fund managers and Ponzi swindlers alike. They all depend upon increasing leverage to increase profitability: Obtaining credit at comparatively low rates and then purchasing assets with values continually climbing seems a terrific operational strategy until the asset prices crash. The markets for assets become less concerned with price discovery than price exploitation: "Buy now to resell tomorrow before somebody else does." Asset prices are continually bid up by funds with access to an abundance of comparatively cheap credit.

Assertions about exceptional returns on investment seem more credible as asset prices rise, and other investment managers—both legitimate and illegitimate—boast of alpha return. An irrational market, such as one characterized by wildly inflating asset prices, promotes suspension of disbelief. It is not a transparent market but a magical one. More and more investors place their savings into managers' custody in the expectation of benefiting from the climb. Funds buy high and sell higher; no harm, no foul.

The key to understanding the usefulness of the asset bubble is to recognize its effect on individuals' decision making. Rational analysis is displaced by rapid opportunism. It does not matter that long-term trends do not support such asset price inflation, such as soaring residential real estate values at a time of flat wage and income growth. What matters is short-term profitability. A manager that does not exploit this investor expectation and vulnerability may be left behind, whereas managers who successfully exploit and time these bubbles are positioned to obtain more clients, press coverage, adulation, and incentive compensation.

Numerous financial institutions received billions of dollars in financial assistance from the U.S. government and the Federal Reserve Bank of New York beginning in October 2008. Many of these bulge bracket institutions,[9] such as Goldman Sachs and Citigroup, control or manage hedge and private equity funds. Interestingly, if Madoff had been bailed out in the same manner as these institutions, it would have been the functional equivalent of handing him an influx of well-heeled new clients whose investments could have been used to satisfy the redemption requests of old investors. Perhaps he would still be a wizard.[10]

Conclusion and Recommendations

The risk of wrongful manipulation of data is manifest in a variety of situations, from rigged markets (i.e., those that are artificially or thinly stimulated) for auction-backed securities to understated contingent liabilities of credit default swaps. Data reliability is paramount, whether market- or model-based. As managers of hedge and private equity funds generally function with light oversight from regulators, the effectiveness of data assurance specialists—credit rating agencies, independent public accountants, third-party service providers—conspicuously used for publicly traded entities is largely lacking for these managers' funds, which benefits both legitimate and illegitimate managers. Legitimate managers are not burdened with excess costs of regulation, and illegitimate managers are not coerced to be transparent.

However, data assurance specialists, such as credit rating agencies, may fail in isolated instances (as in the late downgrading of Enron debt securities) or may fail systemically (as in the market-wide overstatement of credit quality of structured finance vehicles in the recent financial crisis) to provide investors with relevant and reliable data concerning investments. Arguably, their opinions are undeniably vulnerable to the client bias of "he who pays must be pleased." Extending their business models to hedge and private equity funds would seem a reward analogous to the extension of the reach of the accounting profession under Sarbanes-Oxley[11] (in apparent compensation for taking away the accounting profession's ability to provide consultation services to its audit clients). Deficient performance should cause a positive change in oversight, not more of the same.

Nonetheless, the requirement under Sarbanes-Oxley that public filers in the United States be subject to a Section 404 audit of internal controls over financial reporting by an independent registered public accountant is an idea that may be borrowed and modified to benefit investors in alternative investment vehicles such as hedge and private equity funds, as well as their managers, who would otherwise not be subject to such an audit because they are not public filers or they are deemed immaterial under the public filer that controls them.

First, the scope of the audit should include internal controls over financial reporting and operational risks—broader than the Sarbanes-Oxley requirement—as operational risk results when investments are made in bubbled assets, and debt financing is obtained by an already overleveraged entity notwithstanding the accuracy and completeness of financial reporting. Conventional financial reporting focuses on disclosure and presentation of economic events—transactions with outside entities. The accuracy of reporting these events does not require the auditor to opine meaningfully and objectively on the soundness of the reporting entity's broader risk management practices: For example, buying $1 million of General Electric debt is significantly different from buying $1 million of Madoff debt, yet both might have been reported as assets valued at $1 million each. Risk may be inadequately disclosed.

Second, the professionals eligible to perform and supervise such audits should include forensic accountants and fraud investigators; these professionals have by experience, education, or training an enhanced sensitivity to unreliable or fraudulent data. Third, these special purpose audit reports should be confidential and made available only to investors or others with a demonstrable interest and issued to them within 30 days of the measurement date. Fourth, the audit should provide positive assurance (or explain why positive assurance could not be obtained) as to the effectiveness and efficiency of internal controls over financial reporting and operational risks. Fifth, the audits should be financed by the persons who benefit from increased reliability and relevancy of reporting—that is, the industry and its investors (equity and debt capital). A fixed percentage charge against the beginning of the year-total asset value should be levied (e.g., 1 percent of total asset value) and used to fund the current year's special purpose audits. Investors could opt out under penalty of losing the right to bring a civil action against the fund and its manager(s). If investor demand was too low to support a meaningful audit (e.g., less than 0.5% of total asset value) of any given fund, investors would be informed that investment in such a fund requires their waiver of a right to bring a civil action in the United States against the fund and its manager(s). Sixth, auditor selection would be controlled by the SEC and CFTC. Neither the fund nor its managers would have a right to select the auditor, and no auditor would be allowed to audit a given fund for more than one consecutive year.

These suggested changes would likely improve the quality of information reported to investors and others. Although they fall short of fully empowering outside investors (e.g., pension funds), they advance the objective of leveling the current information asymmetry, yet protect proprietary interests, property, and data. Though these recommendations increase compliance costs and shift economic resources to compliance industry professionals, the improved reliability of information, without which there is no relevancy, would greatly enhance the prestige of U.S. capital markets. Maintaining the status quo because air has leaked out of the bubble (and Madoff is in prison) is akin to reckless indifference to the structural cycle of asset bubbles and bursts. Absent the proper tools to distinguish between what is real and illusory, individuals and institutions desiring economic growth must trust that independent and socially responsible individuals will protect them.

Otherwise, *caveat emptor* and you're on your own.

Notes

1. See SEC Litigation Release, http://www.sec.gov/litigation/litreleases/2009/lr20889.htm.

2. See SEC Litigation Release, http://www.sec.gov/litigation/litreleases/2010/lr21489.htm.

3. Unrealized gains also enable funds to increase leverage or borrowings as they appear to have more asset value or collateral value against which to borrow.

4. Reporting entities that actively trade securities report these investments at fair value. Marking to market is a method to discover fair value; that is, securities trading in liquid markets provide daily verifiable evidence of their value (e.g., closing price listed by the New York Stock Exchange).

5. See United States Senate Committee on Banking, Housing, & Urban Affairs, Hearing on September 9, 2009, Testimony of Mr. Harry Markopolos, http://banking.senate.gov/public/index.cfm?FuseAction=Hearings.Hearing&Hearing_ID=7b38b6a3-f381-4673-b12c-f9e4037b0a3f.

6. It was as if Madoff were claiming $100 million in dividend income from owning General Electric shares during 2007 when the total amount of dividends paid by GE in 2007 was $10 million.

7. See SEC Litigation Release, http://www.sec.gov/litigation/litreleases/2009/lr21092.htm.

8. See SEC Litigation Release, http://www.sec.gov/litigation/litreleases/2009/lr21292.htm.

9. Bulge bracket institutions are financial institutions with significant investment banking business activities (e.g., underwriting securities in public offerings).

10. Financial institutions were bailed out without restrictions on the use of these funds. These institutions were comprised of numerous related parties, subsidiaries, and affiliates that could have received credit support from the bailout institutions without anyone being the wiser.

11. See SEC Sarbanes-Oxley Rulemaking and Reports, http://www.sec.gov/spotlight/sarbanes-oxley.htm.

[PART III]

PERVERTED JUSTICE

The most crippling limitation on the regulators', FBI's, and DOJ's efforts to contain the epidemic of mortgage fraud and the financial crisis was not understanding of the cause of the epidemic and why it would cause a catastrophic financial crisis. The mortgage banking industry controlled the framing of the issue of mortgage fraud.

—(Written statement of William K. Black, testimony before the Financial Crisis Inquiry Commission, Miami, Florida, September 21, 2010)

[8]

THE TECHNOLOGICAL ADVANTAGES OF STOCK MARKET TRADERS

LAUREEN SNIDER

With the passage of the Dodd-Frank Wall Street Reform and Consumer Protection Act (Dodd-Frank Act) in the United States on July 21, 2010, the market-banking meltdown of 2008 appeared to have reached the final stage in the typical crisis-reform cycle.

When such disasters occur, nations historically move from outrage to proposals for reform to legislation. Each disaster bequeaths its own "regulatory legacy" (Haines and Sutton 2003), and each new legislative response is hailed as "the" definitive, once-and-for-all solution. Thus, each of the corporate meltdowns in the recent past—the Great Depression of the 1930s, the now-forgotten collapse of the savings and loans in the 1980s (Calavita, Pontell, and Tillman 1997), the collapse of the technology stock bubble in 2001–2002—has motivated "get tough" rhetoric and law. And since stock market crashes and fraud are a regularly recurring phenomenon, opportunities to intervene and "get it right" are lamentably frequent (Banks 2004; Garnaut 2009; Geisst 2004; Reinhart and Rogoff 2009).

During periods of crisis, statutes that were deregulated or ignored during boom times are revived; the budgets and formal powers of relevant regulatory agencies are increased; and the neoliberal antiregulation rhetoric that has dominated the developed world for the last 30 years (particularly the English-speaking democracies) declines in intensity.

But as the media spotlight shifts onto the next crisis, a regulatory status quo ante returns. Regulatory agency budgets once again come under siege, and antigovernment rhetoric and policies increase (Snider 2009).

Throughout each reform period, the omnipresent army of business "enablers"—tax lawyers, accountants, and investment advisors—are kept busy figuring out new ways to evade, avoid, or nullify each new set of regulations (Braithwaite 2005; McBarnet 2004). Their "innovations" proliferate unchecked until the next wave of financial meltdowns occurs and the cycle begins once more (Rosoff, Pontell, and Tillman 2004). The result is that regulators find themselves responsible for enforcing an ever-more complex mass of obscure and often contradictory statutes, provisions, and instructions that provide income for the stable of lawyers who are retained to find loopholes for their deep-pocketed employers and produce mystification for almost everyone else.[1]

Some pundits say, however, that because the 2008 crisis was truly global in its scope and effects, a number of new forces have been set in motion. They argue that it really will be different this time. The financial scandals involving prestigious Wall Street corporations (such as Bear Stearns, Lehman Brothers, Merrill Lynch, and Goldman Sachs), once-reputable financiers (Bernard Madoff and R. Allen Stanford), leading banks (such as Bank of America and Citibank), and prominent mortgage lenders (such as Countrywide) affected not just the United States but the world—triggering a global recession with massive job losses and bank collapses in the United Kingdom, the European Union (particularly Iceland, Portugal, Greece, Ireland, and Spain), and Asia. Many international leaders called for ambitious international measures to prevent such a crisis from recurring (Ojo 2009; Stuckler and Basu 2009).

There are other reasons to hope that out-of-control financial capitalism will finally be brought to heel this time around. New technologies, such as increasingly sophisticated tools that make it possible to track trades and institute systems of panoptic surveillance, including 24-hour video-audio cameras, have been employed for decades against traditional kinds of theft. These same tools could be effective weapons against corporate criminality as well: They make it technically feasible for regulators and investors to render all types of stock market transactions visible, the first step in accountability. Moreover, the pressure on both regulators and traders to "get tough" comes from a variety of sources. Activist investors' groups regularly employ the capabilities of the web to pressure financial institutions on everything from excessive management salaries and bonuses to corporate lack of transparency. Groups such as Democracy Watch (http://www.dwatch.ca/) publicize suspicious transactions and try to name and shame unethical behavior.

Under pressure from environmental groups and labor unions, many CEOs have committed their institutions to "best practices" in the fields of ethics, the environment, and corporate social responsibility (Roberts 2003; Shamir 2008). Moreover, at the sociocultural level, there is deep public anger at the role that corporate and political elites played in causing or failing to prevent the 2008 collapse and at the fact that the perpetrators have not been punished for the social harm they caused. The punitive culture promoted by neoliberal regimes (Garland 2001) in the form of longer jail sentences, welfare cutbacks, and mandatory minimum sentences has intensified the pressure on politicians to take harsh measures against corporate criminals and fraud.

These factors are helping to shape how financial capitalism will be conceptualized, regulated, and controlled in the years to come. While recognizing that it is impossible to predict the "success" of the latest set of regulations, this essay focuses on the new technologies that have transformed stock market governance and their potential use as regulatory tools. It considers what technological resources can be deployed by agencies tasked with regulating financial crime, particularly stock market fraud, and how technology interacts with the political, cultural, and economic (dis)advantages of regulatory agencies.

In the first section I trace this process, its implications, and effects before going on to examine the 2008 crisis and the reforms it provoked. The second section explores the technologies employed by dominant economic actors, specifically Wall Street banks and traders, and how these technologies are used to both maximize profits and resist regulation. It also explores the resources—technological, political, cultural, and economic—that the targets of regulation employ to defeat, deflect, or evade the regulatory gaze.

Technological Resources of the Regulators

To set the stage, we must first examine the business of trading itself and how it has changed over the last 20 years. To borrow a marketing slogan from advertisers, "this is not your grandfather's stock exchange." Equity trading markets have transformed from geographically fixed institutions dependent on face-to-face interactions and paper records into global 24/7 digital and electronically mediated transnational marketplaces. Stock exchanges themselves, originally self-regulating entities established by trading partners to raise capital and facilitate nation-building, have been "demutualized," that is, turned into for-profit corporations competing with new players and venues for listings and the fees they generate (Jackson and Gadinis 2007).

Stock market fraud, a variant of corporate crime that is defined as "illegal acts committed by legitimate formal organizations aimed at furthering the interests of the organization and the individuals involved," has also gone digital (Snider 1993, 15). Demutualization maximizes the potential conflict of interest between the regulatory obligations and the economic interests of the stock exchange, since exchanges, as self-regulating entities, are the first line of defense against stock market fraud. These developments magnify the potential for financial traders to wreak immense financial and social harm and greatly increase the number and geographical spread of primary and secondary victims (Braithwaite 1989; Coleman 1989; Pearce and Tombs 1998; Shapiro 1984, 1990).

It might seem that the digitization of trading systems would have opened up a vast new terrain for regulators, giving them the ability to prevent, track, monitor, and punish a range of stock market fraud at a level that was never possible in the past. With the evolution from paper record keeping to digitized financial flows on vast electronic networks, tracking and monitoring became possible via the digital traces left by every market transaction. The digital revolution, however, was designed and driven by commercial entities to enhance their interests, not those of regulators, small-retail investors, or the police. Efficiencies of time and scale were its objectives.

Thus, it is not surprising that although "a marked proliferation in the use of information technologies and computer programs to monitor, scan and surveil" (Williams 2009, 461) has occurred, the surveillance deployed against dominant economic actors and firms (such as Wall Street traders and the wheeler-dealers of major banks) remains minimal and nonintrusive.

This is particularly obvious when contrasted with the intensive measures routinely used against the embezzling retail clerk or burglar, who steals only a tiny fraction compared with the larceny of corporate titans, and does so with minimal long-term effects on the larger society (Ball and Wilson 2000; Deetz 1992; Sewell 1998; Sewell and Wilkinson 1992; Snider 2003; U.S. Congress Office of Technology Assessment 1987). No surveillance cameras have been installed in executive boardrooms; nor have police, forensic accountants, or regulatory officials been empowered to routinely use "panoptic" surveillance or digitally mine the online activities of CEOs.

Nevertheless, systems of automated, real-time monitoring of trades and trading patterns began appearing in the 1990s. They are now widespread. The first two systems appear to have been the Advanced Detection System, in the United States, and Surveillance of Market Activity, in Australia, which is based on the Stock Watch system used by the New York Stock Exchange (Brown and Goldschmidt 1996; Kirkland et al. 1999). The Financial Industry Regulation Authority (FINRA) is the primary (and largest) independent regulator with jurisdiction over all securities firms doing business in the United States. Created through the consolidation of NASD and the New York Stock Exchange (NYSE), FINRA is tasked with protecting investors and ensuring market integrity through "effective and efficient regulation and complementary compliance and technology-based services" (NYSE 2010). It performs market regulation under contract for the NASDAQ Stock Market, the American Stock Exchange, and the International Securities Exchange. It is also responsible for registering and educating traders and securities firms; enforcing its own rules as well as federal securities laws; educating the investing public; reporting on trades; and administering the nation's largest dispute resolution forum for investors and registered firms (FINRA 2010).

Electronic systems typically use data on "normal" trading volumes and share price fluctuation to catch "abnormal" trades. In the United States, market surveillance divisions often work closely with FINRA and with the SEC, the primary regulatory agency in this sector, in developing and managing their surveillance systems. "Minor" breaches are handled by the exchanges' enforcement units. "Major" cases may (or may not) be referred to the SEC. Recently, FINRA has taken over handling market oversight functions for the NYSE, including providing market surveillance and enforcement.

The effectiveness of electronic monitoring depends on a number of economic and political factors. To keep up with the speed at which trades are made, regulators use surveillance software—programs designed to generate alerts for anomalies—either developed within stock exchanges or, if contracted out, by surveillance software companies. Considering that there are millions of trades in every 24-hour period—average daily share volume on the NYSE increased 181 percent between 2005 and 2009 and the average time to complete an electronic trade dropped to 650 microseconds (Lavin 2010)—this is a formidable task.

The number of alerts issued depends on where the bar is set between the "normal" and "abnormal." Though executed by programmers, high-level executives make this judgment call. Set the bar too high, and the number of alerts issued per day will be astronomical. Set it too low, and thousands of problematic transactions will escape notice. Furthermore, system integrity is affected by a number of factors, such as budget and staff numbers, staff abilities (education and training), the limits set by the official mandate of the monitoring agency, its jurisdictional responsibilities and constraints, and its relative place in regulatory and political power structures within the nation-state. Overall this makes such programs very crude indeed (Williams 2009).

Before the 2008 crisis, video surveillance of traders was virtually nonexistent. The most notable exception was initiated by the SEC in 2006. An SEC investigation identified twenty NYSE traders who, from 1990 to 2003, engaged in "unlawful proprietary trading" through acts of "interpositioning" and "trading ahead" that resulted in more than $158 million in harm to its clients. Because the SEC considered the "parameters and procedures" of the NYSE and its automated surveillance system "too broad," it ordered specialist traders to install audio and video equipment to capture "all floor trading activity" and all activity and interaction "occurring at that specialist's post and panel." The surveillance had to be linked to NYSE's audit trail system, which provided time-sequenced records of all orders arriving at each specialist's trading post that were then stored for a minimum of 2 years. The NYSE was also ordered to retain a regulatory auditor until 2011, to introduce "enhancements" to the NYSE's referral process and to improve the training of its regulatory staff. Finally, the NYSE's chief regulatory officer had to certify annually that the NYSE was in compliance with the SEC's order (Anderson 2005; SEC 2005). However, the program ended in July 2009, 2 years earlier than scheduled. The official rationale, contained in an order issued by the SEC, was that the NYSE needed "greater flexibility in determining the appropriate regulatory usage of its audio-visual surveillance technology." The targets of regulation, declared the NYSE, could decide for themselves how to "maximize the potential benefit to the NYSE's surveillance, examination, and enforcement process" (SEC 2009).

After the 2008 crisis, the SEC responded to widespread condemnation of its failure to prevent the collapse of the banking system or to investigate the egregious abuses that caused it (particularly Madoff's decades-long Ponzi scheme) by forming an office with enhanced surveillance capabilities specializing in large-scale market abuses (the Market Abuse Unit). This Philadelphia-based unit is charged with investigating "complex" frauds, such as "organized" insider trading. It is believed to use surveillance techniques to delve into the backgrounds of certain traders. The system can cross-reference information about where traders went to business school and where they used to work with information about their trading activities. In detecting common relationships and associations, the unit hopes to find patterns of trader behavior across securities that will help it detect trades involving improper access to information (Goldstein 2010; Kaparti et al. 2010).

Legislative Reforms: The Dodd-Frank Act

The 2008 crisis has generated renewed, even frenzied, activity on the U.S. regulatory and surveillance front. Passage of the Dodd-Frank Act was one of the most important responses. The new act, a long and complex document, is intended to reassure investors—and governments around the world—that the American financial system is sound, transparent, and accountable. It also hopes to persuade major corporations to replace the ruinous short-term vision characteristic of their activities with a long-term perspective on their financial health. The act strengthens shareholders' rights by providing them with the ability to reclaim through legal action executive compensation that was based on inaccurate financial statements (Dodd-Frank Act 2010).

American taxpayers, it is promised, will no longer be on the hook to bail out financial firms that are deemed too big to fail. The Volcker Rule restores a section of the 1933 Glass-Steagall Act that was repealed in 1999 by the Gramm-Leach-Bliley Act (Gramm 1999). This rule prohibits banks, their affiliates, and holding companies from engaging in proprietary trading and bans investment in or sponsorship of hedge funds and private equity funds. It also limits relationships with hedge funds and private equity funds and requires "large, complex financial companies to periodically submit plans for their rapid and orderly shutdown should the company go under" (Committee on Financial Services 2010). Moreover, before any emergency loan is approved, the company must demonstrate that it has sufficient collateral to repay the Federal Reserve should the need arise. Brokers and advisors will be subjected to a greater fiduciary duty to act in the best interest of clients. The assets underlying mortgage-backed and municipal securities must be disclosed (Dodd-Frank Act 2010).

The act also streamlined bank supervision so that there will be "clear lines of responsibility among bank regulators" (Dodd-Frank Act 2010; U.S. Senate Committee on Banking, Housing and Urban Affairs 2010, 5). In light of the derivative-caused financial crisis, the Dodd-Frank Act calls for increased transparency and accountability for over-the-counter derivatives. The securitization process, which was a main factor in the development of the banking crisis, comes under tighter supervision. The SEC is also required to examine ratings organizations at least once a year and make its key findings public. Furthermore, banks are expected to ensure that compliance officers not only pass the proper qualifying exams but regularly update their skills. Most important of all, the act forbids the conflicts of interest that allowed ratings agencies to rate funds for clients upon whom they were financially dependent (Dodd-Frank Act 2010).

As noted above, the SEC has been sharply criticized as ineffective. In response to this criticism, the act outlines a series of reforms to the agency, including a requirement that it be self-funded. It also mandates rewards for whistle-blowers. The SEC was ordered as well to tighten its internal controls and management system.

To ensure that such a crisis will never happen again, the act establishes two new agencies, the Consumer Financial Protection Bureau (CFPB) and the Financial Stability Oversight Council (FSOC). The CFPB, to be staffed by experts in consumer protection, financial services, community development, fair lending, and consumer financial products, has been given investigative and enforcement powers, such as the ability to subpoena records and compel witness testimony, and is required to produce annual reports.

Nevertheless, the CFPB's future effectiveness is questionable. First, it has no authority over many of the worst offenders, such as the larger banks, automobile dealers, and real estate brokers ("Times Topics: Bureau of Consumer Financial Protection" 2010). Second, the appointment of Elizabeth Warren, a strong consumer advocate, as the agency's director was so strongly opposed by Republicans in Congress that on July 18, 2011, President Obama announced his intent to appoint Richard Cordray, a former attorney general of Ohio. In January 2012; the president gave Corday a recess appointment that was challenged by the Republicans on the grounds that the appointment is unconstitutional because the Senate was not "technically" in recess. This is hardly an auspicious beginning.

Third, the legislation is dangerously incomplete. For example, the act does not spell out how mortgages will be overseen by the CFPB. Indeed, almost every detail of its day-to-day operation will be left to the regulatory staff (still unhired when this was written) to work out. And as discussed below, this "working out" will occur out of the public view, even as the process is maximally exposed to lobbyist pressure.

The FSOC is aimed at preventing the kinds of financial dealings that caused the bankruptcy of so many investment banks. A Data Center and Research and Analysis Center will make information about the banks' market positions and transactions widely available. The council will also be expected to disseminate the results of its data-collection activities to financial regulatory agencies in an accessible standardized form. At the same time, it must report changes in system-wide risk levels and patterns. Other mandated activities include investigating disruptions in the financial markets, providing advice relating policies to systemic risk, and pursuing research to support and improve regulation (Dodd-Frank Act 2010, 68–78).

These represent an ambitious set of objectives, but with few details on how such an organization would work and whether any private or government body would be *compelled* to act on their recommendations, its overall potential is unknown.

And that's the trouble. The Dodd-Frank Act at present is little more than a "black box." Although one of its primary purposes is to reform the agencies that failed to prevent the 2008 crisis, these same regulators were given formative influence over it. Federal agencies will have to decide the details of at least 243 financial rules (Lichtblau 2010; Morgenson 2010b). Under the act, the SEC alone is responsible for developing ninety-five rules on topics such as trading in derivatives, standards for credit rating agencies, and the disclosure of executive bonuses. The CFTC will develop sixty-one rules, the Federal Reserve has fifty-four, and the two new agencies developed by the act— the FSOC and the CFPB—have eighty rules to establish between them (Lichtblau 2010).

Leaving the regulators to turn the broad mandates of the act into legally binding and enforceable rules of operation is seen as necessary because regulators are the designated, undeniable "experts" in each regulatory arena. However, this rationale overlooks the equally undeniable fact that the rules that make enforcement possible or easy for regulators will typically be very different from those that would be required to rein in dominant financial actors.

Regulators do not shape rules in a vacuum. Since the bill was signed into law, major agencies have been faced with scores of lobbyists (nearly 150 of them former regulators), all of them keen to "help" the regulators shape the rules in the directions most favorable to the corporations they represent. According to the Center for Responsive Politics, total spending by lobbyists continues to be high. Although there was a slight decrease reported during the first three quarters of 2010 (Center for Responsive Politics 2010b), a total of $3.49 billion was spent on lobbying in 2009. The largest amounts were invested by the U.S. Chamber of Commerce, which spent $144.4 million in 2009 and more than $651 million in the preceding 12 years. Over the same period, the number of registered lobbyists has fluctuated, peaking in 2007 at 14,777 lobbyists and slowly declining to 11,916 in 2010.[2]

Former members of Congress, as well as former White House staff, are often recruited by various lobbying firms to look out for the interests of major corporations. Their connections and expertise are considered key to generating results for their employers—and they are paid accordingly, in the range of $300,000 to $600,000 a year. In 2007, following a series of lobbying scandals, new congressional rules for the lobbying of Congress banned ex-members from employment in lobbying firms until a year after leaving office. But even this short "cooling-off" period was circumvented when many former lawmakers worked as consultants or advisors until they became full-time lobbyists when the year was done. In 2009, the Center for Responsive Politics identified 129 former members of Congress as active lobbyists (Center for Responsive Politics 2010a).

The SEC's May 2010 proposal will be a good test of the commission's—and the federal government's—commitment to financial reform. This proposal suggests a series of rules tightening up "Regulation AB," the 2004 rule specifying the information that issuers of asset-backed securities—including the disastrous mortgage securities pools—must provide to investors. The "enablers" of Wall Street had been able to circumvent Regulation AB by issuing one omnibus disclosure statement, then hiding the details of a number of mortgage pools underneath. If rating agencies gave the initial "shelf registration" a top rating, it rendered invisible the possibly dodgy mortgages hidden under its umbrella in subsequent mortgage pools. The SEC proposal aimed to close this loophole by requiring issuers to provide detailed data on all the assets covered by the initial disclosure. And it increases transparency by requiring issuers to provide computer access to the day-by-day performance of their funds (Morgenson 2010a). The SEC solicited "comments" from its "stakeholders" from May to August 2010. Will the proposal emerge intact, and will the SEC be able to follow through when the armies of lobbyists—with their impressive links to key senators and members of Congress—have finished their work?[3]

Technological Resources of the Regulated

In a world with fully digitized trading, where electronic stock surveillance networks have largely supplanted the trading floor, the largest financial actors—in the United States, primarily Wall Street firms—are constantly "innovating," looking for new ways to secure advantages over other traders and investors (and regulators). Smart Routers, combined with algorithms, increase the speed at which trades can be made: through constant, real-time monitoring of market metrics, feedback from market activity, and historic research, they assess price, current and historical liquidity, speed, and stability in order to determine where an order should be placed. In the quest to maximize profits, the firms with the deepest pockets are best positioned to purchase the latest, fastest trading software and the human capital needed to program it. Wall Street firms pay millions of dollars to recruit and retain those equipped to develop the "magical" algorithms that lay the billion-dollar eggs.

Indeed, a recent lawsuit reveals that over the last 7 years, the two top programmers at one firm, Citadel Investment Group, collected tens of millions of dollars in salary and bonuses (Berenson 2009).

In a business where time really does mean money, having the fastest, most complex algorithms provides a huge competitive advantage, since firms can make millions in microseconds from high-volume trades. Thus, each strives to complete its trades, reap the profits, and move on before another firm's algorithms can detect and exploit the same patterns in the market. Some have even gone so far as to co-locate their hardware, that is, to physically locate their hardware closer to the exchanges to decrease the amount of time it takes for trade signals to travel to and from them (Gehm 2010).

High Frequency Trading (HFT) takes algorithmic trading one step further. It combines real-time market data, giving privileged access to pricing information, with particular algorithms that allows traders to buy and sell so quickly and in such quantities that while they may make only pennies per trade, the aggregated profits are huge.[4] Powerful computers, looking for "statistical patterns and pricing anomalies," allow investors to execute millions of orders per second and instantly spot trends within various stock exchanges. This lets the surveillance algorithm probe for the maximum and minimum price a seller or buyer would accept for any given share. Then, in less than a millisecond, automated HFT programs issue millions of buy or sell orders. These "flash orders" happen so quickly that human investors are completely unaware they have occurred. Analysts estimate that such transactions accounted for $21 billion in profits in 2008 alone (the amounts are expected to quintuple in the coming year) and account for over 70 percent of all stock market trading today (Duhigg 2009; Kaufman 2009).

"Market timing" is yet another variant. It occurs when fund managers take advantage of different closing hours or price discrepancies between markets in different parts of the world by quickly buying and selling fund shares. This is often done with mutual funds, the investment vehicle of choice for the small retail investor, unbeknownst to the shopkeepers and pensioners whose savings are tied up in it. Market timing is legal but only when all shareholders have equal opportunities to benefit from it. This is apparently not the case: The benefits of such trades are typically available only to favored insiders with massive portfolios, such as professional money managers and hedge fund executives.

This strategy has also been employed against mutual and pension fund managers, by traders attempting to discover the algorithms they employ, figure out the next big stock purchase they will make, and "front-run" them by scooping up that stock at a lower price and selling it back to the fund at a higher one. As a former NASDAQ vice president put it, these "high frequency bandits" "pump up volume statistics, front-run investor orders, increase transaction costs, and hurt real liquidity" (Lavin 2010, 22; Urstadt 2010).

These algorithmically enabled devices create a two-tiered financial market—one for insiders with access to sophisticated, expensive, up-to-the-minute computers and programmers and another for the average investor whose orders are completed merely as an "afterthought" (Kaufman 2009). High-frequency traders "essentially bully slower investors into giving up profits, and then disappear before anyone even knows they were there" (Duhigg 2009). More serious consequences occur when automated HFT triggers new financial disasters (Salkever 2009) with attendant social harm to smaller and weaker sectors, institutions, and countries. With algorithmic trading constantly increasing the size, speed, and number of trades, and with so many funds traded simultaneously, the speed of trading can become too fast for the computerized system to handle—resulting in both a system and a market crash. As Bernard Donefer notes: "the speed of these equations and their ability to reach so many markets simultaneously could turn even a minor coding error into a spiralling disaster" (Lavin 2010, 22).

The infamous Black Monday, October 18, 1987, when billions of dollars disappeared in the blink of an eye and stocks plunged 22 percent, was an early manifestation of the dangers of automated trading. Automatic market shutdowns were put in place at that time, but on May 6, 2009, an automated cascading effect associated with HFT algorithms caused the Dow Jones to plunge precipitously once again, shaking investor confidence worldwide (Doering and Rampton 2010).

Dark pools are another technologically enabled practice. Here, bundles of shares that allow the largest institutions to trade almost exclusively with one another are put together or "bundled," both to conceal large volume trades from the open market and to temper rapid swings in share prices. These technological applications help trading firms block the regulators' gaze. The absence of visibility and transparency means these markets operate in what are being called dark pools.

But those designed as "truly dark" prevent information leakages by denying entry of orders that are seeking information to trade on, thus allowing "trajectory crossing," an event that gives two opposite algorithmic orders an average price throughout their overlapping time period. "By delivering average pricing over an interval, trajectory crossing helps prevent negative selection and opportunity costs that can occur in gray pools" (Morgan Stanley 2010).[5] Dark pools have expanded from 1.5 percent to 12 percent of all market trades in under 5 years and they too are expected to expand exponentially (Kaufman 2009).

Conclusion

The social harm that an out-of-control financial system can visit upon the world was dramatically illustrated in the 2008 crisis. What potential controls can national governments and international law exert? Where are regulators in the United States, home of financial capitalism and still its dominant economic player? Two short answers: They are worried and outmatched, technologically unable to keep up; and they are fiscally unable to compete (Ministry of Finance 2010).

It is recognized, even amongst themselves, that regulators do not possess the resources to keep up with the financial institutions they regulate. The SEC was seeking a budget increase from $1.119 billion to $1.26 billion for 2011, along with the power to fund itself rather than rely on funding from the Treasury. Yet its requests were making little headway with legislators who believe the SEC should not be "rewarded" with more powers after having demonstrated its inability to prevent the financial crisis (Goldfarb 2010). The SEC has created a Division of Risk, Strategy, and Financial Innovation, a division it hopes will develop a high-tech tagging system able to monitor and track algorithmic trades (Lavin 2010). But access to the technological advances that are (re-)structuring the vast field of finance capital accumulation is wildly disproportionate.

Can any government agency pay programmers the million-dollar salaries they now enjoy? The chair of the SEC, by comparison, earns $158,500 a year, while SEC employees' salaries average $135,099 per year, ranging from $22,000 for clerk assistants to $222,000 for securities compliance examiners, economists, lawyers, accountants, and IT management (glassdoor.com; jobnob.com; usajobs.gov).

Can any agency upgrade its technology on a monthly or daily basis? Obviously not. Agencies that attempt to control the behavior of the financial sector, the most privileged actors in the world, have been and are still funded minimally and reluctantly. The definition of "adequate" funding varies by time and nation. Regulatory budgets have increased over time, but salaries and resources have never come close to those paid by the industry they regulate (which is, of course, why the "revolving door" tends to revolve in only one direction). While every technology is biased by its embedded defaults and assumptions, and no one yet knows the vulnerabilities of algorithmic trading, the potential for controlling it in ways that reflect a general public interest appear small. The algorithms of HFT are specifically designed to serve the institutional agendas of financial insiders, players with the institutional and cultural resources to benefit from them.

The main beneficiaries in this instance are the powerful Wall Street institutions that specialize in the highly secretive and sought-after HFT algorithmic codes. One such firm is Goldman Sachs—and, not coincidentally, it is among those who are lobbying against government oversight of HFT (Doering and Rampton 2010).

For those who would like to prevent the next crisis, or at least lessen its impact, the weakness of regulatory agencies vis-à-vis the world's most powerful economic actors is discouraging. The potential for international bodies to rein in the engines of financial capitalism is unknown. Thus it is tempting to conclude, along with U.S. Senator Ted Kaufman (D-Del), that "the stock markets have . . . become so highly fragmented that they are . . . beyond the scope of effective surveillance" (Kaufman 2009).

Notes

1. And they offer new ammunition for free marketers to decry government "red tape."

2. The top lobbying firm between 1998 and 2010 was Patton Boggs LLP, which spent $373.5 million between 1998 and 2010 (Center for Responsive Politics 2010c).

3. The SEC's May 2010 proposal will be a good test of the commission's—and the federal government's—commitment to financial reform. This proposal suggested a series of rules tightening up "Regulation AB," the 2004 rule specifying the information that issuers of asset-backed securities—including the disastrous mortgage securities pools—must provide to investors. In the past, the "enablers" of Wall Street were able to circumvent Regulation AB by issuing one omnibus disclosure statement, then hiding the details of a number of mortgage pools underneath. If rating agencies gave the initial "shelf registration" a top rating, it rendered invisible the possibly dodgy mortgages hidden under its umbrella in subsequent mortgage pools. The SEC proposal aimed to close this loophole by requiring issuers to provide detailed data on all the assets covered by the initial disclosure.

And it increased transparency by requiring issuers to provide computer access to the day-by-day performance of their funds (Morgenson 2010a). The SEC solicited "comments" from its "stakeholders" from May to August 2010 and pressure from Wall Street's armies of lobbyists—with their impressive links to key senators and members of Congress—has been unrelenting. As of this writing (February 2012), the SEC has made two appointments and set up two of the promised agencies, the Office of the Whistleblower Office in August 2011, and the Office of Minority and Women Inclusion in January 2012, and begun advertising for Directors for the Office of Investor Advocate, the Office of Municipal Securities and the Office of Credit Ratings. It is obviously too early to gauge whether the new agencies will be any more successful in resisting the pressure of Big Money than their predecessors, and since 2012 is an election year, they may all be eliminated should the Republicans win in November.

4. HFT is mostly powered through the hardware of Intel, AMD, and NVIDIA, the same technology that is used for video gaming (Stokes 2009).

5. HFT and "dark pools" are part of the broader context of financialization, a way of recuperating value despite falling markets. Technologies such as HFT (along with public bailout money) help to explain how Goldman Sachs has been able to post impressive profits after the crisis.

References

Anderson, Jenny. 2005. "15 Specialists from Big Board Are Indicted." *International Herald Tribune*, April 13, C2.

Ball, Kirstie, and David Wilson. 2000. "Power, Control and Computer-Based Performance Monitoring: Repertoires, Resistance and Subjectivities." *Organization Studies* 21 (2): 539–65.

Banks, Erik. 2004. *The Failure of Wall Street: How and Why Wall Street Fails—And What Can Be Done About It*. New York: Palgrave Macmillan.

Berenson, Alex. 2009. "Arrest over Software Illuminates Wall St. Secret." *New York Times*, August 23, A1. http://www.nytimes.com/2009/08/24/business/24trad ing.html?_r=2&ref=citadel_investment_group (accessed August 18, 2010).

Braithwaite, John. 1989. *Crime, Shame, and Reintegration*. Cambridge: Cambridge University Press.

———. 2005. *Markets in Vice, Markets in Virtue*. Annandale, Australia: Federation Press.

Brown, Philip, and Peter Goldschmidt. 1996. "ALCOD IDSS: Assisting the Australian Stock Market Surveillance Team's Review Process." *Applied Artificial Intelligence* 10 (6): 625–42.

Calavita, Kitty, Henry Pontell, and Robert Tillman. 1997. *Big Money Crime*. Berkeley: University of California Press.

Center for Responsive Politics. 2010a. "Former Members Turned Lobbyists." Washington D.C.: Center for Responsive Politics. http://www.opensecrets.org /lobby/top.php?indexType=l (accessed August 13, 2010).

————. 2010b. "Lobbying Database." Washington D.C.: Center for Responsive Politics. http://www.opensecrets.org/lobby/index.php (accessed August 13, 2010).

————. 2010c. "Top Lobbying Firms." Washington D.C.: Center for Responsive Politics. http://www.opensecrets.org/revolving/index.php (accessed August 13, 2010).

Coleman, James W. 1989. *The Criminal Elite*. New York: St. Martin's Press.

Committee on Financial Services. 2010. "Brief Summary of the Dodd-Frank Wall Street Reform and Consumer Protection Act." Washington, D.C.: Committee on Financial Services. http://banking.senate.gov/public/_files/070110_Dodd_Frank_Wall_Street_Reform_comprehensive_summary_Final.pdf (accessed August 13, 2010).

Deetz, Stanley. 1992. "Disciplinary Power in the Modern Corporation." In *Critical Management Studies*, edited by Mats Alvesson and Hugh Willmott, 21–45. London: Sage.

Dodd-Frank Wall Street Reform and Consumer Protection Act. 124 Stat. 1376 (2010).

Doering, Christopher, and Roberta Rampton. 2010. "CFTC Weighs Crack-Down on High-Frequency Trades." *Reuters*, July 13. http://www.reuters.com/article/idUSTRE66C6A220100713 (accessed September 13, 2010).

Duhigg, Charles. 2009. "Stock Traders Find Speed Pays, in Milliseconds." *International Herald Tribune*, July 23, A1.

Financial Industry Regulatory Authority (FINRA). 2010. "About the Financial Industry Regulatory Authority." http://www.finra.org/AboutFINRA (accessed May 11, 2010).

Garland, David. 2001. *The Culture of Control: Crime and Social Order in Contemporary Society*. Chicago: University of Chicago Press.

Garnaut, Ross. 2009. *The Great Crash of 2008*. Carlton, Australia: Melbourne University Press.

Gehm, Fred. 2010. "The Lowdown on High Frequency Trading." *Futures*, May, 58–60.

Geisst, Charles R. 2004. *Wall Street: A History from Its Beginnings to the Fall of Enron*. New York: Oxford University Press.

Goldfarb, Zachary A. 2010. "Citing Goldman Sachs Suit, Schapiro Seeks 12% Budget Hike for SEC." *Washington Post*, April 28. http://www.washingtonpost.com/wp-dyn/content/article/2010/04/28/AR2010042805383.html (accessed September 23, 2010).

Goldman Sachs. 2009. *Annual Report 2009*. New York: Goldman Sachs.

Goldstein, Matthew. 2010. "Philadelphia, Where Rogue Traders Dare Not Tread." *Reuters*, February 19. http://www.reuters.com/article/idUSTRE61I39K20100219 (accessed May 1, 2010).

Gramm, Phil. 1999. "Senate Approves Gramm-Leach-Bliley Act: Vote Paves Way for Financial Services Modernization." Washington, D.C.: U.S. Senate Committee on Banking, Housing and Urban Affairs. http://banking.senate.gov/prel99/1104grm.htm (accessed October 25, 2010).

Haines, Fiona, and Andrew Sutton. 2003. "A Sociological Perspective on Juridification and Regulation." *Crime, Law and Social Change* 39:1–22.

Jackson, Howell, and Stavros Gadinis. 2007. "Markets as Regulators: A Survey." Harvard Law School John M. Olin Center for Law, Economics, and Business Discussion Paper #579: 3–81. http://lsr.nellco.org/harvard/olin/papers.

Karpati, Bruce, Robert Kaplan, Daniel Hawke, Kenneth Lench, Cheryl Scarboro, Elaine Greenberg, and Thomas Sporkin. 2010. "Speech by SEC Staff: Remarks at News Conference Announcing Leaders in Enforcement Division." Washington D.C.: U. S. Securities and Exchange Commission. http://www.sec.gov/news/speech/2010/spch011310newsconf.htm (accessed May 1, 2010).

Kaufman, Ted. 2009. "Breaking Wall Street's Boom, Bailout Cycle." *Huffington Post*, November 6. http://www.huffingtonpost.com/sen-ted-kaufman/breaking-wall-streets-boo_b_348494.html (accessed May 18, 2010).

Kirkland, J. Dale, Ted Senator, James J. Hayden, Tomasz Dybala, Henry G. Goldberg, and Ping Shyr. 1999. "The NASD Regulation Advanced-Detection System (ADS)." *AI Magazine* 20 (1): 55–68.

Lavin, Timothy. 2010. "Monsters in the Market." *Atlantic*, July/August, 21–22.

Lichtblau, Eric. 2010. "Ex-Regulators Get Set to Lobby on New Financial Rules." *New York Times*, July 27. http://www.nytimes.com/2010/07/28/business/28lobby.html?adxnnl=1&adxnnlx=1307041725–9HN/39ma+kx3yzzkQQ2fow.

McBarnet, Doreen. 2004. "After Enron: Governing the Corporation, Mapping the Loci of Power in Corporate Governance Design." In *Governing the Corporation: Regulation and Corporate Governance in an Age of Scandal and Global Markets*, edited by Justin O'Brien, 89–111. London: Wiley.

Ministry of Finance. 2010. "Public Sector Salary Disclosure 2010 (Disclosure for 2009): Crown Agencies." Toronto, ON: Ministry of Finance. http://www.fin.gov.on.ca/en/publications/salarydisclosure/2010/crown10.html (accessed August 26, 2010).

Morgan Stanley. 2010. "Dark Pools." http://www.morganstanley.com/institutional/sales/electronic_trading_products_darkpool.html.

Morgenson, Gretchen. 2010a. "BB? AAA? Disclosure Tells Us More." *New York Times*, September 5, B1.

———. 2010b. "It's Not Over Until It's in the Rules." *New York Times*, August 29, B1.

New York Stock Exchange (NYSE). 2010. "FINRA to Perform NYSE Regulation's Market Oversight Functions." New York: New York Stock Exchange Euronext. http://www.nyse.com/press/1272880693677.html (accessed May 23, 2010).

Ojo, Marianne. 2009. "Basel II and the Capital Requirements Directive: Responding to the 2008/09 Financial Crisis." http://ssrn.com/abstract=1475189.

Pearce, Frank, and Steve Tombs. 1998. *Toxic Capitalism: Corporate Crime and the Chemical Industry*. Aldershot, UK: Ashgate.

Reinhart, Carmen M., and Kenneth S. Rogoff. 2009. *This Time Is Different: Eight Centuries of Financial Folly*. Princeton, N.J.: Princeton University Press.

Roberts, John. 2003. "The Manufacture of Corporate Social Responsibility: Constructing Corporate Sensibility." *Organization* 10 (2): 249–65.

Rosoff, Stephen M., Henry N. Pontell, and Robert H. Tillman. 2004. *Profit Without Honor: White-Collar Crime and the Looting of America,* third edition. Upper Saddle River, N.J.: Pearson Prentice Hall.

Salkever, Alex. 2009. "Wall Street Ripoff 2.0: High Speed Trading and Deep, Dark Pools." *Daily Finance.* http://www.dailyfinance.com/story/investing/wall -street-ripoff-2-0-high-speed-trading-and-deep-dark-pools/19116311/ (accessed September 15, 2010).

Securities and Exchange Commission (SEC). 2005. "SEC Charges the New York Stock Exchange with Failing to Police Specialists." Washington D.C.: U.S. Securities and Exchange Commission. http://www.sec.gov/news/press/2005-53 .htm (accessed May 1, 2010).

———. 2009. "Order Amending Order Instituting Public Administrative Proceedings Pursuant to Sections 19(H)(1) and 21c of the Securities Exchange Act Of 1934, Making Findings, Ordering Compliance with Undertakings, and Imposing a Censure and a Cease-and-Desist Order." Washington, D.C.: Securities and Exchange Commission. http://www.sec.gov/litigation/admin/2009/34- 60391.pdf (accessed May 1, 2010).

Sewell, Graham. 1998. "The Discipline of Teams: The Control of Team-Based Industrial Work Through Electronic and Peer Surveillance." *Administrative Science Quarterly* 43 (2): 397–428.

Sewell, Graham, and Barry Wilkinson. 1992. "Someone to Watch over Me: Surveillance and Discipline and the JIT Labour Process." *Sociology* 26 (2): 271–89.

Shamir, Ronen. 2008. "The Age of Responsibilization: On Market-Embedded Morality." *Economy and Society* 37 (1): 1–19.

Shapiro, Susan. 1984. *Wayward Capitalists: Target of the Securities and Exchange Commission.* New Haven, Conn.: Yale University Press.

———. 1990. "Collaring the Crime, Not the Criminal: Reconsidering the Concept of White-Collar Crime." *American Sociological Review* 55 (3): 346–65.

Smart, Barry. 1992. *Modern Conditions, Postmodern Controversies.* London: Routledge.

Snider, Laureen. 1993. *Bad Business.* Scarborough, ON: Nelson Canada.

———. 2003. "Resisting Neo-Liberalism: The Poisoned Water Disaster in Walkerton, Ontario." *Social and Legal Studies,* 5 (2): 27–47.

———. 2009. "Accommodating Power: The Common Sense of Regulators." *Social & Legal Studies* 18 (2): 179–97.

Stokes, Jon. 2009. "The Matrix, but with Money: The World of High-Speed Trading." *Ars Technica,* July 27. http://arstechnica.com/tech-policy/news/2009/07 /-it-sounds-like-something.ars (accessed September 15, 2010).

Stuckler, David, and Sanjay Basu. 2009. "The International Monetary Fund's Effects on Global Health: Before and After the 2008 Financial Crisis." *International Journal of Health Services* 39 (4): 771–81.

"Times Topics: Bureau of Consumer Financial Protection." 2010. *New York Times,* September 17. http://topics.nytimes.com/top/reference/timestopics/organiza tions/c/consumer_financial_protection_bureau/index.html?inline=nyt-org (accessed October 25, 2010).

Urstadt, Bryant. 2010. "Trading Shares in Milliseconds." *Technology Review* 113 (1): 44–49.

U.S. Congress Office of Technology Assessment. 1987. *The Electronic Supervisor: New Technologies, New Tensions.* Washington D.C.: U.S. Congress Office of Technology Assessment.

U.S. Senate Committee on Banking, Housing and Urban Affairs. 2010. "Summary: Restoring American Financial Stability." Washington, D.C.: U.S. Senate Committee on Banking, Housing and Urban Affairs. http://banking.senate.gov/public/_files/FinancialReformDiscussionDraft111009.pdf (accessed August 13, 2010).

Williams, James. 2009. "Envisioning Financial Disorder: Financial Surveillance and the Securities Industry." *Economy & Society* 38 (3): 460–91.

[9]

WHY CEOS ARE ABLE TO LOOT WITH IMPUNITY—AND WHY IT MATTERS

WILLIAM K. BLACK

The defining characteristic of crony capitalism is the ability of favored elites to loot with impunity (and be bailed out). Crony capitalism drives honest competitors from the market, makes democracy fail, and causes recurrent, intensifying financial crises (Akerlof 1970; Akerlof and Romer 1993; Black 2007; Black, Calavita, and Pontell 1995; National Commission on Financial Institution Reform, Recovery and Enforcement 1993; Pierce 1994).

Savings and loan regulators learned the unique advantages of criminal prosecutions in the 1980s. In the Texas "Rent-a-Bank" scandal of the 1970s, two ringleaders—Herman K. Beebe and George Aubin—created a fraud network of fifty lenders that caused billions of dollars of losses (Black 2005).[1] Although the regulators removed and prohibited one of the ring-leaders of the Rent-a-Bank network from working in the savings and loan (S&L) industry, because the frauds were not prosecuted the ringleaders reappeared in the 1980s to create an even larger fraud network. Unless their ringleaders are convicted and imprisoned, sophisticated financial frauds grow ever more destructive. Both of the "Rent-a-Bank" ringleaders were later convicted of crimes they committed in the 1980s, but by then they had cost investors an additional $20 billion (GAO 1993).

The Federal Home Loan Bank Board, the agency for whom I worked during the 1980s, made closing fraudulent S&Ls and prosecuting the elite frauds our highest priorities. We made over 30,000 criminal referrals and helped the Justice Department convict over 1,000 "major" S&L defendants.

We rigorously prioritized cases by creating a "Top 100" list of the worst S&Ls—roughly 700 individuals. These convictions still represent the government's greatest success against elite criminals (GAO 1993).

In 1990–1991, our agency took effective supervisory action against the leading nonprime lenders, particularly those making "liars" loans. At that time, the leading nonprime S&L lender was Long Beach Savings, run by Roland Arnall. He gave up Long Beach's federal charter and turned it into a mortgage bank (Ameriquest) to escape our jurisdiction. His leading competitor was another mortgage bank, Quality Mortgage, run by Russell M. and Rebecca M. Jedinak—whom we had removed and prohibited from working in the S&L industry. Unfortunately, the Clinton administration decision in 1993 to reallocate Justice Department resources from the S&L frauds to health care frauds resulted in thousands of S&L frauds not being convicted, including virtually all of the frauds identified in or after 1991. Ameriquest became the most notorious fraudulent and predatory lender. The nonprosecution of Arnall for his role in Long Beach Savings forfeited an opportunity to deter the creation of the mortgage fraud epidemic. If Arnall had been prosecuted for his S&L frauds, he could not have created Ameriquest. If he had been prosecuted, President George W. Bush would not have made him the U.S. ambassador to the Netherlands. If Arnall and Ameriquest had been prosecuted, Citicorp and Washington Mutual would not have acquired its fraudulent operations and personnel (Hudson 2010).

Seven senior officials of large nonprime lenders who hyperinflated the housing bubble and drove the current crisis have been convicted, all arising from an investigation of Taylor Bean & Whittaker Mortgage Corporation (Bloomberg 2011).[2] The first trial concluded in May 2011—6.5 years after the FBI warned publicly that there was an "epidemic" of mortgage fraud and predicted that it would cause a "financial crisis" if it were not contained (Black 2010; CNN 2004). Taylor Bean was a small lender in 1992 and could have then been closed with minimal losses. In early 2002, Taylor Bean began running overdrafts in its master bank account at Colonial Bank because it could not cover its operating expenses. The trial of Taylor Bean's head, Lee Farkas, occurred 9 years after his frauds were discovered. Farkas was inept, and Fannie Mae promptly caught him in multiple frauds because he double-pledged mortgages. That is an easy fraud to detect because of recordation. If Fannie Mae had filed a criminal referral, Farkas would have been prosecuted and Taylor Bean closed before it caused material losses. Instead it caused large losses. The inexcusable failure of Fannie

Mae to file criminal referrals was typical of how the current financial crisis was handled. The Federal Deposit Insurance Corporation examiners did not discover the frauds so they did not file criminal referrals. The special inspector general for the Troubled Asset Relief Program (SIGTARP) appears to have taken the lead in getting the Justice Department to prosecute. SIGTARP became involved because the conspirators sought to defraud the TARP program through a sham rescue of Colonial Bank. My former S&L regulatory agency, the Office of Thrift Supervision, made zero criminal referrals. The Office of the Comptroller of the Currency and the Federal Reserve made less than a handful. Mortgage and investment banks made only trivial numbers of referrals—and never against their senior officers. Federally insured depositories made tens of thousands of criminal referrals but not against their senior officers.

The result was that the fraudulent liars lenders committed fraud with impunity. The volume of fraud referrals by insured mortgage lenders overwhelmed the FBI (FinCEN 2009, Fitch 2007, Frontline 2009, Gimein 2008, Harney 2007, Lowry 2009, Mayer and Pence 2008, Miller 2007, Mortgage Bankers Association 2007, Pistole 2009, TRAC 2008). As late as fiscal year 2007, they had assigned only 120 FBI agents (spread in "penny packets" among fifty-six field offices) to investigate tens of thousands of criminal referrals for mortgage fraud. In contrast, 1,000 FBI agents investigated the S&L frauds—that is, over eight times the agents were assigned to a far smaller fraud epidemic than are assigned to the current crisis. Unlike in the S&L debacle, there has been no national task force and no comprehensive prioritization (Bloomberg 2007, Lichtblau 2008, Morgenson 2008). This has made it impossible to investigate huge fraudulent nonprime lenders. Since there were no criminal referrals against them, the FBI did not even attempt to investigate them.

The two great lessons from investigating epidemics of "accounting control fraud" are that if you don't look, you don't find; and that wherever you do look (competently), you do find fraud. The FBI was investigating retail, but the problem was being created wholesale. The FBI strategy was doomed to failure and was self-reinforcing. Because the FBI investigated only relatively small cases, it found only relatively small frauds. That caused then Attorney General Michael Mukasey to refuse to (1) create a national mortgage fraud task force, (2) dramatically increase the FBI resources assigned to mortgage fraud, and (3) provide meaningful staff to the FBI to investigate the huge fraudulent lenders. He dismissed mortgage fraud as equivalent to "white-collar street crime" (Litchblau 2008) and never understood that his investigative strategy ensured that the FBI would not investigate the elite frauds driving the financial crisis.

The FBI has been processing 1,000–2,000 mortgage fraud cases annually—but the best estimate is that there were over one million new fraudulent mortgage loans annually by 2006. Mukasey's strategy was equivalent to throwing handfuls of sand on a beach in San Diego into the Pacific Ocean and wondering when one would be able to walk to Hawaii.

The whole effort ended with a whimper. The FBI—deserted by the banking regulators, undercut by the Justice Department, and discouraged from investigating by Treasury Secretary Timothy Geithner—was so desperate that it formed a "partnership" with the Mortgage Bankers Association (MBA) in 2007. The MBA, as the trade association of the "perps," had created an absurd definition of mortgage fraud under which accounting control fraud by the lender is impossible and mortgage bankers are always the victims of the fraud. The FBI and the Justice Department repeated this self-serving definition endlessly and uncritically. Repeat after me: "These aren't the droids we're looking for."

George Akerlof (awarded the Nobel Prize in Economics in 2001) and Paul Romer wrote a classic article in 1993. Their title captured their findings: "Looting: The Economic Underworld of Bankruptcy for Profit." Akerlof and Romer explained how bank CEOs can use accounting fraud to create a "sure thing": guaranteed, record short-term reported income. That fictional income allows the CEO to loot the bank. The bank fails, but the CEO walks away wealthy. We've gone downhill since 1993. We now bail out the bank, leave the corrupt CEO in charge, change Generally Accepted Accounting Principles to hide the massive losses he caused, and renew his bonuses based on the ever more fictional reported income. Here's the great kicker in the accounting fraud recipe: The bank optimizes its short-term (fictional) income by making exceptionally bad quality loans at a premium yield, while providing only trivial allowances for the coming loan and lease losses (A. M. Best 2006). The same accounting fraud recipe maximizes and guarantees stellar (albeit fictional) short-term income and eventual real losses. In criminology, we call them "accounting control frauds," and we know that they destroy wealth at a prodigious rate. There is no "if" about the losses. The only questions are when they will hit, how big they will be, and who will bear them.

The record "income" explains why the accounting control frauds get away with it for years. Private markets do not "discipline" firms reporting record profits; instead they compete to fund them. Fraudulent CEOs can control the hiring and firing of all the "controls" and can create the perverse incentives that produce a "Gresham's" dynamic in which bad ethics drives good ethics out of the marketplace and the professions. Sophisticated accounting control frauds employ these perverse incentives to suborn "controls" and pervert them into allies. They do the same with loan brokers and loan officers. The result is that the large fraudulent lenders, for example, those making large amounts of liars loans, produce "echo" epidemics of fraud (Black 2010). Fraud begets fraud (or in criminology jargon: accounting control frauds are criminogenic).

Notes

1. The scandal involved the use of shills who would be funded by the conspirators so that they could acquire banks and direct loans to benefit the lead conspirators and their associates.

2. The CEO, former president, treasurer, and senior financial analyst of Taylor Bean & Whitaker, Paul R. Allen, Raymond Bowman, Desiree Brown, and Sean Ragland, respectively, and Catherine Kissick, a former senior vice president of Colonial Bank and head of its Mortgage Warehouse Lending Division, and her assistant, Teresa Kelly, pleaded guilty and testified against Lee Farkas.

References

Akerlof, George. 1970. "The Market for 'Lemons': Quality Uncertainty and the Market Mechanism." *Quarterly Journal of Economics* 84 (3): 488–500.

Akerlof, George, and Paul Romer. 1993. "Looting: The Economic Underworld of Bankruptcy for Profit." In *Brookings Papers on Economic Activity*, edited by William C. Brainard and George L. Perry, 2:1–73. Washington, D.C.: Brookings Institution Press.

A. M. Best. 2006. "U.S. Banking Trends for 2005—Signaling End of Peak Industry Cycle." http://www.ambest.com/banks/reports/ambest-bankingtrends2005 .pdf.

Black, William K. 2005. *The Best Way to Rob a Bank Is to Own One: How Corporate Executives and Politicians Looted the S&L Industry*. Austin: University of Texas.

———. 2007. "When Fragile Become Friable: Endemic Control Fraud as a Cause of Economic Stagnation and Collapse." In *White Collar Crimes: a Debate*, edited by K. Naga Srivalli. Hyderabad, India: Icfai University Press.

————. 2010. "Echo Epidemics: Control Frauds Generate 'White-Collar Street Crime Waves.'" *Criminology and Public Policy* 9 (3): 613–19.

Black, William K., Kitty Calavita, and Henry N. Pontell. 1995. "The Savings and Loan Debacle of the 1980s: White-Collar Crime or Risky Business?" *Law and Policy* 17:23–55.

Bloomberg. 2007. "Defaults on Some 'Alt A' Loans Surpass Subprime Ones." July 24. http://www.bloomberg.com/apps/news?pid=20601087&sid=aeWSvfvHw3cQ&refer=home.

————. 2011. "Ex-Taylor Bean Chairman Farkas Found Guilty on All 14 Counts in Fraud Case." April 19. http://www.bloomberg.com/news/2011-04-19/ex-taylor-bean-chairman-convicted-of-conspiracy-fraud-1-.html.

CNN. 2004. "FBI Warns of Mortgage Fraud 'Epidemic': Seeks to Head off 'Next S&L Crisis.'" September 17. http://articles.cnn.com/2004–09–17/justice/mortgage.fraud_1_mortgage-fraud-mortgage-industry-s-l-crisis?_s=PM:LAW.

Financial Crimes Enforcement Network (FinCEN). 2009. "The SAR Activity Review." October. http://www.fincen.gov/news_room/rp/files/sar_tti_16.pdf.

Fitch. 2007. "The Impact of Poor Underwriting Practices and Fraud in Subprime RMBS Performance." November 28. http://www.mortgagebankers.org/NewsandMedia/IndustryNews/58467.htm.

Frontline. 2009. "The Warning." (Originally broadcast in October). http://www.pbs.org/wgbh/pages/frontline/warning/view/.

Gimein, Mark. 2008. "Inside the Liar's Loan: How the Mortgage Industry Nurtured Deceit." *Slate*, July 24. http://www.slate.com/id/2189576/.

Government Accounting Office. 1993. Bank and Thrift Criminal Fraud: The Federal Commitment Could Be Broadened. GAO/GGD (January) 93-48.

Harney, Kenneth R. 2007. "Appraisers Under Pressure to Inflate Values." *Washington Post*, February 3. http://www.washingtonpost.com/wp-dyn/content/article/2007/02/02/AR2007020200712.html.

Hudson, Michael W. 2010. *The Monster: How a Gang of Predatory Lenders and Wall Street Bankers Fleeced America and Spawned a Global Crisis*. New York: Times Books.

Lichtblau, Eric. 2008. "Mukasey Declines to Create a U.S. Task Force to Investigate Mortgage Fraud." *New York Times*, June 6. http://www.nytimes.com/2008/06/06/business/06justice.html.

Lowy, Martin. 2009. *Debt Spiral: How Credit Failed Capitalism*. Lecanto, Fla.: Public Policy Press.

Madigan, Patrick. 2007. "Overview of the Subprime Foreclosure Crisis." September (updated in October). http://www.iowa.gov/government/ag/latest_news/releases/sept_2007/Foreclosure_analysis.pdf.

Mayer, Chris, and Karen Pence. 2008. "Subprime Mortgages: What, Where, and to Whom?" Finance and Economics Discussion Series, Divisions of Research & Statistics and Monetary Affairs, Federal Reserve Board, Washington, D.C. www.federalreserve.gov/PUBS/FEDS/2008/200829/200829pap.pdf.

Mortgage Bankers Association. 2007. "Mortgage Fraud: Strengthening Federal and State Mortgage Fraud Prevention Efforts." http://www.mbaf.org/pdf/2007/StrengtheningFederalandStateMortgageFraudPrevention.pdf.

Miller, Tom. 2007. "Comments to the Federal Reserve Board of Governors on Adopting Regulations to Prohibit Unfair and Deceptive Acts and Practices Under the Home Ownership and Equity Protection Act (HOEPA)." August 14. http://www.iowa.gov/government/ag/latest_news/releases/aug_2007/Fed_reserve_hoepa.html.

Morgenson, Gretchen. 2008. "Fair Game: A Road Not Taken by Lenders." *New York Times*, April 6. http://www.nytimes.com/2008/04/06/business/06gret.html?scp=2&sq=mortgage+fraud&st=nyt.

National Commission on Financial Institution Reform, Recovery and Enforcement (NCFIRRE). 1993. *Origins and Causes of the S&L Debacle: A Blueprint for Reform.* A Report to the President and Congress of the United States. Washington, D.C.: Government Printing Office.

Pierce, James. 1994. "Causes of the S&L Debacle." Unpublished paper presented at the Annual Meeting of the Allied Social Sciences Association. January. Boston, MA. On file with author.

Pistole, J. 2009. "The Need for Increased Fraud Enforcement in the Wake of the Economic Downturn." Testimony before the United States Senate Committee on the Judiciary, February 11.

TRAC. 2008. "Bush Administration's Immigration Prosecutions Soar: Total of All Federal Filings Reaches New High." Syracuse University. http://trac.syr.edu/tracreports/crim/201/.

THE FAÇADE OF ENFORCEMENT

Goldman Sachs, Negotiated Prosecution, and the Politics of Blame

JUSTIN O'BRIEN

The degree of state intervention required to stabilize still-febrile capital markets in the United States has partially changed the enforcement dynamic in the prosecution of white collar crime. Exhortations by industry, backed by funded academic research, to policymakers that high levels of public and private enforcement needed to be curtailed (see, e.g., Committee on Capital Markets Regulation 2006, 32; 2007) on the grounds that a highly litigious culture threatened investor confidence, privileged overzealous enforcement, and contributed to a loss in prestige, have been demonstrated to be at best naive. In the United States, at least for now, the need for security has trumped innovation (Stiglitz 2008). The result is that the governance and accountability deficit associated with "creative enforcement" is once more back on the agenda.

Creative enforcement refers to innovative legal strategies used by prosecutors to secure corporate behavioral change (O'Brien 2007, 2009). Circumventing the necessity of going to trial, these measures often take the form of negotiated consent orders or, more problematically, deferred or nonprosecution agreements, which can include appointment of external monitors (Government Accountability Office 2009a, 2009b). Using these methods to hold executives accountable under the current legal and regulatory framework remains challenging, as the civil litigation taken and subsequently settled by the SEC against Goldman Sachs makes clear (*Securities and Exchange Commission v. Goldman Sachs & Co. and Fabrice Tourre* 2010).

The SEC complaint accused Goldman Sachs of perpetrating a fraud on the market by failing to disclose that an investor with an interest in the collapse of ABACUS, a synthetic CDO securitization offering, played a central role in choosing the referent securities. The former investment bank paid a record $550 million fine to settle the litigation. In addition, it committed to remedial corporate governance reform, including the redefinition of "the role and responsibilities of internal legal counsel, compliance personnel, and outside counsel in the review of written marketing materials for such offerings." The settlement also requires "additional education and training of Goldman employees in this area of the firm's business" (SEC 2010a). The SEC's director of enforcement, Robert Khuzami, claimed that the settlement sent "a stark lesson to Wall Street firms that no product is too complex, and no investor too sophisticated, to avoid a heavy price if a firm violates the fundamental principles of honest treatment and fair dealing" (SEC 2010a).

There can be no mistaking the rhetorical flair of the SEC nor its capacity to reinvent itself as a model regulator. But it remains an open question whether the management of the Goldman Sachs case—or indeed the agency's general approach to enforcement—presents evidence of the possibility of substantive change in either the internal governance or external policing of Wall Street. The SEC, for example, declined to appoint an external monitor. The relative leniency shown to Goldman Sachs stands in sharp contrast to the more aggressive approach taken by the U.S. Department of Justice in recent negotiated prosecutions in the corporate sector, for example, the settlement reached with KPMG over the accounting firm's misuse of abusive tax shelters (Government Accountability Office 2009b). This reflects, in part, the SEC's cognizance of ongoing academic criticism that the mechanism risks "over-powering prosecutorial" privilege (O'Brien 2006; Zierdt and Podgor 2007, 4). At the same time, however, the rush to settle may create the illusion of justice. U.S. District Judge (Southern District of New York) Jed S. Rakoff warned that the SEC's general rush to settle rather than litigate to a conclusion white collar fraud cases risked privileging "the facade of enforcement" (Appelbaum 2010; *Securities and Exchange Commission v. Bank of America* 2010).[1]

This judicial skepticism plays into a growing belief that the operation of investment banks, particularly in the CDO market—and its corollary, the credit default swap—was and remains inherently skewed in favor of those who are packaging complex financial products (Borio 2009).

Simultaneously, institutional investors have long recognized that the protection of legitimate self-interest requires the threat of private enforcement action, notwithstanding the Committee on Capital Markets' analysis, which was funded, in part, by those who are under investigation for governance failures. This imperative is reflected in two outstanding cases taken against the storied Wall Street firm.

Basis Capital, a Cayman Island–registered hedge fund, accused Goldman Sachs of misrepresenting the risk associated with Timberwolf, a CDO described by a Goldman executive—somewhat earthily—as "one shitty deal" (*Basis Yield Alpha Fund v. Goldman Sachs* 2010).[2] The United States District court declined to hear the case as the transactions took place outside the jurisdiction, prompting Basis to refile in February 2012 in the New York State Supreme Court claiming common law fraud. And in *Liberty Mutual v. Goldman Sachs* (2010), the Boston-based insurer Liberty Mutual alleged that Goldman Sachs deliberately underplayed the risks associated with underwriting Fannie Mae, the government-sponsored enterprise charged with providing liquidity to the U.S. housing and mortgage market.[3] The bank strenuously denied the allegations in both cases.

Goldman Sachs is not alone in facing private litigation risk arising from the operation of the CDO market. Cases filed against Credit Suisse, Merrill Lynch, UBS, and Deutsche Bank, whose general counsel for the Americas at the time is now director of enforcement at the SEC, point to significant ethical shortcomings and potential illegalities in the management of conflicts of interest across the entire industry (Morgenson 2010; see also Federal Home Loan Bank of San Francisco 2009, 2010). More troubling for the securities industry, the private litigation coincides with renewed congressional interest in imposing fiduciary standards on the industry (Senate Committee on the Judiciary Hearing 2010).

The Wall Street Reform and Consumer Protection Act of 2010 (section 913) authorizes the SEC to generate uniform fiduciary obligations to retail investors for broker-dealers and investment advisors. At the policy level, whether the bifurcation between retail and sophisticated investors should remain intact remains one of the most controversial issues in regulatory politics (Herbert 2009). In addition, Dodd-Frank mandated the Government Accountability Office (GAO) to assess whether the private prosecution of secondary actors accused of aiding and abetting securities fraud should be allowed. Its even-handed cost-benefit analysis focused on three key factors—deterring fraud, compensating investors, and the effect on the economy (GAO 2011, 37–44). Significantly, the GAO presented Congress with a road map for mitigating the risk of imposing such a liability through the imposition of liability ceilings (GAO 2011, 44–45). The potential salience of this reform is hard to overestimate. It has the potential to reverse legislative restrictions on those authorized to bring enforcement action. It would amend the Private Securities Litigation Act of 1995, the passage of which was widely seen as a significant victory for the securities industry (Partnoy 2003). It could also void Supreme Court precedent (*Central Bank of Denver v. First Interstate Bank* 1994; and, more recently, *Stoneridge Investment Partners, LLC v. Scientific-Atlanta, Inc.* 2008).[4] As a consequence, Wall Street is more exposed than at any time since the crisis metastasized following the collapse of Lehman Brothers in September 2008.

This chapter examines the interlinked securities fraud cases and their impact on the dynamics of regulatory reform. First, the demonstration effect of the staging itself on the political debate is explored. Second, the policy implications of privileging creative enforcement are evaluated via an extended case-study analysis of the Goldman Sachs litigation. Third, the chapter assesses whether the introduction of a specific legislative fiduciary duty that applies to all investors could provide a more stable policy framework than the staging of what amounts to retrospective prosecution (i.e., cases brought for offenses that were not explicitly proscribed at the time they were committed).

Taking on the Street

When taking enforcement action, regulatory agencies need to balance the effect of conviction with the political costs associated with bringing complex and uncertain cases to trial.[5] Beyond the merits of an individual action, achieving wider demonstration effect requires changing both the content and context of the underpinning regulatory regime, which has been defined nicely as the "complex of institutional (physical and social) geography, rules, practice and animating ideas that are associated with the regulation of a particular risk or hazard" (Hood, Rothstein, and Baldwin 2001, 8).

First, the preparation of the case and its subsequent staging—including the critical initial presentation of the evidential base—needs to reconfigure media representations of what constitutes acceptable conduct. This applies despite the legal strength of the material claim. Irrespective of the domain, trial strategies tend to focus on competing (if partially understood) narratives, one of which gains media traction (Cassidy 2010, 21; Malcolm 2010, 36). It is, therefore, essential to "own" the media agenda. Second, the litigation needs to be capable of recalibrating—without credible dissension—the broader policy agenda. The very fact of prosecution can endorse, justify, and legitimize agency interpretation of legal and regulatory authority. To be successful, therefore, prosecutorial strategies need to facilitate the positive framing of policy issues around not only the regulator's own conception of its interpretation of appropriate purpose and accountability but also broader societal understandings, which are intermediated through media narratives (Nash 2006). This coupling is essential to ensure that neither judicial failure nor premature settlement will translate into an incremental erosion of wider support for the legitimacy of the regulator's operational imperatives. Judge Rakoff's concern about the terms of the settlement in the case brought by the SEC against Bank of America over the nondisclosure of agreements to pay bonuses to Merrill Lynch executives (*Securities and Exchange Commission v. Bank of America* 2010) suggests that the reputational risks associated by the failure to manage this process can be substantial.[6]

These interlinked factors were all too evident in the litigation brought by the SEC against Goldman Sachs. Moreover, there was a striking similarity between the media management of this case and those prosecuted by former New York State Attorney General Eliot Spitzer over conflicts of interest in analyst research in the aftermath of the Enron and WorldCom accounting scandals. For Spitzer, the veracity of the legal claim was always less important than the staging of the litigation and its impact on broader policy goals, as well as his own political self-interest (Macey 2004; O'Brien 2005; Walha and Filusch 2005). Spitzer gambled correctly that the sweeping powers afforded to the New York attorney general through the New York Business Law of 1921 (sections 352–353), otherwise known as the "Martin Act," shifted the risk calculus in favor of the state. The law gives the state attorney general unparalleled investigative capacity to probe activities that could be detrimental to the well-being of the state. Until Spitzer's application, the law was rarely used to investigate financial services (although his strategy was replicated by his successor as both state attorney general and governor, Andrew Cuomo). Given the dominance of New York City as a financial center, Spitzer and, indeed, Cuomo were able to use the law to highlight the manner in which Wall Street actually operated. Embarrassed at the time by Spitzer's recurring efforts to set his own policies, and by the political firestorm that accompanied revelations that Wall Street practices had not in fact changed in the intervening period (thus allowing Cuomo to enter into the enforcement arena), the SEC was determined to take a much more aggressive approach. Despite the risk that it could be accused of adventurism by taking the case against Goldman Sachs, the divided and wary federal commission opted to chance litigation failure.

The strategic calculation for both the SEC and Goldman Sachs lay in the reputational implications of proceeding to trial. For the SEC, the risk that a jury would find that Goldman Sachs was following accepted, albeit flawed, rules of the game needed to be balanced with rising public and political pressure to hold the banking sector to account. Along with other regulatory agencies, the SEC had been criticized by President Barack Obama (2009) for its prior failure to police Wall Street. Indeed, regulatory capture plays a central part in the narrative constructed by the Financial Crisis Inquiry Commission (2011). For Goldman Sachs, protesting innocence on technical grounds risked exacerbating reputational damage in the short-term. The bank, like the rest of Wall Street, was also cognizant that to protest its innocence on technical grounds would aid those legislators pressing for enhanced financial oversight. Neither party to the case had an interest in proceeding to trial or in a lengthy appeal procedure. The litigation is best seen, therefore, as part of a calculated bargaining process. Despite the apparent success of the SEC in forcing a $550 million settlement, it is far from clear that the SEC emerged as the winner. It may well, in time, be seen to have won the hand but lost the game.

What was perhaps most surprising about the SEC charges filed in the Southern District of New York was the failure of the bank to disclose that it had been served a Wells Notice several months earlier. A Wells Notice informs "potential defendants of the general nature of its investigation, including the indicated violations as they pertain to them, and the amount of time that may be available for preparing and submitting a statement prior to the presentation of a staff recommendation to the Commission for the commencement of an administrative or injunctive proceeding" (17 C.F.R. § 202.5(c) (2006); see also Atkins and Bondi 2008, 381–82; Naftalis 2002). Although the process is designed to be confidential, there can be no doubting its materiality. Yet Goldman Sachs made the calculated decision not to disclose the existence of the notice, nor did it provide a substantive response before the SEC's Enforcement Division sought and gained permission to proceed from a divided commission (Goldfarb 2010).

Given the exceptional market volatility, the bank's approach to investor and public relations management was uncharacteristically myopic. As a result, neither the bank nor the market was prepared for the media backlash.[7] Having lost the public relations advantage, the bank remained on the defensive. It failed to submit a substantive response (Gallu 2010; Goldman Sachs 2010a, 2010b, 2010c). Despite its protestations of innocence, proffering a legal defense that could change the media dynamic was problematic to say the least. The danger associated with an inability to control the agenda became acutely apparent as news leaked of a potential investigation into a second CDO transaction, disclosed at an exceptionally combative hearing of the Senate Permanent Committee on Investigations 11 days after the ABACUS suit was filed (Gallu and Harper 2010). The tone of the broader debate, which encapsulated the difficulties faced by the banking sector, was set by Senator Carl Levin's opening statement. He claimed that Goldman Sachs had corrupted the industry and despoiled the republic (Levin 2010).

The public stance adopted by Goldman Sachs left Senator Levin incredulous. For the bank "to go out and sell these securities to people and then bet against those same securities, it seems to me, is a fundamental conflict of interest and . . . raises a real ethical issue" (U.S. Senate 2010, 133). As a consequence, he advocated a more aggressive policing of the securitization market than the Obama administration had previously considered. Goldman Sachs's legal and reputational position was further threatened by the private litigation.

The hedge fund Basis Capital made adroit use of the emails released by the Senate, which revealed the derisive attitudes within the bank toward the creation and marketing of some CDOs (Murdoch 2010). Liberty Mutual made similar allegations of deceptive and misleading conduct in a third case filed in Massachusetts (*Liberty Mutual v. Goldman Sachs* 2010). At the heart of the Liberty claim is the allegation that a Fannie Mae offering underwritten by Goldman was presented as a mechanism to raise excess capital. Liberty claimed, with cause, that the government-sponsored enterprise was severely undercapitalized, which should have been apparent to Goldman Sachs during the due diligence process and should, therefore, have been disclosed. Liberty's litigation called into question the capacity of

Fannie Mae's internal management to achieve its stated mission to provide liquidity, stability, and affordability to the U.S. housing and mortgage markets. More problematic for Goldman Sachs, it also renewed questions about the complicity of investment banks in generating the financial crisis at precisely the same time as the horse-trading on Capitol Hill reached a denouement over the Dodd-Frank Wall Street Reform and Consumer Protection Bill.

In all three cases, Goldman Sachs emphasized the sophisticated nature of the investors (Goldman Sachs 2010c). A spokesman for the bank claimed that the Liberty case was entirely without merit, while the litigation brought by Basis was "a misguided attempt by . . . one of the world's most experienced CDO investors, to shift its investment losses to Goldman Sachs" (Gallu and Harper 2010). A similar defense was initially advanced to counter the SEC charges (Goldman Sachs 2010a, 2010b). Goldman Sachs (2010a) noted that the "SEC's complaint accuses the firm of fraud because it didn't disclose to one party of the transaction who was on the other side of that transaction." This was a further example of a case that the bank claimed was "wrong in law and fact. . . . As normal business practice, market makers do not disclose the identities of a buyer to a seller and vice versa" (Goldman Sachs 2010a). Goldman placed responsibility for picking the referent stocks on the independent rating specialist ACA, precisely because it "had the largest exposure to the transaction, investing $951 million . . . [and it] had an obligation and every incentive to select appropriate securities" (Goldman Sachs 2010a). Therefore, according to Goldman Sachs, if ACA placed inappropriate referent securities in the offering, it had not only failed in its obligation; it had also acted irresponsibly on its own account. This transference of responsibility also underpinned Goldman executives' testimony to the congressional inquiry, which had so angered Senator Levin.

The retreat to legal technicalities exacerbated the damage to Goldman's reputation. It also undermined the bank's capacity to wrest control of the media agenda. Warren Buffett, a key Goldman Sachs investor (Craig, Karnitschnig, and Lucchetti 2008) and one of the few to publicly question the SEC's case (Clark 2010), offered qualified support. Despite this, the bank recognized that stonewalling was an insufficient defense (Gallu 2010). Moreover, the Goldman CEO's notion that the firm was merely facilitating "God's work" proved unhelpful (Arlidge 2009, 4). Subsequently, Goldman Sachs announced the creation of a Business Standards Committee. It declared that the results of its review would be made public, a promise fulfilled the following year (Goldman Sachs 2011). The SEC commended both initiatives as sincere attempts by the firm to address the perceived ethical deficit (SEC 2010a). A more realistic assessment suggests that Goldman Sachs concluded that neither the case nor its prior approach was remotely winnable in the court of public opinion. Closure meant accepting that past practices had severely damaged the firm's self-proclaimed reputation for integrity and probity and that it was insufficient to merely state that practices had changed; it had to demonstrate that confidence was warranted. The creation of the Business Standards Committee provided a benchmark against which it was at least theoretically possible to judge ongoing if not past corporate behavior (Goldman Sachs 2011, 62).

Despite the firm's capitulation, the strength of the SEC's legal case is questionable. The extraction of an admission from Goldman Sachs that it was "mistaken" in its management of the conflicts of interest further raises the risk that private litigation will benefit from what amounted to retrospective prosecution. Although there are circumstances in which retrospective prosecutions can and have been defended (Woozley 1968), the danger for regulators is that when the pendulum swings back, as it inevitably will, from enforcement to a focus on facilitating the growth of financial markets, accusations of regulatory adventurism will inevitably also return (O'Brien 2006). The very fact that the SEC has implicitly accepted the retrospective nature of its litigation against Goldman poses, therefore, long-term risks for the authority and legitimacy of the regulator.

Prosecuting Ethics: The Case Against Goldman Sachs

The underlying complaint issued by the SEC against Goldman Sachs raises serious questions about whether the current legal framework can resolve ethical concerns that are not governed by explicit legal prohibition (Greenspan 1996, 2008). If integrity can be reduced to acting within the law, it is arguable that Goldman Sachs exhibited the virtue. If, however, integrity requires more than legal compliance, it is necessary to articulate with more granularity what this entails and why and to secure prior commitment to its restraining force (O'Brien 2010). What is remarkable in the SEC's statement of claim is the looseness of the language and its moral outrage. The offending trade is linked to the Structured Product Correlation Trading Desk, which was established "in late 2004/early 2005" (*Securities and Exchange Commission v. Goldman Sachs & Co. and Fabrice Tourre* 2010, 4). The SEC claims that Goldman Sachs "sought to protect and enhance this profitable franchise in a competitive market throughout the relevant period," which, curiously, is not defined (*Securities and Exchange Commission v. Goldman Sachs & Co. and Fabrice Tourre* 2010, 4). Instead, the SEC cites an (anonymous) e-mail from March 12, 2007, without providing accompanying context. The missive, sent to the Goldman Sachs Mortgage Capital Committee, claimed that "the ability to structure and execute complicated transactions to meet multiple clients' needs and objectives is key to our franchise" (*Securities and Exchange Commission v. Goldman Sachs & Co. and Fabrice Tourre* 2010, 4). Moreover, "ABACUS [the CDO] and others like it helps position Goldman aggressively in the growing market for synthetics written on structured products" (*Securities and Exchange Commission v. Goldman Sachs & Co. and Fabrice Tourre* 2010, 4).[8] Aggressive trading is not illegal, nor was the CDO market at the time of the transaction, which was increasingly dominated by short-sellers. An anonymous employee of Paulson & Co., the hedge fund that sought to create the ABACUS instrument (and which was not named as a defendant in the SEC's action), makes clear in e-mail correspondence that the creation of the synthetic CDO market was essential for those seeking to "short" residential and commercial mortgage-backed asset securities:

> Rating agencies, CDO managers and underwriters [all] have incentives to keep the game going, while real money investors have neither the analytical tools nor the institutional framework to take action before the losses that one could anticipate based [on] the "news" available everywhere are actually realized. (*Securities and Exchange Commission v. Goldman Sachs & Co. and Fabrice Tourre* 2010, 6)

It was abundantly clear to those working on the Correlation Trading Desk at Goldman Sachs that the securitization market had overheated. Fabrice Tourre, a low-level Goldman employee, was not only aware of the looming problems; he was openly incredulous at the naïveté of those still seeking exposure to long-tail risk. Writing to a friend, he said that there was "more and more leverage in the system. The whole building is about to collapse any time now. Only potential survivor, the fabulous Fab[rice Tourre] . . . standing in the middle of all these complex, highly leveraged, exotic trades he created without necessarily understanding all of the implications of those monstrosities" (*Securities and Exchange Commission v. Goldman Sachs & Co. and Fabrice Tourre* 2010, 7).[9] This raises uncomfortable questions about why regulatory agencies (and broader policy communities) were so removed from Wall Street practices that they were unable to stop (or curtail) such ethically questionable activities (Lewis 2009). It does not, however, as noted above, make these activities illegal, if, as Goldman Sachs contended, sophisticated investors could use a private placement to contract out of the general antifraud provisions of the Securities Act of 1933 (section 17a) and the Securities and Exchange Act of 1934 (section 10b).

According to the SEC, the ABACUS product was designed to fail from the outset. "Undisclosed in the marketing materials and unbeknownst to investors," the SEC said, "a large hedge fund, Paulson & Co, with economic interests directly adverse to investors in the product, played a significant role in the portfolio selection process" (*Securities and Exchange Commission v. Goldman Sachs & Co. and Fabrice Tourre* 2010, 2). The SEC noted that 83 percent of the referent securities on which the April 2007 deal was based were downgraded by October, and by January 29, 2008, 99 percent were downgraded to below investment grade. As with aggressive trading, poor performance is not illegal.

In a calculated move, the SEC adopted a narrative that suggested that an amoral culture existed within the bank. Amorality is exceptionally difficult to defend in the context of public resentment toward the actions of Wall Street. But like aggressive trading and poor performance, amorality is not illegal. Hence, a case was being built based on the bank's duplicity. Even here, there are problems given the sophistication of the investors and their willingness to opt out of the protections offered by the underpinning securities regulation architecture in the search for yield. In this regard, the trajectory of the deal at the heart of the statement of claim is particularly illuminating.

As negotiations over the creation of the ABACUS transaction continued, Tourre stressed the need to consummate the deal without delay as "the [CDO] biz is dead[;] we don't have a lot of time left" (*Securities and Exchange Commission v. Goldman Sachs & Co. and Fabrice Tourre* 2010, 270).[10] He also believed that it was necessary to choose an independent party to endorse the referent securities to provide the impression of independence. Tourre noted that not all players in the marketplace would "agree to the types of names Paulson want[s] to use" and put their "names at risk on a weak quality portfolio" (*Securities and Exchange Commission v. Goldman Sachs & Co. and Fabrice Tourre* 2010, 8).[11] An internal memorandum dated March 12, 2007, with an unidentified provenance, declares:

> [The] strong brand-name of ACA as well as our market-leading position . . . [is likely] to result in successful offering . . . [while the] role of ACA as Portfolio Agent will broaden the investor base . . . [which is designed to] target suitable structured product investors who have previously participated in ACA-managed cash-flow CDO transactions. . . . We expect to leverage ACA's credibility and franchise. (*Securities and Exchange Commission v. Goldman Sachs & Co. and Fabrice Tourre* 2010, 8)[12]

This raises the interesting but unresolved question of whether ACA was duped or willingly lent its own credibility to the transaction in return for short-term transactional advantage. The SEC's complaint offers an alternative reading of events that reinforces the latter interpretation. Paulson forwarded an initial list of 123 referent securities. The complaint notes that a series of meetings took place between ACA and Paulson, crucially, without the presence of Goldman's representatives. In an e-mail to Tourre, the ACA negotiator forwarded a list of "86 sub-prime mortgage positions that we would recommend taking exposure to synthetically. Of the 123 names that were originally submitted to us we have included only 55" (*Securities and Exchange Commission v. Goldman Sachs & Co. and Fabrice Tourre* 2010, 10).[13] ACA's admission that it had accepted, based on its own due diligence, fifty-five of the referent securities undercut the prosecution case. Similarly, no evidence was proffered of deliberate deception.

Moreover, Tourre used his appearance at the Senate hearings to deny misrepresentation in the most unequivocal terms (Tourre 2010).[14] "If ACA was confused about Paulson's role in the transaction, it had every opportunity to clarify the issue," he said. "Quite frankly, I am surprised that ACA could have believed that the Paulson fund was an equity or long investor in the deal" (Tourre 2010, 2–3). The significance of this alternative reading of events applies far beyond the contours of this specific litigation.

As noted above, the central policy issue is whether individual investors can contract out of the general antifraud provisions of the Securities Act of 1933 and the Securities and Exchange Act of 1934. If so, then the remit of the SEC is reduced as the investors are deemed to be knowledgeable enough to look after their own interests. Indeed, there is a growing international consensus that the sophisticated/unsophisticated bifurcation is both un-helpful and dangerous (Financial Services Authority 2009). If not, it raises profound questions about the limits of the freedom to contract, which re-mains the underlying rationale of corporate law in the United States and of securities market regulation throughout the common-law world. The settle-ment of the Goldman Sachs case defers for the moment a definitive judi-cial ruling. How the courts and legislature eventually determine this issue will have profound consequences for the future global governance of in-vestment banking activity.

It is in this regard that the SEC's presentation of revised rules for the governance of asset-backed securities creates future problems for the agency. The proposed rules, released while the Goldman Sachs litigation remained alive, undermined the legitimacy of its own case against the bank. They also ignited a broader normative debate about the purpose of the capital markets. In outlining the case for change, the SEC argued:

[I]nvestors have complained that the mechanisms for enforcing the representations and warranties in securitization transaction documents are weak, and thus are not confident that even strong representations and warranties provide them with adequate protection. In the private market we believe that, in many cases, investors did not have the infor-mation necessary to understand and properly analyze structured prod-ucts, such as CDOs, that were sold in transactions in reliance on exemp-tions from registration. (SEC 2010b, 12)

Such a failure to assess risk lies at the heart of the ABACUS transaction and, of course, Goldman Sachs's own defense. The ABACUS marketing materials, including the Flipbook—essentially a PowerPoint presentation—was exceptionally detailed. The contents prompted an influential *New Yorker* financial columnist to remark that they may well have said, "Don't Trust Us" (Surowiecki 2010, 25). Moreover, the materials provided by the bank supplied clear warning to potential investors about the dangers of passive reliance on the representations:

[They] contain statements that are not purely historical in nature. These include, among other things, hypothetical illustrations, sample or pro forma portfolio structures or portfolio composition, scenario analysis of returns and proposed or pro forma levels of diversification or sector investment. These hypothetical illustrations of returns illustrate a range of potential outcomes based upon certain assumptions. Such potential outcomes are not a prediction by the Issuer, Goldman Sachs, the Portfolio Selection Agent or their respective affiliates of the performance of the securities described herein. Actual events are difficult to predict and are beyond the control of the Issuer, Goldman Sachs, the Portfolio Selection Agent or their respective affiliates.

Actual events may differ from those assumed and such differences may be material. Any prior investment results or returns are presented for illustrative purposes only and are not indicative of the future returns on the securities and obligations of the Issuer. The Reference Portfolio selected by the Portfolio Selection Agent on behalf of the Issuer may differ substantially from investments made by the Portfolio Selection Agent on behalf of collateralized debt obligation funds managed by it. Meaningful comparisons between the Transaction and any prior transaction managed by the Portfolio Selection Agent (including those described herein) may be difficult. The Issuer has no operating history. In addition, there can be no assurance that any member of the senior management team of the Portfolio Selection Agent will remain with the Portfolio Selection Agent for the duration of the Transaction. (Reuters 2010)

Just as problematically for the investors (and indeed for any attempt by prosecutors to make a case based on deliberate deception), the investment bank explicitly foreclosed any fiduciary duty to act in the interests of its clients:

Goldman Sachs does not provide investment, accounting, tax or legal advice and shall not have a fiduciary relationship with any investor. In particular, Goldman Sachs does not make any representations as to (a) the suitability of purchasing Notes, (b) the appropriate accounting treatment or possible tax consequences of the Transaction or (c) the future performance of the Transaction either in absolute terms or relative to competing investments. Goldman Sachs may, by virtue of its status as an underwriter, advisor or otherwise, possess or have access to non-publicly available information relating to the Reference Obligations, the Reference Entities and/or other obligations of the Reference Entities and has not undertaken, and does not intend, to disclose such status or non-public information in connection with the Transaction. Accordingly, this presentation may not contain all information that would be material to the evaluation of the merits and risks of purchasing the Notes. Goldman Sachs is currently and may be from time to time in the future an active participant on both sides of the market and have long or short positions in, or buy and sell, securities, commodities, futures, options or other derivatives identical or related to those mentioned herein. Goldman Sachs may have potential conflicts of interest due to present or future relationships between Goldman Sachs and any Collateral, the issuer thereof, any Reference Entity or any obligation of any Reference Entity. (Reuters 2010)

The ABACUS transaction provides a salutary lesson in how incompetence and greed guided investor decision making. It also demonstrates an amoral imperative on the part of the former investment bank, which has now lost its independent status by submitting itself to federal oversight. These dual failures provide a justification for future reform but not necessarily retrospective prosecution, a point implicitly conceded by the SEC. As the agency (SEC 2010b, 22) correctly argues:

[T]he financial crisis has called into question the ability of our rules, as they relate to the private market for asset-backed securities, to ensure that investors had access to, and had sufficient time and incentives to adequately consider appropriate information regarding these securities. However, all our proposals, if adopted, would apply to new issuances of asset-backed securities. Therefore, the proposed rules, if adopted, would not impose new requirements on outstanding asset-backed securities.

These proposed rule changes also include the need to provide "basic material information concerning the structure of the securities thereon, the nature, performance and servicing of the assets supporting the securities, and any credit mechanism associated with the securities" (SEC 2010b, 273). The rule changes are, however, of limited value to investors who fail to conduct their own due diligence. The consultation document suggests clearly the retrospective nature of the Goldman prosecution. As such it also poses exceptionally difficult procedural fairness issues.

The Efficacy of Imposing a Fiduciary Duty at Law

A critical point raised during the 2010 Senate hearings was the need for investment banks to act in the interests of clients. It was suggested that this was best achieved through the imposition of specific professional duties that cannot be transacted around (Senate Committee on the Judiciary Hearing 2010). This issue was at the center of landmark proceedings taken by the Australian Securities and Investments Commission (ASIC) against Citigroup in 2006, which was adjudicated the following year. The proceedings ultimately failed because of the Australian law's silence on the capacity of investment banks to contract out of fiduciary duties. ASIC claimed that Citigroup had breached fiduciary duties to its client, Toll Holdings, by engaging in proprietary trading in a takeover target without securing Toll's prior informed consent. Although strongly sympathetic to practitioner and academic argument that the relationship between an investment bank and its client was implicitly fiduciary in nature (Tuch 2005, 509; United Kingdom Law Commission 1992, 2.4.6), Australian Federal Court Judge Peter Jacobson held that the precise relationship was determined by contractual terms (*ASIC v. Citigroup* 2007, 263–67). According to Judge Jacobson, "but for the express terms of the mandate letter, the pre-contract dealings between Citigroup and Toll would have pointed strongly toward the existence of a fiduciary relationship in Citigroup's role as an adviser" (*ASIC v. Citigroup* 2007, 325).

The decision is instructive. It reaffirmed the ability of investment banks to define the nature of their relationship with clients outside of fiduciary obligation. It also reinforced the critical importance of contractual wording, thus providing banking entities with a mechanism to manage legal risk. This in turn raises questions about whether investment banking could or should be viewed as a profession. A critical determinant of what it means to be a member of a profession is to act in the interests of the client, irrespective of contractual capacity to evade substantive obligation (United Kingdom Inter-Professional Group 2002). In providing advisory services, the professional is mandated not to take advantage of a client's (potential) lack of knowledge of contractual complexities. This is exceptionally problematic in the area of financial services both in Australia and the United States, where conflicts of interest are allowed as long as they are effectively managed and where sophisticated investors maintain a right to transact around generic investor protection.

Fiduciary obligation is, therefore, a remarkably elastic proposition. As Finn (1977, 1) makes clear, "it is meaningless to talk of [generic] fiduciary relationships as such." In determining whether a fiduciary relationship exists, context matters. The failure of the ASIC case demonstrates that in the absence of specific fiduciary duties imposed by legislation, these obligations cannot be assumed to apply through analogous reasoning. The threat of legislatively imposed fiduciary duties is designed, in part, to force the kind of behavioral change in the banking sector that creative enforcement cannot achieve. Unless and until that occurs, it is necessary to find an alternative mechanism to impose restraint. In this context, increasing the potential liability of those to whom fiduciary obligation already pertains offers a potential route forward (GAO 2011).

The SEC already had the capacity to prosecute those who "knowingly" aid and abet securities fraud (Private Securities Litigation Act of 1995, section 104). Now it has a much lower prosecutorial standard. Under the Wall Street Reform and Consumer Protection Act of 2010 (section 9290), the SEC merely has to prove that the conduct was "reckless" to succeed in prosecuting violations of the Securities Exchange Act of 1934 or the Investment Company Act of 1940. Moreover, if Congress accepts the tacit endorsement by the GAO (2011, 44–45) of factors that minimize the risk associated with giving the same right to private plaintiffs, lawyers and auditors, such as capped liability, gatekeepers will face a dramatically increased risk. Countering this risk will require professional intermediaries to demonstrate that their actions did not lead to inefficient and uninformed markets. As such, it offers an immediate restraining action.

The global financial crisis demonstrates the need for *ex ante* prevention of the factors that lead to bouts of "irrational exuberance" (Financial Crisis Inquiry Commission 2011; Greenspan 1996; Shiller 2000). It is insufficient to engage in the politics of blame without offering tangible solutions to embed integrity in market practice. What is required, therefore, is a two-stage process. First, we need to have a greater understanding of how rules and principles are interpreted within specific communities of practice. Second, we need to measure the extent to which practice correlates to or deviates from commitment to stated values, regarding the maintenance of market integrity (O'Brien 2010). This approach offers an opportunity to build organically from principles of self-regulation, but with a more clearly defined conception of business integrity. From a professional perspective, it requires recognition by the legal and audit profession, in particular, of their role as gatekeepers of market integrity. It also requires a willingness by lawyers and auditors to recognize that they are not mere "hired guns" (Carver 2005). Rather, they have a professional obligation to act in the public interest (Kronman 1995; O'Connor 1986). As Jeremy Carver (2005, 224), the former head of international law at Clifford Chance, has put it, "The lawyer cannot escape the commitments inherent in the lawyer-client relationship. It is a contractual one, placing mutual obligations and expectations on both. But the obligation to serve the interests of the client is not unqualified. It is conditioned by a set of public duties, including the duty not to misinform."

The recognition of explicit professional duties could potentially act as a restraining force within financial services. It would provide professionals with a mechanism and justification for refusing to endorse a particular course of action that, although technically legal, may reduce the integrity of the market. Indeed, this constitutive dimension now underpins the thinking of the SEC (Shapiro 2009). To be effective, however, it requires a degree of commitment by the legal and auditing profession to protect values that goes far beyond mere marketing or, indeed, beyond enhancement of public awareness of existing industry approaches to professional obligation. It requires that these communities clearly articulate their broad conception of integrity and then provide granular guidelines on how to operationalize that definition. The scale of intervention required to stabilize capital markets makes it abundantly clear that we cannot rely solely on stated reputation. Reputation has to be warranted.

The importance of securing normative improvements to market integrity underlines the fact that the ongoing transmission of cultural values is as critical to professional obligation as the dissemination of technical knowledge. There is considerable merit in such an approach. For a start, it protects narrow self-interest; that is, it minimizes the risk of conflict between professional obligation and individual corporate practice. More important, it also improves the ethical dimension of practical lawyering. Viewed in this context, professional obligation can be seen as an essential constitutive component of effective governance. What these interlocking questions also reveal is the need to situate the reform agenda within a broader debate on the nature of legitimacy.

As with all markets, capital markets are social constructions, which, to be effective, must be grounded in legitimacy as well as efficiency and competitiveness. As Amartya Sen (2010) reminds us, the answers to the challenge of building constitutive communities are to be found (in part) in rereading Adam Smith's *Theory of Moral Sentiments*. This requires building regulatory frameworks that pay appropriate attention to the need to externally validate the normative dimension, without which trust—the essential basis of exchange—can neither be developed nor sustained. Such an approach demonstrates more prudence than reliance on the illusory promise of an "invisible hand," the "politics of hope," or, more cynically, the enforcement of symbolism.

Conclusion

The decision by Goldman Sachs to establish a Business Standards Committee is a significant admission of past failure. The committee publicly reported in January 2011 on client relationships and responsibilities; conflict management; disclosure and transparency of firm-wide activities; structured products; suitability; and education, training, and business ethics (Goldman Sachs 2011). According to Goldman Sachs, the critical imperative from now on is "not just 'can we' undertake a given business activity, but 'should we?'" (Goldman Sachs 2011, 2). Ongoing evaluation offers an opportunity for the bank (and broader society) to demonstrate whether it, and by extension the investment banking sector, can introduce meaningful restraints and then use these to effectively self-police. This represents partial progress. Although the firm had a technical legal case against the SEC complaint, the ethical deficit within the investment banking industry was clearly no longer sustainable or desirable, as Goldman Sachs (2011, 62) now acknowledges.

As this chapter demonstrates, however, the imposition of direct fiduciary duties on investment banks is exceptionally problematic. The reality of proprietary trading as well as a policy framework based on the management rather than the eradication of conflicts suggests that such an imposition is unworkable. A more robust approach is obviously necessary. In this regard, proposals to enhance the responsibilities of external gatekeepers are to be welcomed. It is, perhaps, unfortunate that it takes the threat of strengthened private and public enforcement action for influential banks to take seriously their responsibility for protecting market integrity. The sad reality, however, is that without such strengthened enforcement, combined with the articulation of professional commitment to market integrity, meaningful change is unlikely to occur.

Notes

The financial support of the Australian Research Council is gratefully acknowledged ("The Future of Financial Regulation," LP100100713; and "The Limits of Disclosure," LP100200573).

1. Judge Jed Rakoff held the proposed settlement described was "a contrivance designed to provide the SEC with the facade of enforcement and the management of the Bank with a quick resolution of an embarrassing inquiry" (*Securities and Exchange Commission v. Bank of America* 2009). He reluctantly signed off on the settlement, citing judicial restraint, but stated that the settlement was "half baked justice at best" (see *Securities and Exchange Commission v. Bank of America* 2009). He subsequently made good on his threat not to endorse further settlements without an admission of wrongdoing, voiding a proposed settlement between Citigroup Global Capital Markets, which he described as a recidivist offender, and the SEC. The settlement, he said was "neither fair, nor reasonable, nor adequate, nor in the public interest" (Henning 2011).

2. The complaint alleges that Goldman Sachs materially misrepresented the value of $38 million of AA and $42.1 million of AAA-rated securities within the CDO.

3. The suit alleges that Goldman acted fraudulently by offering preferred shares in Fannie Mae in late 2007. It claims, "Goldman Sachs not only knew about the serious risks in the mortgage market but it was urgently moving to short the mortgage market. . . . As a knowledgeable and sophisticated investor in the U.S. real estate financial markets and with access to Fannie Mae's financial records, Goldman Sachs knew or recklessly disregarded the actual status of Fannie Mae's capital structure" (*Liberty Mutual v. Goldman Sachs* 2010). Liberty lost $62.5 million in its investment. For Goldman Sachs's response, see Stempel (2010).

4. See *Stoneridge Investment Partners, LLC v. Scientific-Atlanta, Inc.* (2008), in which the Supreme Court ruled 5–3 that "extensive discovery and the potential for uncertainty and disruption in a [class action securities fraud] lawsuit allow plaintiffs with weak claims to extort settlements from innocent companies" and that change "must be a matter for Congress not for this court."

5. In an interview conducted by this author in the aftermath of the Enron accounting scandals, Steve Cutler (2005), then director of enforcement at the SEC, noted the "reluctance on the part of federal prosecutors to take on complicated accounting fraud cases. These are very difficult cases and require lots of resources, lots of time, [are] difficult to explain to juries and that makes for a less than ideal track record as far as a prosecutor is concerned."

6. The proposed settlement "reflected a rather cynical relationship between the parties. The SEC gets to claim that it is exposing wrong-doing on the part of Bank of America in a high-profile merger; the Bank's management gets to claim that they have been coerced into an onerous settlement by over-zealous regulators. And all of this is done at the expense, not only of the shareholders but also of the truth" (*Securities and Exchange Commission v. Bank of America* 2009, 11–12).

7. Goldman released a statement, which contained one substantive line: "The SEC's charges are completely unfounded in law and fact and we will vigorously contest them and defend the firm and its reputation" (Goldman Sachs 2010b). Later that day, Goldman released a more granular statement, but by that stage the media agenda was already set. Arguably, Goldman Sachs had never recovered from a devastating critique in (of all places) *Rolling Stone* the previous summer that described Goldman Sachs memorably as a "great vampire squid wrapped around the face of humanity, relentlessly jamming its blood funnel into anything that smells like money" (Taibbi 2009, 52). The prereleased article was widely cited and, in places, endorsed (Gandel 2009).

8. Citing e-mail sent March 12, 2007.

9. Citing e-mail sent January 23, 2007.

10. Citing e-mail sent February 11, 2007.

11. Citing e-mail sent February 7, 2007.

12. Citing e-mail sent March 12, 2007.

13. Citing e-mail sent January 22, 2007. On January 8, 2007, ACA alerted Tourre that it had previously rated sixty-two of the referent securities, suggesting it was happy with the rating. Just as significantly, when Paulson's representatives met with ACA after the January 22nd meeting, they suggested that ACA neither conducted due diligence nor questioned the purpose of the transaction, prompting Tourre to comment to another employee that he found conduct of the negotiations "surreal" (*Securities and Exchange Commission v. Goldman Sachs & Co. and Fabrice Tourre* 2010). Moreover, the SEC complaint notes that Paulson asked explicitly for the deletion of eight specific Wells Fargo securities but fails to mention that the "flip book" used to market the deal highlighted the fact that Wells Fargo securities constituted the majority of referent stock (Reuters 2010).

14. "I never told ACA, the portfolio selection agent, that Paulson & Company would be an equity investor. . . . I recall informing ACA that Paulson's fund was expected to buy credit protection on some of the senior tranches of the AC-1 transaction. This necessarily meant that Paulson was expected to take some short exposure in the deal. Moreover, from the early stages of the transaction in January 2007 to its completion several months later, none of the offering documents, including the term sheets, flip book and offering circular, provided to ACA indicated that Paulson's fund would be an equity investor" (Tourre 2010).

References

Appelbaum, Binyamin. 2010. "US Judges Sound off on Bank Settlements." *New York Times*, August 23, B1.

Arlidge, John. 2009. "I'm Doing God's Work. Meet Mr. Goldman Sachs." *Sunday Times*, November 8, 4.

ASIC v. Citigroup. FCA 963 (2007).

Atkins, Paul, and Bradley Bondi. 2008. "Evaluating the Mission: A Critical Review of the History and Evolution of the SEC Enforcement Program." *Fordham Journal of Corporate and Financial Law* 13 (367): 367–417.

Basis Yield Alpha Fund v. Goldman Sachs. 10 Civ. 04537 (S.D. N.Y., June 9, 2010).

Borio, Claudio. 2009. "The Financial Crisis of 2007–? Macroeconomic and Policy Lessons." Paper presented at G20 Workshop on the Global Economy, Mumbai, May 24–26. http://www.g20.org/Documents/g20_workshop_causes_of_the_crisis.pdf.

Carver, Jeremy. 2005. "The Role of Lawyers." In *Governing the Corporation*, edited by Justin O'Brien, 223–33. Chichester, UK: Wiley.

Cassidy, John. 2010. "Scandals." *New Yorker*, May 3, 21.

Central Bank of Denver v. First Interstate Bank. 511 US 164 (1994).

Clark, Andrew. 2010. "Warren Buffett Defends Goldman Sachs." *Guardian*, May 1. http://www.guardian.co.uk/business/2010/may/01/warren-buffett-defends-goldman-sachs.

Committee on Capital Markets Regulation. 2006. *Interim Report.* Cambridge, Mass.: Committee on Capital Markets Regulation.

———. 2007. *The Competitive Position of the U.S. Public Equity Market.* Cambridge, Mass.: Committee on Capital Markets Regulation.

Craig, Suzanne, Matthew Karnitschnig, and Aaron Lucchetti. 2008. "Buffett to Invest $5 Billion in Goldman." *Wall Street Journal*, September 24, A1.

Cutler, Steve. 2005. Interview with Director of Enforcement of the Securities Exchange Commission, Washington D.C., May 11.

Federal Home Loan Bank of San Francisco. 2009. "10-K Filing to the Securities and Exchange Commission." http://www.fhlbsf.com/about/investor/ar/pdf/2009/10-K.pdf.

———. 2010. "Statement Regarding PLRMBS Litigation (Updated)." Press Release, June 10. http://www.fhlbsf.com/about/investor/satellite/MBSlitigation.asp.

Federal Home Loan Bank of San Francisco v. Credit Suisse Securities; Credit Suisse First Boston Mortgage Securities; Deutsche Bank Securities; JP Morgan Securities F/K/A Bear Stearns et al. 10 Civ. 497840 (2010).

Financial Crisis Inquiry Commission. 2011. *The Financial Crisis Inquiry Report.* Washington, D.C., January.

Financial Services Authority. 2009. *The Turner Review: A Regulatory Response to the Global Banking Crisis.* London: Financial Services Authority.

Finn, Paul. 1977. *Fiduciary Obligations.* Sydney: Law Book Co.

Gallu, Joshua. 2010. "Goldman Sachs Said to Seek Extension to Reply to SEC Lawsuit." http://www.bloomberg.com/news/2010-06-18/goldman-is-said-to-seek-extension-of-june-21-deadline-to-reply-to-sec-suit.html.

Gallu, Joshua, and Christine Harper. 2010. "Goldman Sachs Hudson CDO Said to Be Target of Second SEC Probe." *Bloomberg*, June 10. http://www.businessweek.com/news/2010–06–10/goldman-sachs-hudson-cdo-said-to-be-target-of-second-sec-probe.html.

Gandel, Stephen. 2009. "Goldman Sachs v. Rolling Stone: A Wall Street Smackdown." *Time*, July 3.

Goldfarb, Zachary. 2010. "SEC Divided on Vote to File Goldman Lawsuit." *Washington Post*, April 23

Goldman Sachs. 2010a. "Goldman Sachs Makes Further Comments on SEC Complaint." Press Release, New York City, April 16.

———. 2010b. "Goldman Sachs Responds to SEC Complaint." Press Release, April 16.

———. 2010c. "On the Issues: Overview." http://www2.goldmansachs.com/our -firm/on-the-issues/index.html (accessed September 20, 2010).

———. 2011. "Report of the Business Standards Committee." http://www.2.gold mansachs.com/our-firm/business-standards-committee/index.html (accessed February 4, 2011).

Government Accountability Office. 2009a. "Corporate Crime: DOJ Has Taken Steps to Better Track Its Use of Deferred and Non-Prosecution Agreement, but Should Evaluate Effectiveness." Washington, D.C.: Government Printing Office.

———. 2009b. Corporate Crime: Preliminary Observations on DOJ's Use and Oversight of Deferred Prosecution Agreements and Non-Prosecution Agreements. Washington, D.C.: Government Printing Office.

———. 2011. Securities Fraud Liability of Secondary Actors. Washington, D.C.: Government Printing Office.

Greenspan, Alan. 1996. "The Challenge of Central Banking in a Democratic Society." Speech delivered at American Enterprise Institute Dinner, Washington D.C., December 5.

———. 2008. "We Will Never Have a Perfect Model of Risk." *Financial Times*, March 17, 13.

Henning, Peter. 2011. "Behind Rakoff's Rejection of Citigroup Settlement." New York Times 28 November. http://dealbook.nytimes.com/2011/11/28/behind -judge-rakoffs-rejection-of-s-e-c-citigroup-settlement/.

Herbert, Bob. 2009. "Chutzpah on Steroids." *New York Times*, July 14, A25.

Hood, Christopher, Henry Rothstein, and Robert Baldwin. 2001. *The Government of Risk*. New York: Oxford University Press.

Kronman, Anthony. 1995. *The Lost Lawyer: Failing Ideals of the Legal Profession*. Cambridge, Mass.: Harvard University Press.

Levin, Carl. 2010. "Senate Floor Statement on Passage of the Restoring American Financial Stability Act." Press Release, May 25. Washington D.C.: Government Printing Office.

Lewis, Michael. 2009. *The Big Short*. New York: Norton.

Liberty Mutual v. Goldman Sachs. 10 Civ. 11150 (D. Mass., July 9, 2010).

Macey, Jonathan. 2004. "Wall Street in Turmoil: State-Federal Relations Post Eliot Spitzer." *Brooklyn Law Review* 70:117–40.

Malcolm, Janet. 2010. "Anatomy of a Murder Trial." *New Yorker*, May 3.

Morgenson, Gretchen. 2010. "The Inflatable Loan Pool." *New York Times*, June 20, B1.

Murdoch, Scott. 2010. "Basis Capital Row Hits Australian Arm of Goldman Sachs." *The Australian*, June 11. http://www.theaustralian.com.au/business/basis-capital -row-hits-australian-arm-of-goldman-sachs/story-e6frg8zx-1225878150987.

Naftalis, Joshua. 2002. "Wells Submissions to the SEC as Offers of Settlement Under Federal Rule of Evidence 408 and Their Protection from Third-Party Discovery." *Columbia Law Review* 102:1912–53.

Nash, Jonathan. 2006. "Framing Effects and Regulatory Choice." *Notre Dame Law Review* 82 (1): 313–72.

O'Brien, Justin. 2005. "The Politics of Enforcement, Eliot Spitzer, State-Federal Relations and the Redesign of Financial Regulation." *Publius: The Journal of Federalism* 35 (3): 449–56.

———. 2006. "Accounting and Accountability Failure: The Impact of the Kaplan Ruling on Corporate Enforcement" *Compliance and Regulatory Journal* 1 (1): 28–38.

———. 2007. *Redesigning Financial Regulation: The Politics of Enforcement*. Chichester, UK: Wiley.

———. 2009. *Engineering a Financial Bloodbath*. London: Imperial College Press.

———. 2010. "The Future of Financial Regulation: Enhancing Integrity Through Design." *Sydney Law Review* 32:63–87.

O'Connor, Sandra D. 1986. "Commencement Address." Speech delivered at Georgetown Law Center, May.

Obama, Barack. 2009. "Twenty First Century Regulatory Reform." Speech delivered at the Council on Foreign Relations, New York, June 17.

Partnoy, Frank. 2003. *Infectious Greed*. New York: Times Books.

Reuters. 2010. "Read Goldman Sachs' Abacus Pitch Book." *Reuters*, April 16. http://blogs.reuters.com/reuters-dealzone/2010/04/16/read-goldman-sachs -abacus-pitch-book.

Securities and Exchange Commission (SEC). 2010a. "Goldman Sachs to Pay Record $550 million to Settle SEC Charges Related to Subprime Mortgage CDO." Litigation Release 21592, July 15.

———. 2010b. "Proposed Rule: Asset Backed Securities." Press Release, April 7. http://www.sec.gov/rules/proposed/2010/33–9117.pdf.

Securities and Exchange Commission v. Bank of America. 09 Civ. 6829 (JSR) (S.D. N.Y., 2009).

Securities and Exchange Commission v. Goldman Sachs & Co. and Fabrice Tourre. 10 Civ. 3229 (2010). http://www.sec.gov/litigation/complaints/2010/comp21489 .pdf.

Sen, Amartya. 2010. "The Economist's Manifesto." *New Statesman*, April 23.

Shapiro, Mary. 2009. "Address to the Practicing Law Institute." Speech delivered at PLI Securities Regulation Seminar, New York, November 4.

Shiller, Robert. 2000. *Irrational Exuberance*. Princeton, N.J.: Princeton University Press.

Stempel, Jonathan. 2010. "Goldman Sued by Liberty Mutual Over Fannie Stock." *Reuters*, July 9. http://www.reuters.com/article/idUSN0915845220100709.

Stiglitz, Joseph. 2008. "Regulatory Restructuring and the Reform of the Financial System." Evidence to House Committee on Financial Services. *U.S. Congress*, October 21, 4.

Stoneridge Investment Partners, LLC v. Scientific-Atlanta, Inc. 128 US 761 (2008).

Surowiecki, James. "Déjà Vu." *New Yorker*, May 3, 25.

Taibbi, Matt. 2009. "The Great American Bubble Machine." *Rolling Stone*, July 9. http://www.rollingstone.com/politics/news/12697/64796.

Tourre, Fabrice. 2010. "Wall Street and the Financial Crisis: The Role of Investment Banks." Evidence to U.S. Senate Permanent Subcommittee on Investigations Hearing. *U.S. Congress*, April 27.

Tuch, Andrew. 2005. "Investment Banks as Fiduciaries: Implications for Conflicts of Interest." *Melbourne University Law Review* 29:478–517.

United Kingdom Inter-Professional Group. 2002. *Professional Regulation: A Position Statement*. Revision. London: UK Inter-Professional Group.

United Kingdom Law Commission. 1992. *Fiduciary Duties and Regulatory Rules*. Consultation Paper 124:2.4.6–2.4.7.

U. S. Senate. 2010. Senate Committee on the Judiciary Hearing. Subcommittee of the Committee on Crime and Drugs. *Wall Street Fraud and Fiduciary Duties: Can Jail Time Serve as an Adequate Deterrent for Willful Violations*. 111th Cong., 2d sess., May 4.

U.S. Senate. 2010. Senate Permanent Subcommittee on Investigation of the Committee on Homeland Security and Governmental Affairs. *Hearings on Wall Street and the Financial Crisis: The Role of Investment Banks*. 111th Cong., 2d sess., vol. 4 of 5, April 27.

Walha, Kulbir, and Edward Filusch. 2005. "Eliot Spitzer: A Crusader Against Corporate Malfeasance or a Politically Ambitious Spotlight Hound? A Case Study of Eliot Spitzer and Marsh & McLennan." *Georgetown Journal of Legal Ethics* 18 (4): 1111–32.

Woozley, Anthony D. 1968. "What Is Wrong with Retrospective Law?" *Philosophical Quarterly* 18 (70): 40–53.

Zierdt, Candace, and Ellen Podgor. 2007. "Corporate Deferred Prosecutions Through the Looking Glass of Contract Policing." *Kentucky Law Journal* 96 (1): 1–43.

[PART IV]

PERSPECTIVES FROM AFAR

Paul Krugman, an economist at Princeton University, told the FCIC, "It's hard to envisage us having had this crisis without considering international monetary capital movements. The U.S. housing bubble was financed by large capital inflows. So were Spanish and Irish and Baltic bubbles. It's a combination of, in the narrow sense, of a less regulated financial system and a world that was increasingly wide open for big international capital movements."

It was an ocean of money.

—(Financial Crisis Inquiry Commission, Final Report of the National Commission on the Causes of the Financial and Economic Crisis in the United States, Official Government Edition, 2011, 104)

[11]

REAPPRAISING REGULATION

The Politics of "Regulatory Retreat'" in the United Kingdom

STEVE TOMBS AND DAVID WHYTE

As the contributions to this volume ably demonstrate, the current economic crisis is a result of a systemic uncontrollability in the international economy. Yet our understanding of how we have reached the present crisis has generally been framed within a macroeconomics that has consciously and systematically distorted what markets are, how markets work, and the role of regulation therein. Of particular interest is the framing of the *idea* of regulation in ways that separate states from markets, indeed subsuming the former into the latter within some crude zero-sum conception of power.

In this essay, we offer a critique of the narrow view that the system is merely an inevitable consequence of "underregulation" and that what is needed to "mend" the system is just "better" or more "responsive" regulation. Further, we argue that this framing also raises questions about the utility of seeking to understand the present crisis through the lens of crime.

This chapter is written, at least in terms of its empirical reference points, from a British perspective. We do not claim that it can be read to fit any situation. However, since our focus is on the nature and idea of regulation in general—what regulation is, and can be, and how the idea is represented, distorted, limited, and reframed hegemonically—we hope that the theoretical argument developed here has a more general applicability.

In many respects, as the chapters in this volume indicate, we know a great deal about the antecedent conditions for the emergence of this crisis. In another sense, however, the details of what happened during and leading up to that period are almost entirely unknown. In the United Kingdom, certainly, there has been no thoroughgoing attempt to re-regulate the financial services sector, nor even to radically alter those parts of it effectively under state ownership; no thoroughgoing inquiry into the potential illegalities involved in the near collapse of this sector; no significant prosecutions developed by the Serious Fraud Office or the Financial Services Authority; and certainly no ideological or material undermining of political faith in "light touch" regulation across all other areas that "affect" business life in the light of our current, very pressing collective experience of its manifest failures.

In the sections that follow, we offer an appraisal of strategies practiced by successive British governments that have all-too-frequently been understood simply as deregulatory. We should emphasize at the outset that our central argument in this chapter is not that the state has, in the neoliberal period, acted as anti-statist but that it has represented itself as such. Thus we have to differentiate between state retreat as a real characteristic and outcome of neoliberalism and anti-statism as a hegemonic device. In this context, it is clear that the period of the past 30 years or so is characterized by complex forms of *re*-regulation rather than simply as an era of deregulation.

The Political Construction of the Idea of Regulatory Retreat

Conservative Governments, 1979–1997: An Idea Rolled Out

The seeds for the present political conjuncture regarding feasible regulation were planted by the governments led by former Prime Minister Margaret Thatcher from 1979 onward. While the policies, practices, and ideological underpinnings of those governments are well known, one aspect is worthy of restatement. The Thatcher cabinet, like the administration of former U.S. President Ronald Reagan and the leadership of other countries that fell under the sway of the neoliberal policies known as the "Washington consensus," was driven by the demand to rebalance the relationship between state and market. To the extent that this provoked intellectual opposition, such dissent tended to focus on the argument that the sphere of state influence should be protected.

Across four successive Conservative-led governments between 1979 and 1997, hundreds of publicly owned companies were sold into private hands. British Aerospace, telecommunications, gas, the electricity and water supply, shipbuilding, freight and ports, coal, railways, and atomic energy were all privatized during this period. In 1979, nationalized industries accounted for over 10 percent of GDP; by 1993, the figure was less than 3 percent. Public sector employment had fallen by 1.5 million. However, this is not simply a tale of governments stepping back from an active role across whole swaths of the economy.

First, at the level of empirical observation, it is difficult to sustain the idea that the state was being rolled back in this period. Under the governments led by Thatcher (1979–1990) and her successor, John Major (1990–1997), public spending increased, and the size and number of different forms of new government institutions grew rapidly (Weiss 2003). As was the case in all governments pursuing neoliberal policies during this period, state intervention increased. Examples include the widening of policing powers and the exponential rise of the prison population (Coleman et al. 2009; Sim 2009). All of those trends went hand in hand with the privatization of public utilities and with "deregulation" policies.

Second, rather than acting to control or restrict markets, regulatory forms that feverishly *promoted* market activity emerged in this period. Thus, the "freeing" of markets in the privatizations of energy, water, telecommunications, and, most tortuously, rail was accompanied by a mass of regulatory institutions designed to establish and maintain what were effectively new, state-constructed markets (Prosser 1997).

Third, there had been, during this period, regulatory efforts aimed at controlling the excesses of capital accumulation. In the sphere of environmental crime, 1990 saw the establishment of the new Environment Agency. Although ultimately ineffective, this agency certainly demonstrated a greater interventionist and prosecutorial commitment than the other key agency of "social" regulation in the United Kingdom, namely, the Health and Safety Executive. In financial services, the deregulatory "big bang" of 1986, a series of reforms in the London Stock Exchange designed to attract overseas financial capital, central to the success of which was maintaining the confidence of large-scale overseas investors, was followed very quickly by the establishment, under the Criminal Justice Act (uniquely for the United Kingdom), of the Serious Fraud Office (SFO). That body demonstrated a remarkable initial prosecutorial zeal, though it was soon to see an erosion of its political mandate. Crucial in this context: within a few months, between 1991 and 1992, the SFO saw convictions over-turned in one high-profile case (Blue Arrow) and the collapse of a second celebrated prosecution against the directors of Guinness. Each of these mo-ments was accompanied by scathing judicial comment, and exaggerated claims of the costs of such failed criminal prosecutions began to circulate politically and popularly. A decisive moment came with the collapse of mainstream political support in 1992 as New Labour, in opposition, em-braced the politics of a business-friendly neoliberalism (Fooks 2003). The SFO retreated into more conservative decisions regarding prosecution. By 1995, its formal relationship with the Crown Prosecution Service had deci-sively shifted. Thus, Fooks (2003) refers to the period from 1992 as a pe-riod of decriminalization of commercial fraud. In the sphere of health and safety, the Thatcher government ultimately retreated from a full-scale de-regulatory assault (Tombs 1996). Meanwhile, at the European level, com-petition law and its enforcement witnessed staggering levels of fines for "anticompetitive" practices levied against some of the world's largest cor-porations, as political leaders across Europe sought to legitimize the proj-ect of the European Union through the creation of an EU-wide market on a "level playing field."[1]

In other words, the empirical evidence suggests that the period spanned by the Conservative governments was a complex, and at times incoherent, era of re-regulation.

Labour Governments, 1997–2010: An Idea as Constraint

The idea of regulatory retreat was an essential element of the pro-globalization attitudes that had become "internalized" in the Labour Party by the time it arrived in office in 1997 (Hay and Watson 1998, 815). Thus, Prime Minister Tony Blair pledged to "accept globalization and work with it" (cited in Holden 1999, 531), as well as to make the United Kingdom the most business-friendly environment in the world. The so-called New Labour government bought into the most naive and exaggerated versions of "globalization," accepting as truth the myth that to regulate is to risk capital flight—a claim for which there is little or no evidence. And this framed its whole approach to the regulation of business while in office: regulation, if a necessary evil, at least had to be reformed along neoliberal lines.

By 1997, with much of the economy (again) in private hands, the ability of the state to manage, regulate, or even hold to account major economic actors—in theory, at least, if having proven problematic in practice—had been all but relinquished. Moreover, the transfers of ownership had created new and significant popular and political dependencies upon private capital, given the centrality of the goods and services formerly in "public" ownership but now being privately produced. If, by 1997, there was little left to privatize (Parker 2004) given the prior scale of privatization, political strategy shifted from formal transfer of ownership to a valorizing of the private sector couched in terms of "choice" and "efficiency." On this basis, a series of measures was also rolled out to attract private capital into the "public sector"—that is, through contracts—to further intertwine state and private corporate activities. The latter, under the guise of programs such as Private-Public Partnerships and the Private Finance Initiative, proved highly controversial. Most crudely, each of these initiatives represented mechanisms for effectively privatizing profits while socializing financial risks in areas previously untouched by private sector involvement, a paradigmatic and infamous instance being in the health care sector.

In April 2001, the Regulatory Reform Act came into force, allowing government ministers to order the reform of legislation with a view to removing or reducing regulatory "burdens." This law set the tone for New Labour's second period in office. In the same month, Tony Blair launched New Labour's manifesto for business before 100 corporate leaders in London. He committed Labour to develop, in its second term, a "deeper and intensified relationship" with business (Blair cited in Osler 2002, 212). Commenting on Blair's pledges, Osler (2002, 212) notes that "policies on offer that day included deregulation."

In the flush of Labour's second landslide victory in 2001, the gloves came off, and a material and ideological assault on regulation was launched. The ideological assault took the form of a long-term, drip-drip type of discursive framing of regulation as "red tape" that created a "burden on business." In 2004, Chancellor of the Exchequer Gordon Brown called for a break with the "old regulatory model" within which "everyone was inspected continuously, information demanded wholesale, and forms filled in at all times, the only barrier being a lack of regulatory resources."

Launching what was known as the Hampton Review,[2] he argued for a new model, which he characterized as "not just a light touch, but a limited touch" (see Brown 2005).

The purpose of the Hampton Review was to "consider the scope for reducing administrative burdens on business by promoting more efficient approaches to regulatory inspection and enforcement without reducing regulatory outcomes" (Hampton 2005). Its ambit encompassed sixty-three regulatory bodies, the largest of which included the Environment Agency, the Food Standards Agency, the Health and Safety Executive, the Financial Services Authority, and trading standards functions within local government (Hampton 2005, 13)—in other words, virtually any body with responsibilities for significant aspects of corporate or white collar crime. The review, published in 2005, called for greater emphasis on advice and education and, in general, for removing the "burden" of inspection from most businesses through more narrowly focused inspections. Specifically, Hampton called for the reduction of inspections by up to one-third—in effect, one million fewer across all regulatory agencies.

The Hampton Review, and the various policies and pieces of legislation that followed it (notably the Legislative and Regulatory Reform Act of 2006), provided a "rationale" for a diminution in the level of inspection activity and for a shift in the kinds of intervention taken by regulators, based on the now formalized, but erroneous, assumption that lawbreaking is marginal and a product of a small minority of business activity (see Tombs and Whyte 2010). The agenda laid out by the Review institutionalized the idea that the key role of regulation, in general, is a *productive* one. Specifically, to paraphrase the report authors, it recognized, as a *principle* of regulation, that economic progress is to be encouraged (Hampton 2005, 43). What this tells us, more clearly than in any previous policy statement, is that regulation is an element in the production of goods and services, rather than an external check on such activity.

The key contradiction that underpins the Hampton Review, and the wider agenda to which it is central, is that while it advocates a productive role for regulation, it draws upon the idea that regulation is burdensome, that the natural position in any thriving economy is less rather than more regulation, and that business and market "freedoms" are both possible and preferable—underscoring the argument that the state is most effective when it is less interventionist in the market.

Collapse and Consensus

The barrage of ideological, antiregulatory messages in the period we have considered in the preceding sections was so strong and constant that one must also take account of their effects "on the ground." It is likely that businesses were emboldened in their dealings with various regulators, while the latter were undoubtedly undermined. Thus, where conflicts over compliance emerged, the shift in the balance of power between the regulated and the regulator made it more likely that outcomes would favor the interpretations and preferences of businesses over regulators.

And this barrage has clearly set limits on what constitutes "feasible" regulation. So well cemented is this new "common sense" (as many called it) approach to regulation that it was not affected by the financial collapse that occurred at the end of the decade. As chancellor, Gordon Brown presided over an unprecedented bailout of the banking system—a massive state subsidy that effectively socialized the consequences of long-term, systematic private greed. Brown, later to become prime minister, underscored the government's commitment to the free-market system even as he issued a plea for corporate social responsibility:

> Our government is pro-business; I believe in markets [and] entrepreneurship, and there are many areas of the economy that need the spur of more competition. But the events of the past months bear witness, more than anything in my lifetime, to one simple truth: markets need morals. (Brown 2008)

In other words, if there were lessons to be learned, they were about eliminating bad apples, not the necessity of restructuring the market through re-regulation. Thus, reflecting upon the causes of the global credit crisis and the international recession, then Financial Services Secretary Lord Myners was able to state,

> The failures have not been failures of the market economy. They have been failures of men and women who forgot that market discipline meant that they had to be disciplined in order to get results out of the marketplace. . . . An unswerving confidence in the efficiency of markets became an excuse for many to simply rest on their laurels. Making money is about hard work. (Myners 2010)

The continuity of approach across pre- and postcrash eras is personified by the figure of Philip Hampton, the architect of the Hampton Review, and knighted for his services to business in 2007. In 2008, Sir Philip was appointed chairman of UK Financial Investments Limited, the firm established to manage the government's shareholdings in banks subscribing to its recapitalization fund (Monaghan 2008). The businessman who had overseen New Labour's flagship reregulatory initiative was thus appointed to oversee the key New Labour body charged with bailing out a financial system that had been brought to its knees by obscene profiteering.

Little wonder that various commentators highlighted how quickly "business as usual" was restored. There is no greater testimony to the power of the reregulatory agenda that had been set over the previous 30 years: "The persistence of this rhetoric of market efficiency is indeed remarkable. The perseverance of both the faith in free markets and the use of that key dichotomy—free versus constrained, private versus government controlled—is simply astonishing" (Harcourt 2010, 87).

Yet the period following the crisis of the fall of 2008 could not possibly be described as a regulatory retreat. The scale of the bank bailout alone indicates government took an active role. Indeed, the scale of the bailout was unprecedented. The £850 billion (approximately $1350 billion) in government commitments made since September 2008 includes purchasing shares in banks to enable recapitalization, indemnifying the Bank of England against losses incurred in providing liquidity support, underwriting borrowing by banks to strengthen liquidity, and the provision of insurance cover for assets. This is hardly the substance of a state rollback. Moreover, during this period, governments effectively allowed the banks to ignore competition law—itself a key regulator of markets—in order to broker an effective takeover of HBOS by Lloyds, two of the country's largest banks.

These actions make it even more remarkable that the idea of regulatory retreat has persisted in shaping government policy, even when faced with crisis. Thus, although a strategy of reregulation was pursued through the bailout, it is a strategy that has been largely reactive, responding to an immediate need to establish stability in the short-term. A thoroughgoing long-term strategy in response to the financial crisis has been notable for its absence.

Of course, there has been much political and popular uproar about "the banks," though in truth this has largely (though not entirely) been restricted to bankers, rather than banks, and more specifically their bonuses and excessive pay—a structural issue reduced to an issue of agency on the part of a few bad apples in relation to a specific phenomenon, that is, their remuneration.

Going into the British general election of 2010, all three major political parties were committed to reducing regulation in general, while each referred to the need to "do something" about regulating banks and financial services—a remarkable (if unremarked-upon) balancing act. Yet, the key terrain upon which approaches to regulation were set out comprised the following elements: Regulation in general was inherently burdensome and only to be an option of last resort, a minimalist necessary evil; in any case, regulation entailed costs for both the state and for business, costs that had to be restricted in the new "Age of Austerity." Thus regulatory costs *had* to be minimized on the one hand as part of the overall attempt to tackle the new fiscal crisis of the state and on the other hand to reduce the costs for the private sector, which was seen as the only vehicle for economic recovery. Absent from this discursive terrain, of course, was any significant weight given to the fact that a particular form of regulation by the state, which in turn fueled unsustainable levels of profit maximization on the part of financial services, had created the very crisis from which these same respective commitments were to forge a recovery.

Oblivious to this point, the Conservative Party went into the general election claiming that "over the course of a Parliament, we will cut Whitehall policy, funding and regulation costs by a third, saving £2 billion a year, and save a further £1 billion a year from quango bureaucracy." It also pledged to reduce regulation:

> Increasing amounts of red tape and complex regulation have eroded Britain's reputation as a good place to invest, create jobs or start a business. A Conservative government will introduce regulatory budgets: forcing any government body wanting to introduce a new regulation to reduce regulation elsewhere by a greater amount. (Conservatives 2010, 20)

Following the election of the Conservative-dominated coalition, the contradiction between arguing that businesses are overburdened and recognizing a need for government action to mitigate the profligacy of the City of London continues to be reflected in government policies. Vince Cable, who in opposition argued for High Street banks to be the equivalent of highly regulated utilities (Cable 2009), immediately established a Reducing

Regulation Committee when he was installed as business secretary in the new government. Its aim is to put an "end to the excessive regulation that is stifling business growth." As Cable put it: "The deluge of new regulations has been choking off enterprise for too long. We must move away from the view that the only way to solve problems is to regulate" (Department for Business, Innovation and Skills 2010).

Those seemingly unsustainable contradictions remain based on a tired, old dichotomy of states versus markets. It is this dichotomy that provides an ontological framework for perpetuating claims that states cannot and should not overregulate and that they have to find a way of controlling capital that does not harm capital.

After all, one achievement of the neoliberal period was to reify the key institutional form of capital—the corporation—as *the* agent of economic success. The financial crisis has exposed governments simultaneously as rabbits caught in the headlights and as the drivers of a car that is careening out of control.

Reappraising Regulation

Ideological mystification has underpinned and then characterized political responses to the rise to international dominance of neoliberalism, commonly referred to as globalization—a period in which politician after politician lined up to espouse the new (all) party line that there was "no alternative." Accordingly, the processes of globalization were increasingly cast as a naturally unfolding reality, impinging upon the functions and capacities of states. "Globalization" was literally represented as a force of nature, so that governments had no choice but to embrace policies of deregulation, low taxation, and declining expenditures as the price of nation-state integration into this "global economy." In so doing, they relinquished control over domestic policy agendas (Leys 2001, 8–37).

By adopting such a fatalistic stance, governments engendered a self-fulfilling-prophecy. The fact that globalization discourses were swallowed wholesale and then elevated to the status of mantra by governments actually helped to bring into existence the very effects that such discourses simply claimed to be documenting as reality. But we should not conclude from this ideological construction of helplessness that state capacities have in fact markedly diminished. If claims regarding the "attenuation of the state" still circulate widely in academic research (Panitch and Konings 2009, 68), these must not remain unchallenged—an observation warranted even by the evidence outlined in this brief review of British neoliberalism.

As we have indicated throughout this chapter, the "rollback" of the state is only part of the neoliberal story. Thus, all of the British "deregulatory" and privatization initiatives cited earlier were accompanied by the creation and re-creation of immensely complex—and, many would argue, highly inefficient—regulatory regimes. And this complexity is exaggerated when the regulation involves the provision of a basic service or infrastructure— such as fuel, health care, or travel. For some commentators, such changes in the role of the state have signaled the "death of the Keynesian state" and the emergence of a "regulatory," "advanced liberal," or "post-social" state. Thus, "privatization combined with new regulatory institutions is the classic instantiation of [the] prescription for governments to steer but not row" (Braithwaite 2000, 50). We can also see in the emergence of the "regulatory state" an apparent paradox: a government committed to privately owned, "free" enterprise that has created a complex web of (re)regulation.

It is evident that regulation, following *de*regulation or privatization of an area of economic activity, necessarily becomes more complex through reconstruction at arm's length. This, itself, is a stunning example of dissonance between the rhetoric and reality of the relationship between neoliberalism and public policy. While the former claims the supremacy of free markets, the latter in fact engages in an awful lot of work to construct and maintain markets so that they may appear to be free.

Empirically, then, the current crisis lays bare what appears to be a curious situation. For over 30 years, British governments have pledged to support "free markets" and to minimize the role of the state in economic affairs while promoting the ideology of their relative helplessness vis-à-vis global economic forces. These commitments have been promoted even as these "free" markets have been feverishly constructed and maintained through a lot of state activity. Further, the government of the United Kingdom has, like many other governments, prioritized, planned, and promoted a wholesale shift away from state spending on public services in the past 2 years: This has been done ostensibly as a means of recovering the costs of supporting the financial services sector, that is, in terms of the necessity of reducing state spending following the costs of the bailout (a process that at times itself looked close to nationalization). Yet even in this context, the political consensus against the idea of regulation has been upheld. How can we make sense of these seemingly paradoxical developments?

If we view regulation in dialectical terms, the contradictions apparent in the relationship between states and markets can be understood as dynamic, producing new regulatory outcomes and new forms of market activity. It is particularly important to grasp the dialectical nature of this process, especially in the context of sociology and socio-legal studies that remain fixated on the limited hypothesis of a "power-over" relationship, whereby regulation is something one set of actors (regulatory agents) does to others (regulated individuals and organizations).

In the past 30 years, a substantial body of work has emerged within criminology, but much more significantly in socio-legal studies, political science, and management studies–related disciplines, that has focused on regulation. And this is of particular interest, since regulation is the empirical link between apparently distinct and separate state and corporate sectors. While in some ways diverse, academic research on regulation can be categorized according to three dominant theoretical approaches (Whyte 2004): a "compliance" school, the neoliberal perspective, and capture theories. In each of these bodies of literature, the state either does not appear at all or is treated as a "black box," a reference point rarely described, analyzed, or theorized. None of this work places a critical analysis of "the state" at its core, although each is based on an implicit theory of state institutions and their role.

A common view across these three apparently very different perspectives is that regulation involves a process of an autonomous (state) agency intervening against an autonomous (capitalist) organization. For compliance theorists, regulatory activities aim to forge consensus across a plurality of competing claims on the part of potentially, but not fundamentally, antagonistic parties ("business," "workers," other "interests"), all of whom are viewed as having a mutual interest in an efficient business sector. For neoliberals the optimal role of the state is to withdraw from economic and social life and to perform any arbitration role as a last resort when market mechanisms have manifestly failed. For capture theorists the state is there to be seized and dominated by powerful, organized external interests and their ways of understanding the world.

Despite the appearance of significant differences between compliance, neoliberal, and capture theories of the state and regulation, what is com-

mon to each is a view of the relationship between the state and corporations, or "business," as one of opposition and externality—that is, the state
stands as an institution or ensemble of institutions that is ontologically
separate and distinct from civil society.

Logically, this approach would lead us to imagine that if the relationship between the state and capital is one of externality, and the regulatory
agency expresses the basic dynamic of the "power over," then state and
capital can be portrayed only in antagonistic terms. Such logic allows the
regulatory relationship to be represented exclusively as a mechanism for
controlling corporate activity. Of course, control efforts are part of this relationship, so there often is struggle between state and capital. Indeed, this
is why we might expect at particular times to see tough regulatory responses against the interests of individual businesses or even new forms
of corporate legal liability emerging at particular moments. However,
while we can see struggle, contradictions, contingencies, and so on, ultimately the role of the capitalist state is to reproduce unequal relations of
power inherent within capitalism.

There is a normative consequence of seeing regulation from this perspective, as the expression of an external, oppositional relationship. Such a view,
albeit untheorized, underpins an orthodoxy in regulation studies that advocates more conciliatory approaches to securing compliance. The dominant
thread in almost all scholarship in this field appears to be the argument that
the regulation of business cannot be organized as other forms of law enforcement are and that, as a consequence, regulatory approaches must be
tailored to be more "responsive" to the needs of the regulated sector. Normally this means offering incentives to regulated parties or reducing
scrutiny in exchange for a more active form of self-regulation. Since this
established wisdom sees the regulatory relationship as fundamentally antagonistic, it embeds arguments that compliance is less likely where more
antagonistic strategies, notably stricter forms of law enforcement, are followed. The logical consequence has been to propose ever-more complex
ways to make the regulatory system less antagonistic and more conciliatory.

The logic of these claims is disrupted if we view systems of regulation
for what they are: a complex and contradictory combination of rules imposed to provide stability for systems of capital accumulation. Such an
approach entails a rejection of conceptualizing, or reducing, regulation as
aiming to "control" or "eradicate" a particular type of harmful or deviant
behavior.

It is too easy to think in terms of a choice between "command" or "responsive" regulation or even an appropriate regulatory "mix." Thinking through whether the former compromises the latter or the latter compromises the former—as we are constantly being asked to do by the leading advocates of this dominant approach—leads us, in fact, into a conceptual and political cul-de-sac. It is the relative power of the various players involved—governments, civil society groups, regulators, and the regulated, all active participants in a regulatory process—that shapes regulatory outcomes, not the style of a particular regulatory approach.

Were there no structural inequalities in regimes of accumulation, then perhaps it might be useful to think through a strategy of choosing between strict enforcement and persuasion or what the appropriate "mix" should be when states try to get private sector actors to be law abiding. Yet, as we have seen, regulatory outcomes are ultimately tested by the stability of a particular regime of accumulation. As our overview of recent UK governments has shown, it is power-brokering by state institutions and private economic agents acting together that establishes particular types of regulatory regime. Economic asymmetries are bolstered, and often multiplied, by the regulatory process. In this context, how can it make sense to disconnect the command-and-control or coercive capacities of regulation from the capacities or techniques of infrastructural power? Or, indeed, from the role of "civil society," since each of those techniques is used ultimately as means of projecting power? Studies of regulation narrow their focus to explaining, analyzing, and dissecting something that we call legal compliance. But what concerns elites (whether they are politicians or business leaders) involved in the process of regulation is power, not law or compliance with the law.

Securing compliance with this or that regulation or law is therefore not the key point to grasp about regulatory outcomes. This also has implications for studying corporate activity through the lens of corporate or white collar crime. While the language of crime has a powerful moral and political salience, and while the analytical and empirical categories of crime lend a seductive, if misleading, clarity to academic work, "crime" or "illegality" simply fails to capture adequately the moving target of our scrutiny. We are dealing with the effects of power, the systematic harms and injustices made possible through economic activity, in which states themselves are frequently intimately imbricated (Tombs 2011).

More broadly, to think through the effectiveness of regulatory interventions, we need to think about struggles around regulation in a more concrete sense. If the key point of regulation is to retain some stability for regimes of capital accumulation under conditions of unequal power, then the key question for those who wish to influence the regulatory process is how particular regulatory interventions have the potential to make adjustments to those power imbalances.

Conclusion: The Struggle "for" Regulation

The central contradiction with which we must grapple is that strong regulatory interventions tend to enable regimes of capital accumulation to remain stronger. But this does not mean we should abandon regulation. Our analysis and argument is not intended to provoke a relativist opposition to any form of regulation as pointless, on the grounds that this merely allows the state to absorb conflict, reconstitute markets, and reproduce social inequalities from a stronger position, and so on. Rather, what it does demand is that regulatory systems must always be subjected to scrutiny on the basis of their ability to change the social and economic conditions that underpin power relations, rather than act as symbolic injunctions to "control" or "eradicate" some specific activity defined as crime or illegality, either actually or potentially.

Thus, demands for more socially just regulatory outcomes remain important, tactically, for at least two reasons. First, such struggles have real effects on the groups of people most threatened by regimes of capital accumulation. Second, and as a means of bringing the real conflict that regulatory regimes seek to absorb to the surface, they allow us to see more clearly what is really at stake when we demand action to curb the power of capital.

If there is a broader conclusion that we might draw from this critical review of the dynamics of regulation, it is that regulation often acts as an accessory to the grotesque inequalities that are currently being reproduced and widened in neoliberal capitalist social orders. In this sense, the regulation of capitalist markets can never adequately guarantee our protection from crimes and harms that arise from and reinforce social inequalities, since regulatory interventions do not, even on their own terms, seek a transformation of the institutional structure of neoliberal capitalism.

Yet a more careful examination of the realities of regulation, as we have attempted here, opens up possibilities for positive reform. Where the "responsive regulation" school closes down such possibilities, arguing that the "realities" of contemporary capitalism mean that state intervention is less feasible, the argument in this chapter tends toward the opposite conclusion. We must remind ourselves of the most glaringly obvious, yet at the same time most stunning, aspect of the present, namely, that at the beginning of the twenty-first century, governments have intervened to prop up their markets, inject capital, and reregulate on a scale never previously seen.

"Seen" is a crucial word, because the active, intense, and ongoing involvement of states in rescuing and re-creating markets and key actors within them renders visible some aspects of the complex and mutually supportive relationships between apparently separate sets of actors. So significant is this moment of exposure that the politics of regulation is likely to remain a highly contested terrain. And, of course, the "solution" to the current crisis or, stated differently, the means to prevent future crises is not simply regulation per se. Rather, an ideological and material assault on the power of capital is required. This is hardly likely to be undertaken by states. That said, the very depth and breadth of the current crisis, and the rendering bare of the basic contradictions between the nature and representations of contemporary capitalism, may prove to be a source of momentum for counterhegemonic movements.

Notes

1. In the United States, competition laws are known as antitrust laws.

2. It is worth noting that Phillip Hampton's career to that point had hardly been uncontroversial. He had been British Gas Group's financial director at the time one of the group's subsidiaries, Transco, caused a gas explosion in Larkhall, Scotland, that killed a family of four. Transco was later fined a record £15 million. The judge presiding in the trial noted Transco's "serious maintenance failure" following significant cuts to the company's maintenance budget. He had also been finance director of Lloyds TSB during the period that the bank was embroiled in a "stripping" scheme in which it falsified its records to mask transactions from Iranian and Sudanese banking clients in violation of U.S. law. The company was forced to pay fines and forfeiture totaling $350 million in a deferred prosecution settlement with the New York District Attorney's Office.

References

Braithwaite, John. 2000. "The New Regulatory State and the Transformation of Criminology." In *Criminology and Social Theory*, ed. David Garland and Richard Sparks, 47–70. Oxford: Clarendon.

Brown, Gordon. 2005. "A Plan to Lighten the Regulatory Burden on Business." *Financial Times*, May 23.

———. 2008. "America Has Embraced the Values of Progress." *Observer*, November 9. http://www.guardian.co.uk/commentisfree/2008/nov/09/barack-obama -gordon-brown.

Cable, Vince. 2009. *The Storm: The World Economic Crisis and What It Means.* London: Atlantic Books.

Coleman, Roy, Joe Sim, Steve Tombs, and David Whyte. 2009. "State, Power, Crime." In *State, Power, Crime*, ed. Roy Coleman, Joe Sim, Steve Tombs, and David Whyte, 1–19. London: Sage.

Conservatives. 2010. *The Conservative Manifesto 2010. Invitation to Join the Government of Britain.* http://media.conservatives.s3.amazonaws.com/manifesto/cp manifesto2010_lowres.pdf.

Department for Business, Innovation and Skills. 2010. *Action plan announced to end excessive regulation. DBIS Press Release, 2nd June 2010.* http://nds.coi.gov.uk/content/detail.aspx?ReleaseID=413620&NewsAreaID=2.

Fooks, Gary. 2003. "Contrasts in Tolerance: The Peculiar Case of Financial Regulation." *Journal of Contemporary Politics* 9 (2): 127–42.

Hampton, Philip. 2005. *Reducing Administrative Burdens: Effective Inspection and Enforcement.* London: HM Treasury/HMSO.

Harcourt, Bernard. 2010. "Neoliberal Penality: A Brief Genealogy." *Theoretical Criminology* 14 (1): 74–92.

Hay, Colin, and Matthew Watson. 1998. "The Discourse of Globalisation and the Logic of No Alternative: Rendering the Contingent Necessary in the Downsizing of New Labour's Aspirations for Government." In *Contemporary Political Studies 1998*, ed. Andrew Dobson and Jeffrey Stanyer, 2:812–22. Nottingham, UK: Political Studies Association.

Holden, Chris. 1999. "Globalization, Social Exclusion and Labour's New Work Ethic." *Critical Social Policy* 19 (4): 529–38.

Leys, Colin. 2001. *Market-Driven Politics.* London: Verso.

Monaghan, Angela. 2008. "Government Appoints Sir Philip Hampton to Oversee Nationalised Banks." *Daily Telegraph*, November 3. http://www.telegraph.co .uk/news/newstopics/politics/3374529/Government-appoints-Sir-Philip-Hampton-to-oversee-nationalised-banks.html.

Myners, Paul. 2010. "The Bankers' Moral Hazard." *Guardian*, March 8. http:// www.guardian.co.uk/commentisfree/2010/mar/08/bankers-moral-hazard-dis cipline-punish.

Osler, David. 2002. *Labour Party Plc: New Labour as a Party of Business.* Edinburgh: Mainstream.

Panitch, Leo, and Martijn Konings. 2009. "Myths of Neo-Liberal Deregulation." *New Left Review* 57 (May–June): 67–83.

Parker, David. 2004. "The UK's Privatisation Experiment: The Passage of Time Permits a Sober Assessment." CESifo Working Paper 1126. www.cesifo.de/pls /guestci/download/CESifo+Working+Papers+2004/CESifo+Working+Papers +February+2004/cesifo1_wp1126.pdf.

Prosser, Tony. 1997. *Law and the Regulators*. Oxford: Clarendon Press.

Sim, Joe. 2009. *Punishment and Prisons: Power and the Carceral State*. London: Sage.

Tombs, Steve. 1996. "Injury, Death and the Deregulation Fetish: The Politics of Occupational Safety Regulation in UK Manufacturing." *International Journal of Health Services* 26 (2): 327–47.

———. 2011. "State Complicity in the Production of Corporate Crime." In *European Developments in Corporate Criminal Liability*, ed. James Pascal and Ana-Maria Pascal. 70–83. London: Routledge.

Tombs, Steve, and David Whyte. 2010. *Regulatory Surrender: Death, Injury and the Non-Enforcement of Law*. London: Institute of Employment Rights.

Weiss, Linda, ed. 2003. *States in the Global Economy: Bringing Domestic Institutions Back In*. Cambridge: Cambridge University Press.

Whyte, David. 2004. "Regulation and Corporate Crime." In *Student Handbook of Criminal Justice and Criminology*, ed. John Muncie and David Wilson, 133–52. London: Cavendish.

12

HOW THEY STILL TRY TO GET AWAY WITH IT

Crime in the Dutch Real Estate Sector Before and After the Crisis

HANS NELEN AND LUUK RITZEN

By 2008, the impact of the U.S. financial crisis had reached across the globe. Stock markets in numerous countries fell drastically and large financial institutions collapsed or were bought out. Even in the wealthiest nations, governments were under pressure to come up with rescue packages for their financial systems. Although economists disagree on many aspects of the global financial crisis (GFC), there is widespread consensus that the collapse of the subprime mortgage market and the end of the housing boom in the United States had a ripple effect on the world's industrialized economies.[1] As other weaknesses in the global financial system became manifest, complex financial products and instruments started to unravel, and trust in the financial system as a whole plummeted.

The crisis of confidence was particularly linked to developments in the real estate sector. Property markets in European countries, the most striking examples of which are Ireland and Spain, suffered a heavy blow. But it is also clear that the financial sector was already under heavy strain. In this essay, we take a closer look at the real estate market, and particularly the *crime-facilitative* features of this sector, some of which predated the crisis.[2] In the Dutch real estate sector, serious forms of crime, such as fraud and money laundering activities, have become endemic during the last decade. The central question posed by this essay is, what has changed in terms of *opportunities*, *incentives*, and *restraints* for committing such forms of crime within the world of real estate as a result of the crisis?

This central question reflects recent developments in the study of crime and crime prevention, which focuses on the opportunities and restraints faced by would-be perpetrators of a criminal offense, rather than on the perpetrators themselves. According to Clarke (1992) and other advocates of the rational-choice approach, crime depends not only on the presence of motivated offenders but also on the presence of facilitating situational factors.[3] Criminologists refer to intervention strategies that aim at eliminating opportunities and creating obstacles to committing crime as "situational crime prevention."

The real estate industry covers a wide range of activities and key players. Some authors even claim that the real estate sector as such does not exist. Brounen and Huij (2004), for instance, suggest that there is no such thing as a heterogeneous real estate market. It is a market that consists of multiple submarkets; and even these submarkets can be divided into smaller markets with their own unique characteristics and (economic) sensitivities. The Amsterdam School of Real Estate (ASRE) divides the Dutch real estate market into two specific markets: (1) the housing market and (2) the commercial market. ASRE further divides the housing market into three activity-specific submarkets: (a) the sales market, (b) the rental market, and (c) the land market. The commercial market can be subdivided into markets that concentrate on (i) offices, (ii) industrial buildings (including factories), and (iii) shops. And these three submarkets can also be subdivided into specific segments.

Major players in the real estate market are project developers, institutional and private investors, brokers, real estate agents, tax advisors, financial advisors, banks, lawyers, and notaries public.[4] Of course, it is impossible to scrutinize the whole real estate market, let alone to focus on all the aforementioned key players. Moreover, as a criminological community, we are just at the beginning of exploring the very complex domain of real estate. Reliable and valid research data are scarce, as are empirical studies that focus on the relationship between real estate and other serious forms of crime. Nevertheless, using some of our own research findings, as well as reports written by colleagues, we will attempt to shed some light on the vulnerability of both the housing market and the commercial real estate sector to criminal abuse. As we have had access only to Dutch research information, the analysis is restricted to real estate in the Netherlands.[5] Yet, despite the Dutch context of our analysis, we are convinced that our major findings and conclusions can also be applied to real estate markets in other countries.

The chapter is divided into four sections. First, we briefly describe the housing and commercial real estate markets in the Netherlands. Second, the empirical research that was conducted before the crisis into criminal abuse of these two markets will be highlighted. Third, the crime-facilitative elements and restraints within these markers will be discussed. And fourth, the (alleged) changes due to the crisis in terms of opportunities and restraints for committing serious forms of crime will be taken into consideration. As these elements cannot be dealt with in full detail, the analysis will only outline the main aspects of recent developments.

Overview of the Dutch Real Estate Sector

Volume of the Market and Economic Developments

The Netherlands is a low-lying country in the northwestern part of Europe. About 25 percent of its area is located below sea level, while approximately 50 percent lies less than one meter above sea level. Significant land area has been gained through land reclamation and preserved through an elaborate system of polders and dikes. With a population of 16.5 million people–401 inhabitants per square kilometer—the Netherlands is the most densely populated country in Europe.[6] Almost half of the population and half of the employment opportunities are concentrated in the Randstad region, a polycentric urban constellation in the western part of the Netherlands, anchored by four big cities: Amsterdam, Rotterdam, The Hague, and Utrecht. This region covers only 21 percent of Dutch territory.[7] The immense pressure for land not only requires governmental spatial policies but also impacts the dynamics (including price movements) of the real estate market.

The total amount of investments in the Dutch real estate industry is considerable and has risen dramatically during the last decades. According to the ASRE data bank, the volume invested in housing rose from €16.5 billion ($22.9 billion) in 1994 to €37.9 billion ($52.5 billion) in 2008. The volume invested in industrial real estate increased from €10.5 billion ($14.6 billion) in 1996 to €20.4 billion ($28.3 billion) in 2008.[8]

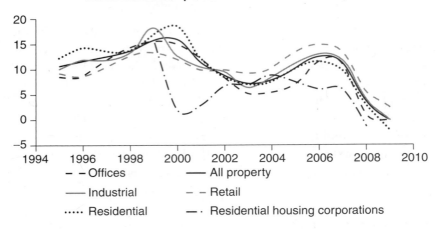

Historical sector performance: total return % p.a.

Figure 12.1
Dutch real estate, 1995–2009. Note: p.a. = per annum. Source: http://asre.databank.nl.

Figure 12.1 shows that both sectors' performances, similar to what occurred in most other countries, dropped significantly after the crisis began in the Netherlands in 2007–2008. In all submarkets, the total return experienced a nose dive.

This drastic decline is likely the result of falling real estate prices. Figure 12.2 illustrates price change in the housing market and variations in the number of transactions from 1995 to 2009. It shows that housing prices dropped 3.4 percent during 2009. In addition, the number of transactions plummeted 30.1 percent in 2009, which can be considered one of the main factors contributing to the decline of the prices. Current data on these developments indicate that these trends have continued since 2010. Housing prices dropped 2 percent in 2010 and 4.1 percent in 2011 and are expected to decrease with another 5 percent in 2012. The number of housing market transactions decreased 7 percent in 2011 (Dutch Central Bureau for Statistics/CBS 2012).

Figure 12.3 illustrates price change and the number of transactions for the commercial office market. It shows that, at time of writing, the office market was less bleak than the housing market.

Prices in the office market actually rose 4.9 percent during 2009, after decreasing in 2007 by 3.7 percent and plummeting by 22.8 percent in 2008.

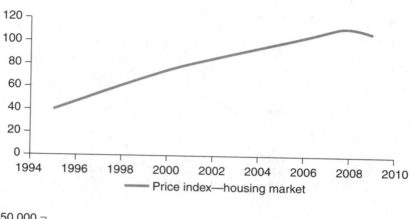

Price index—housing market

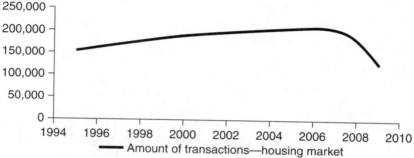

Amount of transactions—housing market

Figure 12.2
Changes in housing prices and transactions, 1995–2009. Source: Statistics Netherlands, The Hague/Heerlen.

Though it is too soon to tell whether this implies that the office market has taken only a minor hit from the crisis, and seemed to be recovering at the time of writing, these findings go against many economists' expectations and against the price trends in the other submarkets. Due to an aging population and inefficient use of many office buildings, 14 percent of office space is unoccupied in business parks, and roughly one in every ten buildings is empty (Eichholtz 2010). According to some leading economists, this fact should have a negative impact on the value of office buildings. Furthermore, in February 2012, a Dutch Central Bank board member forecasted a Dutch "real estate crisis," due to structural over-valuation of office buildings.[9]

Figure 12.3 also shows that the number of office transactions—in line with the observed decrease in office prices during that year—decreased by

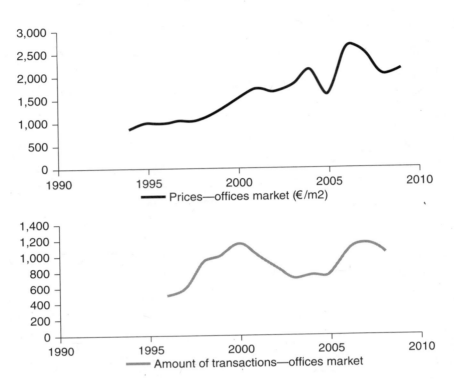

Figure 12.3
Changes in commercial office market prices and transactions over time. Source: http://asre.databank.nl

10.3 percent during 2008. Unfortunately, data on the number of office transactions from 2009 onward are unavailable.

Specific Features

Despite the complex and diversified nature of the real estate market, it is possible to distinguish the value of objects that are being bought and sold as well as the way business is conducted in this sector. Because of the unique characteristics of buildings and land, it is often very complicated to establish the "objective" value of real estate. Specific circumstances and factors may strongly influence prices. The geographical location of the structure is a relevant factor, as are the quality and the practical value of the building. For example, the presence of reliable tenants in an office building will drive up the square meter price, unlike in the housing market where the presence of tenants has a price-reducing effect. The extent to which there is a lack of appropriate real estate opportunities (supply and demand) might also influence prices. In a boom economy, with great demand for high-quality real estate, prices may easily "explode."

In the Dutch real estate industry, three major developments took place during the last decade. First, due to a substantial increase in (wealthy) private investors and private investment funds, the composition of the market significantly changed. After a precipitous drop in stock market prices at the beginning of this millennium, many private investors changed course and switched to the real estate industry. Some of them—alone or in conjunction with other investors—were able to invest large sums of money and gain a firm foothold in the commercial real estate market. Before 2000, this domain was strongly dominated by institutional investors. As a result of this development, both the number and the diversity of key players have increased.

Second, the Dutch real estate market attracted foreign investors from a variety of countries and regions (in particular China and the Middle East). Thus, the real estate industry reflects globalization in many ways. Notably, since 2006, the total annual foreign investments in the Dutch real estate sector have exceeded the annual domestic investments (Nelen, ter Luun, and de Bruin 2008).

The situation in the Netherlands is not unique in this respect. The influx of Chinese funds, for example, can be witnessed in many other European (and non-European) countries as well. Nevertheless, the substantial increase in foreign investment in the Dutch economy, and the real estate industry in particular, is also due to the very attractive Dutch fiscal climate for foreign companies, to good facilities in the financial industry, and to the solid trade reputation of the Netherlands. Of course, economic and financial experts tend to judge these circumstances and developments in a positive light.[10] However, from a criminal justice point of view, the rapid influx of foreign investments can be problematic. Along with an increased volume of legitimate trade, several markets have attracted illegitimate and irregular forms of trade, including serious forms of fraud and money laundering. In this respect, Unger and Rawlings' (2006) finding that the vast majority of the €25 billion ($34.9 billion) that supposedly is laundered annually in the Netherlands is derived from other countries is hardly surprising.[11] After all, the Dutch have created the opportunity structure for this sort of criminal activity: The improvement of facilities in the financial service industry inevitably has been a fertile breeding ground for criminal activities.

The third major development within the last decade, of course, is the financial crisis of 2008. The impact of the crisis on crime opportunities and restraints is discussed below.

Manifestations of Serious Forms of Crime in the Dutch Real Estate Industry Before the Crisis

In 2008, just before the real estate crisis surfaced in public view, a group of researchers from the VU University Amsterdam and Maastricht University published an exploratory study of the crimes and irregularities in the office-building segment of the commercial real estate sector (Nelen et al. 2008). This section is partly based on the findings of that empirical research. Other relevant sources are reports published by Ferwerda et al. (2007) and Gestel et al. (2008) on fraudulent activities involving private homes in the four largest cities of the Netherlands.

In Ferwerda et al.'s (2007) study, a distinction was made between fraudulent activities related to exploitation and speculation. Three different forms of *mala fide* exploitation were found. The first form is unlawful occupation, such as illegal subletting of private homes to individuals who are legally or illegally residing in the Netherlands. The second form refers to "slum landlords" exploiting their tenants, mostly migrants who are not allowed to stay in the country. The third form entails wrongful use, which means that the house is used for purposes other than regular housing. This may range from illegal boarding houses to using the property as a cover for criminal activities such as cannabis farms, human trafficking, money laundering, and illegal prostitution (Ferwerda et al. 2007).

Fraudulent activities associated with speculation can be divided into several categories.[12] The first is linked with so-called ABC transactions. Both Ferwerda et al.'s (2007) study of the housing market and Nelen et al.'s (2008) report about commercial real estate refer to this type of transaction. ABC transactions occur when a deed of conveyance for a specific real estate object is executed a number of times by one or more notaries within a relatively short period of time (sometimes within a day)—that is, a property sold by A to B is then purchased by C. Such transactions are regular features in the property market. And they do not automatically imply fraud or money laundering. However, when the sale from party A to party B and from B to C is accompanied by inexplicable increases (or decreases) in value, the transactions are likely to be part of a property flipping scheme (Gup 2007).[13]

Irregular ABC transactions appear to have played a significant role in a recently revealed major fraud scheme in the commercial real estate sector.[14] One of the most notable aspects of this fraud scheme is a "monster deal" involving a major real estate package originally owned by a major Dutch company pension fund. The mastermind of the fraud scheme persuaded a CEO of this pension fund to buy a Dutch skyscraper that was to be developed at a prestigious spot in Amsterdam. To facilitate such a huge investment, a significant proportion of the pension fund's existing real estate portfolio had to be sold—including a large number of houses and a handful of office buildings. The aforementioned CEO would do so by means of an underhand sale, secretly coordinated by the mastermind of the whole operation.

At the beginning of 2006 the actual transactions took place. The Dutch pension fund (party A) sold 1,525 houses and seven office buildings to a broker (party B). Within minutes the entire package was sold to the mastermind's company (party C) who immediately sold it to its final buyers (party D), who took the package apart and sold parts of it to multiple parties. In total, ownership of some of the real estate changed six times in 35 minutes, each transaction increasing the price. Apart from this, the suspects in this case allegedly accepted huge bribes, falsified invoices, and used slush funds for their illegally obtained profits. It is estimated that the fraud amounted to hundreds of millions of euros.[15]

ABC transactions are also abused for money laundering. In criminological literature many definitions of money laundering can be found, but most definitions concentrate on the concealment of the origins of the proceeds of crime. ABC transactions can be very useful in this respect, as they can create an artificial increase in turnover and profit. As the value of property rises steeply on each occasion, criminals can disguise the illegitimate source of their earnings as profits from successful business transactions. At the beginning of this century, the booming real estate market was extremely appealing to groups and individuals searching for ways to launder earnings from criminal activities.

The same applies to mortgage fraud, the third category of crime related to speculation. The essence of this criminal activity is that individuals or groups try to obtain a (larger) mortgage under false pretenses. In a rising market, a property portfolio can be built up with little risk either to the criminal or the lender, because if problems arise the property can always be sold. Both Ferwerda et al.'s (2007) and Nelen et al.'s (2008) studies indicate that, before the crisis, this relatively safe way of making significant illegal profits did not escape the attention of criminals. A number of mortgage-fraud cases reveal that, at the time, financial institutions failed to expend enough effort to prevent this crime. Again, economic interests prevailed and had a detrimental effect on the vigilance of banks and other financial institutes. Analyses of both Ferwerda et al. (2007) and Gestel et al. (2008) show that commercial interests led to marginal control over documents provided by the borrower. The maximization of profits can be obtained only by a maximum number of mortgages granted against the lowest possible amount of costs. Productivity by individual employees was stimulated by financial incentives, and in order to minimize costs real estate objects were not checked on sight. Thus, financial institutions relied heavily on documentation (including taxation reports) that can be easily manipulated.

A very broad category of crime is tax fraud. This fourth category of fraudulent speculation manifests itself in more than one way. Under-the-table payments for real estate are probably the best known and most widespread manifestation of this fraud (Ferwerda et al. 2007). Parts of the transaction are kept off the books to evade income and property tax.

Another form of tax fraud consists of putting forth a straw person in the transaction chain to conceal the identity of the selling party. In the Dutch fiscal system, individuals who buy or sell property on an occasional basis are less liable to taxation than persons who are registered as professional real estate agents.

The fifth category in relation to speculation is corruption. Research on criminal cases and convictions on corruption charges in the Dutch Criminal Code support the impression that the corruption problem in the Netherlands is rather limited (Huberts and Nelen 2005). However, during the last decade a number of serious corruption cases have been revealed. These cases reflect close relationships between local public functionaries and businesses involved in the construction and real estate industry. The way in which entanglement between public officials and private interested parties seems to be taken for granted in the Netherlands may be a relevant factor (Heuvel 2005).

Crime Opportunities and Restraints in the Dutch Real Estate Industry

Crime-facilitative factors can be found at all levels. The most important factors at a macro level were briefly mentioned earlier. In addition to the fact that the real estate sector attracts large sums of both legitimate and illegitimate money, the globalization of markets and trade has blurred the boundaries between legal and illegal money in international markets. Another relevant factor that was already discussed concerns the difficulty of determining the objective value of real estate.

The fact that the property market offers abundant opportunities for criminal entrepreneurs to conceal their illegitimate activities and proceeds is another relevant crime-facilitative element. In contrast to the financial sector, which is strongly regulated and supervised, the Dutch real estate market lacks sufficient transparency and adequate informal and formal controls. According to Eichholtz (2006), the property market still operates in the same regulatory vacuum as it did 20 years ago. As a result, the market's structural integrity is at risk, as illegal capital is likely to flow to the least-supervised investment market.

It must be stressed that most modus operandi used to hide the origins of investments or to conceal beneficial ownership of property are legitimate. In the property market, disguising ownership by placing property in someone else's name is neither uncommon nor illegal. At times this is done with some sophistication, for example, when corporate structures (legal persons) are used. A striking development—in line with the process of globalization—is an increase of 20 percent in the activities of foreign corporate vehicles in the Netherlands during the period 2003–2006.[16] In some real estate transactions, a long chain of corporate entities can be found, including domestic and foreign corporate vehicles, offshore corporations,[17] and trust companies.

At the market level, the cultural setting of the property market has to be taken into consideration. The research of Nelen et al. (2008) reveals the following features of the commercial real estate industry: It is a closed environment, which makes it difficult for outsiders to obtain access; its members belong to an old-boys network with strong internal ties and frequent contacts on a one-to-one basis, and members rely on reciprocity. Many business relations are made and maintained at informal meetings and places, like golf courses, restaurants, and real estate fairs (such as the MIPIM in Cannes, France[18]). Important business deals are "precooked" during these meetings, and vital information is shared with other key players on a reciprocal basis: One can expect one's business associates to provide vital information in return, now or in due time. Sometimes, tacit deals are made to "stay out of each other's hair," while keeping one another informed of relevant developments in the industry.

The profit margins in the real estate sector are highly dependent on the point in time that reliable information is available on zoning and other governmental plans, as well as on information on the plans that are being devised by potential business partners and major corporations. If a project developer or real estate agent is able to receive this kind of information earlier than competitors, this person has a major advantage. In the described cultural setting, key players are inclined to put pressure on public and private officials to obtain timely access to vital information. Of course, close contacts between real estate agents and high-ranked public and private officials may easily turn into corruption and collusion.

Cases of key players in the real estate sector who want to expose unethical or illegal behavior and blow the whistle are rare. A striking feature of the industry's culture is that most actors are in a constant "state of denial" (Cohen 1993). Bunt (2010) describes participants' shared interests in keeping silent about rumors of misbehavior among their colleagues as conspiracies of silence. The key to a successful conspiracy of silence is that no one has an interest in asking what is going on, and the violators have no interest in telling. Very likely the situation in the real estate sector can be labeled with what Bunt (2010) identifies as "inaction in the face of knowing"—participants and bystanders know something is wrong but have no interest in taking action. According to Bunt (2010), people in this position need to manage their ignorance. This can be done by making sure to have a story ready to explain this ignorance, a type of reasoning Katz (1979) defined as *concerted ignorance*. One way of realizing such concerted ignorance is to look the other way in the face of misdemeanor and to censor your (official) information.

After the Crisis

At the beginning of this chapter, we stated that our analysis is driven by the theoretical notion that the nature and extent of crime in a specific situation depends not only on the presence of motivated offenders but also on the presence of facilitating situational factors—in particular, the presence of suitable targets and the lack of sufficient oversight (absence of a suitable guardian). Obviously, motivation of potential offenders, the targets for criminal activity, as well as the level of oversight are influenced by the dramatic changes that have taken place in the real estate market since 2008. Although it is far too early to present empirically sound and valid data on the current crime situation in various submarkets, in-depth interviews with insiders already indicate some interesting new developments. In this section, we will focus on opportunities and restraints pertaining to three specific forms of criminal behavior. With respect to the housing market, we focus on mortgage fraud and collusion on public auctions. With regard to commercial real estate, the potential incentives for crime in relation to the problem of unoccupied offices will be discussed. At the end of the section, some attention will be paid to the possible effects the deteriorating economy might have on the position of one of the most important guardians in the sector, the notary public.

Mortgage Fraud in the Housing Market

One of the visible effects of the financial crisis is that financial institutions have become far more reluctant to grant loans to consumers, to companies, and to each other. At the same time, mortgage providers have become far more demanding toward their clients. Banks and other financial institutions have tightened their control procedures with regards to information provided by the borrower. In addition, supervision and control by the Dutch Central Bank (De Nederlandse Bank) have increased, partially due to the crisis and partially due to a corporate scandal involving a Dutch mortgage provider. Furthermore, (semi)public institutions issuing mortgage standards have decreased the norm for the maximum amount of mortgage to be granted. An effect of these measures is that commercial interests have aligned with the public interest in fighting mortgage fraud. This has weakened the crime-facilitative opportunity structure and should theoretically lead to a reduction of this type of crime. In this respect, it can be argued that the financial crisis is a blessing in disguise for the prevention of mortgage fraud.

Levi (2010) and Benson (2010) seem to underline this point of view. Both authors question the assumption of the FBI (2009) that the downward trend in the U.S. housing market during 2008 provided a favorable climate for mortgage fraud schemes to proliferate. According to Levi (2010), it is more likely that these fraud schemes originated before the GFC and only came to light after the crisis. Indeed, this type of crime seems to flourish in times of economic growth, rather than economic decline. Yet on the other hand, now that an increasing number of people are facing foreclosures and the prospect of losing their homes, opportunities for fraudsters may have opened up in other areas (Benson 2010). Scams at public auctions may be one of them.

Collusion at Public Auctions

Private consumers who are no longer able to pay off their mortgage debts can lose their house to the financier. In the Netherlands, it is common practice that these houses are sold by financiers through public auctions, which provide great opportunities to buy relatively cheap real estate. At public auctions, private houses are sold for approximately 65 percent of their market value (Brounen 2008), leaving the original owner with a residual debt. The reduction of the price is linked to the risks that public auction buyers run because they lack information regarding the house. In case of unexpected deficiencies, buyers cannot file a claim with the selling party. This is the main reason why public auctions are rarely visited by private consumers. Potential buyers usually consist of the same group of local real estate traders. The situational context in which they operate creates incentives for mala fide transactions. According to Ferwerda et al. (2007), collusion by groups of local real estate traders, setting the prices up front and dividing the real estate among each other, is not unusual. Individual private consumers who try to participate in the bidding process or notaries public who try to contain this form of price fixing are likely to be confronted with intimidating behavior and even violence by these groups.

The aforementioned characteristics also make public auctions very attractive for organized crime. The specific situational context creates possibilities for acquiring cheap housing and for facilitating core activities (e.g., safe houses for human trafficking or the production of drugs) and opportunities for fraud and money laundering. Preliminary findings from ongoing empirical research indicate that organized crime actually utilizes these opportunities.[19] It appears that slum landlords, human traffickers, drug producers, and mortgage and tax fraud networks are participating in these auctions, acquiring undervalued real estate at the expense of private consumers in order to facilitate their activities and launder their criminally acquired money.

In 2009, the Dutch Association for Real Estate Brokers expected an increase of forced sales through public auctions as a consequence of the financial crisis (Dutch Association for Real Estate Brokers/NVM 2009). The annual report of the First Amsterdam Real Estate Auction confirmed this expectation: The number of forced sales through public auctions in Amsterdam increased in 2009 by almost 10 percent. As a result, the opportunities for mala fide real estate traders and criminals to take advantage of this situation probably rose as well.

Unoccupied Offices

Project developers are important players in the commercial real estate market. Their core business consists of (a) buying land; (b) making a development plan and obtaining permits or licenses to build; (c) finding a way to finance the project and attracting funds; (d) giving the assignment to a construction company to build; (e) finding reliable tenants; and (f) selling the project to an investor. Project developers are highly dependent upon people and institutions who want to invest in their projects. Our research shows that the willingness to invest has diminished and the average length of time that office buildings are unoccupied has risen. As the presence of reliable tenants is the main determinant for the value of an office building, project developers and brokers desperately try to attract new clients and retain the tenants they already have. They want to avoid substantial rent decreases, since such reductions may lead to a destabilization or even collapse of the market. So they offer potential tenants informal incentives such as periods free of rent and commissions in order to persuade them to sign a contract. The buyer of an office building is generally unaware of these incentives, as they are kept out of the official records. As a result, to the outside world the commercial market appears to be rather stable. The previously mentioned stabilization of the prices of commercial real estate (cf. Figure 12.3) confirms this impression, although, as was mentioned earlier as well, many economists believe that this stable picture is somewhat artificial and misleading. However, what is clear is that the system of informal incentives within the commercial real estate market has become even less transparent than it was before the crisis. This lack of transparency, in combination with the strain on the market—that is, the relatively high level of unoccupied office space—and poor corporate governance, is a perfect breeding ground for fraud schemes.

Oversight and Economic Pressure

So far our analysis suggests that there are still sufficient suitable targets in the real estate sector for individuals and corporations to commit crimes. On the basis of the central notions of strain theory (Merton 1938), it can be argued that the financial crisis has fostered, rather than contained, the motivation of offenders. After all, the participants' cultural goals—the obtainment of profits —are unchanged, but the legitimate means available to achieve these goals have diminished. But what about the third facilitating situational factor: the nature and extent of oversight or guardianship in the sector?

Despite the long-term emphasis on self-regulation for business, for the real estate market, and within professional groups, the financial crisis has revealed that self-regulation alone is inadequate. Public demand for greater external supervision has increased a number of control mechanisms. We focus on one of the main guardians in the Dutch real estate sector, the notary public.

In the Netherlands, the notary public—a trained legal professional—is an impartial public official. A notary public's foremost legal powers comprise the execution of authentic legal instruments, as stated in the Notaries Act. Notaries public operate in the fields of corporate, family, inheritance, and property law.

Notaries public are required to intermediate in all real estate transactions. Legal ownership of real estate can be transferred only by a notary public's deed, followed by registration of the deed in the Offices of Land

Registry. It is the notary public's duty to ensure proper execution, registration, and payment of the transaction. With regard to the latter, it is possible for involved parties to transfer the necessary funds by means of the notary account. Next to these practicalities, the notary public is obliged to conduct some independent investigations on behalf of the involved parties and society in general. Notaries have a legal obligation to identify the ultimate beneficial owner and to report unusual transactions, including suspected crimes, to the Dutch Financial Intelligence Unit.

Notaries are required to comply with professional standards. One core standard is that of independence. For notaries, independence applies vis-à-vis both the state and the citizen. Independence from the state is regulated via a legal structure.

Dutch law stipulates that notaries have an obligation to provide professional services when legitimately requested to do so, unless their actions would result in unlawful acts or unless the notary's personal or immediate family interests would compromise such a service. On the one hand, the Dutch notary holds a public office and is responsible to the state. On the other hand, the notary is enmeshed in the dynamics of the free market system and needs to be an entrepreneur.

The most lucrative business performed by notaries public is their involvement in major real estate transactions. They receive a percentage of the price for every real estate transaction; hence the higher the value of the real estate, the higher the notary public's earnings. As a consequence of the financial crisis, real estate prices and the amount of real estate transactions have dropped significantly (cf. Figure 12.2). This development has negatively influenced notaries' turnover and profit margins. Thus, the functionary's obligation to be vigilant over the lawfulness of a transaction and the trustworthiness of the parties involved may be compromised by economic stress. It is not inconceivable that in order to survive economically, the integrity of these notary firms may come under severe pressure as well. They might become too dependent on large clients, and notably those in the property sector. In order to satisfy these clients, notaries may jeopardize their role as independent and impartial guardians. Some notaries public might even knowingly cooperate with criminals. This will not only have a negative impact on their reputation but affect their guardianship of all real estate transactions, regardless of the specific submarket or form of criminal abuse involved.

Conclusion

Real estate is still big business. It attracts huge domestic and foreign investments. At the same time, its characteristic of being a closed market dominated by old-boy networks creates enormous possibilities for the concealment of irregularities. A further complication is that the value of real estate is difficult to determine. Regulations, law enforcement, and both formal and informal controls seem to be inadequate. Hence, the real estate sector is less transparent than most other markets, enabling both legitimate and illegitimate entrepreneurs to meet, cooperate, and share expertise and knowledge. Several studies reveal that the situational context in which real estate transactions take place offers ample opportunities for criminal activities ranging from mortgage fraud to price manipulation, money laundering, tax fraud, corruption, and collusion. The crime-facilitative features of the real estate sector definitely meet the standards of what Braithwaite (2005) characterized as "markets in vice." He observed that there is not only a supply side at these markets but also an important demand side induced by competition, an observation confirmed in Dutch studies on criminal activities in the real estate sector. The market demands participants who sometimes look the other way and who, by rejecting any normative rules of compliance with regulations or laws, are able to rationalize their behavior as a requirement for success in a competitive environment. Case studies on criminal activities in the real estate sector reveal a mixture of literal and implied denial (Cohen 1993). Key players either claim that they have not been aware of the endemic fraud schemes in the sector, or they try to portray their actions as a normal part of doing business. Or they simply deny that any fraud has taken place.

The cultural setting of the real estate sector provides the participants with some insurance against mala fide transactions being detected and punished. Another kind of "insurance" is driven by the presence of a guardian who may not live up to the expectations of society at large. The role notaries public play in current real estate transactions may be especially enabling to fraud. As a result of the erosion to their economic position caused by the financial crisis, some notaries have become too dependent on a limited number of clients and may thus be inclined to neglect their duty to control the lawfulness of a transaction and the trustworthiness of the parties involved.

Besides changing conditions for notaries public, the GFC has altered the situational context of the real estate market in a number of other ways. Financial institutions have become more reluctant to grant mortgages, prices at the housing market have dropped significantly, and the commercial real estate market is not as profitable as in the past. Our preliminary findings suggest that these new conditions have created opportunities for, as well as restraints on, criminal abuse. Thus, the GFC may have reduced some types of fraud within the real estate market while increasing opportunities for others. At this stage, it is too early to draw reliable conclusions on the nature and extent of recent crime developments. But since there are still sufficient motivated offenders and suitable targets available, and guardianship is lacking, the metaphor that the real estate sector is a "market in vice" is still fully applicable. We all know that it is difficult to turn a market in vice into a market of virtue (Braithwaite 2005). More research is needed into the dynamics of the market and into the effects of the regulatory strategies that have been developed to contain criminal activities within the real estate sector, in order to be able to say something meaningful about the prospects of such a transformation process.

Notes

1. According to information at www.economist.com/houseprices, both the prices and the sales of houses have declined significantly in the United States. Just 28,000 new units throughout the whole United States were sold during May 2010, the lowest total on record for that month.

2. Needleman and Needleman (1979) introduced the term *two models of corporate criminogenesis*: crime-coercive and crime-facilitative. A crime-coercive system compels its members to commit illegal acts as the price of successful system membership. The crime-facilitative system does not force its members to break the law, but they are presented with extremely tempting structural conditions—high incentives and opportunities coupled with low risks—that encourage and facilitate crime.

3. Rational choice has been linked with Cohen and Felson's (1979) routine activities theory, which has three preconditions for crime: the presence of suitable targets, the absence of capable guardians, and motivated offenders.

4. According to Dutch law, the intervention of notaries public in real estate transactions is obligatory; thus, inevitably they will be confronted with both legitimate and illegitimate transactions. In Anglo-Saxon jurisdictions, the profession of notaries public does not exist. In the United Kingdom, the function, the tasks, and

the competence of a number of solicitors and so-called licensed conveyancers are somewhat similar to that of the notaries public in the Netherlands. In the United States, the tasks of escrow and title agents can be compared to those, in relation to real estate transactions, of the Dutch notaries public.

The notary public must have a master of law (LLM) and undergo a traineeship for a total of 6 years with one or more notary practices in the Netherlands. The title of junior notary is bestowed upon commencement of the internship. Within 1 week of commencing the traineeship, the junior notary registers with the Notaries Disciplinary Board in the relevant district. During the period of internship, the junior notary must successfully complete a Notarial Organisation training course, within a maximum of 3 years (Notaries Act, art. 33, para. 1). The junior notary must have worked during the 3 years prior to the application for appointment for 2 years under the responsibility of a notary or deputy, carrying out the activities of a notary, or him- or herself having acted as a deputy notary. The candidate applying for appointment as a notary must submit a business plan, to be vetted by a panel of experts, that demonstrates that the applicant has sufficient financial resources to maintain a practice and that there are reasonable grounds this practice will cover its costs after 3 years. In principle, an applicant who meets all the requirements will be appointed.

5. The various public and private institutions in the area of financial economic crime, as well as most academics who study white collar crime in the real estate sector, tend to focus on domestically oriented approaches. Thus, social research in this area is still predominantly based on national studies. One of the challenges of the near future will be to conduct comparative empirical studies on irregularities and crime in the real estate sector in various countries. In order to mine the rich field of research on financial economic crime in the property market, a multidisciplinary approach is necessary, meaning that criminologists must build bridges to other academic fields, including economics, tax law, company law, (forensic) accounting, and management studies.

6. Source: http://en.wikipedia.org/wiki/The_Netherlands.

7. Source: http://www.cbs.nl.

8. Source: Amsterdam School of Real Estate: Real Estate Monitor http://asre .databank.nl.

9. For this reason, Dutch professor of real estate financing Eichholtz (2010) calls for an immediate freeze of all plans for new office buildings and business plans.

10. An interesting difference of opinion in this respect became apparent in May 2009, when the Barack Obama administration declared the Netherlands a "corporate tax haven" for U.S. multinationals. The Netherlands, along with Ireland and Bermuda, were accused of sheltering companies' earnings from the American tax authorities. As long as they keep their earnings overseas, U.S. companies are legally exempt from paying U.S. federal taxes. Taxes become due only when the money is "repatriated" to the United States. But after an angry denial by the former Dutch finance minister Wouter Bos, the White House retracted its statement that the Netherlands is a corporate tax haven.

11. According to Unger and Rawlings (2006), money laundering amounts to €3.8 billion ($5.3 billion) of "Dutch criminal revenues," and there is an additional

inflow of €21 billion ($29.4 billion) from crime abroad. Unger and Rawlings' (2006) report was severely criticized by some criminologists, who claimed that most of the assumptions on which they base their calculations are highly questionable. See, for instance, Van Duyne (2006).

12. Using real estate for speculation is not a crime as such, but when speculation coincides with tax evasion, mortgage fraud, or money laundering activities, it is definitely a crime.

13. Gup (2007) defines property flipping as the buying of real estate and then selling the property quickly at artificial high prices (based on false appraisals and documentation).

14. Two Dutch journalists, Van der Boon and Van der Marel (2010), studied this scheme extensively, leading to a very detailed description of the involved alleged criminal organization and the fraudulent cases. They were granted access to the judicial files, including the transcripts of tapped phone records.

15. The investigation, named Operation Ivy, is ongoing and is run by the public prosecutor and the Dutch fiscal investigative unit. Although the prime suspects still await trial, one of them already settled the financial aspects of the case with both the public prosecutor and some victims (major pension funds) for €75 million ($105 million). Another suspect settled his case for €40 million ($56 million).

16. The Dutch Chamber of Commerce counted 6,051 foreign corporate bodies in 2006 (Bunt et al. 2007). Many of them were also registered with the Dutch Land Registry. Most of the registered corporate bodies were domiciled in the European Union (e.g., the English Limited Company and the German Gesellschaft mit beschränkter Haftung).

17. Roughly 400,000 companies were on the offshore registry at the end of 2000 (Nelen et al. 2008). Flourishing offshore economies have emerged in Bermuda, British Virgin Islands, Cayman Islands, Cook Islands, Jersey, Aruba, and Curaçao.

18. The abbreviation MIPIM corresponds to the Marché International des Professionels de l'Immobiliers (the International Fair of Professional Real Estate Agents).

19. The empirical study referred to is part of Luuk Ritzen's PhD research focusing on the entwinement between real estate and serious forms of crime, for example, money laundering. It elaborates on a recent study by Unger et al. (2010) that focuses on detecting and isolating real estate with a high risk of criminal investments by means of data mining.

References

Benson, Michael L. 2010. "Evolutionary Ecology, Fraud and the Global Financial Crisis." In *Contemporary Issues in Criminological Theory and Research: The Role of Social Institutions* (Papers from the American Society of Criminology 2010

Conference), edited by Richard Rosenfeld, Kenna Quinet, and Crystal A. Garcia, 299–306. Belmont, Calif.: Wadsworth.

Braithwaite, John. 2005. *Markets in Vice, Markets in Virtue*. Oxford: Oxford University Press.

Brounen, Dirk. 2008. *The Boom and the Gloom of Real Estate Markets*. Rotterdam: Erasmus Research Institute of Management.

Brounen, Dirk, and Joop J. Huij. 2004. "De Woningmarkt Bestaat Niet." *Economische Statistische Berichten* 89 (4429): 126–29.

Bunt, Henk van de. 2010. "Walls of Secrecy and Silence: The Madoff Case and Cartels in the Construction Industry." *Criminology and Public Policy* 9 (3): 435–53.

Bunt, Henk G. van de, T. J. van Koningsveld, Maarten J. Kroeze, B. van der Vorm, Jan B. Wezeman, C. G. van Wingerde, and A. Zonneberg. 2007. *Misbruik van rechtspersonen; een verkennend onderzoek naar de aard, omvang en ernst van misbruik van buitenlandse rechtspersonen in Nederland*. Rotterdam: Erasmus Universiteit.

Clarke, Ronald V. 1992. *Situational Crime Prevention: Successful Case Studies*. Albany, N.Y.: Harrow and Heston.

Cohen, Lawrence, and Marcus Felson. 1979. "Social Change and Crime Rate Trends: A Routine Activity Approach." *American Sociological Review* 44:588–608.

Cohen, Stanley. 1993. "Human Rights and Crimes of the State: The Culture of Denial." *Australian and New Zealand Journal of Criminology* 26 (2): 97–115.

Dutch Association for Real Estate Brokers/NVM. 2009. *Rapport modernisering executieveilingen*. Nieuwegein: NVM.

Dutch Central Bureau for Statistics/CBS. 2012. *Huizenmarkt*. http://www.cbs.nl/nl-NL/menu/themas/bouwen-wonen/cijfers/extra/huizenprijzen-visualisatie.htm.

Eichholtz, Piet. 2006. "Een AFM voor de vastgoedmarkt." *Justitiële Verkenningen* 32 (2): 67–75.

———. 2010 "Intervention in Real Estate Market Unavoidable." *Maastricht University Magazine* 3:14–15.

Federal Bureau of Investigation (FBI). 2009. *2008 Mortgage Fraud Report*. http://www.fbi.gov/stats-services/publications/mortgage-fraud-2008/2008-mortgage-fraud-report.

Ferwerda, Henk, Richard Staring, Edo de Vries Robbé, and Joris van de Bunt. 2007. *Malafide activiteiten in de vastgoedsector. Een exploratief onderzoek naar aard, actoren en aanpak*. Amsterdam: B.V. Uitgeverij SWP.

Gestel, Barbra van, Ruud F. Kouwenberg, Maite A. Verhoeven, and Mirte W. Verkuylen. 2008. *Vastgoed en fout. Een analyse van twaalf strafrechtelijke opsporingsonderzoeken naar illegale en criminele praktijken in de woningsector*. The Hague: WODC.

Gup, Benton E. 2007. *Money Laundering, Financing Terrorism and Suspicious Activities*. New York: Nova Science Publishers.

Heuvel, Grat van den. 2005. "The Parliamentary Enquiry on Fraud in the Dutch Construction Industry; Collusion as Concept Between Corruption and State-Corporate Crime." *Crime, Law and Social Change* 44:133–51.

Huberts, Leo, and Hans Nelen. 2005. *Corruptie in het Nederlandse openbaar bestuur.* Utrecht: Lemma.

Katz, Jack. 1979. "Concerted Ignorance: The Social Construction of a Cover-up." *Journal of Contemporary Ethnography* 8 (3): 295–316.

Levi, Michael. 2010. "Fraud Vulnerabilities, the Financial Crisis, and the Business Cycle." In *Contemporary Issues in Criminological Theory and Research: The Role of Social Institutions* (Papers from the American Society of Criminology 2010 Conference), edited by Richard Rosenfeld, Kenna Quinet, and Crystal A. Garcia, 269–92. Belmont, Calif.: Wadsworth.

Merton, Robert K. 1938. "Social Structure and Anomie." *American Sociological Review* 3:672–82.

Needleman, Martin L., and Carolyn Needleman. 1979. "Organizational Crime: Two Models of Criminogenesis." *Sociological Quarterly* 20 (4): 517–28.

Nelen, Hans, Bas ter Luun, and Arnoud de Bruin. 2008. *De omgeving van de Rijksgebouwendienst; integriteitsrisico's bij de koop en huur van vastgoed.* Maastricht/Amsterdam: Maastricht University and Vrije Universiteit Amsterdam University.

Unger, Brigitte, and Gregory Rawlings. 2006. *The Amounts and Effects of Money Laundering: Report for the Ministry of Finance.* Utrecht/Canberra: Utrecht School of Economics and Australian National University.

Unger, Brigitte, Joras Ferwerda, Hans Nelen, and Luuk Ritzen. 2010. *Detecting Criminal Investments in the Dutch Real Estate Sector.* Utrecht/Maastricht: Utrecht School of Economics and Maastricht University.

Van der Boon, Vasco, and Gerben van der Marel. 2010. *De Vastgoedfraude.* Amsterdam: Nieuw Amsterdam Uitgevers.

Van Duyne, Petrus. 2006. "Witwasonderzoek, Luchtspiegelingen en de Menselijke Maat." *Justitiële Verkenningen* 32 (2): 34–40.

13

ECONOMIC AND FINANCIAL CRIMINALITY IN PORTUGAL

RITA FARIA, JOSÉ CRUZ, ANDRÉ LAMAS LEITE,
AND PEDRO SOUSA

While economists agree that a financial crisis such as the one that spanned the globe in 2008 is a characteristic of the market system, many believed that instruments to detect and neutralize its noxious effects without undermining the foundations of capitalism were well developed. But the macroeconomic instruments designed to combat instability in the "real economy" in fact proved unable to deal with the complexities that global access to complex financial products present to decision making, particularly when risks are concealed.

Economic decision makers' faith that the tremendous elasticity within the financial markets would dilute risk actually distorted the healthy dichotomy between returns and risk, skewing them toward the pursuit of ever higher profits. In the absence of appropriate instruments to curtail financial crises, intensifying the regulation and supervision of financial markets would be an alternative option. However, state policies during the last three decades emphasized deregulation. At the same time, innovations in communications technology helped to institute a global "real time" financial market, fostering a euphoric climate in which investors believed they could make quick and substantial gains. Financial institutions created paths of elasticity by facilitating credit and by providing a myriad of technocrats who specialized in eliminating the problem of risk. In this highly competitive environment, any threats of inversion were theoretically and "technologically" dismissed. The system was not reality based and was incapable of dealing with the highly risky speculations that were coming to light.

In response, some financial practitioners developed a strategy that involved economic and financial criminality (EFC). Using their informational advantages, they attempted to cover up the problem with even riskier and more aggressive investment schemes, but the elasticity of the system was not infinite, and when the system inevitably snapped, many white collar managers and technocrats managed to escape personal liability for their mistakes. In Portugal, for example, one bank (Business Portuguese Bank) was directly saved from bankruptcy by government (i.e., taxpayer) intervention. Another (Portuguese Commercial Bank, or BCP) was indirectly supported by the state, which authorized a public bank to help it.[1] A third (Portuguese Private Bank) was closed. A few judicial inquiries followed, and a small number of arrests were made (albeit fewer than could be counted on one hand).

The direct and indirect consequences of EFC associated with the financial crisis have been economically and socially harmful for Portugal. The increase in public debt is estimated to be around several billion euros. Portuguese firms now face higher costs for borrowing, which reduces their competitiveness and can lead to insolvencies and unemployment. Portugal, currently experiencing its highest rate of unemployment in 30 years (it was 15 percent in the first quarter of 2012), is also experiencing huge reductions in opportunity costs resulting from the redirection of public resources away from essential goods and services, such as health care, education, the judicial system, and law enforcement agencies (rendering the acquisition and allocation of additional resources to combat crime even more problematic).

Nevertheless, there is a large gray area between bad economic or managerial decisions and economic and financial crime. Uncertainty is an inherent part of business, and many economic and financial decisions that produce negative results cannot even be classified as bad decisions. It is therefore impossible to measure the extent of white collar crime associated with the crisis or to distinguish between "natural" downturns and criminal behavior. In Portugal, the crisis has underlined the need to devote more attention to economic and financial crime (especially to white collar crime), as well as the importance of heeding Sutherland's (1968) appeal for an increased focus on the problem of white collar crime. It also has exposed the failure of Portuguese judicial and legal institutions to address the criminal behavior of those in positions of economic power.

Even before Sutherland's famous intervention, Morris (1968) demonstrated awareness of the threats that eventually would become visible through the crisis. Today his words seem prophetic:

> "[C]riminals of the upperworld" is suggested to define that numerous but never clearly identified group of criminals whose social position, intelligence, and criminal technique permit them to move among their fellow citizens virtually immune to recognition and prosecution as criminals. (Morris 1968, 35)

He then lists several criminal offenses typically committed by white collar criminals that resonate with recent economic crises:

5. Speculating manufacturers who lift the price of their stocks by postponing legitimate operating expenses so that their net earnings may appear high and insiders may sell stocks advantageously. Later, when the addition of the postponed and current expenses apparently depresses earnings, they may repurchase their stocks at bargain prices.
6. Operators who pyramid stocks through holding companies to the point where the paper value of the securities issued is many times the actual value of the basic property.
7. Investment bankers who organize investment trusts to buy securities for their stockholders and then proceed to play both sides of the market with excessive and unstipulated profits to themselves and with loss or ruin to the stockholders. . . .
8. Directors who use inside information to make profits at the expense of the stockholders in whose interests they are presumed to be working. . . .
9. Investment bankers who sell bonds advertised as backed by first mortgages on property worth twice their value when they know that the real value of the property does not exceed the mortgage. (Morris 1968, 36)

The types of criminality that emerge through economic and financial activities are not new, nor are the difficulties they present for criminal prosecutions. However, the overall treatment of this phenomenon is problematic, beginning with definitional concepts. EFC constitutes a large range of offenses, including money laundering, burglary, larceny, embezzlement, crimes against free market competition, forgery, deception, bribes, corruption, insider trading, pollution, crimes against workers, and price collusion. In Portugal (see the appendix at the end of this chapter), EFC is divided into four categories, each of which includes offenses substantially different in nature. Although there has been an effort in the academic literature to take an integrated approach to the EFC phenomena, the difficulties of this are well documented in empirical studies. Even the well-known distinction between corporate and occupational crime proposed by Clinard and Quinney (1963) is not sufficient to address this problem. Moreover, official crime-data collection agencies often establish ad hoc criteria to aggregate and to classify data. For example, it is difficult to understand the impact of the economic crisis in Portugal in terms of EFC because, as demonstrated by the data presented later in this essay, the statistical classification ignores the original causes of the offenses.

Another discussion within criminological discourse focuses on the characteristics of offenders. According to Sutherland (1968), the "status of the offender" is crucial for the analysis, and he defended, therefore, the use of the term "white collar criminal." Several researchers, for example, Shapiro (1990), Ponsaers and Ruggiero (2002), and Bacher (2005), have rejected this limitation on the grounds that economic and financial crimes are not only committed by people with status. They argue that today everyone has access to new technologies and can use them as "the weapon of economic crime." Conversely, Green (2006) and Brightman (2009) indicate that those who possess the power and means to influence economic decisions are required to justify their acts and should be included within the analysis because they can disseminate and promote a culture that facilitates criminal behavior within organizations. Moreover, such powerful players can influence institutions—including those that label what should be considered crime and those responsible for criminal prosecutions. For example, in the context of the financial crisis, the study of white collar criminality makes sense if it is suspected that senior managers and specialized technocrats, as a result of their special decision-making powers and informational advantages, drove the behavior of stakeholders and significantly impacted the markets. A significant limitation for the study of EFC, especially in regards to the impact of the financial crisis, is that published Portuguese statistical data on criminality do not indicate offenders' social status.

However, problems associated with the study of EFC are not confined to the features of the offender; there is also the problem of the nature of the acts and how they are classified. Juridical tradition applies the "crime" label only to acts defined as crimes by penal law. Sutherland (1968) included civil and administrative offenses in the classification of white collar crime, because white collar criminals had the power to influence the judicial system through the determination of what should or should not be included in criminal law. Therefore, these offenders would be expected to exclude from the label "crime" several harmful acts that they practice.

Tappan (1968) refutes this position:

> Our definitions of crime cannot be rooted in epithets, in minority value judgments or prejudice, or in loose abstractions. Within a system of justice under law, crime must be defined quite precisely and in accordance with the explicit formulations of the legislature. (Tappan 1968, 374)

Caldwell (1968) equally defends this legal approach to crime in strong terms:

> It must be insisted that no person is a white-collar criminal or any kind of criminal until he has been properly adjudicated as such in the criminal court. This is as true in the case of a corporation charged with some type of criminal behavior as it is in the case of a person accused of murder. (Caldwell 1968, 380)

In contrast, Hagan (1994) warns that if criminologists treat only offenses under penal law as crime, they become staked to the status quo, which is a result of political choice. According to this view, environmental crimes could not be classified as such until recently in Portugal, because *nullum crimen sine lege*— "no penalty without a law." Ponsaers and Ruggiero (2002) highlight the limitations of the juridical approach when conducting an international analysis that involves more than one juridical system. After all, what is considered a crime differs across nations, and if criminology intends to produce scientific research, universality is needed in its essential concepts. As a solution, Yeager (2010) proposes that the term *crime* be replaced with *lawbreaking*: "My interest is in the explanation of any lawbreaking committed in the pursuit of corporate goals, no matter under which legal regimen the state seeks remedies" (Yeager 2010, 26).

Official Portuguese crime statistics are produced by judicial institutions. But the criminal law is fragmented into several individual regulations, and there are several examples where the only difference between criminal behavior and civil or administrative lawbreaking is the amount of money that is involved.

The question of what should be considered crime is not minor in the study of economic crisis, because the innovative character inherent to economic activities can also be expressed as economic crime. In fact, Schumpeterians define white collar crime as the seeking of opportunities through the use of innovative techniques (namely, exploiting the gray area between what is licit and illicit). As a consequence, white collar crime provides new ways to differentiate among competitors, especially in an environment of crisis and depression, where business ethics interfere with profit goals. An example of this is a fiscal planning scheme in which complex relations between offshore companies are configured to circumvent any direct infraction of the law, but the results ultimately contradict the equity objectives of fiscal law and should therefore be considered as an offense. An example in the financial market involves "licit" complex structured financial products, where the information about the implicit risks is not clear but is predictable according to mathematical models under conditions that are not testable in the "real world."

Misinformation about the risks inherent in many financial products was one of the major harms that emerged from the financial crisis in Portugal. Even public institutions, authorized to use only minimally risky products, were surprised by the "true" risks involved. Therefore, to confine white collar crime only to what is expressed in criminal law is perhaps too restrictive. One solution may be for public authorities to assess schemes before their practical application is approved (this is already applied in Portugal in the case of fiscal planning schemes).[2] However, many legal specialists contend that this approach violates the principles of security, certainty of law, and perhaps even equity.

Criminological literature notes other problems associated with the study of EFC, such as the difficulty distinguishing individual responsibility from organizational responsibility. Portuguese law permits both individuals and organizations to be convicted for certain criminal behavior.

Examples of this are contained in numerous regulations (e.g., competition, pollution, property).

The lack of suitably trained personnel and insufficient resources hinders Portugal's ability to effectively prosecute EFC. In recent years, the recruitment of knowledgeable individuals and an investment in specialized training have somewhat changed this situation. However, when given a choice between investigating conventional street crime, for which they were intensively trained, and dedicating hundreds of office hours to analyzing numbers and accounting data, "traditional" police officers or detectives tend to choose the former option. Meanwhile, Portugal has instituted several other changes designed to tackle EFC, including the establishment of an infrastructure to enable effective data sharing between public agencies and the formation of interdisciplinary investigation teams.

EFC associated with financial crises had a dual harmful impact on Portuguese society. Besides the direct damages to victims, the capacity of the Portuguese government to create new mechanisms to combat criminality—in particular, EFC—as well as to devote more resources to this objective was constrained by the fact that billions of euros were already diverted to propping up a ruined financial sector. Portuguese public expenditure was already severely restricted by euro zone mandates that imposed a reduction in the public deficit of more than 5 percent of the GDP, and about 30 percent of the GDP for the public debt, until 2012.

The challenge facing Portugal is how to shape a social model of dense control and regulation of law-abiding organizations and individuals without restricting or inhibiting private innovation and initiative. It is known that strong regulation and control of economic behavior limit innovative initiatives. On the other hand, it improves confidence in the market and reinforces the collective conscious. What is a fair balance? As Portugal faces serious competitive difficulties and a lack of new ideas for stimulating the economy, many people believe that recovery depends on innovative private investment initiatives. In other words, the economy is in corporations' hands, supported by the financial system. In this context, it is not strange to find institutional indulgence for white collar criminality.

The next section describes Portuguese law on economic and financial criminality, and after reviewing Portuguese research on these matters, we explore statistical data on EFC in Portugal. Unsurprisingly, there is substantial legal fragmentation. Moreover, reported offenses (and EFC detentions rates) are relatively low compared with other types of crime. (This is very similar to what happens in other European countries.) The major justifications for low numbers associated with EFC are explored in the criminological literature and are linked to complexities inherent to EFC and to the impunity of the powerful. But it is not unrealistic to note that a trade-off between economic efficiency and a strong white collar crime control might exist.

The Portuguese Law

Laws governing the prosecution and sentencing of EFC are not located under one single category of Portuguese law. Although many of the relevant offenses are contained in the Criminal Code (established in 1982 and subsequently amended several times), there is no specific definition that deals with these crimes in a systematic manner. This poses troubling questions for the courts in terms of legal interpretation and is an indication of criminal laws' ultima ratio and fragmentary nature. Given the limitations of space, the following is an outline of the principal ways in which the treatment of white collar crime is different from the approach to "primary criminal law" in the Portuguese legal context.

Portugal is part of the continental European tradition, possessing a juridical system whose criminal law is significantly influenced by German legislation and doctrine. The Public Prosecution Service is not authorized by law to choose which crimes should or should not be prosecuted. Most instances of white collar crime are considered to be "public offenses."[3] Insofar as written law is concerned, at least, this form of criminality is a priority. However, difficulties in investigating this type of criminality and the always-present doubts in interpreting some legal concepts, more typical in civil law–tradition countries such as Portugal, combined with the aforementioned legal fragmentation and the lack of available resources for specialized police agencies, result in EFC having one of the highest "dark figures" of all criminal offenses.

The range of penalties that can be applied to EFC is no different from those reserved for other crimes. Main penalties are imprisonment (normally from 1 month to 8 years) and fines (applicable to individuals and to corporations, associations, or foundations). Accessory sanctions include temporary prohibition of the pursuit of certain jobs or activities, the loss of tax benefits, corporate legal dissolution, and the confiscation of assets.

Portugal's Criminal Code covers various types of fraud including, but not limited to, insurance, informatics and telecommunications,[4] "patrimonial infidelity" (the failure to deal with another person's patrimonial interests in accordance with one's duties and intentionally causing significant damage), extortion, and specific forms of credit or debit card fraud. Of particular relevance, especially in times of economic crisis, are "offenses against patrimonial rights," which include intentional or negligent bankruptcy and the favoring of creditors.[5] Portuguese law creates special divisions for "crimes against the public sector," that is, the illicit appropriation of public sector goods, and for "unlawful administration" (similar to patrimonial infidelity, where a person in a senior managerial position intentionally fails to comply with "control rules or economic regulations of a rational management").

Because money laundering is a major concern of the European Union, member states need to adopt EU standards in their national regulations, with the exception of those that are directly applicable to national juridical systems. In addition, Portuguese money-laundering laws must comply with several international conventions and treaties. However, it was only in 2004 that this offense became part of the Portuguese Criminal Code, with a definition spelling out how the offense leads to illicit advantages.

"Influence trafficking" is the act of asking for or accepting—either for the benefit of oneself or for a third party—a patrimonial or nonpatrimonial advantage, or the promise thereof, in order to abuse one's real or supposed influence over a public authority. Another offense is "criminal association," which presupposes that at least three people are joined together to promote or establish a group, organization, or association devoted to committing one or more crimes. Inevitably, all of these offenses are extremely difficult to prove in court and have a nonexistent conviction rate, not due to inaccurate legal description or requirements, but because of significant obstacles to obtaining evidence.

Until 2008, bribery[6] was a "specific crime" for which only "civil servants," as described within the Criminal Code, could be prosecuted. A 2008 law, compliant with a framework decision from the EU (2003/568/JAI, from the Council, July 22nd), established that corruption can also be perpetrated within private activity and international commerce by individuals or corporations.[7] In a recent amendment,[8] the Criminal Code increased penalties and the range of offenders considered to be "civil servants" to include CEOs of public companies and other top public administrators. The law distinguishes between "active" and "passive" bribery. The former occurs when the offender (who may be any person) acts to obtain from a "civil servant" an action or omission that is contrary to the civil servant's public duties. The offender may give or promise to give the civil servant patrimonial or nonpatrimonial advantage, which the civil servant is legally prohibited from receiving. "Active bribery" can also occur if the benefit is not contrary to the defendant's duties but not applicable in the concrete case (e.g., a due subvention paid before its legal term). In these cases, punishment is more lenient. The category of "passive bribery" focuses on the same conduct, but from the perspective of the public servant accepting benefits. Taking into account the civil servant's special responsibilities, punishment is harsher than in active bribery.

In passive bribery cases, civil servants who denounce the crime within a maximum 30-day period after the offer is made and before the legal suit will not be penalized. Nor will civil servants be punished if they voluntarily reject the offered bribe or if they return it before the crime has been committed. If the briber withdraws or requests the return of the illegal offer, no sanctioning will occur. To encourage offenders to desist from their activities, whenever a defendant helps authorities gather decisive evidence to identify or capture other responsible actors, a judge may mitigate penalties.

When the bribery offender holds political office (as defined in the law), the penalties are more severe, on the grounds that such offenders have greater public responsibilities to society. Included under this statute are offenses such as the violation of rules regarding public financial budgets,[9] violations of urban planning rules,[10] embezzlement, and illegal economical participation in a business where the offender is duty-bound to uphold the public interest.

A 1994 statute prescribes general preventive actions to be taken by public prosecutors and establishes a specialized police department for certain offenses characterized as white collar crime. Another crime related to EFC is "illegal business participation," in other words, when a civil servant intervenes in a contract or other legal instrument and provokes a patrimonial loss to the interests that the civil servant is expected to uphold.

Other significant legislation relevant to EFC falls under the category of tax offenses, including violations of tax obligations, customs regulations, tax benefits, and compulsory contributions to social security protection systems. These infractions can be dealt with either as crimes or as administrative offenses (simple or serious), that is, actions that do not violate legal interests protected by criminal law but rather run counter to an organizational interest regulated by administrative law. Such offenses are punishable by a fine and, under particular circumstances, with an accessory penalty.[11] In creating an extension to the general rule in the Criminal Code, the Portuguese legislature, demonstrating concern that tax offenders could escape punishment, declared that the *tempus delicti* is not only the moment in which the offender has acted, or should have acted in cases of omission, but also the moment at which the typical criminal result is produced.

Another interesting aspect of Portuguese tax law concerns corporate criminal liability. The rule applies when the offense has been committed by the company's legal representatives, in its name and in its "general interest." It is noteworthy that the corporation is exempt from responsibility when the offender has acted contrary to a superior's explicit instructions. Corporate criminal liability does not absolve individual responsibility but rather constitutes a possible case of "cumulative penal liability."

Several specific offenses that fall under the rubric of "ordinary tributary crimes" should be noted. "Tributary fraud" relates to attempts to mislead the tax or social security administration by providing false information that leads to the offender's patrimonial increase. "Criminal association" is defined by the law as a union of people whose sole purpose is to act together to perpetrate tax crimes. Contraband (smuggling) is also a punishable offense. "Tax fraud" (with its "qualified variants," depending on the seriousness of the crime) is another offense by which the offender fails to declare income. Under a special clause, the offense does not incur criminal penalties whenever the illegitimate patrimonial advantage is less than €15,000 ($20,400). "Tax embezzlement" is defined as the failure to deliver tax revenues greater than €7,500 ($10,200) to the tax administration when obliged to do so. A special section on offenses against social security includes fraud and embezzlement against that institution.

There has been a considerable effort to penetrate bank secrecy in order to successfully combat the above-mentioned crimes and others, such as money laundering. For example, a law published in September 2010 has significantly increased the number of situations in which a tax administration decision is enough to mandate access to once-protected private data.

Portuguese law is also concerned with offenses against the national economy. These offenses include crimes such as trafficking in fraudulent goods, unlawful monopolization, the destruction of goods "with relevant

interest to the national economy" (not specifically defined by law; therefore, the concept is left to the courts to define), market speculation, and
fraud in obtaining subsidies or subventions or in being granted credit.

Stock markets are also regulated by criminal law, either in terms of
criminal or administrative offenses. Crimes against the market itself include insider trading, with privileged information defined as "all information not to be made public that, being accurate and concerning directly or
indirectly to any issuer or to stock products or other financial instruments,
would be suitable, if publicized, to influence in a considerable way its market price." Also forbidden is market manipulation, such as promoting
false, incomplete, exaggerated, or tendentious information; or undertak-
ing fabricated market transactions that manipulate the functioning of the
market (particularly price determination factors). The Code of Commercial Enterprises penalizes illicit share acquisition, illicit distribution to
shareholders of the company's own goods, and the dissemination of misleading information to shareholders.

The type of criminality that is the focus of this study is frequently com-
bated through the use of intrusive instruments such as wiretapping and
seizures. A 2002 law established a special regime for evidence collection,
breach of professional secrecy, and asset loss in favor of the state for some
crimes, especially bribery, money laundering, and contraband. In an attempt to achieve a fair balance between investigative interests and discovering the truth on the one hand and civil and personal liberties and pri-
vacy on the other, Portugal enacted a new regulation in 2007 that requires
judicial approval for wiretapping to be contingent on the grounds that
there is no other effective means to gather evidence. The regulation also
established stricter rules about wiretapping, judicial monitoring, and destruction of irrelevant material.

A special witness protection statute enacted in 1999 and subsequently
amended is valuable in more serious cases of EFC, where people could
provide evidence that they (or their families) are being threatened. It permits the concealment of witnesses' identity, the deposition by videoconfer-
ence or with a distorted voice, as well as more drastic measures, such as
the relocation of witnesses, the issuance of new identification documents,
or even changing facial characteristics by means of plastic surgery. Undercover police actions for preventive or investigative purposes are regulated
by a special statute and can be used only for serious offenses, some of them
linked to white collar crime (money laundering, bribery, frauds, economic

and financial offenses on an international scale and those connected with the stock markets). These actions are always very sensitive in terms of their final results, given the fact that the line between an undercover (legal) agent and the (illegal) agent provocateur is fluid.

Portuguese Research on Economic and Financial Crime

The few existing empirical studies on EFC in Portugal have tended to focus on corruption. Until recently, criminological research was uncommon in this country. Portugal also has some institutional features that may have made research into these topics even more difficult. Portuguese official crime statistics are flawed in many ways, and public institutions, although directed to practice transparency and disclosure, often did not follow these principles. Banks tend to have strict rules on secrecy and, until recently, were not publicly scrutinized. Moreover, funding for empirical scientific research in areas close to the social sciences is difficult to secure.

Usually, the literature on EFC or even white collar crime has been produced by legal scholars and focuses on the analysis of statutes, rules, and procedures, eventually conveying personal reflections on the causes and mechanisms of such behaviors. Corruption is the subject that is most often reflected upon, due to its impact on the quality of democracy,[12] and of public services.[13] The purpose of this section is to provide a synthetic review of the empirical studies that currently exist in Portugal.

Some studies on corruption use official crime statistics to portray the phenomenon. One of the most common conclusions is that the dark figures of corruption and related crimes (e.g., influence trafficking, peculation, and illegal business participation) are impossible to measure or compare (Faria 2007; Grilo 2005; Maia 2008; Santos 2001, 2003; Triães 2004). Through the analyses of judicial case files, we discover that the typical individual brought before justice for bribing or accepting bribes is a married male over 30 years of age. Bribe givers tend to work for private companies; bribe takers generally come from the lower or higher ranks of public services. Data also tell us that the bribe taker usually is a local government official or works in one of the various Portuguese police forces.[14] In the most common scenario, the bribe or associated gift is of small value, under €100 (approximately $135),[15] and it is usually offered for the purpose of getting a public official to "forget" to impose a fine, to provide a license or permit, or to accelerate a decision process that will grant some right or benefit to the bribe giver (Triães 2004).

Most cases do not lead to convictions, largely because of insufficient evidence.[16] For instance, between 1995 and 2000, for every 100 individuals investigated, only 16 were prosecuted for corruption and 11 of them were found guilty (Maia 2008).[17] Furthermore, only a small number of those convicted receive prison sentences (Santos 2003).[18]

Several researchers explored how corruption and related crimes are treated by the print media (see Grilo 2005, for the period 1999–2000; and Maia 2008, for the periods 2000–2001 and 2005–2006). The two studies cited concluded that, generally, newspapers give little attention to cases of corruption, and when they do focus on the issue, it is usually for a case involving a well-known public figure. However, Maia (2008) saw a small increase in front-page coverage of corruption from 2000 to 2006, as well as an increase in the total number of news reports that contained the word "corruption." Why? One reason appears to be that news outlets increasingly tend to include the opinion of experts, interviews, information on the efforts of the police, or information about legal changes rather than, as previously, limit themselves to mere descriptions of the facts of the crime. Still, most of these news reports do not occupy more than a quarter-page of the newspaper sheet (Grilo 2005). Moreover, the term "corruption" was often used to describe crimes such as money laundering, influence trafficking, misappropriation of funds, document forgery, and other economic crimes. Sometimes it is even used to describe noneconomic offenses, such as terrorism.

Insofar as public perceptions and practices regarding corruption are concerned, Ferreira and Baptista (1992) report that in a nationwide survey conducted in 1990 (sample dimension: $n = 1000$), although three-quarters of respondents condemn bribery, 18.5 percent of them still think that bribery is acceptable and 65 percent have a negative image of whistle-blowers. Furthermore, survey respondents indicate a belief that those who report corruption to the police are motivated by feelings of envy, particularly when large amounts of money are involved. Cases involving small or petty corruption tend to be condoned by the public.

More recently, Sousa and Triães (2008), through a survey on values, attitudes, and practices about corruption and ethics,[19] point out that Portuguese citizens have strong feelings toward situations of "black corruption"[20] that are more similar to offenses prescribed by the criminal law (bribery and misappropriation of funds) and toward practices of nepotism because of their feelings of relative deprivation. Portuguese tend to have ambiguous responses about accepting gifts, conflicting interests, financing political parties, or petty corruption. Finally, they are less likely to criticize public officials who accept bribes or stretch the rules for using public goods if their actions are perceived as benefiting the larger community.[21] More than half consider that if the bribe is for a just cause or to benefit the overall population, then those acts should not be considered corrupt. Still, the Sousa and Triães' survey respondents condemn public actors more strongly than private actors: 64.5 percent of the respondents believe that ignorance of the exact terms of the law is sufficient grounds to avoid prosecution.

Portuguese people believe that the legal system is more lenient toward those in power, namely, members of government (81.9 percent), members of the parliament (79.9 percent), sport celebrities (81 percent), mayors (74.5 percent), and company directors (67.4 percent) (Magone 2008). A more complex analysis by Jalali (2008), using the importance respondents give to the fight on corruption (among a list of governmental priorities) as an independent variable and the satisfaction with democracy as a dependent variable, shows that a stronger critique of corrupt practices is statistically correlated with greater dissatisfaction with the functioning of Portuguese democracy. Lastly, respondents hold a negative view about Portugal's ability to fight corruption (Dores 2008). Eighty percent of respondents do not believe the fight has produced results, while 34.5 percent blame the government for this failure. Another 18 percent blame the failure on ineffective courts, and just over 16 percent believe everyone in Portugal is responsible for the situation.

Trogano (2011) presents a case study of a police investigation into tributary offenses in the scrap-iron sector. The investigation overcame major difficulties, including the large quantity of documentation needed (tax and bank reports and so forth), complexity of the case (numerous facts and actors to investigate over several years), time (some of the facts were more than 5 years old), lack of a clear strategy from the judiciary police, as well as an insufficient number of specialized agents to investigate the case. Tax frauds designed to avoid the payment of value-added tax and other national taxes occur not only in the scrap-iron but also in the car retail sector and in the cork industry.

Tributary scams generally require the offender to create multiple fraudulent documents and transactions. A fictitious commercial chain is created to forge purchases and refundable costs that will later be presented to the tax authorities. A paper trail is produced when documents are forged and simulated transactions are constructed, so that everything seems to be functioning in accordance with the law. Along with this, artificial financial transactions are created through national and international bank accounts in accordance with a specific strategy. An international and organized criminal setting is required to take advantage of the tax system on commercial transactions inside the European Union. Therefore, tributary scams involve companies of different sizes and with functions designated according to their placement in the scam pyramid. Preliminary results show that in two investigations into the scrap-iron industry, the state had lost €153 billion ($182 billion). Estimates of the total loss were as high as €205 billion ($276 billion). In the car retail sector, police investigations returned to the state €4 billion (more than $5 billion) (Trogano 2011).

Portuguese Economic and Financial Criminality in Numbers

Official Data

To understand the EFC phenomenon in Portugal, it is important to analyze the available data. However, in addition to the problem of large "dark figures," we found another limitation: Data are insufficiently organized. The only available official data for crime statistics are annual, covering the period 1993–2009. They provide information on reported crimes, detentions, and completed cases in the courts of first instance (appeals are not included).[22]

From the data provided by *Estatísticas da Justiça* of the Portuguese Ministry of Justice (2010), we have selected crimes that can be defined as EFC without changing their original aggregation. As a result, EFC data are organized into four original statistical categories: offenses against patrimony (against property, against patrimony in general, and against patrimonial rights); offenses against society (forgery, pollution, corruption, and "criminal association," among others); crimes against the public sector (illicit appropriation of public sector goods, electoral frauds, usurpation of public office, embezzlement, peculation, public sector authority abuse, inter alia);

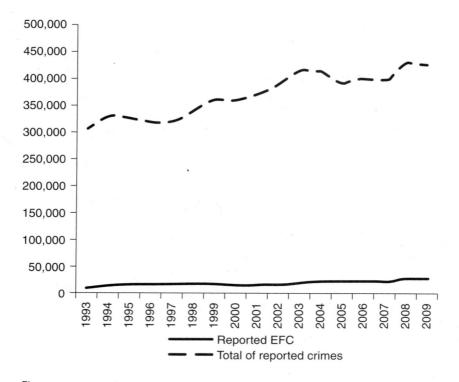

Figure 13.1
Number of reported offenses 1993–2009. Note: EFC=economic and financial criminality. Source: Data from *Estatísticas da Justiça*. Adapted by authors.

and violations of separate regulations (stock market crimes, ordinary tributary crimes, customs crimes, tax frauds, offenses against national economy, frauds in informatics, among others).[23]

During the 1993–2009 period, we observed a clear increase in the number of all reported crimes in Portugal (Figure 13.1), a tendency that is also followed by reported EFCs. Economic and financial crime represents between 3.7 percent and 6.5 percent of the total reported crimes (Figure 13.2). Although the proportion of EFC reported is small, it has been increasing in this period. At the same time, despite a declining trend, offenses against patrimony were dominant, followed by violations of separate regulation. Crimes against the public sector remain the lowest in the group of EFC, representing only 10 percent of the total (Figure 13.3). Despite the small contribution of offenses against the public sector to the total EFC, when we

Economic and Financial Criminality in Portugal

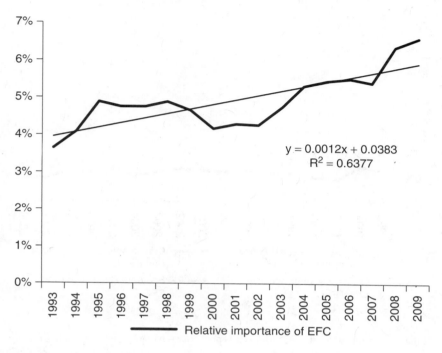

Figure 13.2
Proportion of EFC in all reported offenses 1993–2009. Source: Data from *Estatísticas da Justiça*. Adapted by authors.

take into account subsequent arrests, a different picture emerges, as we will see later in this chapter.

Approximately 8 to 12 percent of reported crimes result in arrests (Figure 13.4). Only a fraction of all reported offenses result in detentions. EFC detentions, which represent 4–5 percent of the total arrests in Portugal (Figure 13.5), do not differ much from the tendency shown by all crimes. These small proportions reflect laws' fragmentation, doubts in interpreting legal concepts, and specialized police agencies' lack of resources, which results in large "dark figures" and in a small number of identified cases.

Among the four EFC categories that are analyzed, crimes against the public sector have the highest percentage of detentions, even though this category had the lowest number of reported offenses. During the period under study, public sector offense detentions increased from 50 to 80 percent of all EFC detentions (Figure 13.6).

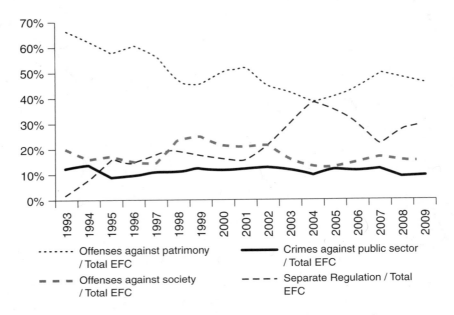

Figure 13.3
Relative importance of EFC offenses types, 1993–2009. Note: For each EFC offense type, relative importance is computed as the number of each type of EFC
offense divided by the number of total EFC offenses. Source: Data from *Estatísticas
da Justiça*. Adapted by authors.

Dividing the number of arrests by the number of reported crimes, we
conclude that offenses against the public sector behave quite differently
from other types of EFC and from other forms of non-EFC (Figure 13.7). In
particular, the proportion between detentions and reported crimes is higher
in these offenses.

Controlling for the increase of population, we computed two indicators:
per capita reported EFC and per capita EFC detentions.[24] Over the period
of the study, both indicators increased, as did the gap between them
(Figure 13.8). In recent years, 9–10 percent of cases resolved in the courts
of first instance were related to EFC. Despite representing only a small
proportion of the total, it is an increasing fraction (Figure 13.9). Since
2004, all four categories of EFC are equally weighted in cases concluded
before the courts, but before 2002 offenses against patrimony and society
represented a higher proportion of concluded cases (Figure 13.10).

Economic and Financial Criminality in Portugal

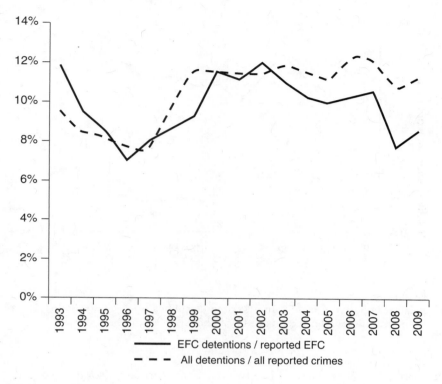

Figure 13.4
Relative importance of detentions in reported crimes, 1993–2009. Source: Data from *Estatísticas da Justiça*. Adapted by authors.

The lack of available data restricts us from investigating the possible links between types of EFC and other variables, such as personal attributes of offenders, namely, the potential link between socio-professional status of suspects and the types and frequency of their involvement in EFC.

Perceptions

Since 1995, Transparency International (TI) has published an annual ranking in which orders countries are ordered according to a Corruption Perceptions Index (CPI). The index, which ranges between 0 (*highly corrupt*) to 10 (*highly clean*), is the outcome of TI's surveys on perceptions of

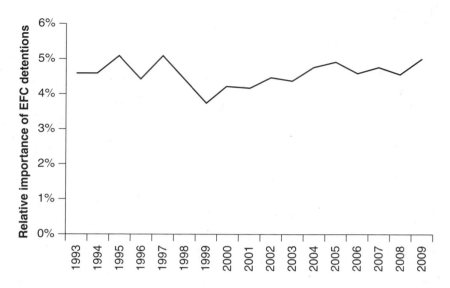

Figure 13.5
Relative importance of EFC in all crime detentions, 1993–2009. Source: Data from *Estatísticas da Justiça*. Adapted by authors.

corruption. These surveys use two types of information sources: country experts (risk agencies and country analysts), both residents and non-residents; and business leaders. In 2009, TI ranked 180 countries, including Portugal.

Although the index is not an appropriate tool to analyze the temporal trends of the absolute values of the CPI for each country, TI's published rankings allows comparisons between countries within a single year.[25] A comparison of results over the past two decades shows a noteworthy change. In 1995, 21 countries were ahead of Portugal in the ranking; in 2009 the number had grown to 34 countries (cf. Transparency International 2010). However, the apparent deterioration of the Portuguese rank doesn't tell the whole story. Two factors should be noted: In 1995, Luxemburg and Belgium (which ranked ahead of Portugal) were classed as a single territory; in 2009 they appeared separately. Second, in 1995 TI did not include twelve countries that appeared ahead of Portugal in the 2009 ranking. Applying these considerations, Portugal's rank is essentially unchanged, but still with a score that is only three-fifths of the CPI score registered by the most non-corrupt country.

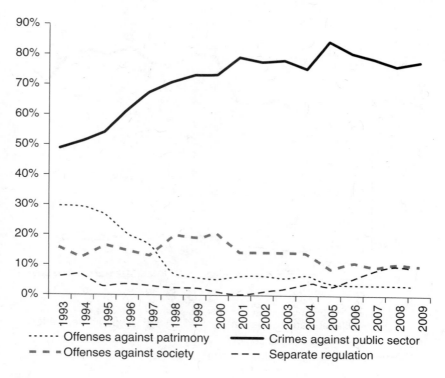

Figure 13.6
Relative importance of EFC offenses in total EFC detentions, 1993–2009. Source: Data from *Estatísticas da Justiça*. Adapted by authors.

In addition to the CPI, Transparency International (2009) administers the Global Corruption Barometer which collects public opinion data about other aspects of corruption. According to its 2009 survey, political parties and the private business sector are most affected by corrupt practices, which follows the pattern of average European (and even world) opinion (Table 13.1).

When asked about personal practice of corruption, the Portuguese people consider themselves to be one of the least corrupt (2 percent of respondents, against 5 percent in Europe and 13 percent in world average). What motivates these answers remains to be discovered, since this figure is not in accordance with Portugal's ranking, as seen above.

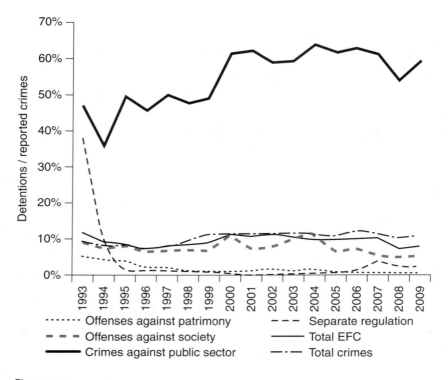

Figure 13.7
EFC offenses: Reported crimes and detentions, 1993–2009. Source: Data from *Estatísticas da Justiça*. Adapted by authors.

Conclusion

In this work, we have attempted to give an incisive yet synthetic overview of EFC and white collar crime in Portugal: a theoretical framework linked to the Portuguese reality, a normative and procedural outline, a review of previous academic research, and some quantitative data available in this country.

We will not try to provide a real conclusion. In view of some of the characteristics discussed about Portugal, it is not possible for us to magically pull from our academic hats an insightful and pertinent scientific finale for this work. Yet, by looking at work already produced by academics from the fields of economics, statistics, law, criminology, and sociology, we have been able to identify several "gaps" or "flaws"—among

Economic and Financial Criminality in Portugal

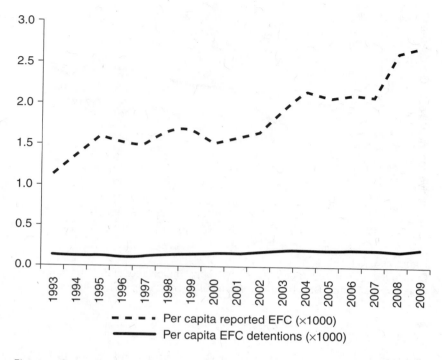

Figure 13.8
Per capita reported EFC and per capita detentions 1993–2009. Source: Data from *Estatísticas da Justiça*. Adapted by authors.

them the absence of previous regulatory work from economics experts, political turmoil, the inferior resources available for investigating EFC, the scattered rules in criminal law, the near absence of scientific research, weak available data, the large dark figures on EFC, which, if we take a minute to appreciate the whole picture "at a distance," are no more than silences tactically situated (as Foucault 2006 would have said) in a deeper structure.

In this structure, which reflects the history of one specific country in an international environment, there are factors that help us to better understand the true nature of EFC. Its political conditions are intimately tied to the functioning of the national and international market, to the regulation of corporations and banks, and to the distribution of wealth. Citizens tend to hold political leaders to blame for corruption and other economic crimes. Portugal enjoys free circulation of people, goods, and capital in a European

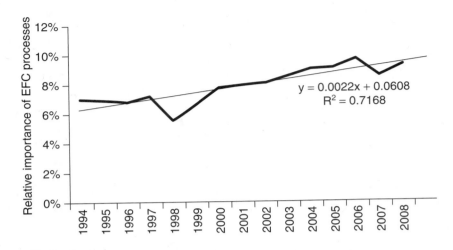

Figure 13.9
Concluded cases in courts of first resort: Relative importance of EFC in total crimes, 1994–2008. Source: Data from *Estatísticas da Justiça*. Adapted by authors.

space that imposes rules and controls and limits public spending and investment.

It is impossible to capture the whole picture if we find ourselves in a state of "liquid modernity" (Bauman 2003) where everything is volatile and changing—unless there is serious, deep, and comprehensive research and inquiry exploring all of these areas. We need "criminological imagination" (Young 2011) to make sense of the sparse available data from official reports or media accounts on major cases of corruption or fraud. We need a critical lens to better understand the causes of EFC and its effects in Portugal.

EFC may well have had a determinant effect on the current global economic crisis. And we are aware of some of the consequences that this international crisis had for Portugal in recent years: bankruptcies; unemployment; an "ashamed poverty" that hides itself and does not seek help; political instability reinforced by the supranational instructions on how to spend or save public money; economical stagnation; strain produced by international markets on the "economical health" of the country; obstructed access to banks by families and small companies; politically imposed cutbacks in public services; strikes and other public manifestations of dissatisfaction.

Economic and Financial Criminality in Portugal

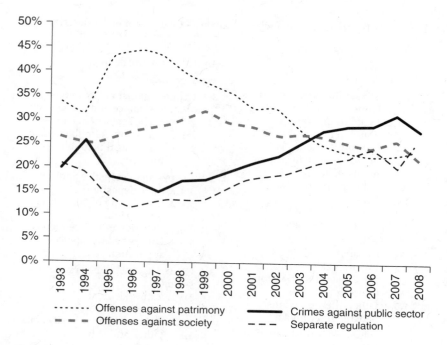

Figure 13.10
Concluded cases in courts: Importance of four EFC categories, 1993–2008. Source: Data from *Estatísticas da Justiça*. Adapted by authors.

Table 13.1
Public Opinion: Institutions Most Affected by Corruption

	Political parties	Parliament / legislature	Business / Private sector	Media	Public officials / civil servants	Judiciary	Average
	To what extent do you perceive the following institutions in this country to be affected by corruption? (1 = *not all corrupt*; 5 = *extremely corrupt*).						
Portugal	4	3.4	3.7	2.8	3.1	3.3	3.4
European average	3.7	3.4	3.4	3.3	3.4	3.1	3.4
World average	3.9	3.7	3.5	3.2	3.8	3.5	3.6

SOURCE: Global Corruption Barometer, Transparency International (2009). Adapted by authors.

Appendix – Economic and financial criminality – Criminal offences description

1. Offences against patrimony	3. Crimes against public sector
1.1. Against property 1.1.1. Confidence abuse	3.1. Influence trafficking 3.2. Electoral frauds

1.2. Against patrimony in general
    1.2.1. Fraud in banking
    1.2.2. Fraud in insurances
    1.2.3. Fraud in informatics and
        communications
    1.2.4. Frauds relative to employ-
        ment and labor
    1.2.5. Other patrimony frauds
    1.2.6. Extortion
    1.2.7. Credit/debit card fraud
    1.2.8. Other offenses against
        patrimony in general
	3.3. Crimes against public authority
	    3.3.1. Resistance and coercion on
	        public sector official
	    3.3.2. Usurpation of public office
	    3.3.3. Others against public
	        authority

1.3. Against patrimonial rights
    1.3.1. Intentional or negligent
        bankruptcy and creditors'
        favoring
    1.3.2. Other offences against
        patrimonial rights
	3.4. Crimes against justice application
	    3.4.1. False deposition
	    3.4.2. Laundering of benefits of
	        illicit origin
	    3.4.3. Violation of justice secret
	    3.4.4. Others against justice
	        application

1.4. Other offences against patrimony
    1.4.1. Other offences against
        patrimony
	3.5. Crimes against public economical
	    sector
	    3.5.1. Embezzlement
	    3.5.2. Peculation
	    3.5.3. Public sector authority abuse
	    3.5.4. Other offences committed in
	        public office
	3.6. Other crimes against public sector

2. Offences against society	4. Offences regulated by separate regulation

2.1. Forgery Crimes
    2.1.1. Money and documents
        adulterations
    2.1.2. Other falsifications and
        forgeries
	4.1. Crimes at stock markets
	    4.1.1. Insider information abuse
	    4.1.2. Market manipulation
	    4.1.3. Other financial offenses

2.2. General danger crimes against
    society
    2.2.1. Offences against nature
    2.2.2. Pollution
    2.2.3. Medicines and food
        adulteration
    2.2.4. Other general danger against
        society
	4.2. Ordinary tributary crimes
	    4.2.1. Tributary fraud
	    4.2.2. Frustration credits
	    4.2.3. Violation of secrecy
	    4.2.4. Other tributary frauds

2.3. Offences against public peace
    2.3.1. Criminal association
	4.3. Customs' crimes
	    4.3.1. Receiving and material
	        assistance
	    4.3.2. Fraud in customs'
	        regulations
	    4.3.3. Marks and stamps breaking
	    4.3.4. Other customs' crimes

	4.4. Tax fraud
	    4.4.1. Tax fraud
	    4.4.2. Confidence abuse in taxation
	    4.4.3. Other tax frauds

(Continued)

2. Offences against society	4. Offences regulated by separate regulation
	4.5. Offences against social security protection system
	4.6. Offences against national economy 4.6.1. Frauds in subventions and others 4.6.2. Market speculation 4.6.3. Other offences against national economy
	4.7. Fraud in informatics
	4.8. Money laundering

SOURCE: *Estatísticas da Justiça (2010)*, Portuguese Ministry of Justice.

If EFC could explain only a small part of these outcomes, it would be important enough for Portugal to produce serious and systematic research, instead of letting silence prevail.

Notes

The authors would like to thank Conor O'Reilly for his invaluable help in reviewing this chapter.

1. CGD (Caixa Geral de Depósitos), a bank owned by the state that has a small share in BCP, helped this institution with an alliance: The CEO of CGD moved to BCP (and was elected CEO) and CGD financed BCP in order to increase its liquidity. The Portuguese government also created a warranty fund to help banks that was used by BCP.

2. According to Decree-Law nr. 29/2008, February 25, under some conditions organizations are obliged to communicate with fiscal authorities about innovative fiscal planning schemes they wish to implement in order to secure prior verification of eventual inconsistencies with the principles, foundations, or the spirit of fiscal law.

3. A "public offense" is a crime in which the public prosecutor has the right (and obligation) to initiate a lawsuit whenever a suspicion exists that a crime has been committed and there is, in general, no possible withdrawal of the process.

4. Informatics is the use of technology to solve complex problems.

5. We have tried to find the most suitable criminal offense in English law tradition in terms of translation. When that is not possible, a specific explanation is offered. Creditor favoring occurs when a person in bankruptcy or close to it pays certain debts before they are due or in a beneficial manner to select creditors, which causes patrimonial losses to others; this is considered an offense.

6. In this chapter, we use the concepts of bribery and corruption interchangeably.

7. Apart from "active corruption resulting in losses to international commerce," provisions concerning "active and passive bribery in the private sector" were introduced in a similar way to those we will describe later. This represents a "Copernican paradigm change" insofar as the legal protected good is not only the trust in the honesty of public administration, but also the honesty of workers even in the private sector. The "illicit contents" is now extended to the offering and/or receiving of "patrimonial or non-patrimonial advantage which is unlawful" and to avoiding concurrence distortion.

8. Published September 2010 and in force as of March 1, 2011.

9. The following are violations of public financial budgets: authorizing debts not allowed by law, authorizing payments without the control of the appropriate public agencies, or using revenue for other than approved specific goals.

10. Since 2011, violations of urban planning rules constituted an autonomous offense in the criminal code.

11. An accessory penalty is a sanction applied along with the fine (in this case) with the aim of preventing recidivism or underlining the offense's seriousness.

12. Intellectual and political elites have constantly questioned the quality and strength of Portugal's democracy since military rule ended in 1974. The country is governed primarily by the two centrist political parties (often in coalition with other smaller parties), which have rotated into power. Yet Portugal has high rates of abstention in every election (be it for the local or central government or to the European Parliament). The lack of civic and political participation is a constant topic of political and media debate.

13. Although Portugal has been unable to transform itself into a welfare state, it is also true that some of the most basic resources, including education, health, unemployment support, and transportation, are provided primarily (if not exclusively) by the state.

14. A well-known case involved several road traffic brigade police officers who received money for not issuing tickets to trucks.

15. This is in about 15 percent of cases where this value is known. Only 2.5 percent of the cases brought to the courts involved more than €50,000 ($67,000) (Triães 2004, from the analysis of sentencing decisions in the years 1999–2001).

16. The Portuguese judicial system still prefers proof produced by personal testimony over documentary evidence. Investigating cases of corruption takes a great deal of time (often extending over several years) and large amounts of paper (from bank account registers to administrative decisions and assets proofs). Interdisciplinary teams are now being established in the police, but judges and magistrates usually do not have special training to deal with these kinds of crimes. Complaints (frequently made out of professional obligation or so that "justice can be done"; see Triães 2004) tend to be anonymous and lack the basic elements that lead to successful police investigations.

17. It is easier to prove the use of public goods for private ends (misappropriation of funds). An example of this would be a mayor who uses machinery belonging to local public services to remodel his house (Triães 2004).

18. For instance: in 1998, of fifty individuals prosecuted, only thirty-three were found guilty and, of those, only eight received a prison sentence; in 1999, five out of

thirty-three individuals found guilty of corruption received a prison sentence; in 2000, of sixty-two individuals prosecuted, forty-three were found guilty, but none was sentenced to prison (Santos 2003).

19. This survey was conducted in November 2006 through a stratified sampling method and involved 1,009 respondents from all over the country between the ages of 18 and 75 years old.

20. According to the categories set by Heindenheimer of black, gray, and white behaviors and described by Sousa and Triães (2008, pp. 62–63):

> Corruption is a social construction, the product of interpretations and perceptions. These judgments are not homogeneous; they are changeable depending on the features of the corrupt act. The analysis of these changes has followed the logics sketched out by Heidenheimer (1970, 1989): to establish a corruption scale (its acceptance, seriousness, etc.) and to identify those behaviors that fall in the black [i.e., those criticized by the majority of the members of a community], grey or white [i.e., highly tolerated] categories.

21. In recent years, some Portuguese mayors have been elected after being arrested and prosecuted for offenses such as misappropriation of funds or corruption. In these situations, political parties generally withdraw public support and candidates run as independents, receiving the necessary votes for reelection.

22. In recent years, the Ministry of Justice has made a great effort to organize data about crime in Portugal (via the Hermes project). However, organized data available are still insufficient to perform a full statistical analysis.

23. For a comprehensive description of economic and financial crimes, see the appendix at the end of Chapter 13.

24. For each year, per capita reported EFC is computed as the number of reported EFC divided by population, and per capita EFC detentions are the number of EFC detentions divided by population.

25. Since the Corruption Perceptions Index's inception in 1995, there have been various modifications in methodology, information sources, and included countries. Therefore it does not offer a stable basis for temporal analysis.

References

Bacher, Jean Luc. 2005. *La Criminalité Économique: Ses Manifestations, Sa Prévention et Sa Répression*. Paris: L'Harmattan.

Bauman, Zygmunt. 2003. *Liquid Modernity*. Cambridge: Polity Press.

Brightman, Hank J. 2009. *Today's White Collar Crime: Legal, Investigative, and Theoretical Perspectives*. New York: Routledge.

Caldwell, Robert. 1968. "A Re-Examination of the Concept of White-Collar Crime." In *White-Collar Criminal: The Offender in Business and the Professions*, edited by Gilbert Geis, 376–87. Piscataway, N.J.: Aldine Transaction.

Clinard, Marshall, and Richard Quinney. 1963. *Criminal Behavior Systems: A Typology*. Austin, TX: Holt, Rinehart & Winston.

Dores, António Pedro. 2008. "Espírito Anti-Corrupção." In *Corrupção e os Portu-gueses. Atitudes, Práticas e Valores*, edited by Luís de Sousa and João Triães, 161–94. Lisbon: Edições Rui Costa Pinto.

Faria, Rita. 2007. "Corrupção: Descrições e Reflexões. Sobre a Possibilidade de Realização de Uma Abordagem Criminológica ao Fenómeno da Corrupção em Portugal." *Revista Portuguesa de Ciência Criminal* 17 (1): 107–46.

Ferreira, Eduardo V., and Maria d. L. Baptista. 1992. "Práticas de Corrupção na Sociedade Portuguesa Contemporânea." *Polícia e Justiça—Revista do Instituto Superior de Polícia Judiciária e Ciências Criminais* II Série (3–4): 75–105.

Foucault, Michel. 2006. *Histoire de la Sexualité*. Vol. 1. La Volonté de Savoir. Paris: Gallimard.

Green, Stuart. 2006. *Lying, Cheating, and Stealing: A Moral Theory of White-Collar Crime*. New York: Oxford University Press.

Grilo, Tânia. 2005. *A Tematização da Corrupção na Imprensa Escrita Portuguesa (1999–2000)*. Lisbon: ISCTE.

Hagan, Frank. 1994. *Introduction to Criminology: Theories, Methods, and Criminal Behavior*. 3rd ed. Chicago: Nelson-Hall Publishers.

Jalali, Carlos. 2008. "Vícios Públicos, Virtudes Privadas?" In *Corrupção e os Portu-gueses. Atitudes, Práticas e Valores*, edited by Luís de Sousa and João Triães, 131–59. Lisbon: Edições Rui Costa Pinto.

Magone, José M. 2008. "Democracia Neo-Patrimonial e Corrupção Política." In *Corrupção e os Portugueses. Atitudes, Práticas e Valores*, edited by Luís de Sousa and João Triães, 101–30. Lisbon: Edições Rui Costa Pinto.

Maia, António J. 2008. *Corrupção: Realidade e Percepções—O Papel da Imprensa*. Lisbon: Universidade Técnica de Lisboa.

Morris, Albert. 1968. "Criminology." In *White-Collar Criminal: The Offender in Busi-ness and the Professions*, edited by Gilbert Geis, 34–39. Piscataway, N.J.: Aldine Transaction.

Ponsaers, Paul, and Vincenzo Ruggiero. 2002. *La Criminalité Économique et Fi-nancière en Europe*. Paris: L'Harmattan.

Portuguese Ministry of Justice. 2010. *Estatísticas da Justiça*.

Santos, Cláudia. 2001. "O Crime de Colarinho Branco: Da Origem do Conceito e Sua Relevância Criminológica à Questão da Desigualdade na Administração da Justiça Penal." *Studia Iuridica* 56, 330.

———. 2003. "A Corrupção [Da Luta Contra o Crime na Intersecção de Alguns (Distintos) Entendimentos da Doutrina, da Jurisprudência e do Legislador]." In *Liber Discipulorum para Jorge de Figueiredo Dias*, edited by Manoel da Costa Andrade, José de Faria Costa, Anabela Miranda Rodrigues, and Maria João Antunes, 963–91. Coimbra: Coimbra Editora.

Shapiro, Susan P. 1990. "Collaring the Crime, Not the Criminal: Reconsidering the Concept of White-Collar Crime." *American Sociological Review* 55 (3): 346–65.

Sousa, Luis, and João Triães. 2008. "Corrupção e Ética em Democracia: O Caso de Portugal." In *Corrupção e os Portugueses. Atitudes, Práticas e Valores*, edited by Luís de Sousa and João Triães, 53–74. Lisbon: Edições Rui Costa Pinto.

Sutherland, Edwin. 1968. "White Collar Criminality." In *White-Collar Criminal: The Offender in Business and the Professions*, edited by Gilbert Geis, 40–51. Piscataway, N.J.: Aldine Transaction.

Tappan, Paul. 1968. "Crime, Justice and Correction." In *White-Collar Criminal: The Offender in Business and the Professions*, edited by Gilbert Geis, 365–75. Piscataway, N.J.: Aldine Transaction.

Transparency International. 2009. *Global Corruption Barometer.* http://www.transparency.org/policy_research/surveys_indices/gcb.

———. 2010. *Corruption Perception Index.* http://www.transparency.org/policy_research/surveys_indices/cpi/2009.

Triães, João. 2004. *Aspectos Sociológicos da Corrupção em Portugal: Actores, Recursos e Mecanismos do Crime de Corrupção entre 1999 e 2001.* Lisbon: ISCTE.

Trogano, António. 2011. *A Investigação da Criminalidade Tributária Organizada— Relato de uma Experiência. In 2° Congresso de Investigação Criminal,* edited by Maria Fernanda Palma, Augusto Silva Dias and Paulo Sousa Mendes, 215–262. Coimbra: Almedina.

Yeager, Peter. 2010. "Understanding Corporate Lawbreaking: From Profit Seeking to Law Finding" In *International Handbook of White-Collar and Corporate Crime,* edited by Henry Pontell and Gilbert Geis, 25–49. New York: Springer.

Young, Jock. 2011. *Criminological Imagination.* Cambridge: Polity Press.

[14]

GREECE "FOR SALE"

Casino Economy and State-Corporate Crime

SOPHIE VIDALI

In contrast to many other countries, the Greek financial meltdown in 2008 was tied not to a collapsing real estate market or a crisis in the banking system but to government deficit spending and illegal refinancing. A key contributing factor was the troubled relationship between the state and the private sectors that had evolved over the previous 20 years, which produced a shift in the state's approach to economic crime. My hypothesis is that while the collapse of the real economy is connected to wider changes related to financial economic expansion and to privatization, these processes, in Greece, took the form of illegal enterprises, which favored political clientele's longevity and their shift into criminal networks; and contributed to illegal wealth redistribution, increased tax evasion, and tax revenue deficits and to the statistical manipulation of the state's budget figures, which was accomplished through the exploitation of preexisting bureaucratic organizational problems.

This essay will analyze aspects of the Greek economic crisis that are related to changes in large-scale economic criminality. The most significant impact of the 2008 world economic crisis on Greece was that the country relinquished control of its fiscal system to the International Monetary Fund. A proper analysis of the crisis must examine how the evolution in the interpretation and enforcement of laws and regulations governing the relationship between the state and private corporations weakened the state's ability to deal with white collar crime at state and corporate levels—and became a major hurdle in addressing the crisis. The cases analyzed here, while among the most serious examples of Greek corporate criminality during the last decade or so, cannot be classified as "typical" white collar crimes. Rather, they are state-corporate crimes, in accordance with the following definition: "State-corporate crimes are illegal or socially injurious actions that occur when one or more institutions of political governance pursue a goal in direct cooperation with one or more institutions of economic production and distribution" (Kramer, Michalowski, and Kauzlarich 2002, 270).

Because law enforcement is rooted in wider political choice, this essay also looks at both the broader sociopolitical origins of the Greek economic crisis and how the crisis interacted with preexisting social relations that helped to generate criminal enterprises, during the transition from one type of economy to another (Taylor 1999).

The analysis is divided into three sections. The first examines the implications and consequences of new attitudes toward the use of capitalist tools to refinance public debt and deficit, especially as it is relates to processes of defining deviance and serious economic criminality. The second section addresses problems with the Greek system of gathering statistics and the way this method undermined how wealth and poverty are measured.

I argue that the manipulation of statistics (specifically debt and deficit figures) allowed social actors to "mask" the impact of Greece's privatization processes and provided an opportunity for criminal exploitation, thanks to a combination of factors: the prevailing ideological attitudes inside Eurostat, structural problems within the National Statistical Service of Greece (NSSG), and the reluctance of Greek governments to reform the NSSG.

In the third section, I focus on some of the most serious criminal offenses committed by the state, public corporations, and the private sector, which have deprived the country of developmental opportunities. I conclude with lessons that can be drawn from white collar and corporate crime theory, which can help rectify the situation and prevent it from recurring.

The Greek Crisis, Finance Capitalism, and Public Debt Refinancing

Greece is characterized as a mixed-capitalist and agriculture-based economy. During the twentieth century, the country's industrial and agricultural sectors largely comprised medium-scale or small-sized family-owned enterprises and an extremely strong self-employed sector (Chalaris 2005; Liagouras 2004; Moisidis and Kamberis 2004; Nikolaidis 2005).

In order to understand the development of the Greek crisis and how state and private interests produce a criminal symbiosis, one needs to know something about the structural characteristics of the Greek political system. Greece's social and political apparatus is typically based on widespread social networks of traditional political patronage and family and friendship relations that strive to protect personal, wider family, and local politicians' interests. This system constitutes a multifunctional scheme of social survival and political control: It forms a reaction to the state's authoritarian interventions, a tool for social mobility, but it also contributes to hidden economic expansion, class conflicts alienation, and human rights violations. Political clientelism was a constant factor of extrainstitutional consensus in the political system throughout the nineteenth and twentieth centuries. Greece's accession to the EU did not change the system's political clientelism. Instead, it adapted to the requirements of the global financial economy. Within this context, aspects of the Greek crisis, at least those related to the "adulteration" of the privatization processes, should be evaluated.

The emergence of casino capitalism in Greece (Calavita and Pontell 1990; Strange 1998) is illustrated by the swap deal between the Greek government and Goldman Sachs in 2001. In effect, Goldman Sachs and the Greek government adopted what was then an innovative practice in the relationship between the state and private sectors that provided cash—first to Greece and later to Goldman Sachs (as interest, etc.) through the off-the-books deals (that is, deals arranged outside the common rules of the market). Core issues regarding this case (see details in Nelson, Belkin, and Mix 2010) include (a) whether the deal was legal and (b) whether its real purpose was to disguise the true nature of Greece's economic health in order to meet the European Monetary Union (EMU) zone's deficit rules *following* the country's adoption of the euro (Story, Thomas, and Schwartz 2010).

Greece's debt-to-GDP ratio at the time was significantly higher than the EU permitted, even after the transaction by Goldman Sachs.[1] Actually, the real problem was not the legality of this swap deal or its off-the books nature but its classification as income rather than a loan in the state budget (Balzli 2010; Story et al. 2010). On the surface, such an arrangement was not criminal; rather, it was understood as a typical intersection of the interests of capital and the state (Kramer et al. 2002, 267).

The media convincingly depicted the arrangement as an attempted fraud against the EU as part of an "economic moral panic" (Levi 2006, 1043) that was then in full swing, and functioned as a 'risk construction' factor (Calavita and Pontell 1990). The panic focused on the increasingly high levels of Greek debt and deficit that were becoming a serious problem, but behind this virtual fiscal economy of shares, stocks, bankruptcy creation and bets on the impending catastrophe lay various forms of white collar and state-corporate crimes. These criminal processes did not always attract the international media's attention, but they still contributed massively to social harm.

Debt and Deficit Data External Revision: A Technical or Political Question?

Since autumn 2009, Greece has been accused of manipulating the data related to its public debt, General Government Debt and General Government Deficit figures, for reasons related to the country's membership in the EMU. At the center of this debate are the computer methods used by the NSSG (Hellenic Republic Ministry of Finance 2003, 15). However, questions about the quality of Greek statistical data are not purely technical. Instead, they reflect institutional and political factors, such as the political economy of fiscal statistics production and regulators' attitudes (Calavita and Pontell 1990).

In the following statement, the Commission of the European Communities speaks to the increasing problems associated with the country's data, which in turn reflects the nature of its "casino economy":

Systemic weaknesses, in the areas of national accounts and public sector accounts, a certain lack of expertise in these matters, and also a lack of reliable basic data had been included among the reasons of the Greek statistics problem. As a consequence of this, the Greek Statistical Office made use of proxies which did not provide reliable results. The revised figures concerning the social security are one example. (Commission of the European Communities 2004, 6)

Problems noted by Eurostat, in 2002, were explained as resulting from methodological changes made in order to comply with the European System of National and Regional Accounts (ESA95), and from the application of securitization operations. As a result, the European Commission's revision of statistics showed a considerable increase in public deficit and debt for the years 2000–2001 (Eurostat 2002a, 2002b). Eventually, the restatements extended to a broader period (1997–2003).

The Commission was explicit in its criticism:

[There] was a lack of awareness of Eurostat to bring promptly the problems to the right public level instead of having a closed discussion between statisticians (who were not sufficiently sensitive at that time to the discussions at the political level). There was also an absence on the need to prioritise and to concentrate on core activities. With the benefit of hindsight, the Commission should have reported earlier and more consistently to the Economic and Financial Committee and ECOFIN Council of the problems encountered. Specifically, already when validating the 1999 deficit data in March 2000, Eurostat could have signaled problems of compliance. (Commission of the European Communities 2004, 6–7)

It was only later, after the Greek statistical system had been completely devalued in 2010, that Eurostat finally included among the causes of statistical inconsistencies the dependent relationship of the statistical services, the NSSG, and the General Auditors Office on the Ministry of Finance (European Commission 2010 4). For the first time, the European Commission inferred that there was deliberate deception:

As far as a possible parallel between the 2004 and 2009 situations is concerned . . . there are some common methodological features between the 2004 and 2009 episodes. In both cases, in the aftermath of political elections, substantial revisions took place revealing a practice of widespread misreporting, in an environment in which checks and balances appear absent, information opaque and distorted, and institutions weak and poorly coordinated. The frequent missions conducted by Eurostat . . . the numerous reservations to the notifications of the Greek authorities, . . . provide additional evidence that the problems are only partly of a methodological nature and would largely lie beyond the statistical sphere. (European Commission 2010, 20)

The topic of Greek fiscal statistical data became a focus of contention between Greece's two major political parties, though its complexity prevented it from becoming a public issue. It was not until October 2009, when Greece's ability to borrow funds from the international markets was questioned, that the "Greek statistics problem" became associated with deficit and debt increases and the Goldman Sachs case.[2]

Any exclusion from the recorded data creates a gray zone in which a wide range of economic and financial transactions appear to be outside any institutional fix or control. The labeling of misleading data as "statistical inconsistencies" results in its disassociation from criminal stigma or even from the submission to civil law's regulations (Sutherland 1945). Under this approach, fiscal statistics assume an ambivalent function as both a means of masking but also as a way to reveal probable occurrences of white collar and state-corporate crimes (i.e., the lavish lifestyles of certain individuals not supported by income data) depending on the wider sociopolitical context, the goals of the presenter, and their interpretations.

The problem of official data collection was compounded by the Greek government's policy, adopted after 2002, in response to regulators' reluctance to enact structural reforms in sectors that fiscal statistics had indicated as problematic, and most of all, by the restructuring of statistical services. The power of inertia, the impact of the processes of privatization, the eventual connection between the enormous scandals that had involved political institutions in Greece and the tolerance of problematic inclusions and exclusions of Greek budget numbers are some of the possible explanations for regulators' reluctance, which I argue also constituted an incentive and an opportunity for the commission of white collar and state-corporate crimes.

In other words, an obsolete and deficient fiscal statistical system is easily manipulated. In the Greek case, the system's deficiency is linked to both the tolerance and/or willful ignorance of statistical inconsistencies, which amounts to a possible "cover-up" of criminal politics related to state-corporate crimes (Calavita and Pontell 1990).

Any evaluation of the relationship between these "technical" issues and the political system should take into consideration the fact that "partnerships" were formed between state apparatuses and financial companies that constituted organized criminal economic enterprises, leading to serious impacts on capital flows, social harm, and wealth redistribution in Greece.

This type of gray economy (one not accounted for in statistics) and its connection to political class contributed to an increase of social inequalities, to the depreciation of state institutions, and to the political crisis. The most serious of these cases are still under inquiry by both the criminal justice system and Parliamentary Specific Inquiry Committees. A review of these cases is essential to understanding the Greek crisis.

The Rise and Fall of the Athens Stock Exchange Market

The formation of the Athens Stock Exchange Market (ASE) led thousands of middle-class small investors to withdraw their bank savings and invest in the stock market in hopes of earning quick and easy profits. This was encouraged by both the media and the Greek state and had broad effects. On the one hand, it complied with the government's strategy to adapt the Greek economy to the requirements of the EMU. On the other, it led to the expansion of financial capitalism in Greece by transforming the demand for goods into a demand for securities (Vergopoulos 2005, 236). The sharp rise and fall of ASE rates between 1998 and 2000 coincided with the transition from drachma to euro, which caused a structural change in the Greek currency and trading systems.

In March 1998, the drachma joined the Exchange Rate Method of the European Monetary System, and it was devalued by 13.8 percent, "enabling" Greece's entry into the EMU. By 1999, an enormous amount of money had changed hands. That year, €11.1 billion derived from increases in capital and the capitalization of 279 listed companies on the Greek stock exchange rose to €197 billion, while the average value of transactions amounted to €692 million. The rate of profit growth by listed companies rose by 87 percent, primarily due to gains from securities and participating interests (*To Vima* April 10, 2005).[3]

The fall of the ASE 2 years later involved two principal processes. The first was the deindustrialization of the country during this period and the displacement of existing productive resources. In essence, the ASE's profits were channeled into offshore companies and to other profit-bearing activities. As a result, the state was unable to refinance the country's debt.

The second process is related to the expansion of criminal networks inside stated-owned or -controlled or state bank–affiliated companies that manipulated shares and created stock bubbles. Among the alleged criminal practices were frauds against investors that created extraordinary increases in share value.

One indication of these nefarious practices was the arrest of the administrators of the Hellenic Capital Market Commission (HCMC) and the ASE and their subsequent acquittal of charges that they had failed to exercise proper oversight (*Kathimerini* February 5, 2006a). As the case proceeded, it was made clear that the stock market lacked sufficient rules or laws governing public offering of shares, qualifications, and certifications. (*Eleftherotypia* November 14, 2004; *Kathimerini* February 5, 2006a; *ANTI* 2003). Moreover, the brokers failed to separate account deposits and the assets of clients from the assets of their company. The HCMC never checked the suspicious transactions in which "relatives and friends of governors and senior executives of agencies and government players bought shares at low prices and sold to gullible retail investors after the extraordinary rise in the price" (*ANTI*, 2003). The lack of rules as well as the selective application of regulations to social and personal networks, were key factors in the exchange's collapse.

As a direct consequence, thousands of small investors, who had trusted the government from 1999 to 2000, lost up to 80 percent of their money, an amount estimated at €30 million. A side effect of this collapse was the loss of 8,000 jobs in that sector (*Kathimerini* February 6, 2005). Thus, state-corporate crime contributed to a redistribution of wealth in Greece for the benefit of the higher-income groups, primarily those involved with financial capital (Vergopoulos 2005, 60). It reversed the function of the ASE, which had developed during industrial capitalism, by destroying the confidence of small investors who had been financially ruined.

The case also exposed a cover-up linked to judicial corruption and data and evidence manipulation on the part of more than twenty-three companies. A 2003 judicial proceeding fined and sentenced a number of the major players to short prison terms *(Kathimerini* February 5, 2006b). As of this writing (early 2012) there have been three acquittals that benefitted administrators of the Securities Public Company. The case should be investigated further, this time, by a specific Parliamentary Inquiry Committee.

The Siemens Case

Another aspect of state-corporate crimes concerns privatization. One of the best-known cases involved corrupt practices in granting award contracts between various branches of the Hellenic state and the Greek branch of Siemens A.G. The aforementioned contracts were related to the construction and supply of high-technology substructures and equipment in critical sectors of the state economy (Hellenic Parliament 2011). These contracts included the digitalization of the national system of telecommunications (Telecommunications Organization of Greece case; called OTE in Greek) in the beginning of the 1990s (€13 million in bribes); the 2004 Olympic Games' security system in the beginning of 2000 (€10 million in bribes); the Greek hospital system's monopolistic supply of high-tech medical equipment; the overpricing of the technical assistance services and the supply of Ministry of National Defense's "Patriot-Hermes System." The total damage to the Greek state is approximately €2 billion according to the Hellenic Parliament Inquiry Committee (Hellenic Parliament 2011, 402).

An additional contract between the National Railways Organization and Siemens for the construction of train wagons (cars) also raised serious questions. The wagons turned out to be inappropriate for the Greek rail system, and the agreed price was two or three times higher than similar products from other companies.

Some of these cases, currently pending in the courts, constitute only part of a wider Siemens scandal revealed in Germany, where the corporation had created a slush fund based in offshore companies that was used to pay bribes to politicians and other authorities in many countries (Teloglou 2009). Money from this fund was also allegedly used to pay members of the media and prominent figures of both major political parties in Greece (Teloglou 2009).

According to the testimony of Siemens's CEO regarding these "services" provided to the corporation, the bribes involved payments of "commissions" ranging from 2 percent to 8 percent of the value of each contract (Teloglou 2009, 23, 37). The involvement of political parties' leading representatives, judges and prosecutors, and even cabinet ministers ensured the longevity of that system. The alleged criminal activities in this case include fraud, money laundering, corruption, and blackmail. The total damage to the Greek state is estimated to reach €57.4 million. The actual cost in the OTE case is estimated to be over €690 million. Total estimated bribes came to about €100 million.

The Vatopedi Case: Monasteries as Offshore Companies

Privatization processes included also forms of "hidden" (i.e., illegal) privatizations. The most well-known example was the so-called Vatopedi case, which involved the exchange of public lands between the Vatopedi monastery of Holy Mount Athos and the Greek state. Employing allegedly questionable (from the legal point of view) methods, the monks took possession of public rural lands in the area of the Vistonida Lagoon in northeastern Greece, which had been set aside because of their important ecological and agricultural value. The properties were exchanged for other state lands of high commercial and investment interest (so-called Olympic real estate). Criminal cases arising from this exchange were brought against five former cabinet ministers, members of the State Legal Council, revenue service officers, and lawyers.

The key points at issue centered on the use of judicial and political corruption to change the status of rural lands to achieve judicial decisions favorable to monasteries and the further economic exploitation of the land by the real estate and tourism industry, and to achieve judicial decisions favorable to monasteries. Offshore companies in which the monks were shareholders, private real estate companies and other private enterprises and public services exponents were involved in this case. Questions were raised about the criteria used by Greek government officials to exchange rural lands for lands with high commercial value. In some cases, the exchanges appeared to be facilitated by reclassifying the lands to obtain undervalued assessments in contracts between the monastery and the government (e.g., an urban estate registered as a forest or rural area or areas outside the urban plan). Although the real value of the lands involved was assessed at more than €320 million, they were assessed at a little more than €40 million for the purpose of the exchange. The damage of the Greek State exceeds €1 billion according to the Parliamentary Inquiring Committee (Hellenic Parliament 2010a; *To Vima* October 3, 2010; elaboration by the author of this essay). The case against individual monks is still pending in the Greek Court.

Embezzlement of Social Security Funds

This case, which took place in the course of only one day in February 2007, concerns the use of the reserve capital of the social security system. Starting in 2004 (after the right-wing party, New Democracy, was elected) the administrators of the Greek Social Security Fund invested funds reserve capital into high-risk financial products (*To Vima* March 25, 2007), despite legal prohibitions (Hellenic Parliament 2010b).

The Ministry of Finance issued a structured bond of €280 million from a swap deal sponsored by J. P. Morgan. In return for J. P. Morgan's agreement to defer receiving coupon payments, the government offered a discount for the bond purchase. Consequently, J. P. Morgan paid 85 percent of the structured bond's nominal value and then resold it at 91.75 percent of its initial nominal value (*To Vima* April 3, 2007). Subsequently, the same structured bond, in the course of a few hours, was resold five times. The final purchaser, the Public Sector Employees' Subsidiary Fund, paid €280 million. For its trouble, the state's cash payment of €280 million (from the Public Sector Employees' Subsidiary Fund's reserve capital) was an overpayment of €42 million for what it had sold some hours earlier to J. P. Morgan for €238 million (*Ta Nea* April 23, 2007). According to media reports, these transactions produced enormous profits in brokerage and transaction fees for J. P. Morgan. Lawyers' commissions alone amounted to €13 million (*To Vima* March 6, 2007; March 28, 2007). The same practice was adopted for investment of other social security funds, such as the Athens and Thessaloniki Newspaper Employees' Pension Fund (€130 million) and the Pharmaceutical Works Employees' Subsidiary Fund (€130 million). According to an expert in the field (Stamatis 2007), the most suspicious aspect of these transactions has been the hidden deals. The interest paid for the first 2 years was higher than the going rate in the free market, but the bond was structured to deliver low-interest rates toward the end of its term. Also of concern was the secrecy of the transaction.

The Social Security Fund, instead of purchasing the structured bond directly from the state, bought it from the free market and paid the over-market value, plus the brokerage commission. Moreover, a very considerable amount of money was paid as "commission" to officials who favored the original transaction (*To Vima* March 28, 2007). This was made possible by the formation of a social network linking the owners or senior officials of banks and brokerage companies to authorities in the stock exchange markets and to state executive personnel. Some of the individuals had also been involved in the Siemens case (*To Vima* June 13, 2010). All were connected by friendship, by family relations, or through their membership in the dominant political parties. Furthermore, ex-ministers and other representatives of the previous government were also involved (*To Vima* March 6, 2007). In essence, the absence of an appropriate system of control combined with the transition to financial capitalism created opportune conditions for these crimes. Although an investigation by a parliamentary Committee of Inquiry confirmed the responsibility of government officials for this hugely profitable transaction (Hellenic Parliament 2010b), as of this writing, only the private "partners" in this case have been convicted and sentenced to prison.

Discussion: State-Corporate Crimes and Culture

State-corporate crimes (as they have been identified in the Greek case) involve networks of horizontal relationships between government and corporations or other entities with autonomous legal personality (like the Mount Athos monasteries; Kramer et al. 2002, 272). The perpetrators of such crimes are able to evade concrete banking rules by exploiting modern communications technology that allows for the establishment of global and transnational networks. The networks link offshore or other financial companies that are controlled by a small number of persons (as in the case of Siemens and the social security funds).

The role of these companies should be regarded as a kind of distribution of criminal labor, where the illegal profits are reaped through security transactions (Ruggiero 1996). Greece is just one node of an illegal financial transactions system that incorporates many other states and facilitates such corporate criminality (Kramer et al. 2002, 271). These are, in effect, transnational crimes in the sense that a multitude of offshore companies and financial institutions are involved in their realization.

The structural change in economic and financial rules governing such transactions created legal opportunities for crime. Since there are no regulations that define or label these types of transactions as criminal, it constitutes an invitation to exploit such networks to the maximum extent.

At the same time, it has spurred competition over the distribution of power and wealth among state officials, political parties, and private companies. All the perpetrators are members of the highly qualified professional elite who are highly goal-oriented individuals (Kramer et al. 2002, 273) and who turned to criminal enterprises after a successful or promising career in the public or private financial sector. It is possible that a preexisting network of friends and family had facilitated this shift since these types of relations ensure confidence. The concept of Sutherland's (1945) differential association helps to explain this shift. In this context, the connection to political parties is extremely significant. In the process of identifying structural opportunities in the new system, for example, political parties finance themselves through the looting of state funds.

Culture has a strong influence on the emergence and the expansion of state-corporate crime in Greece. Cultural definitions of deviance, crime, and ethos are of great significance in understanding further shifts in crime. In a changing world, the traditional cultures of clienteles' social relations constituted one of the methods of social integration. Previously implemented to tackle the state's development challenges, the networks are now responding to the changes in financial practices and the demands of the new global economy (Vidali 2011). The process of transformation since the end of the 1980s has also swept through the existing cultures of political clientelism.

These attitudes, coupled with a competitive and an increasingly risky environment, wherein profit taking has become increasingly opaque, have essentially created the context for the casino economy. In Greece, a broader tacit social consensus in the shadow of corporate media representations has led to a highly anomic situation focusing on the overriding importance of "success," regardless of laws and any law enforcement.

Conclusion

The development of state-corporate crime is related to the processes of wealth distribution between the state and private sectors, set against the landscape of the new financial environment. Therefore, deviance is created by an entire system of relationships linking different institutions, rather than being the result of a single criminal act (Kramer et al. 2002, 272).

The involvement of the Greek public sector in the free-market economy has produced the conditions for minimizing risk for all participants, including the two major political parties. Consequently, the traditional forms of social control were neutralized, and penal law was rendered ineffective, in turn laying the groundwork for institutional impunity, which is one of the constitutive conditions of certain theoretical assumptions regarding anomie. However, behind the "operational" effect of this neutralization, it is possible to reveal the symbiotic relationship (Chambliss 1988, 194; Chambliss 2004) between law and state-corporate crime and to explain the ineffectiveness of formal social control.

Governments and political parties have demonstrated a high level of tolerance of, or complicity with, the actions described in these cases. At the very least, the Greek financial economy has become a source of "gray funds" to support the political system. Tolerance and impunity are directly connected and are easily transformed into the politics of denial (Cohen 2001), which permits the "longevity" of state-corporate crimes.

Further, state-corporate crimes constitute a "normal" collateral effect of anomie and could be considered a typical condition of the transition from one type of economy to another, where deregulation is practiced. Deregulation allows state-corporate criminality to continue in "gray zones" for long periods of time. This situation was permitted by ideological representations of the casino economy that defined social problems as "technical questions." However, when formal social controls are rendered ineffective, it is still possible to prevent criminality by adopting the politics of recognition (Cohen 2001).

Among the other effects of state-corporate crimes is the complete loss of citizens' trust in institutional structures and the law. In Greece, the public has largely responded by retreating from the political arena and abandoning political participation. The long list of administrative malpractice, public sector corruption, fraud, money laundering, tax evasion, and nepotism—just to name a few—frames the illegal and amoral aspect of the Greek crisis.

The effects of state-corporate crimes on normal life in Greece have been clear: an increase in social inequalities, deterioration of the quality of life, creation of a culture of war between citizens (on the basis of employment and unemployment; see Young 1999), distrust of politics, and emergence of illegal behavior as a necessary condition for social and economic survival. The government's strategies for avoiding responsibility can be summarized as "blame the other" or a form of "appealing to higher loyalties." The collective embezzlement perpetrated by the consortia of the state and private sectors has produced a massive victimization of the Greek people, which has in turn undermined their previous guarantees of civil and social rights and led to a widespread sense of frustration and injustice. The resulting ontological insecurity resembles the effects of a war.

Thus the Greek crisis has been transformed from an institutional and financial crisis to a crisis of democracy and, furthermore, a crisis of impunity. The ruling classes have once more shown their inability to find a constitutional way of redistributing power in a society that is now fully in the throes of casino capitalism. Since the end of 2009, Greece has been experiencing the effects of casino capitalism expansion and a new type of authoritarianism (or state crimes) which has had a major, but unquantifiable, impact on the lives of ordinary citizens.

Notes

1. The EU fixed a debt-to-GDP ratio of less than 60 percent. Greece's debt-to-GDP ratio was 105.3 percent before its deal with Goldman Sachs. After the transactions, the ratio stood at 103.7 percent (Wachman 2010).

2. On October 2 and 21, 2009, Greek authorities transmitted to Eurostat two different sets of data related to government deficit and debt for 2005–2008 and a forecast for 2009, which revised upward the debt and deficit figures for the same years in comparison to its April 2009 notification. The Greek government deficit for 2008 was revised from 5.0 percent of GDP in April 2009 to 7.7 percent of GDP. Similarly the planned deficit ratio for 2009 was revised from 3.7 percent of GDP to 12.5 percent of GDP. According to the report, these changes occurred because of a variety of factors: the impact of the economic crisis, budgetary slippages in an electoral year, and accounting decisions (European Commission 2010, 3).

3. During this period, public funds, through the stock exchange market, raised approximately €12 billion. Revenues from tax on stock transactions, which increased the state budget, increased in 1999 to €675 million (*Greek Metohos* November 11, 2006). On September 17, 1999, the General Share Price Index closed at 6,355.04 points (in Greek, *Capital.gr* September 17, 2009). In June 2000, Greece ensured that it met the criteria for membership in the EMU. On December 29, 2000, the ASE closed at 3,388.86 points and then began a gradual decline. In January 2001, Greece joined the euro zone.

References

Balzli, Beat. 2010. "How Goldman Sachs Helped Greece to Mask Its True Debt." *Der Spiegel*, February 8. http://www.spiegel.de/international/europe/0,1518,676634,00.html.

Calavita, Kitty, and Henry N. Pontell. 1990. "'Heads I Win, Tails You Lose': De-regulation, Crime and Crisis in the Savings and Loan Industry." *Crime and Delinquency* 36 (3): 309–41.

Chalaris, G. 2005. "Greece in the Context of Globalisation." In *Economic Changes and Social Contrasts in Greece*, edited by G. Argitis, 27–59. Athens, Greece: Tipothito.

Chambliss, William J. 1988. *On the Take: From Petty Crooks to Presidents*. Bloomington: Indiana University Press.

———. 2004. "On The Symbiosis Between Criminal Law and Criminal Behaviour." *Criminology* 42 (2): 241–51.

Cohen, Stanley. 2001. *States of Denial: Knowing About Atrocities and Suffering*. Cambridge: Polity Press.

Commission of the European Communities. 2004. *Communication from the Commission to the European Parliament and the Council: "Report on the Accountability Issue, Related to the Revision of Greek Budgetary Data."* COM/2004/784/FINAL. http://eur-lex.europa.eu/LexUriServ/LexUriServ.do?uri=COM:2004:0784:FIN:EN:PDF.

European Commission. 2010. *Report on Greek Government Deficit and Debt Statistics*. COM (2010) 1 final. http://eur-lex.europa.eu/LexUriServ/LexUriServ.do?uri=SPLIT_COM:2010:0001%2801%29:FIN:EN:PDF.

Eurostat. 2002a. *Euro Indicators*. News release 116, September 30.

———. 2002b. *Euro Indicators*. News release 132, November 13.

Hellenic Parliament. 2010a. *Findings of the Parliamentary Inquiry Committee 'for the completion of the investigation regarding the Vatopedi monastery's scandal as a whole,'* Year, ΙΓ', session A'.

Hellenic ———. 2010b. *Findings of the Parliamentary Inquiry Committee 'for a full investigation of the bonds case,'* Year, ΙΓ', session B'.

Hellenic ———. 2011. *Findings of the Parliamentary Inquiry Committee 'for the investigation of the siemens case as a whole,'* Year, ΙΓ', session B'.

Hellenic Republic Ministry of Finance. 2003. *Government Budget, Explanatory Report*. http://www.minfin.gr/portal/en.

Kramer, Ronald C., Raymond J. Michalowski, and David Kauzlarich. 2002. "The Origins and Development of the Concept and Theory of State-Corporate Crime." *Crime & Delinquency* 48 (2): 263–82.

Levi, Michael. 2006. "The Media Construction of Financial White Collar Crimes." *British Journal of Criminology* 46:1037–57.

Liagouras, George. 2004. "Successes and Failures of Economic Policy or Crisis and Restructuring of the Development Model? The Greek Economy During the Period 1975–2001." In *Social Change in Contemporary Greece*, edited by Sakis Karagiorgas Foundation, 335–64. Athens, Greece: Sakis Karagiorgas Foundation.

Moisidis, A., and N. Kamberis. 2004. "Productive Modernization and Social Re-Composition of the Greek Countryside." In *Social Change in Contemporary Greece*, edited by Sakis Karagiorgas Foundation, 365–86. Athens, Greece: Sakis Karagiorgas Foundation.

Nelson, Rebecca M., Paul Belkin, and Derek E. Mix. 2010. *Greece's Debt Crisis: Overview, Policy Responses, and Implications*. Congressional Research Service

Report for Congress 7-5700, April 27. http://www.fas.org/sgp/crs/row/R41167
.pdf.

Nikolaidis, Evangelos. 2005. "Agricultural Sector in Greece: Contribution to Its
Real Dimensions." In *Economic Changes and Social Contrasts in Greece*, edited
by G. Argitis, 87–126. Athens, Greece: Tipothito.

Ruggiero, Vincenzo. 1996, *Economie Sporche*. Torino: Bollati Boringheri.

Stamatis, G. 2007. "On Structured State Bonds: A Tale for Smart People." *Utopia*
75:191–202.

Story, Louise, Landon Thomas Jr., and Nelson D. Schwartz. 2010. "Wall St. Helped
to Mask Debt Fueling Europe's Crisis." *New York Times*, February 13. http://
www.nytimes.com/2010/02/14/business/global/14debt.html?pagewanted=all.

Strange, Susan. 1998. *What Theory? The Theory of Mad Money*. CSGR Working
Paper 18/1998.

Sutherland, Edwin H. 1945. "Is 'White Collar Crime' Crime?" *American Sociological Review* 10:132–39.

Taylor, I. 1999. *Crime in Context, A Critical Criminology of Market Societies*. Cambridge: Polity Press.

Teloglou, Tassos. 2009. *The Network*. Athens, Greece: Skai-Book Publisher.

Vergopoulos, Kostas. 2005. *The Seizure of Wealth: Money-Power-Interweaving in
Greece*. Athens, Greece: Publishing Organization Lebanon.

Vidali, Sophie. 2011. "Social Reaction to Crime and Its Limits: Drugs and Organised Crime in Greece." In *Contemporary Criminality, Its Confrontation and the
Science of Criminology*, volume in honor of Professor J. Farsedakis, edited by
A. Chalkia. 2:1751–85. Athens, Greece: Nomiki Vivliothiki.

Wachman, Richard. 2010. "Greek Deal Puts Goldman Sachs in the Firing Line—
Again." *Guardian*, February 28. http://www.guardian.co.uk/business/2010/feb
/28/goldman-sachs-investment-banking-greece.

Young, Jock. 1999. *The Exclusive Society: Social Exclusion, Crime, and Difference in
Late Modernity*. London: Sage.

Greek Press

ANTI (monthly review), December 2003, "The Prosecutor's of the Court of Appeal
inquiry on the Stock Exchange Market criminal network," republ. by http://
www.antinews.gr/2009/09/23/15588/.

Capital.gr, September 17, 2009, "Ten years from the 99's bubble."

Eleftherotypia, November 14, 2004, Papageorgiou, G., "Myths and facts about the
bubble."

Kathimerini, February 6, 2005, Ntokas, A., "The illusory glow of Sofokleous [str.]."

———. February 5, 2006a, Kollias, F., "Entrepreneurs involved in stock exchange
market gambling."

———. February 5, 2006b, "Poor results of the 'first round' of responsibility
attribution."

Metohos, September 11, 2006, "The history of tax and revenues . . ."

Ta Nea, April 23, 2007, "Bonds that 'burning'."

To Vima, April 10, 2005, Kotsis V, "From 1999's heaven to 2005's hell."

———. March 6, 2007 Bitsika, P., Nedos, B., "'Our people' games to fund [reserves]."

———. March 25, 2007, Karakousis, A., "The pyramid of Funds."

———. March 28, 2007, Kroustalli, D., "The bonds' bribery 'pigeon'."

———. April 3, 2007, Karakousis, A, "The hidden bond and its secrets."

———. June 13, 2010, Ravanos, A., "The brokers' group."

———. October 3, 2010, Papapdakou, G., "The Vatopedi cost millions."

[15]

FINANCIAL FRAUD IN CHINA

A Structural Examination of
Law and Law Enforcement

HONGMING CHENG

Financial fraud is increasing in both volume and complexity and, arguably, is now having a major impact on the lifeblood of China's economy and society (Cheng and Ma 2009). Although official statistics are underdeveloped and unreliable in China, financial fraud has been described as "one of the most challenging areas of economic crime" by China's Ministry of Public Security, the nation's top police authority, and is expected to worsen with rapid economic development (Wu 2008). Some analysts suggest that bank fraud alone has cost Chinese banks more than \$2.8 billion annually since 2000 (Zhou 2006).

Although the total costs of financial frauds by offenders outside financial institutions add up to billions of dollars a year, the largest frauds are usually committed or facilitated by insiders, such as bank directors, managers, and loan officers. According to Liu Mingkang, chairman of the Chinese Banking Regulatory Commission (CBRC), insider financial fraud accounts for more than 80 percent of all financial fraud across the country (Liu 2005). In some cases, high-ranking local officials have also assisted outside offenders (relatives, friends, related businesses, and others) in their fraudulent procurement of massive bank loans (CBRC 2005, 2007, 2009a, 2009b). According to the nation's central bank and the CBRC, China's financial institutions still hold \$161 billion of bad loans (CBRC 2008). In interviews conducted online, a midlevel bank officer said: "Many bank managers or loan officers at first passively, and later more actively, seek opportunities to accept bribes or kickbacks. They regard their power to authorize loans as a tradable commodity, to be used for their own profits" (Cheng and Ma 2009, 167).

Western literature provides competing perspectives on whether the powerful and the powerless receive equal treatment by law enforcement authorities. In the tradition of Durkheim (1997), the consensus position suggests that the criminal justice system embodies commonly agreed upon social norms and values (Friedman 1977). From this perspective, decisions are made impartially and determined by legally defined offense characteristics, such as the seriousness of the crime and the offender's prior criminal record. Conversely, the conflict perspective suggests that discrimination in criminal justice processing is a result of conflict between relatively powerless offenders and elite social groups who are able to promote and maintain their self-interests (Coleman 2006; Reiman 2007). Donald Black (1976) argues that offenders with higher "rank" in society experience less severe legal responses. Those with diminished status in multiple stratification categories are hypothesized to be at a greater disadvantage in the eyes of the law.

In the case of white collar crime, it has been frequently asserted that criminal justice and regulatory officials are reluctant to pursue white collar offenders even when financial losses are high (Cheng 2004; Cheng and Ma 2009; Coleman 2006; Snider 1993, 2000, 2005; Snider and Pearce 1995; Sutherland 1949). Levi (1995) compared the dispositions of social security frauds and tax frauds committed by the poor and lower-status social groups with securities frauds committed by entrepreneurs and found that the latter cases are not treated as "real" crimes and are more likely to be diverted from the criminal process into the regulatory one. This reluctance has been attributed to a variety of factors, such as cost of prosecution, limited power and/or resources, difficulty of obtaining evidence, fear of negative effect on market confidence, and sympathy for white collar criminals.

Studies of criminal justice decision making related to white collar crime have largely concentrated on convicted offenses (Copes et al. 2001; Holtfreter 2004, 2005; Holtfreter, Piquero, and Piquero 2008). Although police and prosecutorial decision making in white collar crime cases are equally critical, considerably less research has been conducted in this aspect. One recent study of all fraud cases against businesses that were investigated by police in Montreal from January to June 1991 indicates that fraud against large businesses did not receive preferential response by law enforcement agencies (Bacher et al. 2005). The few studies in this area suggest that further research is needed. Given that only a small percentage of cases handled by the system actually reach the sentencing stage, scholars have cautioned against drawing inferences about the criminal justice decision-making process (Diamond 1995; Holtfreter 2008).

The purpose of this chapter is to examine how law behaves in a clearly defined and bounded social context, namely, police and prosecutorial response to financial fraud in China. Is the law itself biased against certain groups of financial fraud offenders? How many police resources are allocated for dealing with financial fraud? What class-related factors, if any, may influence an investigator's decision making in financial fraud cases? I address these issues through a study of statutes, policy documents, prosecutorial files, court cases, and consultation with legal experts and observers. In addition, I conducted thirty-five semistructured interviews with regulatory officials, police officers, and procurators in China regarding their perceptions of and attitudes toward financial fraud, major challenges they have experienced, and the factors influencing their decision making.

For this study, financial fraud is defined as an intentional act of deception involving financial transactions for the purpose of personal or organizational gain, including loan fraud, mortgage fraud, pyramid schemes, investment fraud, tax avoidance, bank card fraud, check fraud, insurance fraud, and identity theft and scams. Financial fraud can be committed by a person of high social status or by someone from the underclass.

Because the influence of class position on law enforcement is the focus of this chapter, it is important to determine the proper measurement of social class in China. The model of legal response to financial fraud used here suggests that it is a structural position in the social and economic space that influences law enforcement. This is derived from recent Chinese neo-Marxist work on China's class structure (He 2003; Li 2005). The analysis considers three structural positions: a small elite class, an underdeveloped middle class, and a large marginalized class. The elite class includes three distinct groups that possess different types of resources: political, economic, and intellectual. The political elite includes high- and middle-ranking state and local officials and functionaries of large state-owned nonindustrial institutions. The economic elite includes managers of state banks and large-scale state enterprises, the executives of large and medium companies, and the owners of large or medium private firms. The intellectual elite includes top economists, most influential lawyers, and other powerful experts who control important knowledge capital and ally with the political and economic elites.

The middle class is divided between higher and lower strata. In the top level are managers of medium and small firms, lawyers, white collar employees of firms with foreign investment, and employees of state monopolies; in the lower level are specialized technicians, junior scientific researchers, college and school teachers, rank-and-file employees in the arts or media, rank-and-file functionaries in government, lower-level management in state enterprises, self-employed workers, and traders. The marginalized working class consists principally of those who labor in state enterprises, collectively owned firms, foreign firms, joint ventures, and private firms. It also includes farmers, garbage recyclers, and the unemployed poor. It should be noted that family origin is also important in China for our measurement, so the suddenly wealthy who are from poor families may also be discriminated against if they do not develop connections with the powerful elite.

Political Culture and Criminal Legislation Against Financial Fraud

Although Chinese society has been heavily influenced by the West in recent years, the Confucian social hierarchy still remains the main social organization of China, which supports a pyramid-shaped structure where the majority must under all circumstances submit to the few privileged individuals. Confucius believed that by nature all men are benign and therefore famously opposed the coercive rule of law. He argued that the ideal state rested upon a stable and harmonious sociopolitical order achieved by a virtuous and benevolent sovereign through moral persuasion rather than by law (Wright 1960). This political understanding of power and hierarchy arguably still has a fundamental impact on the development of legal thought in modern and contemporary China.

After the Cultural Revolution (1966–1976), the Chinese leadership believed that people had begun to doubt heaven-designated power and thus needed nominal laws to legitimate its rule and the pyramid-shaped class structure. The establishment of a legal system was also necessary as both an instrument and a guarantee for the intended transformation of social and economical life with the economic reform beginning in 1979. Since then, Chinese leaders have increasingly confronted the duality inherent in law: law as an instrument of political power and as an agent for restraining this same power to attract the people's support for the regime.

This dilemma is reflected in financial fraud laws. An offender from a poor or underprivileged family is generally likely to receive more serious punishment, yet occasionally a few greedy officials and capitalists may also be targeted and heavily sanctioned if they pose a threat to the existence of the regime. For example, the first criminal code of socialist China, the Criminal Law of the People's Republic of China (adopted by the Second Session of the Fifth National People's Congress, 1979)[1] classified the offenses of taking advantage of official power to make profits (Article 119) and the misappropriation of state funds (Article 126) as "serious" crimes under the heading "Crimes of Undermining the Socialist Economic Order."

The first major upgrade of Chinese criminal law that took account of financial fraud was the published Decision of the Standing Committee of the National People's Congress "Regarding the severe punishment of criminals who seriously disrupt the financial order" (adopted by the Fourteenth Session of the Standing Committee of the Eighth National People's Congress, June 30, 1995). During its passage, the Standing Committee was informed that the law dealing with financial crime was inadequate and that, if nothing were done, there was a real risk that the Chinese financial market and even the Communist Party's rule could be destroyed. The 1995 decision, which became an amendment to the Criminal Law (1979), introduced seven forms of financial fraud: counterfeiting banknotes, check fraud, bank draft fraud, credit card fraud, letter of credit fraud, as well as embezzlement and bribery of bank officials. The 1997 Amendments of the Chinese Criminal Law, based on the 1990 Decision on Suppressing Drug Dealing, also established the crime of money laundering (Article 191). With the increasing rate of nonperforming bank loans due to major financial frauds committed by the collusion of insiders and outsiders, China again upgraded its legislation under the Amendment to the PRC Criminal Law that took effect on June 29, 2006, which included specific wording that made it a crime to obtain bank loans through fraudulent means. With several other supplementary provisions of the Standing Committee of the National People's Congress, the current Criminal

Law has created a framework for the legal regulation of financial fraud practices.

According to the 2006 Criminal Law, officials in the government or state-owned banks may be sentenced to death if they commit severe graft or bribery. Insider bank dealing (illegally granting loans to related individuals or organizations for self-interest), loan fraud, check and bank draft fraud, letter of credit fraud, credit card fraud, and treasury bill fraud are all criminal offenses, each of which is subject to life imprisonment. However, considering the severe punishment doctrine in Chinese criminal jurisprudence, it is somewhat surprising to see that the maximum punishment for insider misappropriation of bank funds and money laundering is only 10 years' imprisonment. Illegal enrichment (when the property or expenses of officials in government or state-owned companies clearly exceed their legitimate income) is punishable by only 10 years in prison (increased from 5 years following a 2009 amendment that received long debate). It should be noted that the two offenses receiving relatively light punishment are generally committed by high-status officials and/or business executives.

One major problem worth mentioning is the vague definitions of crime, fraud, severity, and criminal liability under the Chinese criminal code. The National People's Congress has set the threshold separating a criminal act from an administrative wrongdoing and differentiating a severe crime from a less severe crime, by specifying the seriousness of the consequences and circumstances (Cheng and Ma 2009). It has occasionally defined the seriousness of the consequences in its interpretations of law by setting a fixed monetary amount or by using other criteria to determine the harm resulting from the offense. However, since this criterion has not been applied in consistent or predictable ways, local courts will set different standards as to the amount of fines reflecting severe punishment. Therefore, it is up to local regulatory or law enforcement officers to make the crucial decision on prosecution before they refer the cases to court.

In practice, a number of cases involving high-profile financial fraud offenders are handled as disciplinary or administrative cases or misdemeanor cases, while powerless offenders are more likely to receive more severe sentences, although in many cases they have stolen relatively smaller amounts of money (Cheng 2009; Huang, Wei, and Meng 2004).

Stealing from a Banking Institution, Insider Misappropriation of Banking Funds, or Illegal Enrichment?

One important consequence of the vague definition of financial fraud is that many frauds committed by street criminals are handled as if they were crimes such as theft, which can make the convicted criminal liable to life imprisonment or the death penalty. For example, malicious withdrawal from an ATM is considered "theft from financial institutions." For "extremely huge amounts," according to China's Criminal Code, the minimum statutory penalty for the accused is life imprisonment.

In *Guangzhou People's Procuratorate v. Xu Ting* (2007), the accused was a migrant worker. While withdrawing cash from the ATM, he was surprised to find that it had only deducted one yuan (13 U.S. cents) from his account for every 1,000 yuan ($150) withdrawn. Apparently, something had gone wrong with the ATM. According to police, Xu Ting subsequently withdrew 175,000 yuan ($26,000) in 171 transactions and ran off with the money. The trial court convicted him of committing an "especially huge amount of theft from [a] financial institution" and sentenced him to life imprisonment. Widespread criticism of this verdict on the Internet led to popular pressure on the courts to review the provisions in the law. In 2008, the Guangdong Provincial High People's Court overturned the ruling and asked the lower court to retry the case. Xu Ting was still convicted of the crime of theft but was sentenced to a fixed-term imprisonment of 5 years.

While it is inspiring to see that public opinion can play an important role in accelerating the progress of the rule of law in China, it raises the question of whether media pressure has an undue influence on judicial trials. Even if public opinion helped the accused to get a fair sentence in Xu Ting's case, in some other cases media coverage has negatively influenced the outcome of trials. More important, the law is still not clear even after this case, as Chinese law, unlike in common-law jurisdictions elsewhere, does not necessarily follow precedent.

The case of Xu Ting sparked an intense debate among scholars, lawyers, and the general public. Some argued that the offense of "illegal enrichment" applied to his actions; others asserted that he should have been tried for embezzlement; still others believed he should have been charged with credit card fraud. At the same time, some argued that the case should be dealt with by tort law rather than by criminal law (Zhou 2008).

The public's perception of injustice in this case was driven by comparisons with the comparatively minor sentences most corrupt officials receive for financial fraud or corruption. A number of high-ranking officials were convicted of "illegal enrichment," which, at the time (2007), was punishable by only 5 years' imprisonment (subsequently increased to 10 years after the 2009 amendment), or of "insider misappropriation of banking funds," which is punishable with only 10 years' imprisonment in spite of the huge amounts involved. For example, in *Liaocheng People's Procuratorate v. Jing Changmin*, the local Land Administration Bureau chief stole as much as two million yuan ($300,000) and was convicted of receiving 80,000 yuan ($12,000) in bribes and of "illegal enrichment" for the remaining major part of the stolen funds. He was sentenced to only 8 years in prison (later reduced to 3 years). There are many such instances of corrupt officials who are convicted of "illegal enrichment" or other serious offenses for fraud and embezzlement or for receiving bribes of millions or even billions of yuan.

Legal Fundraising, Illegal Fundraising, or Fundraising Fraud?

The vague definition of financial fraud has also greatly favored high-status people in getting loans for business. So-called underground banks and Ponzi schemes became more prevalent in 2008 because financial regulators rejected proposals to legalize certain private lenders, and many banks were reluctant to provide loans to small- and medium-sized enterprises (Ye 2009). While those elite individuals and companies can freely get funds from banks, lower-class individuals can raise funds only through private fundraising or underground banks and thus become targets of law enforcement.

Currently, Chinese law lumps all illegal fundraising into two categories: illegal fundraising and fundraising fraud. The main distinction between the two offenses is the intent to defraud. The former refers to an unauthorized form of banking that involves soliciting and raising funds from the general public. In exchange, investors are promised high interest and principal repayments within specified time periods. The maximum sentence for this crime is 10 years. Fundraising fraud, in contrast, involves an intention to dupe investors, so it is considered far more serious and can incur a death sentence. The powerful, even when they committed fundraising fraud, were seldom charged or were charged with the less severe crime of "illegal fundraising."

Since it is difficult in practice to determine intent, the subtle distinction between the two offenses can easily be misinterpreted and even abused by enforcement officials and the courts to favor high-status offenders. In my sample, 74 percent of the illegal fundraising cases involving lower-status offenders were charged with fundraising fraud and only 15 percent were charged with illegal fundraising. Of those charged with fundraising fraud, 91 percent were convicted, and 93 percent of those charged with illegal fundraising were convicted. In 83 percent of the convictions involving low-status offenders, the penalty was more than 10 years' imprisonment. In comparison, 63 percent of the illegal fundraising cases involving high-status offenders were considered legal borrowing and were not charged with any offense, and 37 percent were charged with illegal fundraising. Most of the convicted high-status offenders ended up with a prison sentence of less than 5 years.

It is interesting to note that family origin may also influence interpretation and application of law in this area. In the case of *Dongyang People's Procuratorate v. Wu Ying* (2009), the accused, Wu Ying, was a young woman born to a poor peasant family. Unable to afford a university education, she dropped out of an accountancy program in the 1990s to run a small foot massage parlor and beauty salon and later started a car rental company. She then raised funds from a number of private investors for her business during the following decade and ended up with 3.6 billion yuan ($500 million) in assets in 2007. At first, Wu was charged with having illegally raised nearly 390 million yuan ($57 million) for the "purpose of possession," promising high returns. But as investigators uncovered more evidence against Wu, the charges were changed to fundraising fraud. She was finally convicted on this charge and sentenced to death.

Some observers assert that Wu actually offended local government officials by exposing scandals involving them and local real estate businesses. Some speculate that Wu's humble family origin and lack of close ties to local officials may be related to her severe sentence. Wu's attorney, Yang Zhaodong, insisted that his client was innocent even of "illegal fundraising." He told the court:

> Wu simply borrowed the money but did not cheat anyone. . . . She used the money for business and did not illegally spend it. Wu told the court

she had been investing in highly profitable businesses, including trading companies, hotels, investment guarantee agencies and property developments. The eleven people who lent her money were her friends— not the "general public" as they were defined in the indictments. Wu should not be responsible for the amounts the eleven investors collected from others to give Wu. (Cao 2009, B1)

My analysis of a number of financial fraud cases seems consistent with the family origin hypothesis. When the so-called blue-blooded or second generation of the party or government leaders were involved in financial frauds, their cases were more likely to be handled administratively or incur much lighter criminal punishment.

The Politics of Investigating Financial Fraud

Most financial fraud cases in China are investigated by police departments under the Ministry of Public Security. Criminal offenses committed by government officials, employees, and agencies, however, are investigated directly by procuratorates. The procuratorate's anticorruption unit conducts investigations of bribery, embezzlement, and other public corruption. The procuratorate also has a government employees misconduct unit, which investigates all other criminal conduct committed by government workers while on official business. Executives and managers of banks and of other financial institutions and state-owned corporations are considered government officials or employees and will be investigated by procuratorates if they commit financial fraud.

Police investigation is reactive in nature, relying very heavily on referrals from the CBRC and information from the banking industry. CBRC staff members are required to inspect a certain number of banks and other relevant financial institutions in the region for which they are responsible. The staff is responsible for investigating all alleged offenses and preparing investigation briefs, which are used either for the commission's administrative proceedings or for referral to the police or procuratorate for criminal investigation. The commission's review of the report of its investigators is not a public judicial proceeding, where all interested parties have an opportunity to present their case, but rather a closed-door internal administrative proceeding. A significant enforcement "funnel" operates within the commission: A much lower number of high-profile financial fraud cases are detected and punished than the number actually committed. For example, among the 1,697 employees at financial institutions investigated by the CBRC for financial fraud in the first half of 2005, there were 570 executives and senior managers, including 7 central bank managers and 82 "big four" bank branch heads.[2] However, only 10 percent of the high-ranking managers were referred to procuratorates for criminal investigation; yet 80 percent of the low-ranking employees were referred to the police. Penalties for senior executives and managers were usually limited to dismissal, fines, or simply a reprimand (CBRC 2006).

In the present postcommunist neoliberal atmosphere in China, compliance through cooperation between criminal justice agencies and high-ranking government or business officials alleged to have committed financial offenses is normally more important for the current regime. Criminal proceedings are used only where warnings have failed or for unscrupulous offenders who may threaten the rule and domination of the Communist Party. A CBRC enforcement officer summarized these sentiments as follows:

> Well, my view of it is that insider financial offenses are a regulatory problem. And our job as a regulator is to deal with important problems and try to correct them. We make banking institutions and officials stick to the bottom line of compliance management. The CBRC considers that preventing banking crimes is a major aspect of supervision, and a major part of the regulatory framework on operational risk management. (Interview transcript, case 009)

Similarly, financial fraud involving powerful criminals is not a priority for police, even though on many public occasions senior police officers have expressed concern about the prevalence of serious financial crimes (Meng 2008[3]). In response to the public outrage about corruption and financial fraud, the central government created the Economic Crimes Investigation Department (ECID) in the Ministry of Public Security in 1998, with branches in local police forces across the nation.

However, the subdivisions for banking and other financial crimes are extremely understaffed. For example, in the Public Security Bureau of Beijing, there are only 20 officers in the ECID branch dealing with insider financial fraud, while 300 officers are assigned to investigate outsider fraud

(Wu and Li 2004). In contrast, 10,000 officers are assigned to monitor prostitution. (In China, prostitution in itself is not a criminal offense, and criminal law is not concerned with prostitution unless organized crime is involved. Instead, it is regarded as a "public order" offense punishable via administrative penalties administered by police without public hearing.)

The ECID clearly places a priority on lower-class offenders who are accused of victimizing financial institutions or rich individuals. Because powerful offenders are better able to exploit a complex politically oriented legal system, ECID investigators would prefer poor defendants. They are generally discouraged by local government officials from pursuing high-profile cases involving corporations or high-status individuals. An ECID investigator explained it in the following way:

It is not that we have class bias, and we did find a number of high-profile fraud cases . . . yet such powerful offenders are protected by strong "connection networks" [guanxi wang] and "protective umbrellas" [baohu san]. Local officials have to consider local interests, their personal profits, their political achievement and promotion, so [they] would interfere in our investigation of the cases. It is much safer for us to pursue the small potatoes. (Interview transcript, case 018)

Ironically, such "connection networks" and "protective umbrellas" also include senior police officers who are involved in major financial fraud cases. Zheng Shaodong, the former assistant minister of public security and director of the ECID, was himself convicted of taking more than 8.3 million yuan ($1.2 million) in bribes from several high-profile financial swindlers from 2001 to 2007. In particular, Zheng and his deputy Xiang Huaizhu were charged with taking bribes from Huang Guangyu, one of China's richest businesspersons, for covering up Huang's financial fraud involving the Bank of China's Beijing branch in 2006. Huang's omnipotence in the capital market was reportedly related to his deep connections with central and local government officials through frequent bribes. Huang's case involved not only several ministries in the central government but also senior local officials, indicating that "connection networks" and "protective umbrellas" deeply penetrate the Chinese government both horizontally and vertically (Chen and Zhu 2009).

Some scholars argue that the pursuit of high-profile fraud cases reflects the power struggles within the Communist government: Some controlling leaders use prosecutions as a tool to eliminate rivals and their business supporters, rather than conduct a real "war on financial crimes" (Cheng 2008). In Huang's case, a number of senior officials involved, including the then ECID director, were from Guangdong and had long-standing ties with Huang, who was himself from Guangdong. Some commentators speculate that they might have been punished in a party power shuffle to weaken the Guangdong Faction (*Guangdong Bang*) in China's bureaucracy (Chen and Zhu 2009).

This is a reasonable speculation if we look at many other corruption cases. In a major case in 2008 for instance, Chen Liangyu, the former Shanghai Party Chief and Politburo member and a key member of the Shanghainese Faction (*Shanghai Bang*), was sentenced to 18 years in prison for accepting the equivalent of $340,000 in bribes and for abuse of power related to his role in a municipal pension fund scandal. Chen's challenge to President Hu Jintao's authority played a substantial role in Hu's decision to investigate this case (Cheng 2008).

The class-based or political-based nature of law enforcement has long been singled out by scholars. Sutherland (1949) pointed out that law enforcement was in the hands of members of a powerful class who are likely to sympathize with offenders from a similar class background. Consistent with this hypothesis, officers interviewed for Sutherland's study generally sympathized with higher-status offenders and were reluctant to define them as "criminals," preferring to call them "victims of the imperfect financial system." Most of the officers interviewed considered low-status offenders "real criminals," "bad eggs," or "dishonest crooks" who deserved public blame and criminal punishment.

Such stereotyping is prevalent in contemporary China. With so many "connection networks" existing among high-status individuals in various sectors, the safer approach has been to scapegoat low-status offenders as "folk devils" and to hold them chiefly responsible for financial crime. Media focus on these offenders, even in cases that are spurious, creates the public impression that the government is making great efforts to combat fraud. In 2008, the ECID announced that its nationwide staff had uncovered 9,055 cases of financial fraud during the previous year (Wu 2008). However, it has been suggested that most cases reported were "the easy pickings, the unsophisticated poor criminals, the people under no protective umbrellas" (Interview transcript, case 015).

Some ECID investigators attribute the focus on underclass offenders to a lack of resources and expertise on the part of authorities, as the complexity of financial fraud cases involving high-status offenders often exceeds the ability of law enforcement agencies to investigate them. Most ECID investigators are law school graduates and do not have much experience in, or knowledge of, the financial industry. However, this could easily have been remedied if police leaders had been willing to invest in the training and personnel recruitment necessary to strengthen the ECID's ability to deal with more sophisticated fraudsters.

As mentioned earlier, the procuratorate is empowered to investigate fraud cases involving government officials, employees, and agencies, as well as officials of state-owned companies, and to prosecute all fraud cases including those dealt with by the police. As a result of the political sensitivity of fraud cases involving government officials, the procuratorate's ability to decide who and what to investigate is highly circumscribed. This is despite the fact that, according to law, it is not subject to interference by any administrative organ, social organization, or individual. Consistent with Beare's (2007) hypothesis on the relationship between police and politics, the Chinese Communist Party is able to wield its influence on the procuratorate in a number of ways, including the nomination of procurators and the control of financial resources. Political interference is most evident in major and complex cases, such as those involving high-ranking officials. Final decisions in these cases are made by each procuratorate's prosecution committee, which consists of the chief procurator and deputy chief procurators as well as its divisional or district procurators. Prosecution committees usually make their decisions after consultation with the party's political-legal committees at corresponding levels, which are led by senior party leaders who also serve as deputy party secretaries. This type of decision-making mechanism opens the door for party cadres and government officials to interfere with procuratorates' investigation and prosecution process.

In my interviews with ten investigators in several municipal procuratorates of eastern China, they estimated that 30 to 40 percent of their fraud cases were affected by political influence. Political or party leaders "set the tone" for decision making in almost all major cases involving high-status fraud offenders. One local procurator cited a case in which an investigator courageously ignored senior politicians' demand that he suspend an investigation against a high-status offender. In the end, however, he was fired.

It should also be noted that since almost all senior government officials are party members, the Central Commission for Disciplinary Inspection at the top of the party hierarchy in fact acts as the country's top anticorruption watchdog. Similarly, each regional party committee has a commission for disciplinary inspection to exercise vigilance over corruption. Under such a system, regional party chiefs are virtually immune to supervision by local watchdogs and can hardly be pursued if they collude with top financial officials, that is, unless political concerns make the case a high priority for the central power.

In principle, there is a division of labor between party discipline inspection commissions and government procuratorates. The party discipline inspection commission investigates violations of party discipline and, if such violations constitute a crime, refers them to the procuratorate for further investigation and prosecution. The procuratorate investigates crimes involving officials, most of whom are party members. In practice, however, discipline inspection committees resolve most high-profile cases without turning cases over to procuratorates. The party has its own set of punishments for violations of party discipline, ranging from warning, dismissal from party positions, and probation within the party, to expulsion from the party. Expulsion, the most severe punishment, is nonetheless mild compared with the primary criminal punishments for financial fraud: imprisonment and death.

Conclusion

The findings presented in this study suggest that the class structure limits the independence of the criminal justice system in China. In financial fraud cases, a pronounced class bias exists in both the law and its enforcement by the police, the Banking Regulatory Commission, and procuratorates. The social class bias is exacerbated by the party agencies' direct interference with law enforcement.

Although the influence of class status on criminal investigation is complex in China, the law and its enforcement obviously target low-status individuals more than they do high-status individuals and powerful organizations. Despite political and economic elites committing the most serious and harmful fraud, they are least likely to be investigated and prosecuted in a criminal way. The triple helix of political, economic, and intellectual elites in China, organized to share power and capital assets, may explain why the politicians are so interested in protecting major financial offenders from criminal enforcement.

A number of factors make it more likely that investigators will go after poorer violators. These include investigators' limited power to pursue high-status offenders, discouragement by local officials from pursuing high-status offenders, "connection networks" (*guanxi wang*) and "protective umbrellas" (*baohu san*), sympathy for high-status offenders, the vagueness of law, and the lack of resources and expertise. Consequently, we find that poor or marginalized individuals make up the largest number of offenders charged with fraud, and the government uses prosecutions of their cases to appease public anger about financial crime and corruption. The results would seem to support Black's (1976) central proposition that "law varies directly with stratification." Thanks to the sharp polarization between the rich and powerful and the rest of Chinese society, differentiated law enforcement based on stratification is clearly evident. However, it will be interesting to see whether the growing Chinese middle class will have an effect on this law enforcement model.

My research also reveals a "double-track" government approach that tolerates the windfall profits of the elite while aiming to maintain long-term political and economic stability. In the past, when financial fraud and corruption of the elite attracted little public attention, regulators and enforcement agencies failed to pursue many cases. This is changing—but slowly. The increasing demands from the poor for equitable treatment in recent years may explain why the central party government has instructed party and government enforcement agencies to pursue more high-profile financial fraud cases. However, it is still too early to predict the future trend of financial fraud enforcement in China. Political complications will present substantial hurdles to law enforcement in the coming years.

Notes

The author would like to thank the University of Saskatchewan for providing the President Social Sciences and Humanities Research Council and Tri-Council Bridge Funding for the research presented in this chapter.

1. In Chinese law, only those behaviors prohibited by the Criminal Law of the People's Republic of China (most recently amended in 2009) and the Congress's supplementation to or interpretation of the Criminal Law are considered "crimes." Other legislation cannot provide that a conduct is a criminal offense.

2. In China, these are Bank of China, China Construction Bank, Industrial and Commercial Bank of China, and Agricultural Bank of China, the four largest state-owned banks.

3. Meng Jianzhu is the current minister of public security of China. He emphasized in his article that too many financial crimes involving high-status people would lead to "mass incidents" (*qunti shijian*), a deliberately vague and generic term used by the authorities to describe large-scale public protests.

References

Bacher, Jean-Luc, Martin Bouchard, Pierre Tremblay, and Julie Paquin. 2005. "Another Look at the 'Corporate Advantage' in Routine Criminal Proceedings." *Canadian Journal of Criminology and Criminal Justice* 47 (4): 685–707.

Beare, Margaret E. 2007. "Steeped in Politics: The Ongoing History of Politics in Policing." In *Police and Government Relations: Who's Calling the Shots?*, edited by Margaret E. Beare and Tonita Murray, 313–65. Toronto: University of Toronto Press.

Black, Donald J. 1976. *The Behavior of Law*. San Diego: Academic Press.

Cao, Li. 2009. "Ex-Rich List Woman in $57m Fraud." *China Daily*, April 17, B1.

Chen, Gang, and Jinjing Zhu. 2009. "China's Recent Clampdown on High-Stakes Corruption." Working paper. EAI Background Brief No. 490. East Asian Institute, National University of Singapore.

Cheng, Hongming. 2004. *Insider Trading in Canada and China: Globalized Market Economy and the Role of Law*. Fredericton, N.B.: CLSNA Publications.

———. 2009. "Do the Wealthy Have More Rights? A Socio-Legal Analysis of the Current Constitution of the People's Republic of China and Its Impact on Criminal Law." *China Journal of Law and Economics* 9:67–69.

Cheng, Hongming, and Ling Ma. 2009. "White Collar Crime and the Criminal Justice System: Bank Fraud and Corruption in China." *Journal of Financial Crime* 16 (2): 166–79.

Cheng, Li, ed. 2008. *China's Changing Political Landscape: Prospects for Democracy*. Washington, D.C.: Brookings Institution Press.

Chinese Banking Regulatory Commission. 2005. *The CBRC Calls for Continuous Efforts to Crack Down on the Violations in the Banking Sector*. Beijing: Chinese Banking Regulatory Commission. http://www.cbrc.gov.cn/english/home/jsp/docView.jsp?docID=1594 (accessed August 5, 2010).

———. 2006. *Internal Annual Report*. Beijing: Chinese Banking Regulatory Commission. http://www.cbrc.gov.cn/chinese/home/jsp/docView.jsp?docID=2007 0629B57924013227741CBFFF0431894CBC500 (accessed August 5, 2010).

————. 2007. *Internal Annual Report*. Beijing: Chinese Banking Regulatory Commission. http://www.cbrc.gov.cn/chinese/home/jsp/docView.jsp?docID=2008 04300FB630DC553E65ABFF13F202A6743900 (accessed August 5, 2010).

————. 2008. *Internal Annual Report*. Beijing: Chinese Banking Regulatory Commission. http://www.cbrc.gov.cn/chinese/home/jsp/docView.jsp?docID= 200906016A540A030280DDDCFF4762FBD0BA4F00 (accessed August 5, 2010).

————. 2009a. *Chairperson's Report*. Beijing: Chinese Banking Regulatory Commission. Provided by CBRC Information Office on August 5, 2010.

————. 2009b. *Internal Annual Report*. Beijing: Chinese Banking Regulatory Commission. http://www.cbrc.gov.cn/chinese/home/jsp/docView.jsp?docID=2 0100615A314C942DEE7DD34FF395FFCEB671E00 (accessed August 5, 2010).

Coleman, James W. 2006. *The Criminal Elite: Understanding White-Collar Crime*. 6th ed. New York: Worth Publishers.

Copes, Heith, Kent R. Kerley, Karen A. Mason, and Judy Van Wyck. 2001. "Reporting Behavior of Fraud Victims and Black's Theory of the Behavior of Law." *Justice Quarterly* 28:343–63.

Criminal Law of the PRC (adopted by the Second Session of the Fifth National People's Congress in 1979). http://www.novexcn.com/criminal_law.html (accessed May 15, 2010).

Decision of the Standing Committee of the National People's Congress. 1999. "Regarding the Severe Punishment of Criminals Who Seriously Disrupt the Financial Order" (adopted by the Fourteenth Session of the Standing Committee of the Eighth National People's Congress, June 30, 1995). In *Collection of Current Financial Laws and Regulations of the People's Republic of China*. Shanghai, China: Lixin Kuaiji Press.

Diamond, Shari S. 1995. "The Challenges of Socio-Legal Research on Decision-Making: Psychological Successes and Failures." *Journal of Law and Society* 22:78–84.

Dongyang People's Procuratorate v. Wu Ying. 201 Dongyang Intermediate People's Court Criminal Cases (2009).

Durkheim, Emile. 1997. *The Division of Labor in Society*, translated by Lewis A. Coser. New York: Free Press.

Friedman, Lawrence M. 1977. *Law and Society*. Englewood Cliffs, N.J.: Prentice-Hall.

Guangzhou People's Procuratorate v. Xu Ting. 192 Guangzhou Intermediate People's Court Criminal Cases (2007).

He, Qinglian. 2003. "A Listing Social Structure." In *One China, Many Paths*, edited by Chaohua Wang, 163–88. London: Verso Books.

Holtfreter, Kristy. 2004. "Fraud in U.S. Organizations: An Examination of Control Mechanisms." *Journal of Financial Crime* 12:88–95.

————. 2005. "Is Occupational Fraud 'Typical' White-Collar Crime? A Comparison of Individual and Organizational Characteristics." *Journal of Criminal Justice* 33:353–65.

————. 2008. "The Effects of Legal and Extra-Legal Characteristics on Organizational Victim Decision-Making." *Crime, Law & Social Change* 50:308–30.

Holtfreter, Kristy, Nicole Leeper Piquero, and Alex. R. Piquero. 2008. "And Justice for All? Investigators' Perceptions of Punishment for Fraud Perpetrators." *Crime, Law & Social Change* 49:397–412.

Huang, Kejian, Yun Wei, and Tao Meng. 2004. "Challenges to Economic Crime Investigation." *China Criminal Police* 5:57–8.

Levi, Michael. 1995. "Serious Fraud in Britain: Criminal Justice vs. Regulation." In *Corporate Crime: Contemporary Debates*, edited by Laureen Snider and Frank Pearce, 181–98. Toronto: University of Toronto Press.

Li, Qiang. 2005. "T-Shaped Social Structure and the Structure Tension." *Sociological Research Journal in China* 2:55–73.

Liaocheng People's Procuratorate v. Jing Changmin. 135 Liaocheng Intermediate People's Court Criminal Cases (2010).

Liu, Mingkang. 2005. "Reform, Opening and Development of Today's Banking Industry." Speech Transcription. Nankai University, Tianjing, June 11.

Meng, Jianzhu. 2008. "Deeply Studying Scientific Development Thoughts, Becoming the Party's Faithful Guards and the People's Friends." *Qiu Shi Journal* 21:28–29.

Reiman, Jeffery. 2007. *The Rich Get Richer and the Poor Get Prison.* 8th ed. Boston: Allyn and Bacon.

Snider, Laureen. 1993. *Bad Business: Corporate Crime in Canada.* Scarborough, ON: ITP Nelson.

———. 2000. "The Sociology of Corporate Crime: An Obituary." *Theoretical Criminology* 4 (2): 169–206.

———. 2005. "The Criminological Lens: Understanding Criminal Law and Corporate Governance." In *Governing the Corporation: Regulation and Corporate Governance in an Age of Scandal and Global Markets*, edited by Justin O'Brien, 163–85. London: Wiley.

Snider, Laureen, and Frank Pearce, eds. 1995. *Corporate Crime: Contemporary Debates.* Toronto: University of Toronto Press.

Sutherland, Edwin H. 1949. *White Collar Crime.* New York: Holt, Rinehart & Winston.

Wright, Arthur F. 1960. "Introduction." In *The Confucian Persuasion*, edited by Arthur F. Wright, 3–20. Stanford, Calif.: Stanford University Press.

Wu, Heping. 2008. "Briefing on 2007 National Public Security Situation." State Council Information Office, January 30. http://www.china.com.cn/zhibo/2008-01/30/content_9605527.htm.

Wu, Jing, and Yang Li. 2004. "Increasing Economic Crimes Challenge Police Force." *Beijing Modern Business*, October 11.

Ye, Doudou. 2009. "Ponzi Case Raises Death Penalty Questions." *Caijing Magazine*, January 14.

Zhou, C. 2006. "Revision of Criminal Law: Responding to Six Common Financial Crime Techniques." *China Business News*, January 1, A2.

Zhou, Ya. 2008. "What Is the Aim of Criminal Law? A Discussion of the Xu Ting Case." *Guangdong Legal Studies* 2:32–34.

EPILOGUE

Can They Still Get Away with It?

What has happened in the years since the financial meltdown? Are we out of the woods? Has the debt crisis that long plagued the Third World now become one of the most significant problems facing the First World? What have we learned? Nelen and Ritzen, in this volume, claim that financial crises create both problems and opportunities. Have we taken advantage of the opportunities to restructure the regulatory environment to prevent a recurrence, or can they still get away with it?

The financial landscape has been shifting rapidly ever since the U.S. subprime mortgage crisis and the collapse of Iceland's three major banks made headlines in 2008. It is changing so fast that what is written one day has to be modified the next. Still, general trends and consequences can be identified. Several economies still have unsustainable levels of debt. Many banks, businesses, and individuals are unable to get loans. Unemployment rates, particularly for youth between 16 and 24, have remained high in many industrialized and post-industrialized countries since the crisis began (reaching over 50 percent in Spain, 48 percent in Greece, approximately 30 percent in Ireland, Italy and Portugal, and is 22.3 percent is Great Britain [Thomas 2012]), and wages are stagnant or falling for those who have jobs.

As a result, the standard of living for the vast majority of citizens has decreased. The World Bank calculated that the financial crisis caused the world GDP to fall 1.5 percent in 2009, a drop worse than what occurred during the economic downturns of the 1970s and 1980s (Norris 2011).

During the summer of 2011, as many nations showed signs of returning to fiscal health, economic problems continued to dominate the news in the European Union and the United States. In fact, the economic crises in the euro zone and the United Kingdom appear to be getting worse. Credit ratings agencies downgraded Greek, Portuguese, and Irish debt ratings to junk status, gave Iceland its lowest investment grade rating,[1] and dropped the ratings of Italy and Spain, making it more difficult for those countries to raise capital, stimulate growth, and pull themselves out of an ever-deepening hole. Impatient with Congressional debates over raising the debt ceiling, Standard & Poor's lowered the United States' AAA bond rating to AA+ in August 2011 and the other two rating agencies have threatened to follow suit. The debate over raising the U.S. debt ceiling, at its core, is an ideological debate over the direction the country should take. While some may believe that it makes good economic sense to cut deficits and spending, Nobel economist Joseph Stiglitz warned in 2010 that "'mindless deficit reduction' would lead to greater and longer-lasting national debt" (Phillips 2010). The real problem with economies on both sides of the Atlantic is the lack of jobs, the lack of spending by individuals and cash-rich corporations, and forced cutbacks in government spending (Krugman 2011a).

Europe

Massive debt brought to light by the 2008 financial crisis has hurt the economic standing of Greece, Ireland, Italy, Portugal, and Spain. The bailouts of Greece (initially €110 billion or $156 billion; in February 2012 an additional bailout valued at €130 billion or $172 billion was planned), Ireland (€85 billion or $120.7 billion), and Portugal (€78 billion or $110.8 billion)[2] by the IMF, the European Commission, and the European Central Bank have produced neither political nor economic stability, which in turn raises concerns about the future of the euro zone. In fact, by May 2011, it was determined that Greece needed a second bailout and that Cyprus might be the next weak link.

The European Commission expects Greece's debt-to-GDP ratio to increase from 142 percent in 2010 to 166 percent in 2012. Its fiscal deficit is expected to decline from 10.5 percent to 9.3 percent. Ireland's debt-to-GDP ratio is expected to increase from 96 percent in 2010 to 118 percent in 2012. Its 2010 fiscal deficit of 30.3 percent is expected to decline to 8.5 percent in 2012.

Portugal's debt-to-GDP ratio is expected to increase from 93 percent in 2010 to 107 percent in 2012. On the basis of projected austerity measures, Portugal is expected to reduce its fiscal deficit from 9.1 percent to 4.5 percent in 2012. According to the Bank for International Settlement data, at the end of 2010, the exposure of foreign banks—primarily German and French—to Spanish, Greek, Portuguese, and Irish debt totaled around $2.3 trillion (Marcus 2011, 2).

Greece, Ireland, Portugal, and Italy have adopted severe austerity programs, much to the displeasure of their citizens. Citizens of Iceland, Greece, Italy, United Kingdom. and Portugal have taken to the streets to demonstrate their anger over being asked to shoulder the burden of belt-tightening measures, such as pension reform, tax increases, cuts to public education, and health and reductions in public sector wages, while financial institutions and holders of bank or government debt are not forced to take losses. Neither has anyone from the financial community been sentenced to prison. It is not surprising that the Occupy Wall Street movement resonated with Europeans.

Greece, Iceland, Ireland, Italy, Portugal, Spain, and the United States took different routes into their economic quagmire. Iceland's 2008 financial collapse was caused by "extreme negligence" according to the findings of the Special Investigation Commission (Penfold 2010). Iceland's three main banks collapsed in 2008 following difficulties in refinancing their short-term debt and a run on deposits in the United Kingdom. Since deregulation in 2001, all three banks grew rapidly by borrowing "more than 10 times the country's gross domestic product—$75 billion—from the international wholesale money markets" and quickly expanded their domestic lending (Jackson 2008). They used weak underwriting standards, particularly for loans to large holding companies. They enticed foreign depositors with high interest rates based on stock market performance and issued 100 percent mortgages and car loans, often in foreign currencies. The value of their assets rose from 100 percent of Iceland's gross GDP in 2004 to 923 percent by the end of 2007 (Jackson 2008), a sure sign that something was amiss.

Iceland's response to the economic meltdown, however, was different than the response taken by most countries. Icelandic voters in 2010 rejected a $5.3 billion plan to repay the United Kingdom and the Netherlands for loans incurred during the financial crisis in 2008, and they turned down a similar plan the following year despite warnings that without the debt repayment agreement, Iceland would be unable to obtain loans from the IMF or succeed in a bid for membership in the European Union (Editorial, April 18, 2011; Quinn 2010). Many Icelanders believed that the plan, which would have required each citizen to pay around $135 a month for 8 years—the equivalent of a quarter of an average income for a four-member family—was unfair when the government failed to curtail the reckless behavior of bank executives. Adding to the skepticism, a Special Investigations Commission established by Iceland's state prosecutor in December 2008 to "investigate suspicions of criminal actions in the period preceding the collapse of the Icelandic banks" has already led to charges of gross negligence against seven senior officials, including former Prime Minister Geir H. Haarde. The commission's report claims that Haarde and David Oddsson, former head of the Central Bank of Iceland (Seðlabanki Íslands) "knew that banks were assuming overseas debt but took no action to prevent or mitigate the effects of the accumulation" (Zeldin 2011).

Icelanders' refusal to take on bank debts, forcing creditors to take losses and share in the pain, appears to be very much an effort to ensure that "they" don't get away with it—not to mention a smart long-range move: Iceland's economy is beginning to recover (Organisation for Economic Co-operation and Development 2011).

Greece's debt of $1.2 trillion, amounting roughly to a quarter-million dollars for each working adult, is the result of a variety of factors: a bloated public sector that is paid much better than the private sector, generous pensions, waste, corruption, wholesale tax evasion, cooked books, and creative accounting encouraged by Goldman Sachs (Faiola 2010; Lewis 2010).

Greek bankers, however, "did not buy U.S. subprime-backed bonds, or leverage themselves to the hilt, or pay themselves huge sums of money" (Lewis 2010). Instead, Greek banks lent money to the Greek government, which was their downfall. According to Lewis, who chronicled the Greek crisis in a *Vanity Fair* article, the level of Greek debt has been high since the 1980s. The entry fee for becoming a euro zone country in 2000 was lowering debt levels. To accomplish this, Greece manipulated statistics and its accounting ledgers to make inflation and debt magically disappear. Once its debt was backed by the euro, Greece went on a borrowing spree (Faiola 2010). In 2001, Goldman Sachs taught government officials how to securitize future receipts and aided them in hiding the country's true indebtedness, which in 2009 was 15 percent instead of the required (and reported) 3 percent.

A major contribution to the Greek crisis, as Vidali indicates in Chapter 14, was widespread tax evasion, bribery, illegal debt financing, and other forms of state-corporate criminality. Greeks learned to ignore the law not only because of the absence of law enforcement but also because everyone believed that everyone else was engaged in these activities (Lewis 2010). Clearly, this criminal behavior is socially learned and became the norm. In Greece, in effect, *everyone* got away with it for years.

Everyone was also a victim, as the case of Ireland illustrates. When the financial markets opened the floodgates to almost limitless credit at the beginning of the century, Irish citizens rushed to take advantage. "Lending by banks to Irish residents rose 450% in the decade prior to 2008, compared to a 30% increase in Germany and an increase of 100% in the Netherlands" (Lyons 2010). A housing bubble grew to such an extent that nearly a fifth of the workforce was employed constructing houses. The industry contributed nearly a quarter of the country's GDP, in contrast to what most economists consider a normal proportion of less than 10 percent (Lewis 2011). Loans of the three largest banks—Anglo Irish, Bank of Ireland, and Allied Irish Banks—were tied up in real estate. When the inevitable crash occurred, it had severe consequences. Unemployment, which was 4 percent in 2006, rose to 14 percent in 2012. Ireland recorded a budget surplus in 2007. Today its deficit is 9.9 percent of its GDP, down from a deficit of 32 percent GDP in 2010.

The crisis in Europe is still far from over. Real concern exists over the ability of Italy and Spain (the EU's third and fourth largest economies) to handle their debt. The Spanish economy is larger than that of Greece, Ireland, and Portugal combined, and it has higher levels of bank debt than Portugal. Furthermore, thirty of Spain's banks were derated by Moody's in 2010 (Thomas 2011), and five failed a stress test in July 2011. The sixteen European banks that narrowly passed were concentrated in Spain, Greece, and Portugal (Werdigier and Ewing 2011). The good news is that Spain has taken several steps to stay out of danger—including a pension overhaul and a cleanup of its banking sector (Minder and Castle 2011). Nevertheless, the European banking system's exposure to these countries' debt could result in a systemic crisis in the event of even a partial default. Austerity programs have been offered as the principal solution. But they are certain to worsen standards of living for many Europeans who are used to—and rely upon—a functioning welfare state. Many budget cuts have been achieved by eliminating jobs. In Greece, the unemployment rate was over 21 percent in February 2012. Across Europe unemployment also continued to rise. By December 2011, the unemployment rates were as follows: Spain, 22.9 percent; Portugal, 13.6 percent; Ireland, 14.5 percent (and that is after many of its foreign workers left the country); and Italy, 9.0 percent (Bureau of Labor Statistics 2011). Government austerity programs seem to comport with Canadian journalist Naomi Klein's (2008) "shock doctrine" concept. She argues that governments desiring to replace the existing economic order with a version of a free market economy use opportunities presented by disasters and crises to gain citizen support for slashing social spending and engaging in privatization.[3]

This volume only scratches the surface of how the financial crisis has impacted countries around the globe. While many have identified the financial meltdown as a global crisis, Australian criminologist John Braithwaite (2010) argues that although the financial meltdown has devastated the economies of the United States, Iceland, and many euro zone countries, it is not a true global crisis. True, the recession impacted most countries in the world. However, as he and others note, in countries with better regulatory practices, such as Australia, the recession was not as severe.[4] In those countries, regulators did not allow banks to engage in behavior the regulators did not understand. Avoiding the kind of misbehavior that occurred in the United States, banks and lending agencies in those countries checked records instead of relying on sophisticated quantitative risk models. They also refrained from buying into bad American housing loans. In essence, countries that did not drink the Kool-Aid by jumping on the deregulatory and self-regulation bandwagon tended to escape the worst effects of the financial crisis.

The United States

In the United States, where the crisis began, the picture is just as bleak. The housing market is still depressed in most regions. A large proportion of homes are underwater; that is, homeowners now hold mortgages amounting to more than their homes are worth. Foreclosures are continuing. U.S. Census Bureau data show that 18 percent or 1.6 million of Florida's homes are vacant—an increase of more than 63 percent over the past 10 years (Christie 2011). Housing prices in the state have dropped by more than 50 percent from their peak and are expected to continue to fall through mid-2012. Nevada, the state with the nation's highest foreclosure rate, has a vacancy rate of approximately 14 percent, and Arizona's rate is about 16 percent (Christie 2011).

The U.S. stock market has rebounded, but wages are stagnant. Although the reported national unemployment for January 2012 dropped to 8.8 percent, one questions how many individuals out of work are no longer counted. Cash-starved state governments are cutting jobs, social services, benefits, and demanding labor concessions from their employees. Former U.S. Secretary of Labor Robert Reich warned in his March 30, 2011, blog that the United States was heading toward a double-dip recession. The evidence, according to Reich, is that real hourly wages and housing prices continue to fall in many regions of the country.

The $5.6 trillion in mortgage debt that U.S. households took on during the bubble years is believed to be holding back the economy (Krugman 2011b). Banks are still reluctant to make loans even to good customers. One individual seeking a $120,000 mortgage on a home he built was turned down by the bank with whom he had been a client for over 30 years. He told one of the editors of this volume that he had never missed a payment on a previous mortgage or on the boat loans he had with them. He had $40,000 in savings. But he apparently ran afoul of a new Fannie Mae requirement that borrowers on newly constructed houses must live in the house for 6 months. The fact that he had already owned the property for 2 years and the house was appraised at $280,000 did not help. Although Fannie Mae's new requirement was adopted to prevent the kinds of abuses that led to the crisis, the one-size-fits-all application is problematic. Fallout from the crisis is even affecting customers with good credit.

New scandals involving mortgage-granting financial institutions have appeared. In the fall of 2010, several mortgage lenders engaged in illegal foreclosures using "robo-signers," which mechanically attested that banks had the required documentation to seize homes without verifying whether they actually did (Krugman 2011b). A study commissioned by the San Francisco assessor/recorder found that between January 2009 and November 2011 "84 percent of the files contained what appeared to be clear violations of the law" and a full "two-thirds had at least four violations or irregularities" (Morgenson 2012). These crimes occurred after the government had supposedly increased its scrutiny of the industry. In most cases, the victims were individuals similar to those described by Barnett in Chapter 6.

Politicians reacted to the public's outrage over the shenanigans that led to the financial meltdown by taking steps to plug loopholes and to reregulate the financial industry by passing the Dodd-Frank Wall Street Reform and Consumer Protection Act. The act, aimed at rectifying the problems that caused the financial crisis, is still controversial today and under attack by Republicans on the campaign trail. Another law, the 2009 Mortgage Reform and Anti-Predatory Lending Act, prohibited lenders from engaging in the types of activities Barnett describes in Chapter 6: underwriting loans that consumers do not have a reasonable ability to repay and discouraging exotic, nontraditional mortgages, which were a major factor in the current housing and foreclosure crisis.

Problems with Regulation

Unfortunately, the Dodd-Frank Act has become little more than a hollow promise after it was signed into law in July 2010. As Snider noted in Chapter 8, the financial industry lobbied to delay or dilute several key provisions of the act. Congressional Republicans have done their best to aid the industry in achieving deregulation or a de facto repeal of Dodd-Frank by not adequately funding key provisions of the legislation and not approving the appointments of personnel to several positions the act created to implement and oversee the reform,[5] raising the question of whether the act is merely symbolic legislation. One provision, however, that probably will be adhered to prevents the United States from adopting the newly agreed-upon Basel III capital requirements for banks (Taylor 2010).

The act greatly expanded the already underfunded SEC's responsibilities. But the Republican-controlled House appropriations committee, claiming it wanted to reduce the cost and size of government, actually cut the agency's 2012 budget request by $222.5 million. The total approved this year was $1.19 billion (Stewart 2011). Another agency, the Commodity Futures Trading Commission (CFTC), estimated that it needed $261 million to cover the additional responsibilities assigned it by the Dodd-Frank Act. Congress approved only $202 million (Protess 2011).

Uncertain and insufficient funding creates delays in hiring, training, establishing offices mandated by law, creating and enforcing new laws, and investigating cases. It hardly makes sense that the federal government has spent hundreds of millions bailing out banks that produced the crisis, while it cut spending for enforcement, which could prevent another crisis (Protess 2011). Rather than saving taxpayers money, cutting the budgets of agencies charged with regulating the financial industry may end up costing the treasury and taxpayers dearly.

In addition, financial institutions easily outspend federal agencies in several areas. For example: "In 2009 Citigroup and JPMorgan Chase . . . spent $4.6 billion each—four times the S.E.C.'s entire annual budget—on information technology alone" (Stewart 2011, B7). Under the House proposed budget, the SEC's resources for technology would be cut by $10 million and a $50 million reserve fund earmarked for technology would be eliminated.

Even if the resources were in place, law has difficulty keeping up with innovation and new economic structures, particularly when the political class has little appetite to bite the hand that feeds it (see Chapter 2). As Snider aptly discussed in Chapter 8, innovation in the financial markets, in particular high-speed electronic trading, has presented problems for regulators. High-frequency trading firms (which now account for 60 percent of the shares traded daily on U.S. stock markets) that can turn quick profits producing billions, making the market less stable and hurting ordinary traders, are outside the regulatory purview. Since the May 6, 2010, "flash crash," when the stock market plunged 700 points in minutes before recovering, the SEC and the CFTC increased their scrutiny and proposed curbs on high-frequency trading. Not surprisingly, the industry has mounted a $2 million lobbying effort to limit the proposed regulation (Bowley 2011). On the bright side, Snider reminds us that the same technological tools used by businesses could be effective weapons against corporate criminality.

Prosecutions

An often-repeated refrain among white collar crime scholars is that, with the exception of Bernie Madoff and a few other individual Ponzi operators, no one has gone to prison in connection with this latest financial scandal. Scholars have wondered why there has been a lack of prosecutions against major players in the financial crisis. If Angelo Mozilo (the former chief executive of Countrywide), Joe Cassano (the former head of AIG's Financial Products division), and Richard Fuld (the former chief executive of Lehman Brothers, who approved a bookkeeping scheme that allowed Lehman to hide debt from investors) were not criminally prosecuted for their roles in the financial crisis, who would be? Edwin Sutherland (1940), who introduced the concept of white collar criminality over 70 years ago, claimed that white collar offenders are relatively immune to harsh treatment because of the class bias of the courts and noted that they have the power to influence how law is administered.

The crimes of the wealthy either result in no official action at all, or they result in suits for damage in civil court. Or they are handled by inspectors and by administrative boards or commissions with penal sanctions in the form of warnings, orders to cease and desist, occasionally loss of a license, and only in extreme cases by fines and prison sentences. Thus, white collar criminals are segregated administratively from other criminals and, largely as a consequence of this, are not regarded as real criminals by themselves, the general public, or the criminologist (Sutherland 1940, 8).

In January 2008, the FBI investigated fourteen corporations as part of its Subprime Mortgage Industry Fraud Initiative. Six months later, it reported that more than 400 individuals were charged in a nationwide investigation that included the arrest of two Bear Stearns fund managers, Ralph R. Cioffi and Matthew M. Tannin (Kouwe and Slater 2009). When prosecutors lost the first major criminal case they mounted, against the two former Bear Stearns hedge fund managers, they seemed to lose their appetite to litigate.

As both O'Brien and Geis noted in this anthology, federal prosecutors officially adopted guidelines in 2008 (followed by the SEC in 2010) that encouraged the deferral of prosecutions, rather than charging corporations with crimes. Under the guidelines, companies that investigate and report their own wrongdoing will not be prosecuted as long as they promise to change their behavior. Generally, the agreements require corporations to pay penalties and restitution (Morgenson and Story 2011). Corporate executives are greatly advantaged by deferred prosecutions as they are rarely named as defendants.

Another example of the corporate-friendly environment that continues to have deleterious effects on rational political-economic policy and decision making is that government lawyers often go to companies early in an inquiry to have the corporation itself determine whether it or its officers engaged in improper activities. The companies are then asked to hire law firms to investigate and report back to the government. In an era of limited resources, these initiatives decrease regulators' enforcement loads. But prosecutors who are increasingly dependent on their targets to do the investigative work are less knowledgeable about the evidence (Morgenson and Story 2011). This practice raises questions about how certain regulators and the public can be sure that financial institutions would spot and report all wrongdoing, including evidence related to misbehavior by senior executives or connections to a criminal enterprise. It also raises questions about co-optation and regulatory capture. Not surprisingly, Goldman Sachs, Morgan Stanley, JPMorgan Chase, and others who have cooperated with the government regularly compare notes about government evidence likely to be used against them in what are known as joint-defense calls. Such calls have led to the development of industry-wide strategies to respond to investigations (Morgenson and Story 2011).

Critics complain that the "outsourcing" of investigations and deferred prosecutions let companies off too easily with no real consequences for their actions. For its part, the government argues that harsh treatment would hurt the housing industry and the economy. Noble Prize–winning economists Amartya Sen (2009), Joseph Stiglitz (2010), and Paul Krugman (2011b), along with many white collar–crime criminologists, do not accept this rationale. In an era of diminishing resources, Braithwaite (2010) suggests a focus on preventing a recurrence of the crisis by convincing brokers, bankers, and ratings agencies that the regulator will escalate intervention into their businesses until they fix the problems. This can be accomplished by having financial regulators act as "benign big guns" as they have in countries that were little touched by the crisis. That means regulators would have the power to take over banks, increase banks' required reserves, limit derivatives trading, and impose other conditions. "Big gun" regulators rarely have to use their power; usually they only need to express concern to gain compliance.

We must be mindful of Galbraith's contention, as described by Young, that "it was not only a lack of regulation but the behavior of the major players in the process and their involvement in gross fraud and deception that led to the crisis" (see Chapter 4). In Chapter 11 Tombs and Whyte warn, and the Dodd-Frank Act demonstrates, that regulation is problematic because of the structural relationship between the state and capital. As long as the state believes its interests are intertwined with that of business and it forgets or ignores the need to serve and protect its citizens, it will serve business interests. "Once-and-for-all regulatory solutions" fail as solutions and fall prey to capital's enablers—primarily accountants, lawyers, and lobbyists (see Chapter 8).

Rather than suffer any real consequences for their actions, the major players in the financial crisis in the United States received perverse incentives to take further risks and to skirt and even violate the law. American financial institutions learned that they did not have to be prudent. They could count on federal government to bail them out. Their employees were rewarded, not for careful reviews, but for producing numbers. Convinced that Wall Street would reward the bank for taking on greater risk, Washington Mutual's chief executive, Kerry K. Killinger, amassed bad mortgage loans and did not take action against locations where fraud appeared to be widespread (Norris 2011).

What happened leading up to and during the crisis, and even after the bailout, amounted to a perversion of the capitalist belief that good business would drive out the bad. The Gresham dynamic played out when banks, mortgage companies, and subprime lenders that reduced lending standards appeared profitable, but those that did not lost business (Black 2005).

Even an apparently hefty fine is unlikely to persuade a globally powerful company to change its behavior, For example, $1 billion in fines were assessed by the government in a civil complaint against MortgageIT, a division of Deutsche Bank purchased in 2007, for defrauding the Federal Housing Administration. This fine was little more than a slap on the wrist to a company that had revenues of $42 billion in 2010 (Nocera 2011). The fine amounted to less than 3 percent of the bank's revenue for the year.

The road to financial meltdown has taken many forms around the globe. In Greece, it was triggered by endemic state and private sector corruption. In other countries, it was assisted by factors ranging from the greed of private individuals and companies and an all-encompassing search for profit extraction, as Sassen discussed (in Chapter 2), to the encouragement of a culture that regarded the accumulation of wealth as a means of attaining status, no matter how it is achieved, and to governments' belief that its interests are best served by assisting the business community and the wealthy, as Will and Young suggest (in Chapters 3 and 4, respectively).

The financial crisis has caused great harm to the economy and to millions of people. It has also, however, focused the attention of responsible government authorities and regulators on the criminality and serious defects in oversight that, depending on one's point of view, either caused the crisis or aggravated it. This volume, offering the rich insights and analysis that scholarship can provide, points toward a framework that can guide change.

The question is whether governments (and voters) will embrace the opportunities produced by this crisis to take steps toward supporting real reforms of our regulatory and business structures. Will we, in other words, let them continue to get away with it?

The answer so far has not been encouraging. In the United States, the Dodd-Frank reforms are languishing. Other efforts to strengthen government oversight and protection have hit stiff political opposition. Meanwhile the growing U.S. movement to tackle debt and balance the budget by cutting government entitlement programs and reining in the public sector has found adherents elsewhere in the world. Many experts accept the argument that the economy will recover only if business is allowed to recover—and that excessive regulation will prevent that recovery.

The lack of political will, combined with a culture that seems to accept a degree of financial criminality as the price of prosperity, suggests that we will face endless cycles of regulation and deregulation. The Occupy Wall Street movement has at least awakened the public's consciousness and stimulated discussion about disparities in how individuals and corporation are treated in the United States. While it is hoped that in the time prior to the 2012 national elections candidates will be forced to address basic concerns raised by Occupy Wall Street, politicians and the media seem to have forgotten their message since the encampments have been demolished. Even if politicians listened, there are no guarantees that every loophole will be closed or that shrewd operators will not find new loopholes or technological tools to evade whatever laws or regulations future authorities can develop. And there is certainly no guarantee that we will not experience within the next decade (or next three decades) yet another massive financial meltdown.

What the crisis of 2008 has made painfully clear is that in a globalized economy, the acceptance of criminal, unethical, or amoral behavior practiced by companies and individuals whose reach extends across borders can have devastating effects. There will always be a bill to pay—and most often it is paid by the ordinary consumers and homeowners who were bit players in the Ponzi schemes that nurture casino economies. Such behavior is now as deep a potential threat to the world economy as the new viruses that raise concerns about global epidemics. As the essays here suggest, there is no single answer to the question: "How did they get away with it?" But the authors and editors hope that this volume will contribute to and stimulate additional research and the larger discussion among scholars and policy-makers that can help ensure it never happens again.

Notes

1. Fitch gave Iceland a junk rating. On November 23, 2011, Standard & Poor's announced that Iceland's credit rating remains at BBB–/A-3 on long- and short-term foreign and local currency. It revised its outlook to stable from negative because it believes Iceland's economy is recovering. Moody's rates Iceland at one level above junk.

2. The exchange of euro to dollar was calculated on July 19, 2011, at the rate of €1 = $1.42.

3. In the United States, Congress, reluctant to raise taxes on the wealthy, advocates cutting social programs to decrease the budget deficit despite polls indicating that citizens are against many of the proposed cuts (nearly three-quarters of those interviewed were against reducing federal funding for education and roads), 73 percent are opposed to taxing the value of employer-provided health care, 59 percent are against increasing the age for social security retirement, and two-thirds of those surveyed are in favor of raising taxes on incomes over $250,000 and limiting deductions for large corporations (see Pew Research Center 2011). Yet Congress justifies its actions by warning of severe consequences if the budget is not cut.

4. Australia, Poland, Denmark, and South Korea essentially avoided a recession, and China, India, and Iran experienced only slow growth during that period.

5. As of February 2012, President Obama has not filled several key financial regulatory positions because he been unable to obtain senate approval for his nominees. For example, the Office of the Comptroller of the Currency had been without a permanent leader since August 2010. The Federal Reserve's Board of Governors had two vacancies, and there was an opening at the top of the Federal Housing Finance Agency, which regulates Fannie Mae and Freddie Mac. Also unfilled were new positions of bank supervisor on the Federal Reserve Board and the head of the Office of Financial Research, an insurance oversight position. In reaction to President Obama's announcement on July 17, 2011, of his intent to nominate Richard Cordray, the former attorney general of Ohio, to lead of the new Consumer Financial Protection Bureau, forty-four Republican senators indicated

that they would refuse to vote on any nominee to head the bureau. Instead of a single leader for the bureau, they were demanding it be led by a board of directors (Applebaum 2011). President Obama skirted Congress by using a recess appointment to Cordray into the position on January 4, 2012.

References

Applebaum, Binyamin. 2011. "Former Ohio Attorney General to Head New Consumer Agency." *New York Times*, July 18, B1, B8.

Black, William. 2005. *The Best Way to Rob a Bank Is to Own One*. Austin: University of Texas Press.

Bowley, Graham. 2011. "Fast Traders, in Spotlight, Battle Rules." *New York Times*, July 18, A1, A3.

Braithwaite, John. 2010. "Diagnostics of White-Collar Crime Prevention." *Criminology & Public Policy* 9 (3): 621–26.

Bureau of Labor Statistics. 2011. "International Unemployment Rates and Employment Indexes, Seasonally Adjusted, 2007–2011." *International Labor Comparisons*. Washington D.C.: United States Department of Labor. http://www.bls.gov/ilc/intl_unemployment_rates_monthly.htm accessed February 12, 2012. http://www.cso.ie/releasespublications/documents/labour_market/2011/lreg_may2011.pdf.

Christie, Les. 2011. "Nearly 20% of Florida Homes Are Vacant. *CNNMoney*, March 18. http://money.cnn.com/2011/03/18/real_estate/florida_vacant_homes/index.htm.

Editorial. 2011. "Iceland's Way." *New York Times*, April 18. http://www.nytimes.com/2011/04/19/opinion/19tue2.html?_r=1&scp=13&sq=iceland%20economic%20ocrisis&st=cse (accessed June 1, 2011).

Faiola, Anthony. 2010. "Greece's Economic Crisis Could Signal Trouble for Its Neighbors." *Washington Post*, February 10, A1.

Jackson, Robert. 2008. "The Big Chill." *Financial Times*, November 15. http://www.ft.com/cms/s/0/8641d080-b2b4-11dd-bbc9-0000779fd18c.html#axzz1SZvRoush (accessed June 1, 2011).

Klein, Naomi. 2008. *The Shock Doctrine: The Rise of Disaster Capitalism*. New York: Picador.

Kouwe, Zachery, and Dan Slater. 2009. "2 Bear Stearns Fund Leaders Are Acquitted." *New York Times*, November 11. http://www.nytimes.com/2009/11/11/business/11bear.html (accessed May 8, 2011).

Krugman, Paul. 2011a. "The Lesser Depression." *New York Times*, July 22, A21.

———. 2011b. "Letting Bankers Walk." *New York Times*, July 18, A19.

Lewis, Michael. 2010. "Beware of Greeks Bearing Bonds." *Vanity Fair*, October. http://www.vanityfair.com/business/features/2010/10/greeks-bearing-bonds-201010 (accessed June 1, 2011).

———. 2011. "When Irish Eyes Are Crying." *Vanity Fair*, March. http://www.vanityfair.com/business/features/2011/03/michael-lewis-ireland-201103?printable=true#ixzz1SBGtaoeZ (accessed June 1, 2011).

Lyons, Ronan. 2010. "Ireland's Economic Crisis: What Sort of Hole Are We in and How Do We Get out?" *ronanlyons.com*, November 30. http://www.ronanlyons .com/2010/11/30/irelands-economic-crisis-what-sort-of-hole-are-we-in-and-how -do-we-get-out/ (accessed July 5, 2011).

Marcus, Gill. 2011. "Overview of the South African Economy." Paper presented at the 91st Ordinary General Meeting of Shareholders, Pretoria, June 30. http:// www.bis.org/review/r110711d.pdf (accessed July 19, 2011).

Minder, Raphael, and Stephen Castle. 2011. "Political Divide Poses Risks for Portu-gal in Bailout Talks." *New York Times*, April 7. http://www.nytimes.com/2011 /04/08/business/global/08euro.html?ref=global (accessed April 7, 2011).

Morgenson, Gretchen. 2012. "Audit Uncovers Extensive Laws in Foreclosures." *New York Times*, February 16, A1, A3.

Morgenson, Gretchen, and Louise Story. 2011. "Behind the Gentler Approach to Banks by US." *New York Times*, July 8, A1, B7.

Nocera, Joe. 2011. "You Call That Tough?" *New York Times*, May 7. http://www.ny times.com/2011/05/07/opinion/07nocera.html?scp=1&sq=financial%20crisis %20criminal%20trials&st=cse (accessed May 8, 2011).

Norris, Floyd. 2011. "High & Low Finance; 2 Meltdowns with Much in Common." *New York Times*, March 18, B1, B4.

Organisation for Economic Co-operation and Development. 2011. *Economic Survey of Iceland 2011*. http://www.oecd.org/document/16/0,3746,en_2649_201185 _43946384_1_1_1,00.html (accessed July 15, 2011).

Penfold, Chuck. 2010. "Extreme Negligence Caused Iceland's Economic Collapse, Report Says." *Deutsche Welle*. http://www.dw-world.de/dw/article/0,,5461337,00 .html (accessed June 1, 2011).

Pew Research Center. 2011. "More Blame Wars Than Domestic Spending or Tax Cuts for Nation's Debt." June 7. http://pewresearch.org/pubs/2017/poll-what -created-the-national-debt-wars-spending-tax-cuts-deficit-reduction-proposals (accessed July 20, 2011).

Phillips, Lucy. 2010. "Stiglitz Hits out at 'Mindless Deficit Reduction.'" *Public Finance*, February 10. http://www.publicfinance.co.uk/news/2010/02/stiglitz -hits-out-at-mindless-deficit-reduction/ (accessed July 15, 2011).

Protess, Ben. 2011. "U.S. Regulators Face Budget Pinch as Mandates Widen." *New York Times*, May 3. http://dealbook.nytimes.com/2011/05/03/u-s-regulators-face -budget-pinch-as-mandates-widen/?scp=1&sq=patrolling%20wall%20street& st=cse (accessed May 4, 2011).

Quinn, Ben. 2010. "Iceland Financial Crisis: Voters Reject Debt Repayment Plan." *Christian Science Monitor*, March 7. http://www.csmonitor.com/World/Europe /2010/0307/Iceland-financial-crisis-Voters-reject-debt-repayment-plan (accessed July 5, 2011).

Reich, Robert. 2011. "The Truth About the Economy That Nobody in Washington or on Wall Street Will Admit." *robertreich.org*, March 30. http://robertreich.org /post/5993482080 (accessed March 30, 2011).

Sen, Amartya. 2009. "Capitalism Beyond the Crisis." *New York Review of Books*, March 26. http://www.nybooks.com/articles/archives/2009/mar/26/capital ism-beyond-the-crisis/ (accessed July 15, 2011).

Stewart, James B. 2011. "As a Watchdog Starves, Wall Street Is Tossed a Bone." *New York Times*, July 16, A1, B7.

Stiglitz, Joseph. 2010. *Freefall: America, Free Markets, and the Sinking of the World Economy*. New York: Norton.

Sutherland, Edwin H. 1940. "White-Collar Criminality." *American Sociological Review* 5 (1): 1–12.

Taylor, Mike. 2010. "Volcker: Financial System Is—Yep!—Still Dysfunctional." *New York Observer*, September 24. http://www.observer.com/2010/wall-street /volcker-financial-system-yep-still-dysfunctional (accessed July 15, 2011).

Thomas, Landon. 2011. "Some Weigh Restructuring Portugal's Debt." *New York Times*, March 25, B1, B2.

——. 2012. "For London Youth, Down and Out Is a Way of Life." *New York Times*, February 16, A1, A3.

Werdigier, Julia, and Jack Ewing. 2011. "After Test Results, European Banks Are Urged to Bolster Reserves." *New York Times*, July 16, B1.

Zeldin, Wendy. 2011. "Iceland: Former PM Pleads Not Guilty to Gross Negligence Charges in Banking Crisis." *Global Legal Monitor*, June 13. http://www.loc.gov /lawweb/servlet/lloc_news?disp3_l205402705_text (accessed July 15, 2011).

[APPENDIX]

A SHORT (GLOBAL) HISTORY OF FINANCIAL MELTDOWNS

COMPILED BY ALEX HOLDEN

Government responses are denoted with *italics*; international financial meltdowns are denoted with [square brackets] and those in the United States are denoted with **boldface**.

1637	Tulip mania damages the futures market and Dutch trade in general.
1797	Reserves in the UK fall low, creating a monetary crisis. The Bank of England's hold on cash payments creates a panic.
1819	**The United States' first major financial crisis**
1836	[**U.S. real estate speculation** causes stock markets to crash in the UK, Europe, and then in **the United States**.]
1847	[A credit crisis and bank panic occur when railroad stock prices crash in France and the UK.]
1873	Vienna stock exchange collapses, causing the "great stagnation" on a global scale and lasts until 1896.
1882	France's Union Generale goes bankrupt, causing banking crisis and market crash.
1890	[The UK's oldest bank, Barings, nearly collapses from its exposure to Argentine debt.]
1907	[**U.S. bank panic** spreads to France and Italy after a stock market collapse.]
1923	Hyperinflation in Germany starts monetary crisis.

1929	The Great Depression begins, spreading to the UK, Japan, Germany, and Austria.
1933	*Implementation of Glass-Steagall Act*
1934	*Creation of the Securities and Exchange Commission (SEC)*
1938	*Creation of Fannie Mae*
1944	*Bretton Woods Meeting of 45 countries. They agree on a framework for international economic cooperation to be established after World War II.*
March 1, 1947	*International Monetary Fund (IMF) begins operations.*
1966	**U.S. credit crisis creates deflation and huge economic slump.**
1970	***Freddie Mac created under Emergency Home Finance Act of 1970***
1973	[World financial crisis begins after OPEC quadruples the price of oil.]
1980	***Depository Institutions Deregulation and Monetary Control Act***
1982	Global credit crunch prevents developing countries from paying their debt.
	Garn-St. Germain Depository Institution Act of 1982; Alternative Mortgage Transaction Parity Act
1984–1990	**Savings and loan crisis in the United States**
1987	**Bond and equity market crashes.**
March 31, 1988	***Portions of Glass-Steagall repealed.***
1989	Japanese bubble
	Junk bond crisis
1992	[French Maastricht Treaty sparks crisis in European Monetary System.]
November 1, 1993	*The Maastrich Treaty comes into force, formally creating the European Union (EU).*
1994	***Home Ownership and the Equity Protection Act***
1995	Mexican financial crisis caused by the peso's peg to the dollar during excessive inflation.
1997	[Asian financial crisis begins with the collapse of the Thai baht. It caused currency depreciations and declines in stock markets which spread first through most of Southeast Asia and then to the rest of the region.]
1998	Dramatic inflation of the Russian ruble causes widespread shortages in goods. Russia defaults on payment obligations during major financial crisis.

October 1999	**Washington Mutual buys Long Beach Bank and uses it as its subprime lender.**
November 1999	*The passage of the Gramm-Leach-Bililey Act, in esssence, repealed Glass-Steagall.*
2000	**Dot-com bubble pops, creating a massive fall in equity markets from overspeculation in tech stocks.**
2001	**September 11 attacks create risk by hindering various critical communication hubs necessary for payment on the financial markets.**
	Economic crisis in Argentina, resulting in the government defaulting on payment obligations
October 2001	**Enron announces $1.2 billion loss, leading to its collapse.**
2002	*Euro notes and coins replace national currencies in twelve of the member states.*
	Bond market crisis in Brazil
July 30, 2002	*Sarbanes-Oxley Act passed.*

The Financial Meltdown
2007–2011

| May 5, 2006 | **Possibly the first casualty of the looming subprime crisis, Kirkland, Washington–based Merit Financial Inc. files for bankruptcy and closes its doors.** |

2007

	U.S. real estate crisis causes the collapse of many international banks and financial institutions. Equity markets take a dive.
	Long Beach Bank closed by WaMu.
	GreenPoint Savings Bank shut down by Capitol One.
	NovaStar Financial Inc. stops making mortgage loans.
January 3	**Ownit Mortgage Solutions Inc. files for Chapter 11. It owed Merrill Lynch around $93 million at the time of filing.**
February 5	**Mortgage Lenders Network USA Inc. files for Chapter 11. It is the fifteenth largest subprime lender, with $3.3 billion in loans funded in third quarter 2006.**

February 10	*The Group of Seven Finance Ministers meet in Essen, Germany, to discuss worldwide financial problems. Germany believes the lack of hedge fund regulation could be a source of systematic risk for the financial system, but the United States believes market discipline is the best way to address the issue.*
February 27	**The Federal Home Loan Mortgage Corporation (Freddie Mac) announces that it will no longer buy the riskiest subprime mortgages and mortgage-related securities.**
April 2	New Century Financial Corporation, a leading subprime mortgage lender, files for Chapter 11 bankruptcy protection. Largest U.S. subprime lender in defaults on $8.4 billion in loan repayments. New Century made $51.6 billion in subprime loans in 2006, making it second in subprime lending. It is delisted from the NYSE.
July	Wells Fargo stops originating loans with 2-year teaser rates.
July 11	Standard & Poor's places 612 securities backed by subprime residential mortgages on a credit watch.
August	Lehman Brothers closes BNC Mortgage but continues to make loans via its subsidiary Aurora Loan Services LLC, which is not part of the company's September 15, 2008, bankruptcy filing.
	Aegis Mortgage Corp. and American Home Mortgage Investment Corp. file for bankruptcy.
August 6	American Home Mortgage Investment Corporation files for Chapter 11.
August 9	BNP Paribas, France's largest bank, halts redemptions on three investment funds.
August 16	Fitch Ratings downgrades Countrywide Financial Corporation to BBB+, its third lowest investment-grade rating. Countrywide borrows the entire $11.5 billion available in its credit lines with other banks.
August 31	Argent Mortgage Co., Town & Country Credit Corp., and Ameriquest Mortgage Co., all subsidiaries of ACC Capital Holdings Corp. (the parent company), are sold to Citigroup Inc.
September 14	*The Chancellor of the Exchequer authorizes the Bank of England to provide liquidity support for Northern Rock, the United Kingdom's fifth largest mortgage lender.*

October	Encore Credit Corp. is folded into Bear Stearns Residential Mortgage in October 2007 and stops making loans out of the office in December.
	The Treasury Department and the Department of Housing and Urban Development encourage the formation of the HOPE NOW initiative by an alliance of investors, servicers, mortgage market participants, and credit and homeowners' counselors to help distressed homeowners stay in their homes.
October 15	Citigroup, Bank of America, and JPMorgan Chase announce plans for an $80 billion Master Liquidity Enhancement Conduit to purchase highly rated assets from existing special-purpose vehicles.

2008

February	First Franklin Financial Corp. and NationPoint close all wholesale and retail loan operations.
February 13	*President George W. Bush signs the Economic Stimulus Act of 2008 (Public Law 110-185) into law.*
June	Wilmington Finance Inc. (AIG subsidiary) shuts down its wholesale lending operation.
June 18	Fremont General Corp. (Fremont Investment & Loan) files for bankruptcy and the following month sells the bank branches and deposits of Fremont Investment & Loan to CapitalSource Inc.
July	Countrywide Financial Corp. is bought by Bank of America for $4 billion.
	Martinsa Fadesa, a large Spanish construction company, declares bankruptcy, leaving banks exposed to €1 billion of debt. Spain refuses to bail out Martinsa Fadesa.
July 11	*IndyMac seized by the Federal Office of Thrift Supervision.*
September	*Washington Mutual seized by Office of Thrift Supervision. FDIC "facilitates" the bank's sale to JPMorgan Chase for $1.9 billion.*
September 15	Lehman Brothers declares bankruptcy.
October 3	*Congress passes the Emergency Economic Stabilization Act of 2008, Public Law 110-343. The law authorizes the creation of the Troubled Asset Relief Program and provides*

	$700 billion to purchase "troubled assets" and equity from financial institutions to strengthen the financial sector.
October 7	*Iceland's government takes control of the country's second and third largest banks, Landsbanki and Glitnir.*
October 8	*Iceland's government takes control of its largest bank, Kaupthing.*
November	*[The IMF loans Iceland $2.1 billion, and Nordic countries provide an additional $2.1 billion loan.]*
December 11	**Bernard Madoff arrested.**
December 31	**Wells Fargo & Co. buys Wachovia.**

2009

February 17	EquiFirst, a subsidiary of Barclays Bank stops making loans.
March	**HSBC Finance Corp.'s consumer lending business discontinues loan origination of all products.**
March 19	**OneWest Bank Group purchases IndyMac from FDIC.**
April	*Ireland proposes a National Asset Management Agency to take over large loans from banks to allow the banks to return to normal liquidity.*
October	*The Greek government announces that the 2009 budget deficit will be 12.7 percent, more than double the previously announced figure.*
December	Fitch Ratings reduces Greek debt rating from A– to BBB+.

2010

April	Portugal's debt rating is reduced from A+ to A– by Standard & Poor's.
May	*The EU approves a $146 billion bailout for Greece.*
July 21	**Dodd-Frank Wall Street Reform and Consumer Protection Act is signed into law.**
September 18	**In the United States, Elizabeth Warren is appointed "assistant to the president" to help set up Consumer Financial Protection Board (she later resigns/withdraws).**
November	*[Ireland agrees to a €85 billion bailout from the EU and the IMF. Ireland outlines €15 billion ($20.55 billion) in spending*

*cuts and tax hikes over 4 years, which is intended to reduce
the budget deficit to 9.1 percent of GDP in 2011.*
Portugal announces austerity measures to reduce debt, denies need for bailout.]

2011

January 27	***Financial Crisis Inquiry Commission Report released.***
February–March	***Wisconsin moves to dissolve collective bargaining rights for its public workers.***
March	[Standard & Poor's cuts its debt rating for Portugal from BBB to BBB– (its lowest investment grade rating) and Greece from BB+ (junk) to BB–. Ireland's rating is BBB+. All three countries are dependent on short-term financing from the European Central Bank for their survival.]
April 6	[*Portugal asks the EU for a bailout.*]
June	**Government operations in the state of Minnesota are shut down when the governor and state legislators fail to agree on a package of spending reductions and tax increases.**
July	**President Barack Obama and Republican leaders begin tense discussions about lifting the U.S. debt ceiling.**
July 21	[European community approves a $157 billion bailout for Greece and reduced interest rates on the aid it has given to Ireland and Portugal.]
August 5	**Standard & Poor's downgrade the United States long-term sovereign credit rating from AAA to AA+.**
September 17	**Occupy Wall Street movement begins in New York City and spreads throughout the United States and to many large cities in the world to protest social and economic inequality, high unemployment, greed, corruption, and corporate influence on government. The protestors highlighted the economic and political disparity in the United States with their slogan, "We are the 99%."**
October 31	MF Global, as a result of reported quarterly losses of $191.6 million on trades of European government bonds, files for Chapter 11 bankruptcy making it the largest Wall Street collapse since Lehman Brothers in September 2008. Subsequently, the bankruptcy trustee discovers that approximately $1.2 billion is missing from clients' accounts.

November 15	The Occupy Wall Street encampment in Zuccotti Park in New York City is shut down by police.
November 28	*Judge Jeb. S. Rakoff of Federal District Court in Manhattan rejects the SEC's $285 million settlement with Citigroup in which the bank did not have to acknowledge or deny the veracity of the SEC's allegations.*

2012

January 4	*President Obama uses a recess appointment to make Richard Cordray director of the Bureau of Consumer Financial Protection, watchdog agency created by the Dodd-Frank financial reform legislation in 2010.*
January 24	*President Obama announces creation of a Financial Crimes Unit headed by New York State Attorney General Eric Schneiderman to investigate frauds, including false statements, mail and wire fraud, and failure to comply with the Financial Institutions Reform, Recovery and Enforcement Act of 1989. This unit is distinct from the Financial Fraud Task Force, which the administration created three years ago and has concentrated on small-time fraud and generally settled for civil fines.*
February	[Moody's downgrades Italy and Malta from A3 from A2, Slovakia and Slovenia to A2 from A1, Spain to A3 from A1, and Portugal to Ba3 from Ba2.]
February 9	*A $26 billion negotiated settlement between federal and states authorities and five mortgage servicers—Bank of America, JPMorgan Chase, Wells Fargo, Citigroup, and Ally Financial is designed to provide relief to nearly two million current and former American homeowners harmed by the housing crisis. The states retained the right to pursue allegations of criminal wrongdoing against the banks.*
February 12	*The Greek Parliament passed an austerity measure that, among other things, will cut 5,000 public-sector jobs and lower the minimum wage by 20 percent, from €752 a month to €600, in hopes of receiving a $172 billion bailout. This action was followed by violent protests.*
May 10	J.P. Morgan announced its London offices lost $2 billion trading highly leveraged, risky derivative.

LIST OF CONTRIBUTORS

DAVID C. BROTHERTON is Professor and Chair of Sociology at the John Jay College of Criminal Justice and at the Graduate Center, the City University of New York. His research focuses on social exclusion and resistance, and his most recent book, *Banished to the Homeland: Dominican Deportees and Their Stories of Exile* is coauthored with Luis Barrios. They are also coauthors of *Keeping out the Other: A Critical Introduction to Immigration Enforcement Today* and *The Almighty Latin King and Queen Nation: Street Politics and the Transformation of a New York City Gang* and coeditors of *Gangs and Society: Alternative Perspectives*.

STEPHEN HANDELMAN is an internationally known author, journalist, and lecturer whose work has appeared in newspapers, journals, and magazines around the world. A specialist in transnational crime and organized crime, he has served as a consultant to the United Nations, the FBI, and law enforcement agencies around the United States. Since 2007, he has been director of the Center on Media, Crime, and Justice at John Jay College and executive editor of *The Crime Report*, the nation's first comprehensive news and resource site on criminal justice.

SUSAN WILL is Assistant Professor of Sociology at John Jay College of Criminal Justice and has written about corporate bankruptcy, the Orange County bankruptcy, financial crime, legal culture, and the social impact of regulatory apparatus. Her research interests are in the areas of white collar and corporate crime, sociology of law, and sociology of the environment.

HAROLD C. BARNETT is Emeritus Professor of Economics at the University of Rhode Island. He has published widely on the economics of corporate and white collar crime, including a major study of the Superfund hazardous waste program, *Toxic Debts and the Superfund Dilemma*. He moved to Arizona in 2002, where he was involved in environmental mitigation, real estate development, and mortgage lending. He currently resides in Chicago, where he is a mortgage market consultant and adjunct faculty with the Marshall Bennett Institute of Real Estate, Roosevelt University. His contribution to this volume grew out of his expert research on mortgage fraud. He is currently researching mortgage fraud trends and impacts in Chicago and the relationship between securitizer risk disclosures and default rates on mortgage-backed securities.

WILLIAM K. BLACK is Associate Professor of Economics and Law at the University of Missouri–Kansas City. He is a white collar criminologist, the former executive director of the Institute of Fraud Prevention, a former senior financial regulator, and the author of *The Best Way to Rob a Bank Is to Own One* and of numerous articles and book chapters on "control frauds" and financial crimes.

HONGMING CHENG is Assistant Professor of Sociology at the University of Saskatchewan, Canada. His research focuses on white collar and corporate crime in the context of globalization and regional regulatory cooperation. Recent publications include the book *Commercial Crime and Commercial Regulation: A Comparative Perspective* and articles including "Insider Trading in China: The Case for the Chinese Securities Regulatory Commission" and "White Collar Crime and the Criminal Justice System: Bank Fraud and Corruption in China" in the *Journal of Financial Crime.*

JOSÉ CRUZ is an associate professor affiliated with the Centre for Legal and Economic Research (CIJE) and is on the Law Faculty at the University of Porto (Portugal). He has written about economic crime and corruption.

RITA FARIA is on the Law Faculty of the School of Criminology at the University of Porto. She has written about corruption in Portugal.

DAVID O. FRIEDRICHS is Professor of Sociology/Criminal Justice and Distinguished University Fellow at the University of Scranton. He is author of *Trusted Criminals: White Collar Crime in Contemporary Society* and *Law in Our Lives: An Introduction* and editor of the two-volume *State Crime.* He has published more than 100 journal articles, book chapters, encyclopedia entries, and essays and well over 300 book reviews. He has been a visiting professor or guest lecturer at many colleges and universities, including the University of South Africa and Flinders University in Australia. He served as editor of *Legal Studies Forum* (1985–1989) and president of the White Collar Crime Research Consortium (2002–2004). In November 2005, he received a Lifetime Achievement Award from the Division on Critical Criminology of the American Society of Criminology.

GILBERT GEIS is Professor Emeritus of Criminology, Law and Society at the University of California, Irvine. He is a prolific writer who has authored over twenty books, including leading texts on criminology and white collar crime, and over 300 articles and book chapters. He is a former president of the American Society of Criminology and recipient of its Edwin H. Sutherland Award for outstanding research. He has also received research awards from the Association of Certified Fraud Examiners, the Western Society of Criminology, the American Justice Institute, and the National Organization for Victim Assistance.

ALEX HOLDEN recently completed a master of arts degree in criminal justice at John Jay College of Criminal Justice. He is currently interning for the New York City Department of Investigation.

ANDRÉ LAMAS LEITE is an assistant professor on the Law Faculty at the University of Porto. He has written about criminal law and criminal justice.

HANS NELEN is Professor of Criminology and Chair of the Department of Criminal Law and Criminology of the Faculty of Law at Maastricht University, the Netherlands. Between 1986 and the beginning of 2001, he was employed as a senior researcher and research supervisor at the Research and Documentation Centre of the Ministry of Justice in the Netherlands (WODC), mainly involved in drug, fraud, organized crime, corporate crime, and police research. Between 2001 and 2006, he was associate professor and senior researcher at the Institute of Criminology of the Vrije Universiteit, Amsterdam. Nelen has published several books and articles on a variety of criminological subjects, including corruption and fraud, occupational crime, the administrative approach to organized crime, the proceeds-of-crime approach, drugs, and evaluation.

JUSTIN O'BRIEN is Professor of Law and Director of the Centre for Law, Markets and Regulation, at the University of New South Wales in Sydney, Australia. A specialist in the dynamics of financial regulation, he has authored three books on regulatory politics: *Wall Street on Trial; Redesigning Financial Regulation;* and *Engineering a Financial Bloodbath.* In addition he has edited several anthologies on corporate governance, including *Governing the Corporation; Private Equity, Corporate Governance and the Dynamics of Capital Market Governance; Corporate Business Responsibilities;* and *The Future of Financial Regulation,* which he coedited with Iain MacNeil. Prior to his career in academia, Professor O'Brien was an investigative journalist for a range of national and international broadcast networks.

LUUK RITZEN holds a bachelor's degree in health sciences and a master's degree in forensics, criminology, and law. Currently, he is working as a criminological researcher and lecturer at Maastricht University. He is specializing in organized crime, white color crime, corporate crime, and money laundering. His doctoral dissertation focuses on the entanglement between real estate and serious forms of crime. In addition, he participates in the Regional Intelligence and Expertise Center, Limburg, an organization responsible for gathering intelligence and expertise to combat organized crime.

SASKIA SASSEN is the Robert S. Lynd Professor of Sociology and cochair of the Committee on Global Thought at Columbia University (www.saskiasassen .com). Among her books are *The Global City* (2001) and *Territory, Authority, Rights: From Medieval to Global Assemblages* (2008). She has now completed for UNESCO a five-year project on sustainable human settlement based on a network of researchers and activists in over thirty countries; it is published as one of the volumes of the *Encyclopedia of Life Support Systems* (http://www.eolss .net). Her books are translated into twenty-one languages. She has written for the *Guardian,* the *New York Times, Le Monde,* the *International Herald Tribune, Newsweek International,* and the *Financial Times,* among others. She contributes regularly to HuffingtonPost.com and OpenDemocracy.net.

DAVID SHAPIRO currently leads the corporate investigative unit for a major international corporation. He is also an adjunct lecturer at John Jay College of Criminal Justice, where he instructs in the field of forensic analysis of financial records and reports. Previously, he was a corporate investigator for Kroll Associates in New York; an assistant prosecutor in Essex County, New Jersey; a special agent and assistant legal advisor with the FBI in Albany, New York; and a certified public accountant and management consultant.

LAUREEN SNIDER is Professor of Sociology (Emerita) at Queen's University, where she specializes in corporate crime, surveillance, and legal reform. Recent publications include "The Conundrum of Financial Regulation," *Annual Review of Law & Social Sciences* (2011); "Moral Panics Deflected: The Failed Legislative Responses to Canada's Safety Crimes and Market Fraud" (with Steve Bittle), *Crime, Law & Social Change* (2011); "Framing E-Waste Legislation: The Obfuscating Role of Power," *Criminology & Public Policy* (2010); "Tracking Environmental Crime Through CEPA: Canada's Environment Cops or Industry's Best Friend?" (with Suzanne Day and April Girard), *Canadian Journal of Sociology* (2010); "The Challenges of Regulating Powerful Economic Actors" (with Steve Bittle), in *European Developments in Corporate Criminal Liability*, edited by James Gobert and Ana-Maria Pascal (London: Sage, 2011); and "Mega Events and Mega-Profits: Unravelling the Vancouver 2010 Security-Development Nexus" (with Adam Molnar), in *Surveillance Games*, edited by Colin Bennett and Kevin Haggerty (2011).

PEDRO SOUSA is an economist who is an auxiliary professor on the Law Faculty, School of Criminology, at the University of Porto. He has written about central banks and monetary policy.

STEVE TOMBS is Professor of Sociology and co-director of the Centre for the Study of Crime, Criminalization and Social Exclusion at Liverpool John Moores University. His primary research interests are the incidence, nature, regulation, and harm of corporate crime. He is also interested in the politics of knowledge. He is on the Steering Committee of the European Group for the Study of Deviance and Social Control. Recent books that he coauthored with David Whyte include *Corporate Criminal (Key Ideas in Criminology); Regulatory Surrender: Death, Injury and the Non-Enforcement of Law; Safety Crimes;* and *A Crisis of Enforcement: The Decriminalisation of Death and Injury at Work.* He coedited *State, Power, Crime* with Daniel Dorling, Dave Gordon, Paddy Hillyard and Christina Pantazis; *Criminal Obsessions. Why harm matters more than crime* and *Beyond Criminology? Taking Harm Seriously.* In addition, he has written numerous articles and book chapters. He currently edits a column, Crimes of the Powerful and Insurgent Resistance, with Frank Pearce, on Crime Talk, http://www.crimetalk.org.uk/library/section-list/38-frontpage-articles/174 -crimes-of-the-powerful.html.

SOPHIE VIDALI is Associate Professor of Criminology and Crime Policy in the Department of Social Administration at Democritus University of Thrace, Greece. She is the author of several books, book chapters, and articles on a wide range of criminological topics, including crime policy, criminological theory, forensic investigation, terrorism, organized crime, drugs, crimes among youth, crime control, and crime-control institutions (police and policing).

DAVID WHYTE is a reader in sociology at the University of Liverpool. His primary research interests are in the area of corporate power, corporate crime, and corporate legal responsibility and accountability. Recent books that he coauthored with Steve Tombs include the *Corporate Criminal (Key Ideas in Criminology); Regulatory Surrender: Death, Injury and the Non-Enforcement of Law;* and *A Crisis of Enforcement: The Decriminalisation of Death and Injury at Work,* and *Safety Crimes.* In addition, he has written numerous articles and book chapters. He received the 2007 *British Journal of Criminology* Leon Radzinowitz Memorial Prize for his article on corporate crime and the rule of law in Iraq. In 2005, the Scottish justice minister appointed him to the Scottish Government Expert Group on Corporate Homicide.

JOCK YOUNG is Distinguished Professor of Sociology and Criminal Justice at John Jay College of Criminal Justice and the Graduate Center, City University of New York, and Professor of Sociology at the University of Kent, in the United Kingdom. He is best known as the coauthor of *The New Criminology,* the 1973 book that founded a new school of thought about the subject. His theoretical interests have been oriented to the development of the new field of cultural criminology, of which he has written widely. He received the American Society of Criminology's Sellin-Glueck Award in 1998 for Distinguished International Scholarship. In 2003 he received a Lifetime Achievement Award from the Critical Criminology Division of the American Society of Criminology. A prolific writer, he has written numerous books, articles, and book chapters. His recent trilogy, *The Criminological Imagination, The Vertigo of Late Modernity,* and *The Exclusive Society,* offers a critique of social exclusion in contemporary society.

INDEX